MYTH AND CULT AMONG PRIMITIVE PEOPLES

MYTH AND CULT AMONG PRIMITIVE PEOPLES

By Adolf E. Jensen

Translated by
Marianna Tax Choldin and Wolfgang Weissleder

THE UNIVERSITY OF CHICAGO PRESS
CHICAGO & LONDON

This book was originally published in 1951
by Franz Steiner Verlag, Wiesbaden, under the title,
Mythos und Kult bei Naturvölkern

Library of Congress Catalog Card Number: 63-20909

THE UNIVERSITY OF CHICAGO PRESS, CHICAGO & LONDON
The University of Toronto Press, Toronto 5, Canada

Composed and printed by THE UNIVERSITY OF CHICAGO PRESS
Chicago, Illinois, U.S.A.

PREFACE TO THE AMERICAN EDITION

Regrettably, there has been little contact or collaboration between the anthropologists of the United States and Germany. Although German anthropology, in its American sense, has a rather unique position among the ensemble of nations, it has met with little sympathetic understanding in America. This may be the result of the philosophical orientation of German anthropological thought, but a certain part of the suspicion against German ethnology undoubtedly is a holdover from the days when the so-called *Kulturkreislehre* held sway, especially in the dogmatic interpretation of Father W. P. Schmidt. American anthropologists are now likely to feel that history has proven them right in rejecting the *Kulturkreislehre* as an aberration that no longer needs to be considered. After all, even the staunchest adherents of the doctrine, the so-called School of Vienna, have arrived at a similar interpretation.

Such a radical rejection seems to me an overly facile evasion and hardly does justice to the meritorious work of Frobenius, Graebner, and others. Some credit must be due, at least, to Graebner's sweeping vision in which the entire history of mankind is seen as a system of coherent and articulated phases and strata. It is only the overweening optimism with which Graebner presented his vision of the succession of cultures and which seduced him into seeing his *Kulturkreise* as an ultimate solution rather than a working hypothesis that is not shared by the Viennese school of today. Only the ready-made, Procrustean system into which Graebner, and later on Schmidt, forced the major anthropological problems has been rejected. German anthropologists have never recanted the fundamental idea of culture history in its entirety.

As early as 1921, Heine-Geldern published a paper which took critical issue with the arbitrariness of the *Kulturkreislehre* and with the dogma of Schmidt that, wherever headhunting and human sacrifice exist, motherright (a concept of which Schmidt gave a vague definition at best) must also be expected. Nevertheless, Heine-Geldern tried to demonstrate that the many cultural manifestations, in the New World as in the Old, which have so much in common must have emanated from a single point of origin.

This was, of course, a fundamental tenet of the *Kulturkreislehre*. It was in this sense that the culture-historical tradition **was** carried on by most German diffusionists.

It seems to be an opinion widely held in the English-speaking world that the assumption of common origins requires proof while the converse may be accepted as a matter for which proof is superfluous. This seems a misplaced confidence; that dispersed, but similar, occurrences are *not* evidence of a common history likewise would appear to call for proof. Both arguments would then face the same problem: in anthropology, where most information pertains to populations that have no form of writing or datable historical documents, any appeal to rigid formal proof must fail. Ultimately, we always have to choose between a greater or lesser likelihood. Neither the belief in a common origin nor its rejection is more or less "natural" or self-evident. The choice will ultimately be left to the discretion of the questioner and his decision will largely depend on the degree of confidence he has in the human capacity for invention. We refer, of course, only to the invention of something fundamentally new, whether object, practice, or institution. Only the discovery of a hitherto unknown principle qualifies as an invention in this sense; none of the countless secondary elaborations that modify, embellish, or develop known solutions will do.

Essentially, then, the acceptance and the rejection of inventiveness have equal claims to consideration. Yet the partisans of both views continue to dispute the issue without either converting the other. It seems high time to aim at some peaceable and fruitful coexistence which would permit each side to make the most of its viewpoint.

I shall try to illustrate my point about "equal claims" with two examples, though they may appear somewhat simple-minded to the convinced diffusionist. I am referring to the distribution of the bull-roarer and the blowgun. The latter is found in Indonesia as well as in the Amazon regions of South America. It may be said, of course, that the principle of the blowgun is so simple that, wherever it may occur, it must have done so almost of necessity. But, on the other hand, all instances of its occurrence may be referred to a *single* conception which radiated from a *single* geographical origin. Supporting this interpretation is the fact that those cultures which have knowledge of the blowgun are nearly of the same *level of culture*. Similar arguments may be offered regarding the bull-roarer. Here, too, simplicity of the basic principle justifies the assumption of multiple invention while, on the other hand, bull-roarers may have been diffused by cultural transmission. We cannot neglect the uniqueness of its characteristic function: it always represents the voice of a spirit at an initiation ceremony.

As I have indicated, this book shares some fundamental assumptions with ideas long ago expressed by Heine-Geldern. I am, however, only peripherally concerned with culture history or questions of cultural diffusion. Emphasis here is given to another aspect of our discipline, one that should be of interest to all anthropologists, diffusionists or not. We shall deal mainly with the intercultural comprehensibility of certain phenomena that have so far eluded interpretation. Especially in the area of religion, anthropologists are confronted with odd and curious manifestations which defy understanding and often seem so absurd as to belie the profound solemnity and the significance accorded them in the ideology of primitive peoples.

The path we are about to take was first explored by Leo Frobenius. He, properly, was the originator of the anthropological theory that later became known as the *Kulturkreislehre*. Early, however, he dissociated himself from the doctrinaire rigidity which others imparted to it (1905: 88 ff.). All of his later works are dominated by a profound concern with sense and meaning. His attention was, therefore, engaged especially by the regularities of cultural processes. Frobenius distinguished two phases in the full realization of a culture: a *creative* phase in which a new insight spontaneously assumes its specific form and experiences its period of florescence; thereafter a phase of degeneration during which the original significance of the new insight gradually fades and finally decays. Its form, however—be it a rite, institution, mythic concept, or whatever—may persist with metamorphosed significance and altered function once it has become established and integrated into the cultural continuum. The form will be "utilized"; it will continue to be "applied."

When we encounter cultural phenomena in the phase of *application*—and this will be the case almost consistently in the sphere of primitive religion and ideology—their announced meanings and "purposes" must of necessity appear absurd and incomprehensible. Quite in contrast, then, to a once pervasive, naïve confidence that historically early ways of thinking may be read directly from the statements of primitive man, the recognition of these two culture-historical phases provides us with a methodology to discover meaningful contexts.

Frobenius correlated the historical sequence of these phases with the concepts of *expression* (of an insight) and *application* (its semantically depleted form). With his conception of the nature of culture, Frobenius cleared a path that could lead to fuller "understanding." *Kulturmorphologie*, the designation which he gave to this approach to ethnology, grew in close spiritual association with Oswald Spengler, cofounder of the Institut für Kulturmorphologie, now the Frobenius-Institut.

This volume is rooted in the idea of *Kulturmorphologie* and will, above all, be an attempt to extend our understanding of the religious conceptions and practices of primitive peoples. Obviously, its interpretations must remain hypotheses. However, no more can be said for any other treatment given to the subject, and this in itself encouraged me to embark on this new and different approach to the known data. I believe that it will more adequately do justice to the essence of culture as well as to the nature of man as a creature of reason and creative abilities.

It only remains for me to thank the Wenner-Gren Foundation for the financial assistance which made possible the publication of the book in the English language. I also wish to thank the translators, Mrs. Marianna Tax Choldin and Dr. Wolfgang Weissleder, who also acted as editor, and Mr. Wolfgang Lindig, assistant at the Frobenius-Institut, who helped with suggestions in the final draft of the translation.

FRANKFURT, GERMANY
December 1962

CONTENTS

CONTENTS

INTRODUCTION

Recent ethnological literature shows little understanding of the way in which the life of prehistoric or primitive man presents itself to the observer. The wildest assertions are made and repeated, contrary to all good sense, simply because any kind of absurdity seems possible and will be taken for granted where non-Western cultures are concerned. In a recent work (1949) on psychology and prehistory, we read: "When the hunter obsecrates the painted animal [the reference is to prehistoric rock paintings] he does so not because the picture is a symbol of reality but because picture and object are identical in his mind. There is no distinction between image and reality." Such statements are neither rare nor found only in inconsequential writings; they are numerous and often occur in works which have merit in areas of substantive research.

What are we to make of such statements? Are we to believe that the hunter has completely forgotten that he himself painted the colored image and that he now considers it to be an animal of flesh and bone? Would he not feel the urge to skin it and eat it? Imagine the daily disappointments! But this absurd notion aside, what is left of the "identity" of the animal and its image? If the hunter does not try to eat the painted image, he must distinguish between it and living reality. It is time to stop making broad generalizing statements which are not even supported by reasonable conceptualizations.

Other types of misstatement are no less frequent, even in substantial scientific works. Grotesque notions of early man's capacities (or, rather, incapacities) recur in the numerous attempts to explain the peculiarities of early forms of society through allegations of a collective conscience, the absence of realized individuality, or the wide and open realm of "magical usages."

The consequences of these distortions continue to plague the study of religion. In the economic and technological sectors, the astonishing successes of so-called primitive peoples have been admitted for some time. We have learned to measure their achievements—in these areas—with the yardstick used for "reasonable" human beings. Where intellectual propensities are concerned, however—in the realm of art, for instance, and especially in that of religion—primitive man is supposed to have been destitute of all reason and hardly seems to deserve to be called "human." K. T. Preuss gave this attitude its most extreme formulation when he spoke of "*Urdummheit*," primal stupidity, as the state of intellect from which the early forms of religion arose. Unfortunately, the evils inherent in this type of thinking do not affect theory alone; they influence field research to this day. In consequence, the data on which ethnology must rely are fundamentally distorted and falsified or, at best, are not presented in the form of purely phenomenological reports. This situation is all the more deplorable when we remind ourselves that the coming decades may well offer the last opportunities for gathering solid and authentic data, on the quality of which all future research into the history of mankind will have to rely.

At present, three general theories characterize ethno-religious studies. Each claims to have uncovered the origin of religion. The oldest of them is E. B. Tylor's theory of animism (1872), which concerns itself primarily with the concept of soul among primitive peoples (cf. chap. xiii). It was followed at the turn of the century by the theories of pre-animistic magic (cf. chap. x) and *Urmonotheismus* (cf. chap. iv). Since I intend to raise fundamental objections to all these views, thorough discussion of each of them will be given in appropriate sections of this book. Here, mere mention will serve to sketch out the proposed task.

Analyzing into century-old theories may seem a thankless task, and so it would undoubtedly be if later theories had freed themselves of the harmful effects of older ones. Astonishingly enough, this is not the case. It is not that there have been no notable recent contributions to the history of early religion. Significant works appeared in Germany, for instance, about the time of World War I. Since they were not written by ethnologists, they had little effect on ethnological theory. Thus, Rudolph Otto's *Das Heilige*, in spite of its significance, made almost no reference to ethnological material. On the other hand, authors who have drawn heavily upon ethnology and even professorial ethnologists have not gone beyond modifying the three earlier theories. Only very recently has the picture begun to change, notably in the publications of Mircea Eliade and Werner Müller.

The science of religion, more than any other, stands to gain from ethnology, if only because of the preservation in primitive populations of forms of religious expression that antedate the archaic high cultures. Because the contemporary manifestations of primitive religion are usually mere petrifactions, they can be understood only with the help of insights offered by ethnology. At the moment of their genesis, these forms were undoubtedly spiritually potent; all of the highly developed cultures of later times built upon them. In the sphere of religion, understanding of the higher demands knowledge of the primitive forerunners. Occasionally, but significantly, the inventory of the high culture shows us phenomena obviously taken over from previous cultural stages but not meaningfully integrated into the new world view. They can only be explained as misinterpreted vestiges, drained of their former significance (cf. chap. viii).

My skepticism is directed mainly toward the image of man's nature with which all three of the theories operate; and this image affects not only specific interpretations, such as the obsecration of animals mentioned above, but the very fabric of the theories. For this reason it becomes necessary to enter into detailed discussion of attitudes toward spiritual matters both in primitive and in occidental cultures, and these discussions take up the first part of this book. We need to find out, for instance, whether a rock painting carried connotations for the primitive hunter that differ materially from those it carries for us. Furthermore, can we hope to resolve this question? And, if a difference can be established, can it be precisely formulated?

This approach is made necessary by the historical nature of our science. Spurred by the wish to arrive at a better "understanding" of religious phenomena in the non-Western world, I have felt sure for some time that we need to find new paths. As usual, there is a lag between the recognition of a need and its fulfilment.

Much depends on the possibility of reconstructing the original state of cultural phenomena; today these phenomena appear metamorphosed and only highly qualified conclusions can be drawn regarding their origins. It is one of the great merits of Leo Frobenius that he insistently reiterated this historical situation. He directed attention to the fact that the creative act at all times presupposes a specific psychic situation which he tried to characterize as *Ergriffenheit*,[1] an engulfment of man by his environment. Creative processes never take place as later descriptions would have them, and this is true not only of early times. It applies as well, for instance, to scientific insights insofar as they have creative origins; they are never conceived in the formal outlines of scientific treatises. Demonstration and proof, indispensable for the convincing transmission of ideas, owe their origin to secondary reasoning, while the bright flash of insight, the creative moment per se, arises quite independently of them as an uncontrollable psychic event, without rationalism or deliberate intent.

Although we may not be able to share the experience of the creative process and must let *Ergriffenheit* serve us as an approximation of understanding, we do recognize the results of creativity in cultural configurations. Originally, these must have been more or less perfect "expressions" of *Ergriffenheit*. When a new aspect of reality has revealed itself to man in this manner, the resulting cultural configuration follows its own course, chiefly because the initiating impulse is spent and no longer acts to maintain the configuration during its continuing "application." Every cultural manifestation is ultimately passed on didactically. It remains the living part of a culture to the precise extent that the original creative spirit is still felt by master and disciple. The converse is equally true: when creative awareness has been extinguished, any cultural configuration will appear as a petrified and empty isolate.

It puzzles me that a reviewer of the German editions of this book has accused me of having produced a new degeneration hypothesis after the model of Andrew Lang or W. Schmidt (Mühlmann, 1952, 1962; cf. Jensen, 1963). I fail to see what might have caused such a bizarre misunderstanding. Nowhere have I advocated the opinion that religion had its greatest efflorescence in prehistoric time or that all other religions in the history of mankind—even the institutions of Buddhism, Christianity, and Islam—are merely degenerate offshoots of the great prehistoric religion. On the contrary, I am convinced of man's undiminished creative capacities. Throughout history new aspects of reality have revealed

---

[1] *Ergriffenheit* has been translated as "seizure" in various English-language discussions of the work of Frobenius, and "seizure" is therefore—reluctantly—retained in the following—Trans.

themselves to man, spurring the innate creativity of his nature to express new insights through new cultural formulations. Yet, at all times, these formulations have had to submit to the law of degeneration, the "decline from expression to application." I have, as a matter of fact, set myself the task of showing by a number of examples that it is indeed possible, under certain conditions, to make cogent statements about original creative acts. To understand means, however, to uncover the initiating creative forces. When, for instance, an African peasant states that he performs a certain ritual so that his field will bear more fruit or that it would not bear any if the ritual were omitted, we learn little about the original meaning of the ritual act. Similarly, a European Christian may make a pilgrimage to a sacred shrine in hopes of being blessed with offspring. Both instances show us "states of application"; a religious custom is "used" for the attainment of a goal. However, the ethnologist cannot satisfy himself with such "pseudopurposes." He will either arrive at his own conclusions from evidence not contained in the statements of those involved or he will find explanations in similar practices at other localities where relevant meanings are more clearly apparent. Both approaches have inherent difficulties and call for caution. Yet, we have hardly any other paths to "understanding."

Primitive settings rarely offer us cultural configurations in the state of "expression"; and this, more than anything else, expresses their state of "petrifaction." In contrast, for instance, many members of the Western cultural community would be able to sum up the whys and wherefores of their characteristic scientific world view: it is the central expression of an active and vital culture. Primitive peoples often reply laconically to questions that ask the reasons for actions: our ancestors did it this way. Actually, that is the sole motive for many human actions. Even in our own culture we hold fast to traditional customs and for no other reasons. This is true especially at weddings, funerals, and other solemn occasions. Rarely is there full awareness of the original meaning of customs. Why, for instance, do we consider black the color of mourning? (In China it is white!) Why are there a best man, bridesmaids, a bridal bouquet at a wedding? Often ethnology has the explanation, though it is unknown to the man in the street—and this is significant for comparison with primitive peoples—who does not even care to ask the question. We, too, feel tradition to be a sufficient reason.

For all that, it makes sense that man goes along "in the way of the ancestors." Solemn occasions call for solemn behavior and the time-honored practices of the past meet this requirement, even though their original significance is forgotten. At the same time, however, we persist in customs which defy justifications of this kind. Why are men's clothes buttoned on the right while women's clothes are buttoned on the left? Confronted with a sudden "why" we might easily react exactly as primitive peoples are wont to react in similar situations and name any handy or imaginable reason, whether actually related to the origin of the custom or not. The eating of horseflesh, for instance, meets with widespread aversion among us and is supported by all sorts of reasons which are maintained with strong conviction: it is un-wholesome, unsavory, or, it may be said, the horse plays so different a role for the human community that eating it would be an abomination. It so happens, however, that we know where the roots of this particular aversion are to be found. The proscription of eating horseflesh goes far back into the Middle Ages, when it was taken as a sign of adamant persistence in paganism and its ceremonia, which often involved the eating of ritually slaughtered horses. The church vehemently fought the custom (Steller). It was considered the height of infamy to eat horseflesh and this attitude was passed on through generations. Today it finds jus-tification only in pseudomotivations.

We are led to the conclusion that motivating statements on the part of primitive peoples can be accepted only with a great deal of skepticism and that we do better if we secure understanding by other approaches. One of these is to be found in the myths, stories, and tales of primitive peoples in general, a treasury which up to now has hardly been exploited. This book makes extensive use of myths and narratives; their intrinsic value for the task of "understanding" and the methodological difficulties involved in their adduction will be discussed in detail later on. For the present we must keep in mind, however, that the law which we shall come to call the "law of semantic depletion"— the gradual shift from a state of "expression" to one of "appli-cation"—applies, of course, to myths and narratives as it applies to all other cultural manifestations.

Since we have credited the forms of "application" with very limited value in solving problems of meaning, it is natural to demand objective criteria by which the two polar stages may be ascertained in any case. This will constitute another major concern of our presentation, but we should anticipate even now that such criteria do not exist and in all likelihood cannot exist. Where a subjective capacity for experience forms the sole basis of value judgments and where values are not even quantifiable, "communication" is limited and can take place only if it meets with a correlative capacity for experience. Someone able to relive the magnificence of a Shakespearian tragedy cannot communicate his experience to another who does not possess the same subjective capacity. This may be said of all forms of art, of music, painting, sculpture, and it applies with possibly even greater force to all forms of religious expression. One of the greatest achievements of early mankind was this "invention" of a means of communication among members of a cultural community. Taking the form of cultic action, it proved more effective even than language in transmitting certain cognitive insights (cf. chap. ii, sec. 2).

The lack of objective criteria and the limitations inherent in verbal communication characterize those spheres of man's intellectual history to which the forms of religious expression belong. Not even Dilthey, who more than almost any other philosopher was devoted to the attainment of "understanding" in historiography, seems to have made the attempt to set objective criteria. How much importance he gave to this attitude which we share with him—though on the strength of a totally different background and interests—he expressed in a talk given on the occasion of his seventieth birthday. He said: "World views are rooted in the nature of the universe and in the relationship to it which the finite, comprehending mind assumes. Thus each world view expresses, within the limitations of mind, one aspect of the universe. Each is true, but each is biased. . . ."

We do not set out here on a systematic discourse on the science of religion. Rather, we are seeking for a new way to a better understanding of what the intellect of non-Western man has created. Since this will require a detour, the reconstruction of the creative processes, our efforts must for the most part remain in the realm of hypothesis. A critique of the prevalent theories, however, will show that *they too are purely hypothetical con-*

structs. We therefore shall ask whether there are not far more natural and straightforward explanations for religious manifestations among primitive peoples than they have given. This, in turn, will depend on the image of man that we are willing to accept as correct. I assume that man was in primal times essentially what he is today (cf. chap. i). Religious expression can in any event only be formed by minds commensurate with the magnitude of the objective. Concepts of God, in our view, cannot have developed from ideas unrelated to the idea of divinity.

On the other hand, we are not ignoring the actuality of "primal stupidity." *Urdummheit,* however, is not confined to one phase of human evolution; it has its representatives at all stages of culture. But it is characteristic of primal stupidity that it is spiritually uncreative and there is no evidence that it was ever different. Always relegated to the stages of "application," it was in most instances a significant force in the degeneration of originally meaningful phenomena into semantically depleted routines. Empty routines have supplied the main body of data for the theory of pre-animistic magic. It fashioned them into an "origin of religion" that proved to be one of the most fateful dead-end roads in the history of the sciences—all the more disastrous because it met with such wide acceptance.

Since we are not embarking on a systematic treatise on the science of religion, the religious phenomena with which we shall deal are to be considered as examples, selected to illustrate the culture-morphological approach. Specialists may notice a certain partiality in favor of examples from cultures of the archaic root-crop cultivators. The bias is admitted; its main reason is the author's long acquaintance with this culture stratum and a consequent greater confidence in making assertions regarding it rather than any other. It should be self-evident that *this implies no limitations in principle.* The selection of examples arises quite naturally from the requirement that understanding must be based on copious data and that we must have worked with them long and intensively.

I shall not go into the problem of the origin of religion, which was the focal point of all earlier theories. I am convinced of the impossibility of making any statement, on the basis of available data and methods, concerning the substance and contents of the pristine form of religion. It seems far more important at this point that we recognize the basic problems with which the respective forms of religion are concerned; for by their very nature religious configurations are answers to fundamental questions regarding existence that cannot be replaced by any other answers. It will then become apparent that the course of history offers a profusion of questions posed and answered. Although we might be able to place them in relative temporal sequences, we would not be able to state categorically which is the first and oldest one.

From this skepticism follows one more restriction which I set myself in the writing of this book. The present situation of ethnology can best be characterized by the two main questions to which all research into primitive culture has addressed itself during the last decades. One is phrased historically and aims, by a variety of methods, at least for a relative, possibly for an absolute, chronology of culture strata which are believed to be isolated. As an avowed culture historian I affirm the extraordinary importance of this question. An answer to it is, however, not the object of this book. The second of the main questions, then, asks the meaning of cultural phenomena and searches for the "understanding" of which we have already spoken. *This, and only this, is the aim of my investigations.*

PART I | Man and Reality

1

THE DISTINCTIVE WAYS OF PRIMITIVE CULTURES

Any of us who study the life ways of primitive peoples pass through a first impression of their alien quality. We sense that our world view ill equips us to understand these odd activities. This is true of the artistic creations of primitive peoples no less than of many precepts and customs which rule their lives. A piece of African sculpture appears just as strange to us as the widespread practice of knocking out the incisors.

We tend to overlook the many instances where primitive peoples conduct themselves in ways which seem completely reasonable and comprehensible to us. In technological activities, such as house building or the tilling of fields, they proceed in a manner which seems quite proper to their various cultural levels as the behavior is subordinated to clearly recognizable ends. The element of strangeness is limited to certain spheres of activity and does not extend to all aspects of life.

To define these spheres of activity more precisely, a useful criterion for differentiation is the concept of ends or aims, i.e., purpose. Practical economic activities in primitive societies are obviously regulated by norms which seem quite reasonable. To be sure, such matters as hunting, house construction, the cultivation of fields, and the preparation of foods may be surrounded with ceremonies incomprehensible to us, but these appear to be of secondary significance, since—to our way of thinking—their absence would not affect the economy. The primitive hunter may think that success depends on strict ceremonial observance, but he does not neglect to set his traps or kill his prey with spear or bow and arrow.

Some actions, however, permit no reasonable interpretation from our point of view and we can ascribe to them no rational purpose. What purpose is served by the knocking out of incisors, by circumcision, by the prohibition of certain marriages, by the use of masks? The multitude of theories offered in answer to each of these questions in itself attests the difficulty of assigning purposes. Each theory sees purpose in some psychological association of the behavior with an end mistakenly conceived as its result.

13

But no single theory turns out to be more convincing than another. Rarely is the question asked—and scientifically it has never been broached—whether the curious ways of primitive cultures must, indeed, have "purpose" in the pragmatic sense of the word. Perhaps we must seek for motives in other areas of man's nature. As we progress, we shall repeatedly come face to face with the irrelevancy of the search for purpose. We will, however, deal especially with the reasons behind the curious ways of primitive peoples.

1. THE DISTORTED IMAGE OF EARLY MAN

We have already alluded to theories which purport to explain some of the strange doings of primitive peoples. Divergent as the theories may be, they have in common a particular attitude toward man. Every scientific investigation formulates a very definite *image of man,* and the importance of this for the scientific study of culture can hardly be exaggerated. Even the reporting of facts is usually unconsciously influenced by the "image," which—uncontrolled—often subsumes interpretations not inherent in the situation itself. The effect of the "image of man" becomes even more pronounced in the realm of the purely theoretical.

One theory undertakes to explain most of the oddities in the religions of primitive peoples through a concept of *pre-animistic magic.* It assumes that early man arrived at totally erroneous conclusions regarding cause and effect. Considerations for his welfare misled him into translating his false notions about nature into particular and peculiar actions. Thus, he tried to solve problems beyond his reach by employing inadequate, i.e., magical, means, in themselves explicable only as the result of defective reasoning. The origin of early religions is laid solely to the intellectual deficiency of primeval man, as it can still be studied in living primitive populations. Such an image of man's early stages must inevitably lead to a disparagement of his intellectual life, which W. Hellpach (1947: 19) calls *"Hokus-pokus."*

The main features of this image of man may be given:

1. Man is viewed as oriented exclusively toward *practical goals.* No cognizance is taken of the many activities for which no purpose

in this pragmatic sense can be stipulated. We need think only of the theater and other branches of the arts in our own culture, which have no practical (economic) purpose and yet are of great significance for our cultural life. Man has carried on activities of this nature as far back as we can trace his existence and hence, probably, at all times.

2. Man's intellectual capabilities are considered to the exclusion of almost all others. Again and again we are told of early man's striving toward mastery of nature by means of knowledge. Forgotten is the fact that the image of causally oriented man, personified in the rationally proceeding scientist of today, is no more than an abstraction. The question remains unasked whether early man's seemingly bizarre utterances may not have sprung from entirely different aspects of his multifaceted nature than his intellect.

3. Strangeness—insofar as it is regarded merely as the result of ratiocination—can be made intelligible only by imputing intellectual deficiency to early man.

4. The necessary result of such views is a *negative valuation* of all those expressions of early man's thinking which we do not find immediately comprehensible.

This characterization is not limited to theories focusing on magic. In scientific literature there are other types of theories which explicitly or implicitly share essentially the same image of man. Animism, for example, as an explanatory theory also sees man as a searcher for causes, whom ignorance of true relationships leads to false conclusions. Man comes to believe in the existence of independent souls, separable from the body, and directs his actions toward goals never to be realized with the means at his disposal. Thus, according to Tylor's view, religion as the central expression of early man's mentality is no more than the result of incorrect modes of thought and is of only negative significance.

Distinct and different from these theories is the idea of *Urmonotheismus*—of original, primal monotheism. The hypothesis, however, that belief in a Supreme Being dates back to the very beginning of human history, as framed by Andrew Lang and Schmidt, does not imply rejection of the two theories discussed before. Both remain essentially unaffected. *Urmonotheismus* merely denies that the particular concepts with which they operate are properly to be assigned to the beginning of human history. They are relegated to later stages and regarded as degenerations of mankind's initially rational behavior.

The theory of primal monotheism, too, judges early man almost exclusively according to his intellectual abilities, though it does not assign negative value to the spiritual attainment of this very earliest period. Most of that which is odd and strange is said to belong not to the rational and comprehensible first stage of human history but to have grown up later. Since magic and animism are accepted as sufficient explanations of incomprehensibility, we see that this theory partakes of the same image of man which we have discussed previously but assigns it to the second and third stages of human history. Among the advocates of *Urmonotheismus*, Radin (1927) takes a different view—one which we consider more natural—accepting primitive man as just as human as modern man. Differences between the primitive and modern capabilities are not taken as rooted in human natures but in the respective culture-historical settings.

Inevitably, however, the implicit caricature of man was to find scientific formulation. In France, Lévy-Bruhl devoted several works to examining those ways of behavior among primitive peoples which to us had to appear particularly outlandish. His researches, undertaken with great care and acumen, led to results which depart in some respects from the unexpressed assumptions underlying the above-mentioned theories. To Lévy-Bruhl, prehistoric man is not a "protoscientist" who arrived at false conclusions but another type of man entirely, whose mental life differs from ours in kind. The thought processes of primitive peoples are assumed to obey other laws, and our logic has no validity for them. Primitive man is said to possess a prelogical mentality. Some basic regularity, a so-called *loi de participation*, established mystical relationships among the things of the world, relationships which have passed out of our own scientific thought.

Lévy-Bruhl explains the strangeness of much of what we are discussing by seeing it as the result of modes of thought essentially different from our own. Thus, he makes distinctiveness the point of departure, searching the data for regularities of mental processes which may have engendered them. The scientific study of culture undoubtedly is here face to face with an important decision: whether to resign itself to an acceptance of the bizarre and incomprehensible or else to seek a way out of the difficulty by a fundamentally different path.

We are citing Lévy-Bruhl as the most prominent spokesman for the generic differentness of early man, though it may be objected that this view, contained in earlier works, was negated in the posthumous publication of his diaries (1949). The publication of his diaries, however, did not nullify his earlier works and especially not their effect on other branches of science. Lévy-Bruhl still remains the pre-eminent ethnopsychologist for those areas of the science of religion which we are discussing here.

2. OBJECTIONS TO THIS IMAGE OF EARLY MAN

For our approach, differences in principle between early and later man can be ruled out. The physical record supports us: Homo sapiens, as he has populated the earth since Upper Paleolithic times, is generally regarded as a single species, in contrast to some of his predecessors. Distinctiveness of the various races does not justify the assumption of parallel differences in fundamental human capabilities. Distinctive ways of life and modes of behavior occur even within related and immediately contiguous cultural regions, though never so divergent (within the occidental cultural community) that mutual intelligibility ceases. Unity, then, extends only over the basic human capacities and should not be taken to mean that all peoples are equally gifted when it comes to the solution of specific problems. This applies to entire populations as it applies to their individual members.

Speaking of the familiarity and comprehensibility of our own culture, we must, however, note that among (folk) customs and superstitions we meet with beliefs and actions which defy rational explanation, though we may ourselves perform them either playfully or sometimes even with some gravity. We knock on wood three times to ward off evil; raise three fingers when we swear an oath; express approval in the theater by clapping our hands together or whistle when we are displeased; and we drink to someone's health. In none of these cases is there a rational connection between the action we take and the situation which evokes it. To such instances Tylor applied the term "survivals." The quality of strangeness is no less evident here than in many of the activities of primitive peoples. We know these survivals do not originate in contemporary culture but come from older strata. Their original significance must be read from the older cultural context. Tylor (I, 20) demonstrates with an example from the British right of succession of his own day how a provision which had been quite sensible at the time of the Norman conquest, when it had been instituted, clashed with the patrilinealism of the nineteenth century. He therefore demanded that survivals be approached from a historical point of view. Most of them, however—especially those which appear the most quaint—would seem to go back to so remote a period of human history that the historical method, here understood in the narrowest sense, could not possibly discover the original meaning. They are taken either as one with their absurdity from their beginnings or as vestiges from an epoch of prelogical thought.

We should, however, entertain—at least as a possibility—the initial reasonableness of all such actions. Their present apparent irrationality may be due to their continued existence in cultural settings where the concepts which gave them meaning have been displaced or replaced. This raises two new questions regarding the nature of cultural forms.

If an apparently meaningless act may be meaningful in some other conceptual context, we may ask: *Whereby does any manifestation of culture acquire significative character?* An answer may help us understand how a given act may have meaning in one setting but lack such meaning where it appears as a survival without at the same time compelling a denial of rationality to either of the two cultures.

The idea of survivals rests on the presupposition that a cultural form can exist in a totally changed cultural environment. This leads us to inquire into the particular laws that govern continuity. We will not deal too extensively with this second question, since it has only limited connection with our subject, the strangeness of primitive ways. We note, however, that in the history of culture extraordinary importance must be granted to "inertia," the obstinate clinging to that which once has taken form, to the extent that a lack of inventiveness seems to be a dominant principle of the human mind.

We have asked, "Whereby does any manifestation of culture acquire significative character?" and this question is central to our inquiry. Survivals also occur in primitive cultures. No better than we, can the contemporary primitive give a rational account of the motives for many of his actions. If he does give one at all, it rarely stands in a logical relationship to the action itself. The Miao in Indochina, for instance, claim that success in the hunt can be augmented by smearing the weapons with the blood of the last prey (Bernatzik, I, 186) and the Eskimos say that a sick child will not recuperate unless his father abstains from all work (Rasmussen, 1929: 197). In explaining these beliefs, it is commonly agreed that the native either has committed an error or thinks in ways alien to us. The underlying assumption is that the statements must be independently meaningful. It should be considered, however, whether the actions could not originally have been expressions of specific meaningful experiences, so that the associated usages would have acquired meaning from them.

In other situations—for instance in dialectical discussions—European observers have often stressed the keen logic of the native. Livingstone relates a conversation with a Bechuana rainmaker (an excerpt is given in chap. xii below), which he characterizes as follows: "The above is only a specimen of their way of reasoning, in which, when the language is well understood, they are perceived to be remarkably acute."

By dispensing with the concepts of "prelogical" or "defective" mental processes of primitive peoples, we do away with much of the derogatory prejudgment of their spiritual life. The sacred earnestness which characterizes the actions of primitive men and which has been attested again and again by serious students of their way of life runs counter to all such theorizing.

3. PSEUDOPURPOSES

The claim of prelogical or irrational behavior freely uses the statements of primitive man in evidence. The view urged here does not have such direct documentation at its disposal. First of all, therefore, we must take the question of precisely how much significance should be attributed to direct statements on the part of "primitives."

It is often useful to seek analogues to primitive usage in our own cultural environment. Many examples are found in Catholic ecclesiastical practices. Rosaries, for instance, upon which the Pope has conferred his blessing seem to be desired before all others. A visitor to St. Peter's found a great crowd assembled in the square. Among the people was one man, kneeling, his hat filled with rosaries before him. During the Pontiff's blessing he stirred the rosaries with his hand, obviously concerned that the entire contents be touched by what he seemed to think of as the effective chemical substance of the blessing. Undoubtedly this man's action is comparable with many similar ones known from primitive peoples. There is evidently an unconscious thought in it which aims at the attainment of a substantive purpose: in this case, to heighten the desirability of the rosaries and to maximize their value. The rosary vendor apparently saw in the papal blessing an effective "magical" power which can be transferred as a substance. Obviously, his action had little in common with the principles of logic. His way of thinking is better characterized as "mystical participation." The enlightened and the scientifically oriented would not consider such behavior "rational."

We see it is not difficult to find in our own cultural setting correspondences with practices with which some of the above-cited theories of primitive mentality are concerned. The behavior of the rosary vendor can hardly be thought unique. Western culture, both in urban and rural environments, provides an abundance of other illustrations just as characteristic. Such actions may be collected from all historical periods, the earliest as well as the most recent, and from all peoples, primitives as well as the most civilized. We leave open whether "prelogical mentality" or *"Urdummheit"* applies to any of them. They do lack an important detail: The rosary vendor acts out of a devout faith whose roots cannot be determined from his superficially observable actions. Obviously, however, the actions are not the result of scientific and logical mental effort.

Our basic question is aimed toward the *understanding* of important cultural manifestations. In our example it is undoubtedly the significance of the blessing that concerns us primarily, though a discussion of the fundamental meaning of blessing and related phenomena would go beyond the task we have set for ourselves. It is sufficient if we establish that we cannot with any degree of certainty deduce the meaning of the action from the action itself. Where primitive peoples are concerned, exactly the opposite is naïvely assumed again and again. If we grant that the rosary vendor's actions partake of the meaning and significance of the blessing—possibly even of its original sense—we must not disregard such indirect connections with the creative event in primitive situations. But the event at the heart of a cultural manifestation, which is the result of a creative process, is never to be explained as a "prelogical act." Such "prelogical acts" are possible only where the basic phenomenon—in our case the blessing —is already present. The reinterpretation of the blessing in line with "prelogicality" has ancient antecedents. Jacob's way of gaining the paternal blessing intended for his older brother reveals the same belief in the substantivity of the blessing.

Where dealings with primitive peoples are concerned, informants are generally such "rosary vendors." We would not accept an interpretation of our own culture based on this one example, and by the same token we should not feel justified in explaining and interpreting the spiritual life of primitive peoples on the basis of similar evidence or even from statements by natives themselves. Direct statements are only of indirect value to science and require the greatest caution if they are to be used as evidence. They already constitute reinterpretations of the original meaning, as we can see when we draw upon other sources. Such sources are the *myths,* which often provide statements of a totally different nature concerning significant spiritual phenomena, different especially from the rituals which are said to serve only secular ends. Myths speak of grave deeds of gods and man; before that grandeur the accusation of prelogicality vanishes, even though myths present the same difficulty to immediate understanding as the actions which accompany them.

We already have spoken of the error of presupposing purposive motivation for all actions. Modern thinking considers purposes as given and concedes to them superordinate explanatory significance. The "pseudopurposes" indicated by primitive man are on the same *niveau* of utility as the actions of the rosary vendor, at best offering only secondary explanations.

The spiritual creations of Western culture—religions, great works of art, the *Geisteswissenschaften,* for example—know of no such practical purposes. We cannot reasonably assert that things must have been different in early cultures.

21

4. NON-INTERCHANGEABILITY OF MYTHIC AND SCIENTIFIC PROPOSITIONS

We come close to the roots of our question when we concern ourselves with the thought processes which underlie the supposed strangeness of behavior. According to the theorizers, primitive man rejects logical thinking and searches for mystical connections—besides empirical causality—in line with his special mental disposition. Lévy-Bruhl, whose work can stand for many, in *Die geistige Welt der Primitiven* ("The Intellectual World of the Primitives") discusses a topic which often recurs in ethnological literature: the imagined causes of pregnancy held among primitive peoples, especially the Australians. According to Spencer and Gillen, the Australian is unaware of any connection between the sexual act and pregnancy. Spirit beings, so-called "spirit-children," are said to enter a woman's body. (It so happens that this report of Spencer and Gillen, though not impossible, seems to be based on an error. Strehlow [II, 52, n. 7; III, xi] relates that the very same tribes are fully aware of the connection between copulation and reproduction where the non-human animal is concerned.) Lévy-Bruhl writes: "We must not conclude from this that [primitive mentality] does not know the role of the sexual act, but rather that it does not believe that conception is really dependent upon it, despite their more or less vague insight." He sees the explanation for their belief in *spirit-children* in an irresistible urge to find causes of a mystical kind. "Even if they had noticed that children come into the world only when fertilization has taken place they would still not arrive at conclusions which, to us, would be the only natural ones. They would persist in the belief that a woman becomes pregnant because a spirit . . . has entered her."

He formulates the difference between primitive peoples and modern men thus:

No question regarding natural phenomena presents itself to them in the same way as to us. When we require explanations, we search among the phenomena for the necessary and sufficient causes. When we succeed in determining them, we do not ask anything more. *Knowledge of the natural law is sufficient for us.* [Emphasis added.]

The primitive's attitude is, however, completely different: he invariably seeks for the "real cause" in the realm of invisible forces.

The citation—one of many possible ones—invites detailed discussion. Our supposed satisfaction with knowledge of the natural law, to which we would refer in the given example, would not account for the fact that pregnancy does not attend each sexual act or that it never does so in the case of a barren individual. Scientific thought would never stop at the mere correlation between the procreative act and pregnancy but would search for additional causation. Assuming even that all concomitant causes had been fully established, what would the whole cerebration have to do with the question raised by the event itself? Are the conception of a living being, pregnancy, birth, not miraculous events indeed? Does science really provide answers which are sufficient as they stand? "If, in the eyes of the primitive, death is never 'natural,' then it is self-evident that birth is not either" (Lévy-Bruhl, 1927: 345). But, who among us feels that science has any satisfactory statement to make about the meaning of birth or death?

If we want to investigate more closely the difference between primitive man and us, we must take a multiple approach: First, in what context do the strange manifestations of primitive life occur? Second, could the concepts behind the strange actions be replaced by scientific-logical ones? Third, is it demonstrable that primitive man prefers mystical irrationality to reason? Fourth, is it indeed true that logic permeates all spheres of our existence?

Lévy-Bruhl, in the example just quoted, equates the attitude toward birth with the attitude toward death. Scientific research has not diminished the mystery of either by any statement of higher rationality. Man's spiritual and physical existence contains many mysterious enclaves. The growth process, metabolism, maturation, all are in a way mysterious happenings. Questions of cosmogony and creation, the relationship between the animate and the inanimate world, between plants, animals, and man only multiply the examples. *Exactly in this sphere, however, we encounter most of that which seems strange and incomprehensible to us.* It all has a common element: *the basis of our existence is involved.* Significantly, concerning such matters no answer has ever been devised by rational thought that would transcend cultural boundaries.

We have not attempted to enumerate all areas to which the strange ways of primitive peoples show an affinity. The realm that is unattainable to logical thought processes is immense and permeates all of human life. Though much is open to rational explanation, though success, for instance, may be clearly attributable to skill and intelligence, who would deny that there are those among men who enjoy a special "good luck." There is no rational explanation for such instances, and they are therefore either not taken into scientific consideration or are glibly dismissed. It is given to the poets to recognize this gift: Goethe called it "natural" or "ingenerate merit." Primitives, urged by no preconceptions, have frequently shown intense awareness of it. The often-discussed quality of "mana" draws at least part of its meaning from "good fortune."

Even these brief allusions give answers to some of our questions. "Exoticism" among primitive peoples centers about phenomena for which satisfactory logical statements cannot be made. Hence for the vaunted "prelogical behavior" there really is no equivalent "logical behavior" in most cases. Knowing this does not dispel the strangeness of primitive behavior. If primitive people have found answers to questions which are inaccessible to causal logic and if these answers cannot be replaced by causal-logical ones, then the answers may well be irrational and differ from our rational ones to just this extent.

This leads us to our fourth question: Does Western man make use of logical thought in all situations? Doubtless, rational actions could often be made to substitute for irrational actions, but the decisive point remains that Western man often acts irrationally. The rosary vendor and his equals in all cultures are characterized by a similar disregard for available rational modes of behavior. Horoscopy has no equivalent in the causal-logical world of our discourse, for its significance had its origin in astral mythology at a time when man behaved in accordance with appropriate myths. Belief in the correctness of a horoscope in a time when astral myths no longer carry any weight demonstrates only the irrationality of the believer. Neither he, however, nor his forerunners among the primitives are objects of our discussion. We are to deal only with people who stand in a living relationship to the essentials of their culture. In our own cultural setting we can more easily define two such groups, but we must learn to differentiate them also in alien cultures if an ethnological science of culture is to have meaning. The methodological means for such differentiations do not concern us here. Certain strange modes of behavior, indeed, will remain closed to interpretation by categories of analysis derived from an alien culture and will appear to manifest only that *Urdummheit* already characterized in our Introduction. As we have shown, *Urdummheit* in itself could never have been creative but has always taken possession of existing forms and further adulterated their meaning.

5. *A DISTINCTION EMBEDDED IN THE NATURE OF CULTURE*

At the beginning of the previous section we asked: Is there a fundamental difference between primitive man and ourselves in regard to spiritual matters? We shall illustrate the problem by an example from Talbot (pp. 31 ff.). The Ekoi, a West African tribe, claim that kinship ties exist between persons and trees. One Sunday evening an Ibo man by the name of Oji, who served in the police force under Talbot far away from his home, suffered an attack of a sort of insanity during which he ran from his quarters after taps had sounded and headed for the woods in great excitement. A corporal and five constables tried to stop him, but he resisted violently. At Talbot's appearance he requested permission to be allowed to leave immediately, *since his tree was calling him.*

On further questioning he stated that in his homeland there were so-called Oji trees which at certain times of the year sounded a call to all those who—just as he—were named Oji. When the call is heard, the subject must get up and run until he comes to the place where the trees grow. This night, after he had gone to bed, he had heard the call in his sleep: Oji, Oji; and when he awoke he kept hearing it. Then he ran into the night. When the men tried to stop him, he had only tried to free himself, as the call of the tree had grown louder and louder.

A member of our cultural community, offering this explanation, would undoubtedly be certified as a mental patient. And yet, on second thought, the whole episode should not strike us

25

as so totally alien. Our own poets are quite capable of speaking of the call of a tree.

Obviously, poets make statements about reality that cannot be derived through causal logic: the root of poetical communication consists of just this.

We can hardly overstate the degree to which man must rely on all the different means of expression at his command if he wants to communicate about all aspects of the reality which he is capable of experiencing. The behavior of Oji is odd indeed if we look only at the externals of his actions and measure them against our standards of purposes and causal-logical consistencies. The absurdity comes about when we assign the event as a whole to a totally inappropriate category; the eccentricity tends to disappear when we recall that not every event in our culture is measured by causality and logic.

We touch here at the core of our problem. It is not that primitive man is not able to differentiate clearly one expression of reality from another. Much evidence bears this out. Shirokogoroff (p. 179) mentioned the importance of distinguishing between such evaluations of reality on the part of primitive people. Of the Tungus he reports that kin ties between men and animals are frequently mentioned and that many stories deal quite concretely with the rape of human females by animals, especially bears and tigers. From this one might conclude that in the mind of the Tungus ancestry is thoroughly understood in biological terms and that this—in this instance—would be evidence for their complete misconception of what is biologically possible: another instance of a false sense of causality. Shirokogoroff, however, indicates that the stories are considered untrue or, rather, that the bears and tigers actually are known to be human beings who have taken on the appearance of animals: "Thus they are not real and common animals." Shirokogoroff considers it improbable, on the basis of his knowledge of Tungus views, that they would concede the possibility of impregnation of human females by animals, just as they are aware of the impossibility of impregnation of female animals through a sexual act with human males.[1]

In the eagerness to find evidence of prelogical behavior, much material has been overlooked which would tend to show the actions of primitive man to be much like ours. We may become

[1] I owe this reference to a conversation with Professor Hentze.

deeply engrossed in a performance of "Macbeth," when—on another level of awareness—it should be clear to us that "it's only a play." From my own experience with natives I can well imagine what a continued conversation with the Ibo constable might be like. If one asked him if he had heard the call of the tree as one hears a human voice, he might well have answered: "Not like the voice of man, for then I would have had to assume one of my comrades was calling me. It was different, and I knew that it was a tree that was calling me." Our poets do not explicitly say that their statements are not to be taken literally but that is taken for granted. Why then should primitive peoples add such a caveat to each mythic statement? At another occasion I have shown that behavior toward masks, in a primitive setting, can be understood only on the basis of this psychical intermediacy, in which things are experienced according to their representational intention, while at the same time there is awareness of the means by which the affect is created (cf. chap. ii, sec. 3a).

It can be objected that no occidental would be likely to run into the night at such a call as Oji received and that in one respect at least the difference between the primitive and us is basic. But in the final analysis, this difference is not anchored in human nature either. If an occidental actually felt disposed to follow such a call, pressures would at once force him to act in a manner totally different from the Ibo. Our culture indoctrinates us from childhood on to apportion our drives and longings in accordance with a particular scale of values. In the Western world, causality and logical relations take precedence over all others. If some deviate from the norm—and among artists such individualists are relatively numerous—they are not considered representative members of the cultural community. Behavior such as that of the Ibo constable, if it were acted out in our society, would be seen as alien to our culture, and every response by others would reflect opposition. Ibo culture, from earliest childhood on, teaches the priority of such a call over all other considerations and demands obedience. Talbot perceptively relates how the incident was judged by those present, each in accordance with his own culture. The Yoruba, who know nothing of the summons of a tree, found the Ibo's behavior no less foolish than we might. The Ekoi enthusiastically confirmed the urgency of obeying such a call; they also knew of such trees in their own homeland.

Thus we have stated a concrete difference between us and primitive peoples. It is not rooted, however—and this should be emphasized—in human mentality, "logical" in one instance, "prelogical" in the other. It lies in the essence of the respective cultures, each formulating a scale of values by which it ranks the canon of experiences according to an order of precedence. In the example with which we have been working greater attention was given by the Ibo to some aspects which, among us, find poetical expression because they do not lend themselves to causal-logical interpretation; on the other hand, the Ibo neglected aspects which are more particularly part of the scientific sphere of experience. Many configurations of his culture must, therefore, appear to differ from ours without, however, necessitating a fundamentally different mentality as their basis.

There is one other difficulty to the understanding of the actions of primitive peoples for which the case of the Ibo police constable offers an illustration. We have seen that no single element in his conduct is outside the canon of our own experiences, if only we abandon the assumption that our minds function in causal-logical ways exclusively and—what is still worse—that everything must be comprehended by those categories. Scientific thinking is merely one possible facet of man's mind; our culture stresses it—perhaps excessively so and probably to our misfortune—while primitive man knows it but attaches a different value to it. Actually, purely scientific man does not exist: he is an abstraction.

The incident reported by Talbot belongs to a group of cultural manifestations which we designate as "totemism" or "nagualism." A totem relationship here binds man and tree and is emphasized by the identity of the names. The close affinity between man, animals, and plants will occupy us later. We shall be convinced that all such relationships are traceable to experiences quite rationally rooted. There happen to be real ties between men and trees and where they are given weight, i.e., where man is affected by them, they have found cultural expression. We are not concerned with the Ibo constable's experience per se, which is purely the result of indoctrination's having given him certain canons of belief upon which he acted. The psychological problem, therefore, is essentially one of culture; we disregarded it because we are concerned with fundamental psychological differences between ourselves and primitive peoples.

Natives often can clearly describe the spirits with whom they are conversant and whom they may even be able to see in broad daylight; the unrelenting insistence of the tree's summons belongs to the same category of experience, which we are quite ready to call "hallucinations." Yet, some of the most exalted moments in the history of mankind are related to us in just such terms. Moses receiving the commandments, Jacob's struggle with the angel, Apollo or Athena appearing to the Greek heroes—all present us with the same enigma. The only protection against such experience is a surrender of one's imagination to those aspects of life which are exclusively ruled by purpose and which can be described solely as chains of cause and effect. The incidence of hallucination is in all likelihood inherent in a specific cultural and historical situation. For each individual, the form taken by the hallucination is determined by the inventory of ideas making up his particular culture. We will not discuss here the purely psychological aspects of hallucinations but are interested rather in the conceptual presuppositions to the extent that they are cultural formations.

6. THE STRANGENESS OF SOME INTELLECTUALLY GAINED INSIGHTS

So far we have dealt with man's propensity to reify spiritual propositions (cf. chap. xiv) and with the many actions subsumed under rites, cults, and ceremonies. There is still another, though smaller, category of phenomena to be discussed: those which are amenable to treatment as intellectual, purposive behaviors yet have all the attributes of oddity. Let us take, for instance, the concepts of time and space. We shall discuss them in the following paragraphs, emphasizing the role of the intellect in the creative process leading to culture.

The limited consideration so far given to pure reason should not lead to the assumption that intellect plays no part in the creative processes of culture. Creativity draws on *all* human capabilities. The separation of poetic from scientific aspects of the human mind was chosen to demonstrate only that the assignment of certain phenomena to the category of "pure thought" usually fails to do justice to their significance.

Max Planck, in his chancellor's address, characterized reality as

29

"measurability." If this definition is or was valid for the natural sciences, then—to be applicable to man as a vital being—it can mean no more than: As a physicist, I am interested only in those aspects of reality which can be measured. Other aspects of reality —beauty, for instance—are disregarded by definition; there is no yardstick for beauty.

In his earlier writings, dealing with the work of Ernst Mach, Planck referred to the historical direction of all human knowledge as "de-anthropomorphization." Early man, he assumed, was incapable of extricating himself from the reality he tried to comprehend. The slow process of extrication—de-anthropomorphization —ultimately cleared the way for objective knowledge. Incontrovertibly, the emphasis on one aspect of reality—especially the natural-scientific—has produced astonishing results which basically distinguish Western culture from older stages of history.

A brief digression now seems indicated, for de-anthropomorphization raises an important methodological point. Can the emancipation from the *menschlichen Bedingtheiten* (this too, is Planck's term) be carried out absolutely; i.e., can a given description of reality be carried through to the exclusion of all other possible ones? Planck probably believed this to be attainable in the not-too-distant future (he lived in an era of optimism in the natural sciences), for otherwise certain of his formulations would not have been possible: "Let us suppose that a physical view of the world had been achieved that would satisfy all demands, hence be capable of expressing all empirical laws to perfection" (p. 78). Unity would be the characteristic of such an ideal world view: "Unity with regard to all individual features, unity with regard to all places and times, unity with regard to all scientists, nations, and cultures" (p. 28). Physical reality would be purged of anthropomorphisms to such a degree that the remaining constants "must, of necessity, be stumbled upon even by the Martians and, for that matter, by all intelligent beings that inhabit nature, if they have not, indeed, stumbled upon them already" (p. 25).

Obviously, modern physics no longer shares this optimism. In his utopian view of the future, Planck thought it possible to completely eliminate the fact that, ultimately, all measurement passes through the human mind (note his reference to Martians). However, even the most rigorously performed experiments presuppose the experimenter. The absoluteness of quantification is always destined to be frustrated.

Many other considerations militate against this optimism. Nonphysical sciences, especially experimental biology, in trying to apply the methods of natural science and encountering obstacles, have found that the totality of life sets a limit to complete quantification. (Compare Jacob von Uexküll, *Der Sinn des Lebens*, especially *"Ausblick,"* by Thure von Uexküll, p. 79 ff.) Nevertheless, with respect to the historical attainment of intellectual knowledge, de-anthropomorphization undoubtedly was at work.

We may again turn our attention to primitive situations and can now hope to find criteria that will help us to make meaningful distinctions between primitive cultures and our own. It is often claimed that primitive peoples lack *history*. The word is obviously carelessly chosen, for it would be sheer nonsense to assume that migrations, wars, and cultural changes have existed only since the time of their first appearance in an historical record. Not history, but historical awareness, is lacking. Ratschow (p. 88 ff.) holds the rise of historical awareness responsible for the collapse of the magical *Lebensgefühl* of prehistoric man, which was replaced by the religious *Lebensgefühl* of historical times. Ratschow takes the distinction to be a basic one, though perhaps it has less extreme implications for human nature than the distinction between prelogical and logical thought involves.

We shall turn to a brief discussion of man's relationship to time in early and late cultures. One example, from the Totela of the Zambesi, South Africa, which may stand for many interpretations has already been quoted by Frazer and Preuss (*Myths,* p. 13):

Yes, it was a long time ago. It was so long ago that at that time no white men had yet come to this country. It was before my father's days, even before the days of his father, and both died old men. Yes, it was so long ago that now only the old people speak of these past times. It was before the time when people got old and died.

This, then, is the image of a time long gone, when death first made its appearance.

An occidental might justifiably call this childlike. But being neither a mark of stupidity nor of a different mentality, it reveals only childlike ignorance in matters to which more recent cultures have attached great importance but in which earlier cultures saw little of interest. The native's relationship to time is perceptual: He concretely "sees" his grandfather, perhaps his great-great-grandfather and, in the opposite time expanse, his grandchildren and great-grandchildren. These boundaries are filled in with observable data. Anything beyond this can be known only through intuition. It requires particular values, inherent in the cultural background, to turn man's mind in the direction of the non-perceivable.

The abstract, non-perceptual relationship which characterizes our own historical awareness developed in consequence of the invention and development of written records. In those social strata of Western culture which place little weight on the written or printed word, we find a relationship to time similar to the primitive's. Only vague school memories prevent modes of expression like that of the Totela. True historical awareness is even less developed than in most primitive communities, in which there are at least small groups of individuals who maintain an outstanding oral tradition, often of amazing accuracy, over long periods of time.

The Icelandic Sagas, recorded long after the historical events, are the records of an oral tradition; the extensive genealogies and lists of kings among recent native states belong to the same category. But we shall forgo further discussion, for it would lend nothing fundamentally new to the argument.

Intuitional, non-perceptual cognition cannot have been points of departure for older cultural stages; perception must always be the first step. Let us imagine the Robinson Crusoe situation in a somewhat altered form: By some catastrophe Western man is suddenly annihilated, except for one-year-old children—children, at any rate, of an age before they can have received any enculturating instruction. Undoubtedly, the human potential of these children would be the same as that of their parents. And yet, all the books in all the libraries would be of no use to them. Before the enigmas of existence, they would fare very much as the members of the oldest cultural communities had fared. They would have to begin with perception and observation. Their relationship to time would be the same as that of the Totela.

Again, as Max Planck pointed out, the history of intellectual knowledge moves from observation and perception in the direction of de-anthropomorphization, the abstract. Western culture has progressed farther than any other along this path, which reaches back—without break—to that instance of original perception. In other words, the differences between our culture and that of early peoples are distributed along an historical gradient. Nothing in the record bespeaks fundamentally different mentalities.

The relationship of early man to geographical space illustrates the progression from perceptual to abstract thought even within primitive cultures. Orientation in space is primarily achieved through intellectual activity. Our own concepts of space have little direct relation to perception, while our theoretical views are in direct contradiction to it. As far as perception is concerned, the sun, moon, and stars move across the sky from east to west; the movement of the earth is outside of perceptive experience. But, even though we reject the Ptolemaic universe as false, we would never think of accusing Western man before Copernicus of having a prelogical mentality. We must even reckon with the possibility that future times will find flaws in our own view of the universe, and yet our *Lebensgefühl* is in no way distressed by ignorance of what later generations are likely to know.

The ancient culture stratum of cultivators knows nothing of orientation by the course of the stars. Rivers, oceans, and mountains, i.e., immediate observational data, suffice as landmarks (cf. Jensen, 1947: 38 ff.). To such people, the sun does not seem to rise from an established point of the compass but rather from various places, depending on the observer's own location—an idea which is quite in accord with direct perception. The concepts so produced differ from ours, though all cognitive activity must ultimately stem from perceptions.

We have seen that primitive peoples—even without the aid of writing—have "progressed" from perceptive to abstract awareness, for many make use of celestial orientation. More recent cultures, then, had already arrived at the abstraction that the sun is not an immediate element of human life but that its course is traced at such a distance that it may be used as an abstract point of reference regardless of man's geographical location. This has no correspondence in perception and can only be "intuited." Once apprehended, the knowledge was transmitted like any other part of learnable culture.

All these instances show primitive man's progression toward

intellectually achieved knowledge through "exact thinking." An element of strangeness is not due to mentality but is a variable dependent upon the degree of perceptivity which differentiates cultural epochs, always characterized by progression in the direction of abstraction.

7. THE CONCEPT OF PROGRESS

Progress implies movement along a path but does not specify a defined goal. Progress in this sense means no more than departure from a certain location. Progress, then, suggests a unilineal evolutionary path for humanity—always away from where man had previously been.

It has long been apparent that the idea of progress could contribute statements of only limited value to culture history. Who would apply "progress" to a comparison of the work of Beethoven, Bach, and Corelli? The description of physical reality has, however, shown "progress" from the days of Newton, to Helmholtz, and then to Planck; but "progress" is not a term applicable to the essence of culture. Every culture is at ease with its intellectual *niveau*. Could classical Greece have been dissatisfied in lacking cognitive values which are part of every school curriculum today? From our own experience we know there is no such disquietude; and neither could there have been such unrest in the intellectual life of primitive peoples, at least until they became acquainted with Western culture. And even then change was not inevitable. If Michelangelo could exist without knowledge of the cognitive values of the twentieth century and yet be able to express something that carries meaning for all time, then the nature of man and the essence of a cultural epoch can hardly be sought in cognitive contents.

Resistance to the idea of progress and to its application to culture history needs only to point to those spheres of culture which preclude quantitative comparison. The depiction of an animal, created in the Upper Paleolithic, holds its own with the artistic creations of any period. The idea of progress may be applied meaningfully only to technological and other quantifiable facts but never to the essence of cultural configurations. These are not sums of elements and, therefore, can never be dissected into elements. Historical comparison of rational-cognitive elements can investigate the quantity of such elements and the degree of de-anthropomorphization. But the inalienable, individual worth of a culture, which permits no comparison with other cultures, is not fundamentally (and never solely) determined by the sum and the distinctiveness of rational cognitive elements; it lies in a genuine creativity which can never be any the truer, more beautiful, or better, for belonging to a more advanced period. Cultures owe their truth, beauty, and excellence to the creative source alone, from which they sprang.

The creative aspects of primitive cultures must be the true object of any scientific treatment of culture. The history of progress, i.e., the quantitatively identifiable changes in the cultural inventory, will never be understood unless this difficult problem is solved. We refused to take the detour through the supposedly alien mentality of primitive man. On the contrary, we have attempted to demonstrate that the understanding of primitive culture is forever closed to us if we consider all phenomena as objects of intellectual cognition in the light of Western ways of thinking. If we see them as creative events and compare them to analogous events in our own culture, there is at least a possibility of dispelling the aura of exoticism and to attain true historical understanding. This presupposes, of course, that earliest man possessed, no less than contemporary primitives, the same capacity for experience that we possess. We will be open to this experience only when we remember that for us, too, a tree can be more than an object of scientific study and that it may affect us through cultural reformulations which are intellectually incomprehensible. In the numerous instances where such genuine, spontaneous understanding cannot be realized, it is better, temporarily, to desist from interpretation, rather than distort the data to suit questionable theories which act as obstacles to understanding.

At the center of our discussion, then, is a basic distinction between quite different experimental foundations of cultural formulations. In reference to intellectual cognition, we have taken over Planck's idea that progress seems to be connected with increasing de-anthropomorphization, although we cannot share his optimism that there will be an ultimate and absolute description of reality in terms of the natural sciences. In the non-intellectualized perceptions of reality—its qualitative appearances and configurations which defy analysis—de-anthropomorphization does not exist in the course of historical transformation. The experience of full participation in nature and life, as for instance when man feels a state of oneness with certain trees, cannot be tested by any instrument, not because such an instrument has not yet been invented but because no such instrument can exist. If one could be invented, it would mean the end of humanness. Not "method," but a capacity for subjective experience, is the only approach to understanding.

To assert the totally different mentality of primitive man, we would first have to deny modern man the capacity of appreciating the qualitative aspects of reality. We can hardly deny it to the primitives, since many of their cultural configurations are comprehensible only as expressions of particular qualities of reality and as means of communication concerning them. Who would seriously believe that the occidental either cannot so experience or cannot give Gestalt to such experiences?

All such forms contain statements regarding the "truth" of reality which is of the greatest importance for man, and it may therefore appear unobjectionable to call them statements of "knowledge," though their source and the test of their verity do not accord with scientific standards. The verity of a poetic statement about reality, for example, is practically of the same nature as the question about the origin of the authority which is granted to certain prominent members of a cultural community; for, this authority can be based only upon the truth of the statements made about it. The difficulty of finding objective criteria for this kind of truth is attested by the readiness with which the members of some cultural communities grant authority to anyone who lays claim to it. We have already mentioned the believers in horoscopes and similar "sects" and have come to realize the impossibility of discussing with them the truth contents of their beliefs. No rational argumentation could bear out the authority which Western culture has granted to Shakespeare and Goethe. Nor has philosophy, as far as I can see, contributed anything to a scientific answer to this question. We must content ourselves with a statement that is applicable to all cultures, namely that the verity of dominant ideas is acknowledged by the representatives of their respective cultural communities.

At the outset we asked what it is that gives meaning to any

cultural phenomenon. At this point in our discussion, we would answer: Each phenomenon, in its pristine state, contains one or several statements of reality and is at the same time a means of communicating the contents of that statement—giving both to "statement" and to "means of communicating" the broadest possible interpretation. We have tried to show that statements of essential cultural expression in early cultures are neither knowledge of causal-logical provenance nor replaceable by such knowledge. A cultural phenomenon is meaningful when the statement it contains is *true*. For our discussion this means only that *the creative members of a cultural community knew, or know, experiences of reality which justify corresponding behavior.*

Beyond this, meanings within a given culture often depend upon relationships to other statements about reality, within the same culture. Culture is a system of such statements from which single statements cannot arbitrarily be detached. The "fit" of any manifestation of culture into the over-all system is the second characteristic of meaning; its absence marks a *"survival."* Survivals, having their origin in earlier culture strata, make statements about reality which are no longer experienced as true. Even where they are still comprehensible, they often contradict the central ideas of the newer world view.

Our second question concerned the difference between early cultures and our own. We attempted to show that the idea of progress can be employed only regarding matters of the intellect. Knowledge begins with perception and progresses to the abstract. In this respect, the contrast between the most ancient cultures and our own is that of lesser advancement to maximal advancement (to date). We also tried to demonstrate that this distinction, at least where the older cultures are concerned (but, in our opinion, even in Western culture), does not penetrate to the core of culture history. At all times and independent of progress, man was capable of the qualitative discernment which is the essence of culture. Distinctions between cultures are not to be measured by any yardstick of progress and cannot be reduced to qualitative differences in mentality. Rather, proper distinctions are innate factors, so numerous that they defy enumeration. Important, however, is man's capacity for experiencing and representing the grandeur and nobleness of life. The presence or lack of this capacity is not a variable, dependent on technical means, but depends on the magnitude and nobleness of the formed and forming experiences. In this respect, no difference exists between older and younger cultures. From this point of view, cultural change is nothing but a change of *Weltsicht,* of the attitude toward the environment. Man has again and again asked questions bearing on the foundations of his existence; he has sought answers to the changing aspects of the reality about him and has thereby produced the documents of culture history which, at the same time, are a self-realization of original creativity.

2

MYTH, CULT, AND PLAY

We have stressed the basic changelessness of the nature of man from the moment that the word *man* can justifiably be applied to him. What differences there are relate to the contents of cultural configurations. We now go on to describe the content and nature of a world view still deducible from the life ways of contemporary primitive peoples. In the area of religion, myths and cults undoubtedly stand in the foreground of such considerations, although there seem to have been religious ideas at all times which found little or no mythic or cult expression; this we shall see when we discuss the "High God" concept (chap. iv).

1. MYTH AND CULT AS HOLISTIC WORLD VIEWS

In most early forms of religion, myths and cults are closely related. Mythic perception has decisively influenced all of man's life patterns. We find it at the base, not only of cults in the narrow sense, but also of many other areas of life which we cannot consider cults but which in form and content are determined by mythic attitudes. The often complicated social organization of primitive peoples may serve as illustration. These were not invented for practical ends; they were, no less than cultic religious activities, reactions, felt to be sacred duties, to experiences of a mythic reality. Dual organizations, for example, in which the social macro-unit is divided into exogamous moieties, are often traced back to divine twins, reflecting in mythical guise the polarity of the world, the antitheses of day and night, male and female, right and left, fauna and flora, and a multitude of other polar opposites (cf. chap. vii, sec. 1).

Much the same may be said of house building, settlement patterns, or economic activities. We find the obligatory nature of the myth and of the world view which it contains expressed by analogous regularities in cults and in other spheres of life.

What is said here concerning the two religious forms of expression—myth and cult—has even more generalized application and can embrace some of the most variant forms of *Lebens-*

gestaltung. Myth and cult have long been recognized as inseparable, although the proper implications of this fact have often
been overlooked. K. T. Preuss, in his later works, saw the connections clearly, especially in his book on the religious content
of myths (1933). He gave numerous illustrations and developed
some noteworthy concepts around them without, however, coming
to recognize the untenability of the hypothesis of primal magic.
The most significant contribution to our topic was made by
W. F. Otto. In the Introduction to *Dionysos* (1933), he elaborated a profound conception of these phenomena, doing justice
alike to the nature of man and the magnitude of the subject. He
shows convincingly that myth and cult constitute a unity. (See
also Kerényi, "Was ist Mythologie" and [with C. G. Jung] *Einführung in das Wesen der Mythologie,* or Eliade, "Mythus der
ewigen Wiederkehr.")

Primitive religion offers so much evidence for the intimate
connections between the two modes of expression that the fact
itself can hardly be contested. At times, cultic activities are no
more than dramatic representations of a corresponding myth. We
will often speak of examples of this kind. Even the recitation of a
myth may occasionally be an act of a pronounced cultic nature.
Recitation occupies the center of the festive proceedings associated with the ball games of the Witoto (South America); it
fills the nights of the long ceremonial period, while the days are
given over to the games. " 'We don't only dance,' say the Witoto,
'though you say: 'they do nothing but dance'; rather, we tell our
tales at the festival' " (Preuss, 1921–23: 644–56). Questions are
asked and answered by the telling of a myth; and only then do
they dance and play ball, for " 'the tale shows that we do not dance
without reason.' " Thus, for example, one group will bring red
Vacuri fruit to the "master of the feast," chant an old traditional
song, and ask about the origin of the Vacuri tree. The "master of
the feast"—he has this function because he "knows much"—
"fixedly looks (at the fruits), explains the song and tells about
the origin (of the Vacuri tree). . . ." Then all dance until dawn.
Thus the "master of the feast" tells "without tiring" of the origin
of numerous fruits, of the origin of the ball, and also of the
origin of man.

This stressing of the myth in cultic feasts impressively reveals
its relationship to man. It would be wrong to compare myth

telling with the telling of fairy tales despite some external similarities. We could sooner establish a parallel with the reading of the Gospel on a Christian holiday when the past reality upon which the festival is founded is revived in the minds of the congregation. In the instance of the Witoto, the tribal community "celebrates" profound concerns of its members who—without any doubt—perceive the myths as satisfying and therefore true answers to questions which seem to them of the greatest importance. The festive character of the event is thus in itself of basic significance, for festive experience is different from everyday experience. Mythic truths are of a kind revealed only in a festive atmosphere. In a prosaic setting, translated into the language of science, for instance, they are robbed of that splendor which literally constitutes their significance. Later on we shall deal with the relationship between myth and ceremonial. For the present, we shall start with the "measure of truth" which the genuine myth contains. We believe that we can "empathize" with it only if we let the festive mood of the primitive celebrant find an echo within ourselves.

As we have seen, the mythic world view radiates over many sectors of man's existence, but it is most directly connected with those activities which we designate as cults or ceremonies. They do not differ basically from other forms of behavior insofar as these carry the imprint of the mythic world view. All share the religious-ethical attitude which tries to realize human nature in an awareness of its divine provenance and its partaking of the divine (see below, chap. ix). Cults emphasize this aspect. They serve a fundamental need of man, lifting that which he recognizes as an essential value in life beyond the sphere of the ordinary, placing it at the focus of festive observances, thereby attesting to the overwhelming significance of the fact before himself and before the community. This can hardly be overemphasized. Social order, settlement patterns, and the like may be regarded as *adaptations* to an understood order. Cults, however, are a *demonstration* of this order; through them the community gains a heightened awareness of it. The need of giving fitting formal expression to the essential values of life is not only the motive force in the origination of cults—as in the originations of all creative processes, for that matter—but a major motive for their continuance as regularly repeated customs. Every ceremony, every solemn occasion depends on it. Our own environment offers many illustrations: family gatherings foster the "family spirit"; the members demonstrate a need to "represent" the cohesiveness of the family unit and the "belonging" of the individuals. Many examples are found in public life. One need think only of patriotic celebrations and their manifold ceremonial.

In all cases the given order exists per se. Everyone knows the order and his role in it, but it is nevertheless considered necessary to raise it to a level of heightened awareness. This inner drive can originate new forms of expression. Once they are in existence, however, it is natural that they be employed. That man feels this urge especially to express essential values of life, relating him to the divine, needs no further explanation. The cults of the great religions are eloquent evidence. To the same extent, however, this applies to the cults of primitive peoples.

2. CULT AS A MEANS OF COMMUNICATION

We shall here discuss only two of the essential characteristics of primitive cults, the first of which has received little attention heretofore. Living in a community, man needs a means of communication by which he can transmit all of his important concerns. Among ourselves, speech takes on this function with astonishing exclusiveness, though we are well aware of other forms of communication and occasionally make use of them. Facial expressions, gestures, glances often say more than words. When we note a peculiar expression we may tell ourselves: I could not express in words what I see, but I do understand what the expression conveys. There are expressive contents which cannot be transmitted through speech. We often prefer—not only on "ceremonial" occasions—a gesture or movement to the use of words.

Naturally, speech is an important and probably the most important means of communication among contemporary primitives, just as it surely was in prehistoric cultures. The great significance of myths, which after all utilize speech, proves it. And yet, other forms of communication have far greater importance in those cultures than in ours. In the sphere of religious expression, cults occupy the foreground. They were the great religious "language" of early times whose meaning has declined more and more in the course of time. Only in an "applied" form has this means of communication been carried into later cultures, where it has served to unite large-scale population gatherings through communal experience. Even in the earliest periods of history, its most prominent function was the linking together of communities through collective activity. To this day, archaic peoples have practically no social stratification, a fact which has often led to a mistaken overemphasis of the collective aspect of their lives. Archaic peoples have even been denied the possibility of individual experience, and a "collective soul" has been declared responsible for all their cultural configurations—particularly cults. Such a collective soul is hard to imagine, unless we mean to find it in the dependence of individuals on principles accepted by the community as a whole; but this dependence has applied at all times and applies now to the life ways of all people. In any case, there is enough evidence that "individuality" is of decisive importance even among the most archaic populations of culture history. The place of the shaman in the community is strong evidence (chap. xi), but myths affirm even more insistently that important events are to be attributed to single great personages.

"Collective soul" aside, cults nonetheless were the preferred means of communication in socially unstratified and hence homogeneous communities. Primitive peoples' statements concerning the origin of cults favor the assumption that the activity of a prominent personage, assigned by them to "primeval time," lies at the basis of each cult. Among some peoples, cult rules the religious life to the exclusion of the pertinent myths, which seem to have been lost. In any event, we often possess detailed descriptions of the ceremonial life with no indication of mythic connections which might make the activity itself comprehensible to us. Among other peoples, again, myths predominate. It is probably no accident that so archaic a people as the Witoto give precedence to myth telling and place it ahead of other forms of expression in their cultic feasts; according to K. T. Preuss, the Witoto are remarkably given to philosophical speculation, in contrast with others of similar cultures. This may be the cause of their preference for verbal communication. It must be said, however, that ethnology is of course particularly vulnerable to the individual inclinations and interests of its researchers and that a dearth of myths as well as the insufficiency of some cult descriptions may often be traced to the ethnologist.

Were it not for all-embracing communication between persons and especially between generations, there would be no history of culture. Joining in the activities of the cult is of decisive importance for the transmission of the essential world view to the rising generation. Puberty ceremonies, after all, have no other meaning than the initiation of youth into full membership of the community. This applies especially to the initiation into the secret men's cults of the root-crop cultivators. To show how cultic activity serves as a means of communication in primitive culture, we shall refer briefly to a few significant features of the mythic world view which underlies the culture of most of the cultivator populations. Accordingly, the present condition of the world was preceded by one totally different. Among other differences, man did not yet have his present form of being, and there was no such thing as foodstuffs. An event of great import, centering about the killing of a deity and involving the origination of food plants, terminated primeval time and instituted the present form of life including mortality and the procreative capabilities of man. Often the murdered deity is identified or associated with the moon. At this point, we must limit ourselves to such seemingly disconnected details. They are properly part of a system of concepts which I have presented in another work (Jensen, "Weltbild"; see also chap. viii, sec. 3).

Among the Konso, a population of cultivators in southern Ethiopia, the great initiation feast at which all the boys who have grown to maturity are initiated into the cult secrets takes place only every eighteen years—apart from a few intermediate festivals. A few days before the celebration the young men are sent without any food into the uninhabited bush to kill a hare. We should interpret this phase of the ceremony in the following way: The young men directly experience the absence of foodstuffs in primeval times, re-enact the first act of killing by bringing down a hare—an animal which African mythology almost universally associates with the moon—and thus they obtain the first food. Only now may they participate in the ceremonies and "only in this way do they attain their procreative faculties." Then they are true men and full members of the tribe. Even a married man who has not participated in the cultic re-enactment of the mythic events cannot—according to belief—beget children, for his seed is as water: so little do they value biological fact, with which they are doubtless acquainted, and so strong is their belief in the order-producing primeval myth.

I chose this illustration though we do not possess the corresponding explanatory myth and only the cultic actions are known. I chose it quite deliberately: there are enough other populations whose cults, myths, and the associations between the two are known. If, however, as in this instance, we know only the course of a ceremony, we are tempted to take a stab at theoretical explanations which set out from incomprehensible details, each of which is explained as magic for some practical end. The explanation which we offer, referring to a mythic background which is not in the record, must naturally remain quite hypothetical; *but so are all the explanations which invoke magic.* If hypothetical explanations are to be admitted, then at least admit such that bring us closer to an understanding in terms of rational actions. In other words, we accept the connection between a mythic world view and independently incomprehensible cultic activities to the extent that we feel constrained to seek for mythic explanations even where such myths are not recorded. Obviously, such mythic backgrounds may not be freely invented. We must be able to separate out comprehensive mythic images, larger in scope than has been done hitherto. Then many of the actions of primitive peoples will explain themselves as meaningful cultic references to mythical events.

We will frequently have to return to the interpretation of uncomprehended cults through references to mythic accounts (for instance, chap. xi, sec. 4). Here we are interested specifically in the communications function of cults. Many years, for instance, the young Konso lives under a strain of expectation; then come the great events of the long ceremonial period and finally marriage, which comes immediately upon the occasion of the feast. Hence marriages are concluded only once every eighteen years and then simultaneously by all who have reached a certain level in the age-class system. All this raises cult participation far beyond the efficacy of verbal instruction. The initiates are not "taught" a world order; they *live* it with utter intensity.

45

3. CULT AS PLAY

The "play" aspect of cult has been clearly set forth by J. Huizinga in *Homo Ludens*. Brilliantly and convincingly he shows to what extent play enters into all cultural configurations and goes on to deal with cult at some length. It seems particularly fitting to discuss Huizinga's work in this context chiefly because it makes a statement about the play character of cult in a manner which cannot easily be improved upon and, moreover, because his work makes it especially obvious that satisfactory results cannot be achieved if one focuses predominantly on the external and formal elements of cultural phenomena and overlooks the fact that human activity in creating new cultural forms is primarily determined by spiritual cognition.

A. Huizinga's Conception of Play

Huizinga himself expresses his initial ideas on the nature of play as follows:

In tackling the problem of play as a function of culture proper and not as it appears in the life of the animal or the child, we begin where biology and psychology leave off. In culture we find play as a given magnitude existing before culture itself existed, accompanying it and pervading it from the earliest beginnings right up to the phase of civilization we are now living in. We find play present everywhere as a well-defined quality of action which is different from "ordinary" life. We can disregard the question of how far science has succeeded in reducing this quality to quantitative factors. In our opinion it has not. In all events it is precisely this quality, itself so characteristic of the forms of life we call "play," which matters. . . . We shall observe this action in play itself and thus try to understand play as a cultural factor in life [p. 4].

Huizinga makes a point of locating the play element in various cultural phenomena, particularly in cultic activities, or, more precisely, he makes a point of tracing these activities to play.

Huizinga then examines the concept "play" and establishes some main characteristics: play is above all voluntary activity. "Play to order is no longer play." "Child and animal play because they enjoy playing, and therein precisely lies their freedom." "Play is superfluous." "It is never imposed by physical necessity

46

or moral duty" (p. 8). Later (chap. ix) we will attempt to show that playing—insofar as it is indeed cultic—can be exclusively traced back to religious-moral obligations. This freedom implies that play "is not 'ordinary' or 'real' life. It is rather a stepping out of 'real' life into a temporary sphere of activity with a disposition of its own" (p. 8). An example will illustrate this proper sphere of play: A father hugs his four-year-old son who is playing "trains." The child says: "Don't kiss the engine, Daddy, or the carriages won't think it's real" (p. 8). This realization of the "only-pretending" quality of the world of play is one of the most significant marks for all who play: "We play and know that we play, so we must be something else besides merely rational beings, for play is irrational" (p. 4). The consciousness of "only pretending" does not prevent it "from proceeding with the utmost seriousness . . . with an absorption that passes into rapture . . ." (p. 8). Play may "rise to heights of beauty and sublimity that leaves seriousness far behind" (p. 8). Furthermore, play is always disinterested. It stands "outside the immediate satisfaction of wants and appetites." It interpolates itself as a "temporary activity" (p. 9). The disinterestedness of play is the core of Huizinga's ideas. It constitutes the bridge which leads from play to all those actions which so tenaciously resist biological explanation. Cults and myths lie just as far outside the area of "immediate satisfaction of wants and appetites" as play and for that reason alone would belong to its sphere. "Now in myth and ritual[1] the great instructive forces of civilized life have their origin: law and order, commerce and profit, craft and art, poetry, wisdom and science. All are rooted in the primeval soil of play" (p. 5).

A further characteristic of play is its spatial limitation. "All play moves and has its being within a play-ground marked off beforehand either materially or ideally, deliberately or as a matter of course" (p. 10). This, too, constitutes an important link with the sacred observances. Formally, the sacred precinct cannot be distinguished from the playground. "The arena, the card table, the magic circle, the temple, the stage, the screen, the tennis court, the court of justice, etc., are all in form and function play-grounds, i.e., forbidden spots, isolated, hedged round, hal-

---

[1] The English translation of *Homo Ludens* regularly employs *ritual* where the German version has *Kult*. Despite divergent terminology, the meanings clearly coincide.—Trans.

lowed, within which special rules obtain" (p. 10). Play creates order and is order. Among other elements of play Huizinga mentions tension, the propensity to form clubs, and the urge to secretiveness and mummery. "Tension means uncertainty, chanciness [p. 10]. . . . With a certain amount of tension something must 'come off.' . . . The club pertains to play as the hat to the head" (p. 12). "The exceptional and special position of play is most tellingly illustrated by the fact that it loves to surround itself with an air of secrecy" (p. 12). "The differentness and secrecy of play is most vividly expressed in 'dressing up.' . . . The disguised or masked individual 'plays' another part, another being. He *is* another being" (p. 13).

Huizinga states:

Summing up the formal characteristics of play we might call it a free activity standing quite consciously outside "ordinary" life as being "not serious," but at the same time absorbing the player intensely and utterly. It is an activity connected with no material interest, and no profit can be gained by it. It proceeds within its own proper boundaries of time and space according to fixed rules and in an orderly manner. It promotes the formation of social groupings which tend to surround themselves with secrecy and to stress their difference from the common world by disguise or other means [p. 13].

There is no question that Huizinga succeeded in arriving at insights basic to the cultural sciences by his characterization of play. It is important for our context that he finds all the essential criteria of play repeated in cult. Earlier, ethnologists had pointed out that a large number of sacred activities of all religions had assumed the forms of play, and Huizinga himself cites several such observations. (Naturally, we are not referring to the repeated statements which rely on a play instinct in explanation of everything and anything that won't "fit.") Primitive man himself makes statements which show him aware of the link between sacred acts and play. Huizinga even adduces the exalted authority of Plato who unreservedly recognized "the identity of ritual and play . . . as a given fact" (p. 18). Though there were predecessors, it was Huizinga who expanded the connections between play and cult into a system. Nowhere had a thorough proof been given that play had so extensive and significant a function in the history of culture. We shall let Huizinga himself demonstrate the step-by-step intergradation that lies between play as such and sacral ritual play:

We are hovering over spheres of thought barely accessible either to psychology or to philosophy. Such questions plumb the depth of our consciousness. Ritual is seriousness at its highest and holiest. Can it nevertheless be play? . . . Our conclusions are to some extent impeded by the rigidity of our accepted ideas. We are accustomed to think of play and seriousness as an absolute antithesis. It would seem, however, that this does not go to the heart of the matter. . . . Let us consider for a moment the following argument. The child plays in complete—we can say, in sacred—earnest. But it plays and knows that it plays. The sportsman, too, plays with all the fervour of a man enraptured, but he still knows that he is playing. The actor on the stage is wholly absorbed in his playing, but is at all times conscious of "the play." The same holds true for the violinist, though he may soar to realms beyond this world. The play-character, therefore, may attach to the sublimest forms of action. Can we now extend this line to ritual and say that the priest performing the rites of sacrifice is only playing? At first it seems preposterous, for if you grant it for one religion you must grant it for all. Hence our ideas of ritual, magic, liturgy, sacrament and mystery would all fall within the play-concept. . . . The ritual act has all the formal and essential characteristics of play which we enumerated above, particularly insofar as it transports the participants to another world [p. 18].

I believe that ethnology can accept Huizinga's ideas without the slightest hesitation. The most sacred acts are play. Play is "a contest *for* something or a representation *of* something" (p. 13; emphasis added). These are the two basic aspects under which we may describe cultic acts in terms of play.

B. Cult as Celebration

Having followed Huizinga's ideas to this point, we must now turn toward a criterion of the play concept which Huizinga specifically rejects. All cultic activities, he states, are play. How about the converse of this statement, however? Is all play cultic activity? Doubtless no. Hardly anyone will equate a card game or a soccer match with a sacred ceremony. Huizinga never made it entirely clear whether or not he would stand by the inversion

of the statement. In some instances he seems to deny it unequivocally; in others he leaves it uncertain.

Now if the inversion does not hold, what then is the distinction
between simple play and sacred play? There should be some in-
dicator which sets one off from the other. This criterion would
be of greatest significance to the scientific study of culture since,
being the essence of cultic activity, it would express the very
nature of the activity. At one point Huizinga himself stresses this.
He says:

Passing now from children's games to the sacred performances in
archaic culture, we find that there is more of a mental element "at
play" in the latter, though it is excessively difficult to define. The
sacred performance is more than an actualization in appearance only,
a sham reality; it is also more than a symbolical actualization—it is a
mystical one. In it, something invisible and inactual takes beautiful,
actual, holy form. The participants in the rite are convinced that the
action actualizes and effects a definite beatification, brings about an
order of things higher than that in which they customarily live. All the
same this "actualization by representation" still retains the formal
characteristic of play in every respect [p. 14].

There is agreement that cultic activities have all "the formal
characteristics of play." But what is that additional "mental element" which enters into play and is so "excessively difficult to
define"? According to Huizinga it is a mystical actualization,
though he does not tell us anything more specific and leaves us
without an answer to this question which is so decisive for the
scientific study of culture. Only in the passage quoted above does
he mention this "mental element." A little further along in his
book he states that "such ritual play is essentially no different
from one of the higher forms of common child-play or indeed
animal play" (p. 17). We do not learn, however, what "higher
forms" signifies here. Other passages lead us to assume that the
difference between higher and simpler forms of play is in no way
fundamental. Neither is there any doubt that Huizinga does not
accord undue importance to the additional "mental element"
which is said to elevate cultic activities above simple play. One
quotation will clearly show his views: "Archaic society, we would
say, plays as the child or animal plays. Such playing contains at
the outset all the elements proper to play: order, tension, move-

ment, change, solemnity, rhythm, rapture" (p. 17). (I doubt, though, that we may carry the notions of order and solemnity over into animal play and related child play; they seem to pertain only to traditional play. Later we shall have to say a word about the necessity of distinguishing between several categories of play.)

Only in a later phase of society is play associated with the idea of something to be expressed in and by it, namely, what we would call "life" or "nature." Then, what was wordless play assumes poetic form. In the form and function of play, itself an independent entity which is senseless and irrational, man's consciousness that he is embedded in a sacred order of things finds its first, highest, and holiest expression. *Gradually the significance of a sacred act permeates the playing. Ritual grafts itself upon it; but the primary thing is and remains play* [p. 17; emphasis added].

This then is the decisive statement to which our objection was addressed and which we must discuss in some detail. One cannot help but feel that the rising of cults is here seen as something quite inconsequential and incidental, which is superadded to primary play "in a later phase of society." The transformations of play into sacred act, which is the focus of interest for the study of culture, is of secondary importance according to Huizinga. In theory, a cult could graft itself onto any play activity. It seems to us that a very essential nexus has quite escaped him, though he had encountered the problem. He takes issue at great length with ideas contributed by Leo Frobenius (p. 15). Before we give the problem detailed attention we shall, however, let a work of K. Kerényi make its point concerning the nature of celebration. It deals with our problem and is mentioned by Huizinga though without detailed evaluation.

Huizinga emphasizes how much his views of play have in common with Kerényi's views of celebration and feast. Both share a character of primacy and a certain indefinable quality.

In the very nature of things the relationship between feast and play is very close. Both proclaim a standstill to ordinary life. In both mirth and joy dominate, though not necessarily—for the feast too can be serious; both are limited as to time and place; both combine strict rules with genuine freedom. In short, feast and play have their main characteristics in common. The two seem most intimately related in dancing. According to Kerényi, the Cora Indians who live not far from the Pacific coast of Mexico call their sacred feast of the young corn-cobs and the corn-roasting the "play" of their highest god [p. 21]. . . . There is no question, feasts are play; and Kerényi himself has already expressed this with all clarity.

It seems to us, however, that Kerényi has expressed very much more. All cults are feasts and all feasts are play. But that something which differentiates them is an "additional mental element" which carries through the entire work and was, as a matter of fact, the author's main concern. To transform human effort into a feast

something divine must be added, whereby the otherwise impossible becomes possible. One is raised to a plane where everything is "as on the first day," "shining," "new," and "occurring for the first time," where one is together with gods, indeed where one is divine oneself, where the breath of creation is blowing and where one participates in creation. That is the nature of the feast, and that does not exclude repetition. On the contrary, as soon as one is reminded of it through signs of nature, through tradition and through habit, then one is capable again and again of taking part in a heightened state of being and creating. Time and man become festive. . . . In the background of the corn festival stands—no matter whether it is bringing forth this idea for the first time or remembering it over and over again —the reality of the fate of the corn. Why does the idea of that fate arise as a reality for people who exist in a life-unity with the corn —why does it arise just at the "high time" of the corn, and take the form of the fate of a divine being: that would be idle speculation. *From something present something still more present has arisen, from a reality an even higher reality.* . . . Between the serious and the playful, the strictly bound and the arbitrarily free extends the festive atmosphere. This paradox can be solved only if we focus our attention on the central idea. A reality becomes a psychological actuality and we experience it as a convincing insight. . . . In this instance the idea is objective actuality become psychological reality and, in the process, slightly distorted by its contact with the human substance, adulterated, as it were, by fears and desires [Kerényi, pp. 70, 71, 73, and 70].

Two things then differentiate the sacred feast from other play. First, there is a deeper and more fundamental relationship to reality; then a special psychological state is indicated, a spirit of celebration and solemnity without which the creative process would be unthinkable. This spirit intimately links all men to their gods according to their respective beliefs. Man relives primeval times when deities, or men who were like gods, made the world as it is today. Thus cult is not just any order re-enacted but the true order, the order under which man lives and which shapes his image of reality. Indeed, feasts and festivals are repetitious, but they are imbued with the creative spirit of primeval times, or else they could not be what they are.

Such "self-recreating" is naturally repetitious. Primitive man knows it; consciously and painstakingly he repeats the religious deeds of the ancestors: This is the guiding principle of his religion. Repetition saps the strength of life and drains life of living. With each repetition of a religious act, however, an element of creativity is retained which is irretrievably lost once the act has ceased to be repeated [Kerényi, p. 61].

Here Kerényi evidently comes to grips with that "additional mental element" which Huizinga mentions only to neglect. As a matter of fact, he quite deliberately obliterates it again when he deals with the term *Ergriffenheit* ("seizure") which Frobenius coined. *"Ergriffenheit,"* however, refers to just those two criteria of which we speak. "To be seized" means (even in common usage) to experience a psychological state that lifts man out of the customary. It is a festive sense which is to a certain extent characteristic of man in the creative moments of his life. "To be seized" points toward a reality oriented toward man. Frobenius said that man was seized by the essence of things. One might say that at an inspired moment in time man won a deeper knowledge and had revealed to him the order of reality—that which is divine in things.

C. Reality and Play

In contrast to Kerényi, Huizinga feels that the process which leads to the institution of a feast is

altogether inaccessible to our observation. It is only by fanciful metaphors that Frobenius and Jensen force an approach to it. The most we can say of the function that is operative in the process of image-making or imagination is that it is a poetic function; and we define it best of all by calling it a function of play—the *ludic* function, in fact [p. 24].

Accordingly, it would be quite a forlorn effort to tackle the problem of creative effort, since—as Huizinga reasonably observes— it is hidden from observation. Yet there is an abundance of data readily accessible.

There are, for instance, all those statements which will be made by the members of the primitive society itself. No one will doubt that the mood of participation in a board game differs materially from the attitude toward a tribal ceremony. Huizinga acknowledges this, but we wish to show that there is more to the difference than a matter of "higher forms" of play. Primitive man insists on relating the sacredness of festive occasions to events in the primeval past. K. T. Preuss (*Religiöse Gehalt der Mythen*) demonstrates this convincingly. Griaule (*Dieu d'eau*, pp. 233 ff.) reports that the Dogon, a tribe in the Western Sudan, give an annual cultic representation of the mythical theft of fire. The myth tells of a divine smith who broke off a piece of the sun to carry it to a storehouse on earth. In his flight he dropped some of the fire but picked it up again with his cross-shaft. In his fear he ran three times around the storehouse until he finally found the entrance and hid the brand. The celestial spirit, angry over the theft, hurled two bolts of lightning, which, however, failed to catch up with the thief. During the cultic feast this event is re-enacted: A torch bearer plays the thief. He runs around the fields, here and there setting fire to the grass. Two masked men swinging knives represent the bolts of lightning. Three times this scene is repeated until the torch bearer at last reaches the sacred precinct. Such parallels between cults and myths are plentiful (cf. chap. iii, sec. 1). Kerényi's contention that festive experience reflects the creative process of the time of its institution is amply borne out by the statements of primitive man.

But we need not even seek our evidence among the primitives. Holy Communion, for example, receives its sanctification only from the event that led to its institution. It is, therefore, repetition and reminiscence of an event which—in the parlance of primitive man—would be assigned to the primeval past. Re-enactment recalls the prototypical experience.

Though the close linkage between prototype and re-enactment is removed from direct observation, we do know that such primal events must have taken place. Unless we assume that man has, from the beginning of time, been just as he was upon his entrance into history (and who would assume such a thing?) then any cultural phenomenon must have occurred at some "first time." *This initial occurrence marks an actual moment of cultural crea-tivity.* Acknowledging the creative element, we establish a base-line for our analysis: creative events can be dealt with only in terms of creativity.

At any given creative period it is only one aspect of reality which seizes man's imagination to such an extent that others are obliterated. One particular reality is abstracted from total reality; the others are never actualized. This is by no means a sign of primitive mentality. Any modern law, for instance, codifies a specific aspect of reality. In extreme cases, the rigidity of cere-bral logic may lead to conflict with other realities. We need only remind ourselves of the callousness with which, in our most re-cent Western history, family ties, regional bonds, and other deep-rooted values were pushed aside so that other principles, which were deemed more essential, could be enforced. Abstraction from other realities is characteristic of all cognition, and archaic formu-lations are no less cognitive for having arisen from "seizure." We can neither accept the purposive explanation which primitive man is wont to offer for puberty rites, for example, nor can we call them products of a generically different mentality. At the same time, it is next to impossible to see them originating as play in the manner of children's and animal's play onto which "non-ludic" meaning is grafted at a later stage of society. We must see them as formulations of a perceived reality. Procreation and death are not connected by *logic* only; the close bond be-tween them is a fundamental aspect of life. It was revealed to man in a creative primal event and found formal expression in myth and cult. Puberty ceremonies make statements concerning the essence of male procreativity. They represent the recognition of an order in the human environment. At that, it is not just any order but a certain "real" order; and for this reason ceremony is more than "mere playing." The relationship between a cult and reality must under no circumstances be confused with an explanatory purpose. Man's *Ergriffenheit* by "cosmic phenomena" and other realities, his representations of them in human transformations, his cognitive awareness of a world order and its enactment in the form of a human order, all this is no less purpose-free than the performance of a modern stage play. It partakes of the same freedom of action which Huizinga saw as an essential criterion of play. At the same time, it shares with it a measure of bondage, if we take account of the compulsion inherent in man's representational nature (chap. ix).

D. The Difference between Cultic and Other Categories of Play

Huizinga sees difficulty in separation between actions which precede cognition of reality from those which express or represent a known order. He asks: "What are we to make of a mental process that begins with an unexpressed experience of cosmic phenomena and ends in an imaginative rendering of them in play?" (p. 16). The question sounds more difficult than it really is. We know very well the difference between unexpressed experience and its conscious formulation. It can be demonstrated in the life cycle of a child. The child moves and lives in a world whose order it comes to understand only gradually, piece by piece, and in discrete stages. Nonetheless, it disposes and acts through unexpressed experience. The genesis of culture must have taken the same course. Man—to return to the example of the puberty ceremony—procreated and multiplied before he became aware of the nature of the process. He acted through unexpressed experience. At some moment he was "seized" by the process; he had become conscious of its nature. "From something present has come something still more present" (Kerényi). About the steps of the process, however, leading from one level of awareness to the other, we know as much or little as of any creative process. We are certain, in any case, that they do exist, that they have existed in archaic society, and their formalizations have all the criteria of play. When we call to mind how all those conscious values which adults and professional teachers today instil in our children were once—and without the aid of pedagogues—spontaneously discovered, we realize how overwhelming must have been the wealth of creativity in early and later periods. The origin of the sacred acts must conjure up truly "great times" and just for that reason the spirit of festival and celebration approaches them most closely.

Against Huizinga's contention that cult has grafted itself belatedly onto forms of play which originally may have been equatable with child play and even animal play, we have raised serious objections. The spiritual content of sacred acts vanishes and only formalism remains. One is led to assume that every kind of play can assume cultic dimensions. Then cult, however, loses all meaning and we are back where we started. Huizinga seems hardly less committed to the basic senselessness of all sacred acts than those scientific theories of religion which both he and Frobenius deny.

Huizinga's premise seems to us unproven. Play is taken to be primary, older than culture, for "animals have not waited for man to teach them to play" (p. 1). Culture supposedly is a universal human possession. If animal and child play are to be equated—and this might be justified to a limited extent—then we need to distinguish between different types of child play. Children and puppies tussle and, to this extent but not beyond, child and animal play may be comparable. However, from such primarily biological playing no path leads to cultic acts. To find the path we must turn to two other types of children's play.

We can readily define these types by asking questions concerning the content of children's play. There are the predominantly improvised games which youthful inventiveness always dreams up in great profusion. The element common to all is a reference to reality. Be it mother and child, trains, steamship, dressing-up, selling, cooking, cowboys and Indians, cops and robbers, or whatever—in every single instance the environment and the still strange reality of the adult world is played out by the child. Exact imitation of all features of the reality that reveals itself to the child, and which it has abstracted as most significant, is the characteristic of all such playing. Children play the order of things as they see it and thereby conquer reality, enact it, and adsorb it in purpose-free, non-utilitarian activity— just as archaic society saw and enacted reality in cultic play.

Improvised children's games and cultic games are specific expressions of awareness. Even by themselves they would affirm man's creative nature, for can there be a more decidedly creative process than a child's acquisition of an entire world view? The fact that this takes place in the course of play is significant. In freedom of action and in dissociation from all purpose, utility, and anxiety about success, we find man's proper posture in regard to creativity. Formal schooling, which is so often hostile to play, would most quickly and thoroughly attain its goal if it were to present itself to the child in just that sense.

Yet there is an important difference between children's play and sacred act. Children play an order of things which has already been actualized; they react to well-formulated situations. However, though their creativity is limited in extent, the gift of empathy is nonetheless an aspect of the creative process and is indeed impossible without it. Now, it is indeed true, as Huizinga points out, that any contemporary cultural community receives its imagery as traditional material just as "ready-made" as the child does (p. 24). To this extent the creative content of sacred acts is equally secondary. But cult gains its sacred character precisely as a reminiscence of a far more elemental event in "primeval times" and as a recapitulation of that seizure. At that time when the mythic conception was born (no less than at any other creative period in history) man must have received the revelation of reality as such or, at least, of a facet of reality; what is represented in the sacred observances is the essence of this revelation rather than any man-made order. As long as the world view, so described, retains its validity, later repetitions will reverberate with a residuum of the original creativity. It is this residuum which marks the *sacred* play with the "additional mental element" which distinguishes it from "mere play."

Our second category, traditional children's games, includes such stand-bys as seesaws, Maypole swings, spinning tops, kites, stilts, etc. They are inherited by each generation as part of the stable cultural inventory and are never the child's own invention. In the following chapter we shall discuss them in detail to show that they are to be viewed as "survivals" of cultic games.

3

MYTH AND CULT IN THE STATE OF APPLICATION

Cultural phenomena are meaningful when they have a point of reference in reality. We maintain that any such phenomenon must by necessity be older and more basic than traditional play, in which established formulations continue to exist outside of any meaning context. Our view is opposed by one of wide currency which maintains that the historical process might just as well have taken the opposite direction. There can indeed hardly be any unequivocal evidence either for one side of the argument or for the other. It cannot be said, however, that the prevalent view is, so to speak, the more natural one. For my part, I would consider it most unnatural, since it rests entirely on a caricature, i.e., primitive mentality. In either case, however, the views are purely hypothetical and for that reason alone we must of necessity examine all alternate possibilities and test their validity with care.

Huizinga can by no means be called an adherent of the particular theories of the science of religion with which we are taking issue here.[1] In fact, his intentions are in direct opposition. But since he sees a non-ludic element in any link to reality which a cultural phenomenon may possess and since he further sees in such a link a threat to his favored definition of pure play, he must necessarily arrive at unsatisfactory conclusions.

1. "MERE GAMES" AS "SURVIVAL" OF CULTIC PLAY

We have spoken of the "traditional games" in our own culture, those which are played "for fun" or for sport and contest, as for instance the many kinds of ball games. Most, if not all of them, form parts of cultic acts in other cultures. They will aid us in

---

[1] I should mention that Huizinga corresponded with me during the war on the occasion of a book review of mine which I had published in *Paideuma* (II, 124). He wanted me to know that we are in much greater agreement on some major questions than I had assumed in the review. He expressed the hope that we might discuss them someday in calmer times; the great scholar's untimely death forever precluded this exchange. (The letter itself fell victim to a bombing raid.)

answering the question whether cults were grafted onto play or whether play is integral with the nature of cult and has developed into "mere play" and sport through a process of semantic depletion.

Karsten gives us a detailed description of a dice game (1935: 478) played by the Canelo of Ecuador. Its name, *huayru,* is a Quechua word; the game itself was therefore in all probability taken over from a Quechua-speaking people. The Canelo play it only at the death vigil for the master of the house, held the night after he has died. No women or male members of the family participate. Only the invited male guests range themselves in two rows on both sides of the corpse, which is placed on a bier in the center of the hut. The first man in one line throws a die across the corpse to the first man in the opposite line who returns it to the second man in the starting line, and so on. The die is an irregular cube cut from the leg bone of a llama, about 6–8 cm. long and marked with a different symbol on each side. The rules of the game differ from locality to locality. The winner is determined on points or by a single lucky throw on which the die remains perpendicular. The winner receives one of the domestic animals of the deceased, which is immediately slaughtered, prepared by the women, and eaten by all.

Bowls with the greatest delicacies are placed near the deceased, who is considered effectively present and very much the central personage of the ceremony. So, for instance, a particularly lucky player is thought to be an intimate of the dead man, while a chronic loser is thought to be disliked by him. A long run of unfavorable throws is attributed to the deceased. Everyone covers his head then and the presiding officeholder carries out a ceremony in the course of which he converses with the dead man and entreats him not to be so unsociable to his guests.

It is important that everyone present stay awake throughout the night; sleep is considered very dangerous and is tolerated only in the youngest children. All the livestock of the deceased is thus gambled away, save a few animals which are kept as breeding stock. The animals are evidently identified with the deceased in some respect, for the widow treats the remaining sheep or hog with particular tenderness. She even takes it to bed with her, embraces it, expressing by this that she is embracing her dead husband.

It is undoubtedly extremely difficult—and at this time actually impossible—to give the original sense of such a game ceremony. We will not risk the attempt here at all. A great number of heterogeneous images, all linked to a particular cultural world view, must have contributed to this particular configuration of cultic game. We would have to know and understand them all and their interrelationships and ties to reality besides, if we would give a meaningful interpretation. But since we know none of this, it is decidedly better to forgo theorizing.

That, however, which mainly interests us can be stated with a high degree of probability: the ceremony, formally identical with our games of chance, is inseparably part of the death cult. It is inconceivable that the game of chance is the sole carrier of meaning and that the death cult is "merely grafted on," or that the death cult merely introduces "an additional mental element" to the "game." It is contradicted by the fact that the game is played only during the death vigil. (Karsten mentions similar games played in the Gran Chaco *only* during the period of ripening of the *algarobba* fruit.) If the game was independently meaningful, its combination with the death cult can be understood only with a further proviso: the game must have contained an essential element which virtually demanded the combination or, at least, made combination appear sensible. This would strongly imply that it did indeed have its proper meaning through a connection with the cult. Among us, few would think of playing games of chance at a funeral, indicating only that the nexus can hardly lie in the element of "mere play."

So frequently are games encountered as essential parts of a cult and as vivid expressions of central religious concepts that even the skeptic must be persuaded. As far as ball games are concerned, the unique material which Preuss collected on the Witoto convincingly bears witness. We must forgo discussion of the religious concepts of the Witoto at the length which alone could make them comprehensible. A few details must suffice to indicate connections: the ball game is associated with the annual fruit-harvest feast, which also gives it its name (p. 26). At the feast, the *Urvater*, the primal father, reveals himself in the fruits (p. 131). The ball itself, as its name shows, is thought of as the fruit of the caoutchouc tree, of whose sap it is made. At the same time it is the actualization of the divine, the "soul" of the "father" revealed (pp. 29, 134, 135). The sanctity of the ball game is indicated in the following quotation:

[A]s a result our father gave us the ball and told us the good word which one may not use profanely, the word of our caoutchouc ball. We do not forget the words . . . with the help of these words we play ball. —When we play ball we are not making mischief, for the good word is a holy thing and he who toys with it is punished by the master of the ballgame; for he watches the players and knows when someone harms it.

The ball game can have arisen only in homogeneous unity, along with the other cultic configurations. When the concepts which lie at its root will have lost their validity in the eyes of the Witoto, the ball game will probably live on as "mere play" and popular amusement. It will pass out of its state of "expressivity" into one of "application."

Stilt-walking is another example. We know it only as a children's game played for fun. Some primitive peoples know it in exactly the same sense. It occurs among the Pangwe (Fang) (Tessmann, 1913: II, 294) and the Bena Lulua (Wissmann, p. 80). The Nyam Nyam (Zande), on the other hand, are said to have a practical use for stilts. Their watchmen use them to guard the fields (K. Lang, p. 276). At the same time, however, stilts had cultic application among many African peoples. For the Chokwe in south-central Africa, stilts symbolize the *mbongo*, a protective spirit who guards the village. A crude cylindrical effigy, carved from a post, represents him at the village entrance or a pair of stilts may take its place. Belief has it that the *mbongo* grow to giant height in the darkness, stretching to the clouds till they reach Kalunga, lord of the sky. In addition, stilt-walking plays a basic role in certain secret male initiation rites for which we cannot ascertain an exact meaning. During this ceremony of several days' duration the novices chiefly learn to walk on stilts (Baumann, 1935: 120, 203 ff.). Another author (Melland, p. 176) reports of the Kaonde (farther to the east) a stilt-dance feast which is called *mbongi*: At the time of the death of an important man, before a successor has been chosen, a drum is carried into the forest by moonlight and a dance begins. Naked men, painted white from head to foot, appear on tall stilts among the trees and scurry between the branches "like the spirits of the dead." Many of the onlookers flee to the village in fright, though they know well that the ceremony is a performance put on to please the dead.

Though we do not have corroborating myths here, as we had for the Witoto ball game, we need not doubt that the semantic nexus in which we find stilt-walking among the Chokwe and their neighbors is older than the sense of "mere playing" in which we find it among the other peoples mentioned. We are here closest to the root concept of the "game." The cultic representation of stilt-walking sentinel spirits may well continue into profane life—after the religious associations have faded—in the actuality of field watchmen equipped with the very useful stilts. Their function might be assigned an intermediate position between watchman and sentinel spirit. A ceremony which, as cult, had agitated and terrified may well live on as popular amusement. The converse, however, whereby watchman becomes sentinel spirit and stilt-walking becomes mortuary ritual, is very unlikely. Lindblom, in his research concerning stilts, comes to the same conclusion, although he, as he himself emphasizes, is not among those who consider the cultic significance of the activities of primitive peoples primary (p. 31). On the contrary, he started with the assumption that the origin of stilts must be sought in practical purposes. The data, however, have convinced him of the opposite —especially regarding Africa—and he now interprets the occasional use of stilts as children's toys as "survival" (p. 27).

Top-spinning is likewise linked to cult among some populations. The Kajan on Borneo, who use heavy wooden tops 30 cm. high, play exclusively during the great planting feast; only men participate (Nieuwenhuis, I, 330 ff.). Among the Naga tribes of Assam, "tops" is also a man's game and is allowed only at specified times. While the rice is growing, for example, it is forbidden "because the earth is pregnant" (Mills, 1926: 150). On certain holidays, when the village community may be said to be in a state of taboo—no one may work, leave the village, etc.—the men spin the tops (pp. 220, 221). A myth transmitting the ceremony of the founding of a village gives a hint that the future inhabitants will spin tops (Mills, 1937: 45, 123). In some tribes, tops are buried with the warriors (Hutton, 1921: 244). Even though the original significance of the game cannot be deduced from such isolated practices and customs, these practices are nonetheless unmistakably linked to solemn religious concepts. We are of the opinion that their significance can only have stemmed from such concepts. This applies to any traditional "mere game," of which hardly one is found in the Western world which does not have a sacral counterpart among primitive peoples. The significance of string games (cat's cradles) has been demonstrated by Höltker.

Play drive is insufficient to explain traditional games, and neither can pleasure in orderly motion explain formalized dances. How primitive people view their dances becomes clear from a statement made by a Witoto: "[Myths] are the words of our father, his own words. By means of these words we dance, and it would not be a dance had he not given us the words" (Preuss, 1921–23: 625). All true dances, be they animal dances, labyrinth dances, or whatever kind of imitative movement, aim to "express" some essential trait in the image of reality. All our athletic activities occur among primitive peoples (cf. Meuli, "Olympische Spiele"), even in their sense of contest; however, they are never contests for their own sake but always part of a ceremony in which they *must* take place since they belong to the enactment of a mythically perceived world order (cf. Jensen, "Wettkampf-Parteien").

Nothing in the nature of games makes their development into cults inevitable. However, they eloquently exemplify the degree to which cults may be "enactment" of a cognitive knowledge of reality as well as opportunities for expression. The active presence of expressivity in all cultic activities, which makes them adaptable to human nature and its predispositions, also gives them longevity. Man will nurture them even when all the original referents to reality have been supplanted and their primary semantic nexus has been totally lost.

2. THE ETIOLOGICAL MYTH

What has been said so far is especially applicable to art. Art cannot be characterized as pure play or encompassed by the slogan "l'art pour l'art"; it is in all of its early manifestations a means of expressing a heightened sense of the world. About prehistoric rock paintings we have no certainty; but of sculpture, dance, and of myth as the earliest form of the narrator's art, we know that the aim is beyond mere sculpture, dance, and narrative representations of perceived verities. Art constitutes one of the few spheres of life where the expressive apparatus links our cultural epoch with early mankind. It retains its unique position throughout the length of human history, as long as man is anxious to experience and represent the world's divine aspect. Yet nothing can prevent works of art—like all cultural manifestations—from undergoing within each major historical epoch a process of degeneration from expressivity to semantically depleted application. The category of mythic narrations offers parallels to the course of events. In the solemn, magnificent myths, which we regard as the true expression of mythic experience, the nature of the world is clarified, brought to life, and made vivid in very singular ways. Implicitly or explicitly, all events took place in a primeval setting. How could it be otherwise! The world shows itself in an order that has always existed; i.e., as long as there has been man and as long as human memory can extend backward into time. Mythic thinking presupposes, however, that everything that exists has passed through a becoming and is the product of creative forces which fashioned the present order from disorder; they transformed an alien, improper order into the existing order; that which was different in kind into that which now is. It is astonishing that this idea, familiar to science, should have guided the human consciousness at a time when neither geology, paleontology, nor prehistory could lend it concrete support. On the other hand, mythic consciousness differs in kind from scientific consciousness: there is no searching for developmental stages or for continuous progressions from primordial beginnings to terminal configurations. The mythic occurrence is in almost every instance unique and unrepeated, a majestic event in the primal past. Its result is the presently sanctioned formulation of the mythic manifestation.

The mythic idea of how things have come to be as they are is by no means self-evident, as one might be inclined to think. Entire systems of completely different propositions about reality are imaginable, some of which we would have to credit with *ab initio* existence, without giving a thought to morphological change. A tremendous upheaval must have taken place to engender the new world view. It must have consisted in the profound insight that nascency as such, the initial entrance into reality, is of the greatest significance. Any initial event is distinguished from its repetitions by the quality we call creativity; early man's attention must have been strongly drawn to it. The realization of nascency can have originated only in an awareness of creative processes. This suggests—as the myths themselves suggest—that the shapers of the mythic world may have been creative personalities in their own right who themselves experienced the impact of the creative process.

We cannot doubt that there is a mythic reality. How, otherwise, could myths have met with belief? How could they have become sacred convictions which gave man the strength to undergo the harsh and inhuman consequences often attendant upon them? How could this have been if they had *not* contained a valid truth? The truths of a proposition can be tested only against the background from which it arose and against the course by which man was led to its acceptance. Mythic propositions concerning the genesis of a phenomenon are rooted in the nature of the phenomenon itself; the course toward formulation is the intuitive and spontaneous experiencing of the specific nature. The creative force which engendered the present configuration is seen to be still latent within it. Thus the mortality of all living beings is traced back to a primeval event which, in fact, does no more than paraphrase the actual condition which permits man to think of existence as mortal. The truth contained in the descriptions of the primeval event rests on cognition of the essence of living reality as it is gained from direct observation.

To emphasize that the primary cause of mythic propositions is religious, we might call them formulations of revelations which may be derived from observation of reality under the influence of specific experiential predispositions. We are thinking of revelations of creative forces which have been phenomenologically realized "so, and only so," and constitute today the nature of things according to their contemporary order. For this reason, the essence and by the same token the creative spirit may be read directly from the phenomenological record without detours by way of concrete prehistoric researches, as long as man is at all responsive to their revelations. Myth always begins with a condition antecedent to concretization, when the creative idea is already in existence and finally manifests itself through the mythic event.

This may be said of all the great genuine myths which we must consider related to reality even without observational corroboration. The fact that the myth exists and carries conviction for a more or less numerous population lets us assume such a relationship.

Naturally, the same applies to individual features of myths. Thus we find that Sedna, the most important deity of the Central Eskimos, who consider her "mother of all sea animals," passionately hates all land animals. The Eskimos, referring to this, faithfully observe a profusion of rules and prohibitions which have the strict segregation of land and sea animals as their objective; and this irrespective of the difficulties they add to a struggle for existence which is harsh enough as it is—for the Eskimos are, for better or worse, equally dependent upon land and sea fauna (Rasmussen, 1929: 67, 183 ff., 190 ff.). There is no mistaking that the Eskimo is deeply committed to a belief in the "truth" of this character trait of his deity. Doubtless, we may take this as a symptom of the fact that the concept is rooted in a cognition of the essence of reality, and we must stand by this assumption even if our attempts to discover the reality come to nought.

Primitive peoples possess in their stock of narratives an abundance of stories which obviously lack truth contents, though they externally resemble myths to the extent that they want to give explanations by assigning events to a primeval past. The Ungarinyin of northwest Australia, for instance, tell a story which gives the "reason" for their tribal exogamy: Banar and Kuranguli lived at a time when men still married without selectivity. One day Banar returned from the bush with a girl with whom he shared his camp. Kuranguli did likewise. In contrast to others, however, Banar and Kuranguli had done the proper thing. Banar, who belonged to the "gray kangaroo," had taken a woman of the "red kangaroo," and Kuranguli, who belonged to the "red kangaroo," had taken a woman from the "gray kangaroo." But when they had children, Banar did wrong: he had intercourse with his daughter and even wanted to give her to his son as a wife. Kuranguli, on the other hand, did the right thing. He suggested that his son receive Banar's daughter for a wife. Conversely, Banar asked for Kuranguli's daughter as wife for his son. And so it was done thereafter (Petri, *Sterbende Welt*: 132).

This tale clearly makes only a single statement which we may consider mythic: the naming of primeval personages who, for

67

the first time, engaged in the "proper" marriages. Besides that it contains only some information about the marriage-class system of this people. Ideas travel so exclusively along the path of mythic narrative that even the simple proposition, "two-class exogamy is proper," appears in the trappings of a myth. To be a genuine myth, however, would require something additional that would illuminate the sense of this order, as happens very frequently in other explanatory myths on the subject. We bring to mind those several social systems in which the two founders are associated with the sun and the moon so that the polarity which is at the base of the system is placed as an essential element at the point of the genesis of all things. In such cases something is said about the nature of a phenomenon which actually relates to its creative origin (cf. chap. vii, sec. 1).

Tales are not produced by a simple inclination to report in mythic forms. The primal past, as a period of divine activity, has both sanctifying and sanctioning power. There exists a tendency, therefore, never to discuss certain spheres without reference to primeval time. Because of this, we have reports of many customs —as for instance cutting the hair in a ceremony of mourning— which were instituted by a deity in the primal past, though no reasons are given for the deity's action. The tendency to sanction petrified custom through assignment to a primal past is found in the archaic high cultures to our own days. The enumeration in the Old Testament (Deut. 5:16–29) of all the customs hardened into "law," without a word of justification, shows the seriousness with which the past is regarded. It was done under the proper assumption that the suggestion of "our father doing it that way" is sufficient reason. However, the culturally creative periods which brought forth the customs cannot have possessed this comfortable formula. The contemporaries must still have pondered these matters. If we do not succeed in finding out some of their thoughts—and how seldom can we hope to succeed!—we shall have no key to understanding.

In the following we shall deal with a group of tales which we usually separate from true myths by calling them etiological or explanatory. Such a separation seems indicated since the resemblance of this type of tale to true myths is entirely superficial. They lack such basic characteristics as religious content and the criterion of being believed as established truths.

An example will define the type for us: The Barotse of South Africa tell a tale according to which, at some occasion in the primal past, the long fur of the hippopotamus caught fire and it jumped into the river to quench the flames. As any genuine myth would, this tale begins with the assumption of a fundamental dissimilarity between the primeval and the present condition. In the past the hippopotamus had long fur and lived on land where mammals, by the present order of things, have their proper habitat. If the hippopotamus does not now conform, an explanation seems in order, and the tale is designed to provide one.

The truth of the mythic formulation is, however, no more based on a revelation of the nature of the hippopotamus than it is based on scientific research into its normal behavior. The tale is an episode in an extensive myth (cf. Jensen, 1933: 75) which does indeed deal with divine events, though none of their splendor is reflected in this episode. It merely explains a phenomenon which transgresses the rule—an answer is given to the very reasonable question: how is it that . . . ? The explanation recognizes the practicality of the animal's seeking the water, though it should be natural to assume that it would climb back on land once the flames are extinguished. To enhance credibility, a motive should at least have been added to explain why it stayed in the river for all time. The fact that such a motive is not needed is in itself a formal trait of mythic narration. In genuine myths, every primal event would be an organizing act instigated by creative forces which requires no motivation but that it be derived from the nature of the phenomenon itself.

Accordingly, etiological myths seem mythic in form only but seem to lack foundation in religion and a belief that they state a truth. We have said before that the mythic proposition relates to questions and areas in which they cannot be replaced by other, truer propositions. To a certain extent this applies also to the etiological implication of the cited episode: science would be hard put to shed light on the causes of the amphibious way of life of the hippopotamus. And yet there is a distinct difference from the genuine myth; it is the causal character of the explanation which shifts the question regarding the truth of the proposition in the direction of causality. The tale is thereby subjected to a test of its integral truth to which it is not equal.

It is appropriate that we narrow down the differentiating criteria between both kinds of myth. I choose another example which clearly shows its connection with genuine myth. The tale comes from the Wemale on the East Indonesian island of Ceram (Jensen, 1939: 125). It tells how the rooster acquired his splendid plumage, a matter of interest to the Wemale, who take the adornment of the body—especially at festive occasions—very seriously. The festive ornaments of the men, made chiefly of feathers of many colors, are reminiscent of the rooster's plumage; this bird plays an important role in the entire inventory of Wemale myths. It is said that the Ulisale, a very plain bird of the forest, had at one time worn the rooster's finery. One day, when an as yet unadorned village rooster sees the Ulisale in a bamboo tree, he is very much upset and runs back into the village. The following day he returns to ask the Ulisale why he, in his beautiful garb, lives among the weeds rather than go to the village. Only when the Ulisale shows no inclination to do so does the real action begin. The rooster offers his friendship and to confirm the pact goes with him to the palm tree where they indulge in the palm wine till the Ulisale is quite drunk. Then the rooster asks him for the loan of his comb, his red wattles, and his splendid tail, that he might show off in the village. After three days, he says, he will return everything. The distrustful Ulisale is persuaded at last. The rooster puts on the splendid attire and gives his own plain one to the Ulisale. Then—this is the most charming part in a pleasant and amusing tale—the rooster dances with joy and asks: "Now, am I handsome, or not?" The Ulisale declares: "You are handsome." Returning to the village, and from a safe distance, the rooster calls to the forest bird: "I have deceived you; henceforth I shall wear your beautiful clothes." The Ulisale weeps and calls a large bird of prey to begin a war with the domestic fowl and continue it through all eternity.

With the final sentence an additional fact is linked with the tale, namely the hostility between domestic fowl and bird of prey; it is purely explanatory and not very different from the tale about the hippopotamus. The emphasis lies, however, on the splendid adornments of the rooster, and this part of the narrative undoubtedly contains rudiments of a genuinely mythic element. The nature of the rooster and the nature of the Ulisale are important components in the explanatory tale. Were it different, were the Ulisale the possessor of the magnificent ornaments while the rooster was the unassuming one, what nonsense! Who in the world would wear his finest attire to move about in the wilderness! No, ornamentation belongs to the essence of sociability, belongs to village life, and if the Ulisale refuses to wear his festive garb at the proper place, i.e., the village, then it is only fitting that it be taken from him by one who knows how to make the right use of it. Only so do regulations regarding dress make sense. For that reason the story presupposes correctly that the rooster has an immediate powerful desire for that which is so very germane to his nature. Only through his success does the rooster fully become that which lay predetermined in his nature, as it were. To this extent we might be dealing here with a genuine myth. On closer observation, though, it becomes apparent that the tale is concerned not so much with the rooster as with the relationship of man to festive dress. We shall return to this; for the moment we must digress.

The exchange of adornments between the two birds could undoubtedly be made plausible by numerous narrative devices. Neither a ruse, common cheating, nor the betrayal of a just concluded and confirmed friendship were absolutely necessary for the continuity of the tale. A serious quarrel might have started between the two, could perhaps even have been caused by the Ulisale, so that the rooster would have gained the booty in an honest contest. A heroic age would doubtless have preferred such an expedient. The introduction of deception is, however, not an accident. The frequency of its appearance in the narrative art of primitive peoples speaks against that. As inconsiderable as heroic elements are in this early art, so important and even characteristic is deception. It seems that man has become aware of his superiority over other creatures in the exercise of cunning. The hunter's success depends on his outsmarting the animal. Everywhere, cunning and success belong together just as intellectual incapacity and failure belong together. To the extent that success is esteemed desirable by a culture, cunning seems to be an indispensable part of action.

The strong emphasis on cunning might give rise to the supposition that the tale of the two birds is not a genuine myth and possibly not even the degeneration of a myth but must be counted in another category. Ruses do not appear to fit into the religious sphere of which myth is a part. Alien as the mutual outwitting of the Greek gods may appear to us, there is no doubt that the frequency of ruses in the mythology of early peoples need not be a sign of degeneration. In some myths it is such an intrinsic component that a different course of the action cannot be imagined. I am thinking of the wide-spread myth of the purloining of the cereal grains from heaven by a divine thief. Between the sky deity and his divine antagonist arises a situation as between Zeus and Prometheus. The superior might of the sky god is presupposed; and yet the *heilbringer,* the culture hero, bringer of good fortune and material benefits, triumphs in bringing about that which constitutes part of the present order of things. The ethical judgments which are occasionally adumbrated need not have been originally connected with the respective myths; they are in no way unequivocally directed against either thief or victim. Rather, two deities are in contest with each other, one of which tries to get something away from the other through cunning— the same situation as in our tale of the rooster and the Ulisale. It speaks in favor of the more cunning of the two that he instituted a condition which is correct and proper; therefore it continues to persist. A "punishment" certainly follows the cunning theft but it does not consist in nullification, only in a lessening of the blessing. The sky god might, for instance, send a plague of mice to curb the joy of victory, or the Ulisale may call on the birds of prey to make life difficult for the rooster. The festive plumage, however, is kept by the rooster, as man keeps the cereal grains. Some forms of the genuine myth occasionally make ethical judgments exclusively in favor of the thief, especially where no reason is given for retention of the cereal grains by the sky god and the idea is suggested that only envy and ill-will make him withhold from man what is due him according to a reasonable order of things (chap. iv, sec. 8).

These observations certainly do not exhaust the intricate subject of cunning. Here we were interested only in the fact that its occurrence is insufficient cause to deny a mythic narrative the predicate of genuineness. Indeed, ruses have at all times been a very important element of man's way of life without inviting ethical judgment. This can easily be established if we observe human behavior. Man's ability to "adapt" to other people, to present something persuasively—though quite within the bounds of truth—always contains a bit of cunning in the same sense in which the hunter outwits his prey. The hunter starts with a precise knowledge of the animal and its habits and hunts it down through means which his ingenuity tells him are the most suitable. The art of "convincing" a partner in negotiation or conversation makes use of the same means. Superiority is often demonstrated in the use of a shrewdness which makes use of the knowledge of likely reactions without provoking ethical judgment. An inferior partner is convinced by different arguments than an equal one. Thus there is shrewdness in all pedagogy. Life is permeated by it down to the smallest details.

The tale of the rooster and Ulisale resembles the unquestionable myths in more than the motive of cunning. Other features of it place it close to the genuine myths: it is set in primeval time when the world was different from today. The mythic events make reference to the essential nature of the "personalities" and affirm the new order instituted by the action of the tale. The possibility is actually considered that the Ulisale enter the village and play the role of the rooster. The Ulisale's nature makes him unsuited for that, and only because of this unsuitability does it seem right that his finery is gotten away from him by a ruse.

Still, we are not ready to call this tale a genuine myth. Because of its subject matter, it most definitely lacks stature. It deals with festive attire, a matter which—though not completely irrelevant in this setting—lacks sublimity. Certainly it is not a fundamental aspect of life, ranking with birth, death, or sustenance. For the rooster the matter of attire could have quite different significance, and we may imagine a truly mythic formulation of the theme. Undoubtedly, the natural experience of even early peoples revealed to them that the rooster's splendor had nothing to do with his domestication but that related, though far more basic, forces are at work than a social drive in the form of vanity. Just those elemental forces have often become the subject of mythic treatment. A genuine myth would without doubt have placed the rooster's masculinity, his outstanding trait, at the center of the plot. But our story pays no attention to this. Rather, it views the problem from its human side and sees the rooster's garb as mere decoration and a cause of pleasure and boasting. More than anything else it is the insignificance of the subject matter which stamps the tale as etiological. Religious ideas are not kindled by matters of such small concern, for the creative, divine spark is revealed in them only in very mediate form.

Thus, the difference between etiological myth and myth proper lies, not in form, but in the theme itself and more particularly even in the manner of its development. As there is no definable boundary between the sublime and the commonplace, so is there no strict boundary between the etiological and the genuine myth. Sustenance, for instance, can be quite a commonplace theme but may also be treated as a fundamental problem of existence. Among the themes of the magnificent myths of the ancient cultivators, sustenance appears chiefly in this life-supporting sense. But there are, in addition, a great many explanatory myths in which color or shape of foodstuffs, for example, is rationalized in a manner analogous to the tale of the hippopotamus which we mentioned earlier.

Decisive for the relationship between etiological and genuine myth is their formal congruency. They belong to the same type of narration. In consequence, there can be no sharp boundary line between them. Where a given myth may be inserted in the continuum only analysis can decide.

Some cosmogonic myths, despite their mighty and world-encompassing theme, are predominantly explanatory. Conversely— and to return to our example—we might imagine a narrative concerning the rooster's ornateness which would present his rooster qualities in quite a different manner so that we would not hesitate to classify the tale as a genuine myth.

Etiological myths are closer to our understanding than myths proper. The explanations given are usually quite transparent and rest on associations which are combined with playful intent for the sake of the artistic effect. To this extent they are typical folk art, i.e., not products of single great poets without whom the genuine myth is unthinkable, but the work of a reflective imagination which utilizes the formal apparatus created by the genuine myth. It, too, wants to provide explanation for the "just-so" of the world and is thus essentially explanatory. But true myth focuses on a deeper essence and never is purely associative. To the extent that associative ideas do occur in genuine myth, they are probably and chiefly later incorporations and contribute nothing to the central thought.

Etiological myths have been called the oldest narratives in

human history, arguing that they ask about the "why" and the causes of events. The question, it was pointed out, is so intrinsically part of human nature that it must have come to the fore at the beginning of human history (Lehmann-Nitsche, p. v). Possible, even probable, as the last assertion may be, its consequences for the interpretation of etiological myths are precarious. The question "why" is without doubt at the heart of it, but what would the answer be like? Even pleasant and vivid presentations cannot conceal the fact that the explanatory answer contained in them is totally meaningless. It is not conceivable that there have been human beings who believed the hippopotamus lived in the water for the reasons given. But that is exactly what the proponents of those theories maintain; they consider these explanatory ideas just fantastic and primitive enough for early mankind.

Etiological myths lack all verity, mythic or otherwise. They do not owe their existence to the perception of any event which at some time was considered true; at least there is no plausible reason to assume this to have been different in the faraway past. They owe their *existence* to their literary charm which is as tangible to us as it is to primitive peoples. But is it conceivable that they should also owe their *origin* to this charm, i.e., that they arose independently of myths and prior to them? The answer to this question cannot disregard formal congruency. At some time, perhaps in the dim past, there developed the mythic narrative which sees all things as products of a "becoming" and describes the process of nascency itself as the course of an action. When this style of narrative originated, it must have contained meaning, i.e., must have told a "true" tale. We are not saying that man cannot also have acted absurdly, but the great and serious creations of the human mind never have been sponsored by absurdity. This applies particularly to the age of mythic creativity. Only in our time are we beginning to reread myths and to reopen our minds to their deeper meaning, now that they have resisted so long and successfully all attempts at rationalistic decoding.

The criterion of verity does not apply to the extreme type of the etiological myth. Their independent and prior development would imply that the meaningless would have given birth to something that only subsequently acquired specific meaning. This seems impossible to us. It is possible, however—we have already given a number of examples—that a meaningful phenomenon loses its specific meaning but does not cease to exist since it has not lost *all* meaning. Of the abundance of meaningful interrelationships which any cultural configuration contains, one or several nuclear clusters may have crumbled away, but enough remain to assure a frequently most tenacious continuity.

The relationship between etiological myth and genuine myth proper is similar to that between cultic play and children's play. When the true myth had engendered a narrative form of definite style and schema which, among other things, provided an answer to the question "why," it constituted an art form which, as an art form, contained the justification of its own existence. It became an artistic form in its own right, independent of the "truth" of its statements. In this type of narration the question "why" and the explanatory answer are merely an excuse to display the charm of presentation which is its very life.

The etiological or explanatory myth is not the only degenerative form of the genuine myth. Without a doubt, all historically younger types of narrative ultimately go back to it. This applies to adventure stories as well as to fairy tales, which, moreover, have usually borrowed their motives from myths.

3. THE PROCESS OF SEMANTIC DEPLETION

In concluding our ideas on the process of degeneration, especially where it pertains to religious expression, let us touch upon the factors which have influenced its course. Some we have already mentioned though without striving for completeness. Steady repetition—though it is an irreplaceable part of religious expression—makes it inevitable that cultic observances, such as prayer and myth, suffer a loss of vigor. But repetition of a cult does not, by itself, deplete its meaning. So long as its world view retains validity and its reality has not been displaced or supplemented by another reality, or its order by another order, elements of the original creative event and of its sacral character will survive. The decisive event which leads to semantic depletion is the changing of the world view and man's orientation toward other aspects of reality and other possibilities of expressing them. Culture history would appear quite differently if all creative productions of a given epoch were expunged with the collapse of a world view and its loss of validity or else received a new significance along lines conforming to the new image of the world. The first case almost never occurs, the second only rarely. As a rule, each culture drags with it a considerable ballast of "survivals" from earlier epochs. Their persistence stands in odd contrast to their state of semantic depletion. We have already seen that the play element is of significance for the continuance of many phenomena and that "having been passed down from our fathers" is a sufficient reason for the respectful observance of many customs. But even without an impetus of this kind, obsolescent cultural phenomena persist, subject as it were to the law of inertia. Without special stimulus, man does not think of jolting that which is established or of re-examining its intellectual foundation.

We should claim that no cultural phenomenon, though drained of semantic content, dies a natural death. If it does not gain new life by acquiring new meaning or if it is not eliminated by opposing forces, it will continue to exist in spite of its semantic deficiency.

Religious forms usually carry the germ of their own degeneration from the beginning. The general expectation of salvation, the hope for happiness and reward which man associates with each deed, often obstructs the true sense of a religious act. As we will show later (chap. ix), the true religious ethic is not primarily concerned with interpersonal relationships. Ethical bonds of this kind are found in the earliest human societies without requiring justification of a religious kind. The primary religious-ethical postulation in primitive religion constrains man to be constantly aware of the divine origin of the world and of the human partnership in divinity. The initiation of awareness and the vivid preservation of a special "knowledge" of the nature of reality are therefore the truest forms of the religious attitude. This is achieved by rites and ceremonies. With respect to their origins, religious festivities make sense only as reminiscent internalization and as actualization of a mythically perceived state of being and its regularities. We have shown this by examples (chap. ii): puberty ceremonies are not magical means of favorably influencing fertility but are, according to their origin, feasts at which— "occasioned" by the maturity of the young men—the community actualizes those mythic events which made man a procreative and

77

mortal being. Pious action, therefore, is first of all an act of reflection. Impious and without religious morality are those who do not possess the "knowledge" and are not willing to reflect upon it. Such behavior is beyond redemption, not because the god will punish it, but because such a person places himself outside human nature. Only reflection on the divine origin of all phenomena actualizes in man that which is inherently in his nature. The deity need not punish the unredeemed; they cannot attain the higher state under any circumstances, for it is integral with reflection. In the following we shall repeatedly attempt to show that ceremony and other religious practices have only this one true and original sense.

A good example of what primitive people think when one of them does not take part in the ceremonies or speaks of them derisively was given me by the Baka in southern Ethiopia in a tale intended to show why one of their clans is related to the monkeys. Once upon a time, a man of this clan had gathered his family to sacrifice a sheep, a lengthy ceremony of great importance in the religious life of the Baka. One of his sons became impatient. He called the sacred rites unnecessary and demanded his share of the sheep without waiting for the end. The old father became angry. He pointed his stick at his son and ordered him to leave the place of sacrifice. He was to go into the wilderness where he belonged. At that the boy changed into a monkey and ran into the forest. In all its artlessness, this story shows that in the thinking of the Baka it is first of all religious sensibility and devout performance of ceremonies that differentiate man from the animals.

As we have seen from the Konso (chap. ii), primitive people are wont to say that puberty ceremonies are necessary, since otherwise procreativity could not be attained or because the deity would punish the whole community for any offense against the established order. (It never occurs to anyone to ask why the deity would take such a step!) Here we doubtless have an indication of an early stage of semantic depletion, for utilitarian purpose or fear of divine punishment cannot have been connected with the cause of a religious ceremony.

In such cases it is not difficult to establish how the reinterpretations arose. We can frequently see similar processes at work in the history of thought and ideas. First of all, good and evil, originally part of the act of reflection, are linked with the external cause of the action. The true significance is thereby displaced onto the realm of visible events, a process which we can observe in our own environment. We are reminded of the rosary vendor (chap. i) who reinterpreted the gesture of blessing as a concretely effective force. The ceremony no longer lends actuality to a deeper form of existence (in which salvation and the higher good are immanent), but it *effects* an expected salvation and benefits as a consequence of reverential action. The logical converse is the calamity which *follows* such impious behavior as the neglect of the sacral act.

This particular form of expectation, i.e., its link with a causal ceremony and in particular with the externals of it, set up the conditions for most degenerative features in the realm of religion. The hypothesis of pre-animistic magic was made possible only because it found here material for its thesis of early man's absurd faith in his ability to influence natural processes through ceremonies. Preferentially cited are ceremonies that let this interpretation appear plausible, as for example instances of analogical magic (cf. chap. xii, sec. 8). A large number of ceremonies were overlooked, however, which such interpretation does not make at all comprehensible. They would find much more natural explanation in the assumption of an originally creative attitude and of later degeneration into utilitarian and purposive acts.

We hope to have made clear the course of events by which the original myth and the semantically intact cult have deteriorated to the state in which we are accustomed to find them today. To understand them we must try to gain a measure of rapport with those phases in which the original sense was still alive. We believe and will attempt to document that it is possible to penetrate to the roots only if we approach the intellectual achievements of the primal past with a requisite reverence. We must assume that behind them stood a being "man" who deserved the name and who was gifted with the same powers of cognition as men of the higher cultures.

PART II | Deity, Sacrifice, and Ethos

4

HIGH GOD AND DEMA-DEITY

Not too long ago it was still frequently said that there existed populations that possessed no religion whatever. Today argument on this point, which often had become quite heated, has died down. However, a claim that some populations know nothing of gods and that their religions consist solely of ceremonial practices (which often is equivalent to claiming the absence of all religion) is still found in ethnological literature. Especially with respect to the culture of the ancient cultivators it has often been stated that no concept of a deity is in evidence but only fear of spirits and worship of ancestors. It so happens that this culture stratum, so important in the history of mankind, is quite uniformly distributed over the entire earth; since quite definite ideas of gods have been documented for many of its most typical representatives, the stubbornly repeated assertion that one or another group lacks the concept has little likelihood. Since theoretical ethnology is dependent on very heterogeneous field data, it can only be hoped that later reports will correct what may well be incorrect information in each such instance.

Of the three theories which dominate the scientific ethnological study of religion—we have critically discussed them in the Introduction—only *Urmonotheismus*,[1] primal monotheism, has placed the concept of the deity among primitive peoples at the center of its system. It has the merit of having discovered the significance of the concept of God for all scientific study of religion in ethnology. It has provoked less criticism than other theories, partly because it is devoted to the determination and distillation of a single idea of God for which it tries to prove culture-historical antiquity. One of the advocates of the theory, Gusinde, simply places the vast realm of religious manifestations which ethnology endeavors to understand outside of religion proper (cf. sec. 5, below). Some phenomena which are the subjects of our discussion are consequently not considered by him. They are regarded as degenerations, and W. P. Schmidt is of the

[1] This designation, though current in the literature, has not been used and has even been disavowed by the representatives of the "School of Vienna." But since it suits the facts quite well it will be used here for the sake of simplicity.

opinion that animism and magic sufficiently explain these young-er manifestations. *Urmonotheismus* will therefore concern us only while we deal with the concept of a deity, since it has noth-ing to contribute to any other area of our study. Although the theory of *Urmonotheismus* has set unjustifiable limits to the defi-nition of religion, it nonetheless has directed attention to the ideas which primitive peoples have of divinity; it has, through a wealth of supporting data, confirmed the almost undeniable fact that even the most ancient peoples still accessible to our re-searches possess such ideas.

If in the face of this evidence it is still claimed that many peoples are without a god—especially among the cultivators—there may be a number of reasons. Among primitive peoples, as among ourselves, there exists the injunction against employing the name of the deity in everyday usage; this belongs to the essence of the concept of the divine. These very sensible inhibi-tions are not the only reasons why so often no concept of a deity is reported. Frequently, the idea has been relegated to the back-ground and some activity—originally oriented toward the deity—has taken the spotlight and is, alone, still taken seriously and observed conscientiously. Finally, however—and this is only too often the case—a traveler may observe activities most carefully without ever encountering the concept of a god, even if it is quite alive, for instance, in the myths. Exact description of externals without attention to underlying spiritual content still predomi-nates in ethnography.

Our discussion of the concept of a deity among primitive peoples does not aim at completeness. Especially in discussing the idea of God among the ancient cultivators will this incom-pleteness become apparent. Behind the names of bringers of benefits and culture heroes are hidden very different kinds of personalities (cf. chap. vi, sec. 1). Primitive peoples, just as those of high cultures, have specifically elaborated, if not created, their own ideas of a deity. Typologies can only do violence to these ideas; we cannot disregard them, however, if we wish to "empathize" with the spiritual conditions which have led to particular formulations of the concept of God in given cultural epochs. Only concerning the High God do we possess an extensive literature, which we owe to the advocates of the theory of *Ur-monotheismus*. We shall deal with it here in conjunction with another concept which we shall call the "Dema-deity," quite different from the High God in all important particulars and originating in other spheres of the human psyche. A comparison will clearly show the typical features of both concepts and their fundamental differences. First we shall turn to the concept of the High God and of a Highest Being.

1. URMONOTHEISMUS

The assertion, based on ethnographic data, that at the beginning of all religions there existed the belief in an ever benevolent, omnipotent Being was first made by Andrew Lang (1898). It was W. P. Schmidt, however, who expanded the theory, offering his evidence in an imposing, twelve-volume work, *Der Ursprung der Gottesidee.*

One of Schmidt's basic theses is the statement that the belief in a Highest Being is to be met with in its purest and clearest form precisely among the ethnologically most ancient populations. This is to be taken as evidence that we are here dealing with the oldest concept of a deity. Gahs, his disciple, brought in prehistoric materials in support of the thesis. Finds from the Lower Paleolithic were interpreted as sacrifices to the High God (cf. the critique by Meuli, 1945: 283 ff.). Not a single one of these highly specific interpretations has remained unopposed. It would be a thankless task to recapitulate all the polemics. It would be just as unsatisfactory, however, to dismiss the theory of *Urmonotheismus* with the statement that though it might possibly be true it has by no means been convincingly proven. In our context we can only give a few hints which show the justice of the doubt. Who could, in any case, convincingly present the original religion of even one of the archaic peoples, e.g., the Bushmen of South Africa? The paucity of the sources precludes it. The only good, extensive, and unbiased sources are the myths recorded by Bleek. They contain nothing, however, that would let us assume the belief in a High God, a conclusion with which Schmidt agrees. The sources are more than meager but, in all their contradictions, at best show that the religion of the Bushmen was quite complex and that a Highest Being may have played a role in it.

The same complexity may be seen, as Radcliffe-Brown had shown, in the religion of the Andamanese, another typically archaic people. In my opinion we have no methodological means of arranging the heterogeneous data about the "Puluga" deities worshiped by various Andamanese groups into a diachronic order in which the belief in a single male Puluga-being may be placed at the beginning as Schmidt tried to do. The Southeastern Australians, as Howitt had described them, provided another central argument in Schmidt's deductions. But in Howitt's work the belief in a Highest Being does by no means appear as the sole expression of religious experiences. The profusion of magical practices is to be found there in peculiarly Australian forms as is initiation. The resemblance between the High Gods of the Southeastern peoples and the spirit-beings (who are not regarded as High Gods) in the central Australian initiation rites has been stressed—as I see it, justifiably—by Spencer and Gillen (pp. 492 ff.).

All of these doubts are only intimations and therefore hardly convincing. But even detailed discussion of the pros and cons in the argumentations of Schmidt and his critics cannot produce full clarification because there are too many uncertainties in this matter of the religion of the ethnologically most archaic peoples (cf. Martino, pp. 185 ff.). We hardly possess a description that outlines a sufficiently complete and convincing picture of the religious expression of archaic peoples to enable us to speak of it as uniform in all parts of the world. All data are so fragmentary that some few correspondences can be ferreted out only with great effort; most clearly they concern the so-called bush spirits, in the guise of a "Master of the animals" (cf. chap. vi). Even if a Highest Celestial Being should be a part of these concepts, serious doubts remain concerning Schmidt's thesis that the purity of the concept must be acknowledged in direct ratio to the assumed culture-historical age of the population. One glance at the religious forms of the African peoples, for instance, shows that the sky-gods of the pastoral culture stratum which I associate with the Nilotes stand out much more strongly and dominantly in their religious formulations than among any hunting-and-gathering populations. The only Hamitic-speaking cattle breeders who have remained pagans, the Galla of northeast Africa, believe in a sky-god Waq who—according to all we know—reminds us of Old Testament religious concepts. To illustrate briefly this idea of a celestial God, I quote from one of the prayers which the Galla address to Waq, as taken down by Paulitschke (II, 42 ff.):

O God! Thou hast allowed me to live this day in peace, permit me now to pass the night peacefully, O Lord, who hast no Lord above Thee. There is no strength except in Thee; Thou alone hast no commitment. In Thy hand I pass this day, in Thy hand I pass the night; Thou art my mother, Thou art my father.

It so happens that the religion of the Galla—like that of all northeast African cattle breeders—has been portrayed quite differently in newer works than in the older ones. But the striking similarity between the religious views of these cattle breeders—especially of the Galla—and those of the people of the Old Testament has remained. The geographical proximity of northeast Africa and Palestine suggests direct connection, though we leave it open whether the connection was through contact or through a common cultural substratum. Even if African High Gods cannot all be traced to the continent-wide spreading of cattle-breeder cultures, the vividness of the particular concept of deity among them remains a notable fact. In any event, the concept of God as, for instance, held by the Galla conforms far more closely to the High God in *Urmonotheismus* than do the concepts held by any of the culture-historically older peoples.

Similar conditions can be shown to exist in Indonesia. The idea of a sky-god, the return of the dead to the heavens, and mythical celestial journeys are essential parts of religion among peoples of a Middle-Malayan stratum; among the older cultivators we find other concepts of a deity of which we shall speak next. The Middle-Malayan stratum, which probably is also responsible for the pre-Indic diffusion of the water buffalo in Indonesia, belongs to the younger ethnological cultures (cf. sec. 8, below). In America, too, the sky-god is most palpably present in the more recent culture strata. An example is given in the Kwakiutl who, despite their acquisitive economy, count among the youngest cultures in North America. Boas (II, 182) reports among other things the following prayer at sunrise: "Welcome, Great Chief, Father, as you come and show yourself this morning. We come and meet alive. O protect me that no evil may befall me this day, Chief, Great Father."

87

By these examples we only mean to touch on the fact that emphasis on the High God is most pronounced among the less archaic peoples; that the High God—besides other ideas concerning the deity—is most significant among the cereal growers and cattle breeders; that is, among the great mass of the younger primitive cultures in many parts of the world. Later we shall touch once more on the question of whether or not the idea of a Highest Being might go back to older concepts (see chap. v, sec. 2). For the present we shall consider that image of deity which we place in contrast with the concept of the High God. We shall come to know it under the name of Dema-deity, an addition to the terminology which we hope to justify in the next section.

2. THE DEMA-DEITY

Even Andrew Lang had to deal with the fact that primitive religious forms exist in which the Highest Being does not occur or is totally insignificant. Since the belief in a Highest Being is thought to constitute the *oldest* form of faith, it follows for Schmidt that the culture-historically younger peoples, who do not possess the concept, must have lost it. Lang and Schmidt agree that this fact can be explained only by hypothesizing a retrogression of intellectual capacities. According to Lang (pp. 281 ff.), it was man's laziness which made it seem easier to deal with venal and corruptible spirits than to live up to the strict laws of a High God. So, it is said, man developed the "lesser mythology" and those spirit-beings gained ascendancy which the animistic hypothesis sees as the first phase of religion. On closer inspection of the religious forms on which Lang concentrates, it becomes quite incomprehensible how he could have arrived at his claim. If man expected only advantages from the lower spirit-deities, he certainly placed the greatest possible difficulties in the way of their attainment—such that one must ask if the stakes are in reasonable balance with the expected gain. Cults often demand the highest stakes of man, sometimes even his life.

I am not at all sure that man—if one can look at the problem from this point of view at all—did not make a poor bargain when he bartered away life according to the laws of a High God for the seemingly cruel cults of another religion. This view is also expressed by K. T. Preuss (1932: 247), who assumes that the cultic religions were displaced by the purely supplicative religions because of the excessive demands which cults had made on man. In this manner, the idea of a High God who demands only prayer gained ascendancy. We have already stated our views of the origination of forms by which religious attitudes find expression and therefore need not explicitly point out that such motives cannot possibly have played any part.

What Lang labels "degeneration" is, in a larger view, the substance of the beliefs held by the early cultivators, which are far better known to us than those of the archaic hunters and gatherers, for example. By "early" or "ancient" cultivators we mean a culture stratum which to this day spreads over almost all the tropical regions of the world; it is chiefly characterized by slash-and-burn soil preparation, cultivation of tubers, and the use of arboreal fruits. Cattle breeding, plowing, fertilization, megaliths, and, presumably, the planting of cereal grains form *no* part of their cultural inventory. We are dealing with the most archaic form of tropical cultivation. Representatives of it correspond not only in important traits of their technology but of their culture as well. I have attempted a full description of their forms of religions in another work (cf. Jensen, "Weltbild") and shall cite it frequently, not only here but especially in the next chapter. The animistic hypothesis has paid practically no attention to the concept of God in this culture; it focused on the belief in spirits and ancestor worship, which are indeed of eminent importance in the religion of these peoples, though by no means in theirs exclusively.

Overemphasis on spirits and ancestors by European travelers has often obscured the very definite idea of a deity which is intrinsic to the religion of the cultivators and is the commanding influence at the great cultic feasts. These divine figures are kept clearly distinct from spirits and ancestors, quite often by specific designations.

We will not go into details about spirits and ancestors at this time. It shall only be said that they obviously are not primary formulations, as the animistic hypothesis would have it and as they would appear in most descriptions; they received their significance only secondarily through the truly divine beings and their particular natures (cf. chaps. xiv and xvi). We must mistrust the frequent assertions that some tribes of this culture stratum had no concept of a god but knew only a fear of spirits and the worship of ancestors; one explanation for the one-sidedness of this view is the relative importance of spirits and ancestors in the daily activities of the people, but the major reason is our deficient knowledge of the mythic ideology of the peoples in question. Were we to know the myths that, as we have already stated (chap. ii), must be viewed as the ideological foundations of the ceremonies, divine figures would come to the fore whose nature and essence would transform the multifarious religious notions into "religion." It is they that lived on earth in the mythic primal past and effected the present order and the origination of that which is crucial for existence.

To exemplify divine beings among the cultivator cultures, I cite my work "Das religiöse Weltbild einer frühen Kultur." For the Wemale on the island of Ceram (Moluccas), three female deities stand out among mythic personages: Satene, Rabie, and Hainuwele (pp. 34 ff.). The fact that the deities are female is by no means the rule everywhere. In the myths of the Marind-anim and the Kiwai—both living on the southern coast of New Guinea —there are a great number of such figures, male as well as female. Examples are: Jawi (in Marind-anim mythology), who suffered the first death and from whose head grew the first coconut palm (pp. 46 ff.); the "mother of the cult" who is represented at the annual fertility feast by a girl who is killed and eaten (p. 49); among the Kiwai, the outstanding figure of Marunogere, who introduced death and procreation (pp. 60 ff.), and his daughter Pekai, from whose dismembered body sprang the useful plants; these are only a few of the deities and only a few of their characteristics. Among the Witoto, in South America, we find the primal ancestor and creator Moma and the related figure of Husiniamui (pp. 109 ff.); among the Southern California Indians especially the personage of Wyot (pp. 93 ff.). The enumeration could be continued, especially if we bring in Melanesian examples. In central Africa, too, such figures are found—particularly the Kakaschi-Kakullu—in the mythology of tribes of the southern Congo basin (Frobenius, *Atlantis:* XII, 74 ff.). We have restricted ourselves to these illustrations merely because we happen to possess sufficiently precise descriptions to allow a clear exposition of the nature of the deities.

So far we have simply spoken of deities, but now we have second thoughts, though by no means because of doubts about the divine character of these gods, which is fully confirmed by mythic statements. However, our concept of God and gods—rooted in acquaintance with the high cultures and our Christian education —is so specialized that we cannot make room for a totally distinct kind of deity. To demonstrate the contrast, these deities have often been called tribal or culture heroes, innovators, or the like. In my opinion, such designations fail to meet the full measure of the phenomena. The element of their divinity deserves to be stressed in the terminology, and they might well be given a collective name, in the same way in which we speak of Indic or Greek gods and of the Old Testament or the Islamic God and connect quite concrete concepts with them. The Marind-anim have a term for the collectivity of primal beings and for the divine and creative figures among them. Their word is *Dema;* and *Dema-deities* seems to be an appropriate designation, assuming that the uniformity of the concept has been successfully demonstrated.

The first question must be: what is the main characteristic that differentiates a Dema-deity from our concept of God? This, I believe, may be found in the temporal aspects of the actions of the Dema-deities. We know the omnipresent God who guides the world's fate and to whom man may relate himself in prayer, sacrifice, and devotion. Dema-deities, in contrast, are not *present* in this sense—either in heaven or on Mount Olympus; *their presence is of a different kind.* Their active effectiveness goes back to an ancient primal past or, better, to the end of the primal past. We have seen that myths portray the existent as something that "has become," thus presupposing a contrasting antecedent state of the world (cf. chap. iii, sec. 2). The dominant beings of primal time are the Dema, sometimes possessing human shape, sometimes appearing as animals or plants. Among them, the Dema-deities, outstanding through their creativity, bring about all that exists and the order in which it exists and thereby set an end to primal time.

At this level, too, the creative process is basically different from that with which we are acquainted in the sphere of the High God concepts. Nothing existing is "made" as an artisan makes things, only later to be animated. Among the heterogeneous mythic descriptions of how that which exists came to be there is a peculiar "mythologem" (mythic theme) which confronts us in many variant forms and must be considered the basic formulation of the world view of the archaic root-crop cultivators. The decisive event, resulting in all the significant phenomena, is *the killing of the Dema-deity by the Dema*. The background which this killing of the god finds in the philosophy of religion will be discussed later (chap. viii). In any case, there is no doubt that it constitutes—as do all the great genuine myths—a truthful statement concerning the nature and lawfulness of existence. As a further prerequisite the mythologem of the killing of the Dema-deity must be genuinely religious in nature, i.e., must be a description of the existence of man, beast, and plant and must be traced to a divinely creative act. With the end of primal time, the Dema cease to exist. In place of immortality enters mortal, earthly life, the ability to propagate, the need for food, and a form of existence when life is extinguished. The murdered Dema-deity transforms himself into the useful crop plants but also embarks on the first journey into death and transmutes himself into the realm of death as represented by the terrestrial image of the cult-house. Moreover, we are told, the deity turns into the moon, symbolizing in its waning and reappearing the constant renewal of life.

A deity such as this is not "present," and it would be senseless to address prayers to it, for it does not control fate. Man's religious attitude consists chiefly in continued awareness of the divine origin of the order which the deity engendered. Thus, cultic life is in the main a dramatic presentation of primal events. The many ritual killings with which we are familiar among peoples of this culture and many other phenomena can be understood only in the sense embodied in the given mythologem.

3. *PRIMEVAL LABORS AND CONTINUING PRESENCE OF THE DEITY*

So far we have mainly stressed the Dema-deity's effective action at the termination of the primal past and, in contrast to other concepts of God, the fact that the deity has no *presence*. This cerainly requires limitation, though even when limited it will be seen that the *presence* is of quite a different kind than we would commonly think. We have already stated that the slain Dema-deity continues to exist in various guises, as plants or as the realm of the dead.

The ceremonial eating of fruit or sacrificial animals, in fact only representations of the deity, or—as a particularly drastic replacement—the cannibalistic meals are ways of actualizing the divinely caused primal event. For this reason it is possible for a coconut palm or the fruit of the field to convey the immediate presence of the deity, as is done in great religious festivities when the Dema appear in the shape of their creations and when the portrayers of the deities illustrate under cover of masks or fantastic disguises the coconut-Dema, the banana-Dema, or other mythic figures.

More immediate even is the "presence" of the Dema in man himself, for man has sprung from the Dema at the end of the primal past. A long chain of ancestors links present-day man to the primal Dema, and in death man has the opportunity to be reaccepted forever into their community. This, then, is the root of ancestor worship, which plays so important a part in the religious formulations of the root-crop cultivators (cf. chap. xv, sec. 1). The world of spirits, too, is anchored in these firmly established concepts. As one variant of the myth clearly states, spirits, like the animals with which they are frequently equated, stem from those Dema who could not pass a test demanded by the deity and who therefore could not attain human form (cf. chap. xvi).

Such tests differ from one people to another. According to a widespread belief the dead who cannot solve a riddle posed by the sentinel at the gates of death may be refused entry into the nether world and may turn into spirits. The philosophical thought behind this—to be mentioned only in passing—is oriented toward the ethical imperative that man be conscious of the divine origin of the world order, for all religious ceremonial is preparation for the journey into death and ultimately has only one sense: compliance with the ethical imperative (cf. chap. ix). Among the Kayan of Borneo, tattoo marks, for instance, are considered a sort of visa which facilitates entry into the realm of the dead, since the marks show the deceased to have been a successful headhunter (Hose and McDougall, II, 41). Labyrinth dances are also related to the special test or ordeal which governs entry into the land of death. The various musical instruments in whose tones the voice of a deity is said to reveal itself are special actualizations of the Dema-deities. In most such instances, a drum, a bullroarer, or a flute is expressly related to the primal deity in the narrative of a myth and is, as a cultic instrument, withdrawn from all secular use. Often the relationship is symbolized in the wood from which the instrument is made, for the wood is taken from the kind of tree into which the Dema-deity was transformed upon his murder. A very fine and telling myth of this type comes to us from the Yahuna in western Brazil and was taken down by Koch-Grünberg (*Zwei Jahre:* 386 ff.). It tells of a boy, Milomaki, who sang so beautifully that many came to hear him. Grown to adolescence, he was cremated on a funeral pyre. He still sang in ringing tones when his corpse burst asunder. From his ashes grew the first Paschiuba palm, from which tree large flutes are carved which render again the marvelous tunes once sung by Milomaki. Women and children may not see these flutes, used at the Yurupari feast where one dances in honor of Milomaki, creator of all fruit.

Egon Schaden (p. 164) had this *presence* of the Dema-deities in mind when he stated in his meticulous study of South American Indians that the spirits of their mythic primal "heroes"— they are typical Dema—are alive to them in a quite real sense. "They live in the ornaments which represent them and in the musical instruments which reproduce their voices."

In comparing the characteristic Dema-deities of the archaic cultivators with the Highest Being of *Urmonotheismus,* differences obtrude themselves even in externals. The present-day cultic center is usually regarded as the spot where the primal event took place. The land of the dead is subterranean in almost all instances. Omnipresence of the Dema-deity can be understood only as a presence in the men, animals, plants, or even inanimate objects into which they turned themselves. It is not a workaday awareness but is reserved for specific cultic and festive occasions. Another aspect of the High God of *Urmonotheismus,* his benevolence, can be applied to the Dema-deity only in a completely different sense, for the order established by the Dema encompasses all aspects of reality, the hostile and the amicable, mortality and propagation. Religious faith and constant cultic repetition of the creative moments of the primal past allow us to suppose an essentially optimistic view of life. The "So-being" of the world is praised in its entirety as the outcome of divine work. The idea of a diabolical antagonist or of divine punishment for sinful acts to explain the unfriendlier manifestations is lacking. The Dema's nature places it beyond good and evil. It is also notable that the mythologem which is associated with the cultivators hardly ever is concerned with the creation of the earth, which is almost always counted among the deeds of the High God. Generally, the earth is assumed to have been pre-existent. Interest is concentrated on the origin of creatures and especially of the sociocultural order. Thus, the two ideas appear quite disparate. Can we really consider the religious world view of the cultivators as degenerative? Our answer must be negative. Even if we were to permit ourselves the generalization that Western revulsion at human sacrifice, head-hunts, and cannibalism constitutes a nobler humanity, we cannot shut our eyes to the grandeur of the religious conception. We must acknowledge that experiences have here found cultural formulations which carry their own justification. It is therefore not surprising that concerns which met with vivid religious elaboration among those archaic cultivators have found their way into later religious forms even in the high cultures. They have retained their firm hold even within the structure of quite alien systems of religion.

We shall have occasion to deal intensively with the intimate link between Dema-deities and the gods of the polytheistic high cultures. A single reference to a contribution by K. Kerényi ("Kore," pp. 341 ff.) must here suffice to point out that Demeter and Persephone of Greek mythology and even the Eleusinian mysteries reflect the same mythic idea as dominates the world view of the archaic cultivators. Like all cultural formulations, the Dema-based religious world view has its moments of decadence, as for instance the mass slaughter of men and beasts of which we shall take account later. It is, however, impossible to assign the belief in a High God as a sublime form of religion to the initial phase of human history and then declare all later forms which are not unequivocally related to this belief to be manifestations of corruption. Both concepts of God have, in their respective creative epochs, found majestic expression and in times of cultural impoverishment shown signs of degeneration.

4. MONOTHEISM AND POLYTHEISM

The most important question concerning the relationship between Dema-deity and sky-god would have to inquire—at least from the standpoint of Western theoretical thought—into the number of gods worshiped. Judaism, Christianity, and Islam have rested claims of superiority on the oneness of their God. Lang and Schmidt believed that uniqueness was already an essential characteristic of the idea of God in primal culture (*Urkultur*). For the present we offer no opinion as to whether singularity, the "monon," has been of such conscious importance in the belief-systems of early mankind as, for example, in those of the Old Testament. To my knowledge there is no direct statement to that effect. The sky-god of the African cattle breeders rarely occurs in isolation. At times there is a duality of gods, as among the Masai and Hottentots; more often there are divine figures of another order ranged beside the sky-god. However, the outstanding preponderance of a specific deity may have suggested a natural monotheism without elevating singularity to a principle or attaching special significance to the isolated situations. It must also be conceded that the specific idea of God, as it confronts us in the Highest Being, suggests in a special sense the idea of a *sole* God. The designation "Highest Being," which is quite appropriate in most cases, as well as the special character of a *prima causa* inherent in this idea of God, stresses uniqueness.

In contrast, the Dema-deities almost never stand alone, so that even according to this external feature a certain relationship to polytheism obtrudes itself. But this comparison in particular points up a significant distinction. The Dema-deities, appearing in different myths under different names, are so similar from one people to another that one cannot help but regard them as mere variations on a single theme. I have shown in another work (1939: 11 ff., 32 ff.) how many threads connect the three female deities of the Wemale (Ceram), how they only reflect different aspects of a single reality, how one can substitute for another, and how even their names may blend. The same unity can be demonstrated for the very numerous Dema-figures of the Marind-anim. Here the unity of the various idea-complexes is revealed even more in the cults. There are a great number of them and each dramatizes a particular myth. The course of the ceremonies shows so close a degree of relationship among the underlying concepts that one inclines to postulate a single seminal ceremony which, in time, subdivided into several different but still similar cults (cf. the discussion of the Rapa, Imo, and Majo cults, in Jensen, "Weltbild": 49 ff.). Among the Kiwai we are basically dealing with a single cult; but a large number of Dema-deities appear in the pertinent myths, so similar that the same episodes recur in different myths (cf. Sido, Soido, and Marunogere, in Jensen, "Weltbild": 58 ff.). The diverse myths and various cults of the Witoto have been collected and reported by Preuss, who repeatedly interpreted them as variations on the single theme of the killing of a moon deity (*Witoto:* I, 144).

The question arises how such variations can come about if *one* firmly established myth and *one* pertinent cult are assumed at the outset. I do not find it difficult to imagine courses of history which could lead to such variation, particularly among illiterate tribes who preserve established lore only by oral tradition. We know by experience how rapidly variants arise in oral communication. A variant, returning to its point of origin, may well depart so far from the first version that it becomes independently viable, though it still is similar to the original.

However, myths of Dema-deities which go back to one original version imply that there perhaps has been only a single Dema-deity. This is difficult to prove conclusively, but acquaintance with the data makes me inclined to accept the premise. The fact that variants were perpetuated alongside each other and that frequently distinct, though similar, cults exist side by side clearly shows that the "monon," the element of uniqueness, carried no great weight with the people of that culture. That this was actually never the case among primitive peoples before the time of the Old Testament is, in my opinion, documented by all available sources, including those about the sky-god.

Uniqueness, so central to *Urmonotheismus,* may possibly not be tied to the concept of a Highest Being exclusively but may rather be a natural characteristic of early forms of religion. The "Master of the animals" (cf. chap. vi) among hunting peoples may well have possessed it. Nowhere before Old Testament evidence, however, does uniqueness assume the proportions of an uncompromising principle.

Insistence on principle always presumes a certain measure of intolerance. The coexistence of heterogeneous conceptions of deities among most primitive peoples constitutes an acknowledgment of many ways of experiencing God. Even if the germinal idea of Dema-deities may have been linked to a natural monotheism, there nevertheless is a type of Dema-deity that is rooted in duality even in its inception. We mean those pairs of heroes and twins of mythology who personify the principle of polarity in the world; often they are associated with sun and moon or with other paired contrasts of the phenomenological world. They seem to belong to a specific culture stratum and are often regarded as the founders of dual social organization (moieties), with which we shall deal in chapter vii, section 1. Instead of natural monotheism we may here speak of just as natural a dualism, which in that early stratum had found purest cultic expression—for we must think of dual social organization in that sense (cf. chap. ii, sec. 1).

It is certainly appropriate to draw a generic parallel between this thinking in dualities and the paired contrasts in the religions of later cultures which may be reduced to the formula of God and devil. It is difficult if not impossible, however, to interpret the Zoroastrian teachings of the binary division of the world as a sublimation or "enhancement" of older "primitive" ideas. The doctrine of the benevolent God whose creation is upset by a diabolical adversary ultimately rests on a rather problematical criterion; it divides the world into factors favorable and unfavorable to man, and one cannot say that this principle does justice to the nature of things. Purely phenomenologically, however, the later pairings of deities are rooted in dualistic thinking.

5. DISTINCT CAUSES IN INTELLECTUAL HISTORY

Even if the idea of the Dema could be traced to an origin in a single deity and if this should have external similarities with a single High God, the fundamental distinctness of the two concepts of God must still be emphasized. Both stem from totally different attitudes which can be shown within fairly clear cultural settings. The sharp typological difference between the two ideas of God is made graphically clear by their untroubled coexistence within a single culture. There are numerous examples. We shall cite one which was reported by an adherent of the hypothesis of *Urmonotheismus.*

Gusinde describes in detail the culture of the very archaic Selknam (also known in the literature as the Ona), who live on Tierra del Fuego at the southern tip of South America. According to Gusinde, a Highest Being whose name is Temaukel occupies the center of the religion of this hunting tribe. "Only this personage and the reverence accorded him make up the religion of the Selknam in the proper sense of the word . . ." (p. 495). Temaukel resides in the sky; no one can ever see him. He has no body; neither does he have wives and children. He has always been, and he never dies. He never comes to earth. He sees everything that goes on on the earth and knows the most hidden thoughts. Creative achievements are attributed to him, "small in number as they may be" (p. 501). The fashioning of the phenomenological world, however, is the work of other creative figures, and so Temaukel can be credited only with the creation of the "starless sky and formless earth."

The almost total absence of any relationship between God and man conforms to the theory of primal monotheism. The Highest Being does not occupy himself "with the particulars of individual lives; he withdraws, as it were, into a state of inactive and impenetrable aloofness" (p. 504). The sole religious attitude of man is expressed in the reverence shown whenever his name is pronounced, though even this is usually avoided out of awe. "Prayers of supplication are almost totally lacking." There are "neither temples nor communal religious celebrations, neither idols nor cultic rites of any kind" (p. 508). The sacrifices related by Gusinde (p. 512) are highly suspect and in this form, i.e., as sacrifices, meaningless. Besides this rather abstract figure of Temaukel, the beliefs of the Selknam allow for several "great personages," who lived on Tierra del Fuego as the first beings in primal time but were not yet contemporary man. Among them the person of Kenos stands out most vividly, having been sent to earth by Temaukel. Out of clumps of earth he formed a male and a female genital organ whose union resulted in the first humans. These, however, were unlike contemporary man but were Dema beings, since many features of the human condition, as for instance death, did not yet exist. Kenos raised the sky, which at that time still stretched low above the earth. He taught man to

99

speak. When men grew old, they did not die but wakened rejuvenated from a deep sleep to grow old once more. When they chose not to waken any more, they turned into a mountain or a bird, the wind, or a sea animal, a rock, or a star, like Kenos himself, who after his creative deeds turned himself into a star in the sky (pp. 571 ff.). Man's ethical laws also were created by Kenos.

Gusinde placed great value in the statement that Kenos carried out his beneficent activities at the command of Temaukel. For our purposes this is inconsiderable, since the statement merely links the activities of Kenos with the existence of Temaukel and once more stresses the first-cause aspect of the Highest Being. Kenos himself and the "great personages" who are of his kind are typical Dema-deities from whom stem, not only all things real, but the ethical order in which man moves. Significantly, the creativity of the Dema lies in effecting transformations of phenomena which thereby enter into existence for the first time. The actual ancestors, i.e., Kenos and others of his class of beings, continue their existence in the shape of natural objects (p. 579). With the institution of death by another Dema, an end is put to the primal order.

All descriptions clearly show two very different ideas of God existing side by side. (I am passing over the fact that Gusinde credits the "great personages" with neither divinity nor any kind of religious experiential significance. His own description can hardly be made to harmonize with this view.) Gusinde himself calls Temaukel a typical "Highest Being." Kenos and the other members of his class are typical Dema-deities, though the myths which record their deeds are not the best or most vivid examples of their type. The one link between the two is the already mentioned statement that Kenos acted on Temaukel's orders, but this causal nexus cannot negate the fundamental difference and the actual disjunction between the two.

In all this, we are not even considering whether the Dema-deities belong to the original stock of religious ideas of the Fuegians or if they were taken over at a later time from other peoples of different cultural affiliation. I consider the latter probable (as does Gusinde), despite the relative vitality of the religious contents. The same question might, of course, be asked regarding the Highest Being, but we are here concerned only with the contiguity of the two ideas of God which seem not to interfere with each other to any extent and exhibit little tendency to amalgamate. The Selknam illustration may stand for many others that could as well demonstrate that fundamental difference between the concepts is a prerequisite for their coexistence. That the possibility was not always given is reflected in many mutual influences and hybrid forms. These will be discussed in the following section.

6. FIRST CAUSES

Singularity seemed to us not to be the major criterion of the Highest Being; what distinguishes the sky-god we find in the particular manner in which he shows his effectiveness and in his continuing presence as an individual, active personage, the guide of fate who through punishment or reward determines human fortune. So he was described to us by Schmidt. Often, however, the High God is presented as an otiose deity, too far removed to bother with the affairs of mankind. Otiosity has to do with the second criterion that distinguishes the High God from Dema. The sky deity is a being without associated cult, a condition which probably corresponds to the myths which are told about him. They usually deal with the creation of heaven and earth. The creative activity of the Dema-deity, on the other hand, is almost exclusively concerned with the animate world, especially with human existence; the earth is either thought to be pre-existent, or its origin is not even touched on in the myth. The creative activity of the sky-god stands in absolute contrast to this. When "God says 'let there be light' and there was light," the creative act springs from omnipotence. The description of the event contains no mythic element. Man and beast are formed by an artisan's hand. God himself remains outside of his creation as the Great Instigator.

The Dema too are instigators. They transform themselves into phenomena in which they continue to exist. The event is *of a truly mythic nature*, containing statements concerning the essence of things which are to be known through the myth and only through the myth. Seen mythologically, the Highest Being is a *deus ex machina* whose will alone, without any motivation, can bring about the created phenomena.

Any concept of God formulated by man must necessarily have its correlates in human psychological propensities. It readily suggests itself that both concepts of God were linked to quite distinct realms of human reality. The psychological potential which is inherent in the conception of a Dema-deity constitutes the human ability to experience the divine content of the phenomenological world. Essentially, the world view of the cultivators represents the world as something that has come about through divine actualization. At the center of the presentation is the human condition which is revealed in its most dramatic situations: death, propagation, killing, and the need for sustenance.

In contrast, the Highest Being depends to a greater extent on man's intellectual capabilities. The experiences which underlie the concept of the Dema-deities are more immediately beholden to observation. Questions about the origin of all things and the sense of all that happened—and that happens even in the present —led to the idea of an originator, of a first cause, and of a God who controls destiny. One might ask with some apprehension how mankind could be content with an idea of God which to a large degree was a product of ratiocination. However, a counter question arises here: has mankind ever been satisfied with that idea of God alone? Christianity would certainly be a point in contradiction; alongside the Highest Being it places a completely mythic concept, the person of the murdered Son of God. Cult, as true and profound expression of religious experience, is not kindled by the image of the Celestial Deity. Only prayer will establish an active relationship between God and man. (I intentionally refrain from mentioning blood-sacrifice,[2] which, in the form that has come down to us, is a "survival," i.e., a misinterpreted and empty repetition of ritual killing. We shall return to it in some detail [cf. chap. ix].) The cult of Christianity is, therefore, almost entirely pre-empted by the divine life and works of Christ himself.

Schmidt, too, discusses how the idea of a Highest Being might have been conceived. The only difference of opinion between him and Andrew Lang turns on the subject of primal revelation. Lang refused to admit it as explanation of the origin of the idea of God. Schmidt is here—rightly, I believe—of a different opinion.

[2] This term is used throughout the book. It might be more correct to speak of "bloody sacrifices," as R. H. Lowie does in *Primitive Religion*, for not blood but an animal is sacrificed, at the killing of which blood is shed.

It is interesting to read (I, 185 ff.) that in his view mankind may have penetrated to the concept of a Highest Being in a purely rational way, even prior to any primal revelation. The abstractness of this idea of God makes me strongly sympathetic to it.

I should like to return once more to the question of the antiquity of the idea of a Highest Being. Without giving up any of the points of doubt raised before, Schmidt's thesis of the priority of the idea of a Highest Being as creator and disposer of all things seems quite reasonable from a purely psychological point of view. Lehmann-Nitsche once said that "why" is the oldest of all questions. We could then agree with Schmidt that early man, having the mental endowment with which we credit him, should have been capable of giving form to such an idea of God. If root-crop cultivators make statements which lead us to include the presence of such conceptions, we must admit the possibility of their primary origin. We place all the more value, therefore, on the two earlier findings, namely that this concept of God never appears *alone* among the archaic cultivators and that it never constitutes the core of their religious life.

Gusinde acquainted us with one of many examples of the compatible coexistence of two concepts of deity within a single culture; it is only natural to ask what mutual influences have taken place. I see a decisive influence of the High God concept on the Dema concept in the culture-historically significant process by which primeval deities were transmuted into polytheistic gods. It may be that this influence was only one of many factors at work there, but it should hardly be disregarded (chap. viii, sec. 4).

The occasional fusion of the two conceptions is not of very great importance to the history of culture. Among the Witoto, the figure of Moma has certain features of a Highest Being, though its Dema-character still dominates. Frequently, one of a pair of polar Dema-deities, the one identified with the sun, is "raised" to a High God status. A clear example is found among the Apinayé (cf. chap. v, sec. 2). In their mythology, sun and moon are Dema-deities with typically dualistic implications. In the everyday, however, prayer and worship are directed to the "sun" alone as the superior deity.

Conversely, the Dema *concept* has doubtless had influence on the High God concept. All that has been said so far suggests that the following traits of the High God may be referred to such influences: (1) Otiosity which often makes the sky-god so aloof that he becomes of small concern to man. It does not correspond to the image of a punitive or rewarding ruler of destiny but rather forms a parallel to the cessation of Dema efficiency at the close of the primal period. (2) When the High God is taken to be the ancestor of man, he takes on characteristic traits of the Dema. Through these, man usually traces his descent quite directly, while the craftsman-like fashioning of first man, so often associated with the High God concept, excludes direct descent. (3) The last characteristic deserves more detailed treatment in the next section. It refers to the High God's activity during a paradisaical phase on earth which also is assigned to a primal past.

7. PRIMAL ERA AND PARADISE

The myths which the archaic cultivators tell of primal time have on occasion been called variations of the story of Paradise (cf., for example, Fischer, pp. 204 ff.). The assumption is that we are sure enough of what we mean by Paradise to base on it the explanation of the unknown. As so often, we take our evidence from the high cultures and extrapolate it to the less well known archaic cultures. Not rarely, however, this hampers understanding instead of furthering it; concepts with which we are familiar are by no means always the most reasonable, and the true sense of a cultural phenomenon is often revealed only when we trace out the historical progression from primitive to high cultures.

The change which takes place at the threshold between primal past and present condition suggests the Old Testament story of Paradise. As "Edenic tale" it has entered the terminology, and the entire class of tales has thus been placed in an old familiar frame with the understanding, of course, that the tales are either variants or primitive prototypes of the perfect Old Testament version. Paradise conjures up a multitude of associations, the Fall of Man, the Expulsion, i.e., the primitive event which marks the inception of the present condition of existence, miserable, sinful, and deplorable when compared with the paradisaical past. Parallels with primitive myths, down to the least detail, were easily established. The killing of the Dema-deity is equated with the Fall or on occasion with the first sexual act, which—as we have seen—is closely related to the act of killing, for mortality and procreativity simultaneously became man's destiny. Thus the comfortably familiar leads us to the understanding of the uncomprehended; myth becomes an innocent fairy tale.

In spite of obvious similarity we must not obliterate basic differences between the types of narrative. We can limit ourselves to a few important points. Have the archaic cultivators had an image of a paradisaical primal past? This we must deny. The mythic view proceeds from the present state of things, and in the interest of narrative technique, it places before it a different, possibly even contrary, situation. The genuine mythologem does not elaborate the description of the primal era but concentrates on the final phase when events took place which initiated the "Just-so" of the world and the beginning of the human condition. The substantive descriptions of primal existence are therefore essentially etiological and not properly mythic.

In any event, the world view of the archaic cultivators dispenses with any evaluative juxtaposition of reality and primal past. The Old Testament dwells on the negative aspects of the loss of Paradise: in pain Eve shall bring forth children and the fields shall bear thorns and thistles. The image which the world view of the archaic cultivators produced would better be expressed as follows: with the end of the primal condition, man achieved true life; though destructive of life and a mortal being, he procreates and propagates; though henceforth he requires food and sustenance, the deity provides it through his own transmutation.

The Old Testament does not emphasize the act of killing but rather the act of eating at the termination of the primal era; the killing becomes associated with the later events about Cain and Abel. In terms of narrative technique this constitutes a complication; to present the act of eating as a sin that demands expiation through mortality requires explanation, as does the prior divine interdict. One is tempted to ask why the tree was placed near Adam and Eve if they were not to eat of its fruit. All such individual features show that we are not dealing with a genuine myth; that the mythic pattern has been taken over and retained, though explanatory and fairy-tale–like traits dominate. Through it all are woven philosophical speculations and allegorical allusions devised on the basis of a totally different world view. To give proper due to the sincerity and undeniable grandeur of this other world view lies outside our immediate task. I am only concerned to demonstrate that whatever was taken over from the older religious image—and that is not little—has in many instances lost all grandeur and even semantic context.

Much could be said for and even more against the contention that the character of sin attaches to the first act of killing. I will limit myself to a single argument. The fact that the mythic event *must* be repeated in the form of cultic killings shows sufficiently that we are not dealing with "sin." Had the killing been an objectionable and contemptible act, it would be completely senseless to re-enact the offense voluntarily and thus bring down the punishment again. A *feeling* of sin is certainly a universal human trait and is called forth with particular intensity by such acts as killing or the sex act; but it always *follows the deed*. If it were vehemently evident beforehand, the deed probably would never be done. Many of the customs belong here, presumably, by which head-hunters protect themselves from the revenge of their victims *after* the deed; before the hunt they had to conform to many rules and precepts in order to insure the success of their undertakings.

A comparison between the mythologem associated with the archaic cultivators and the Edenic tale cannot be carried through in any of the decisive points. The two are linked only by a specific literary style which undoubtedly originated in the older cultural epoch.

The fairy-tale–like story of Paradise never bore the character of a particular religious commitment. Psychologically, it is imaginable only as emanation of a relatively pessimistic world view. In this it contrasts sharply with the mythologem characteristic of the cultivators. Among primitive peoples we often find descriptions of the realm of the dead which are quite reminiscent of Paradise. But even in these cases the psychological premise seems to be a pessimistic, even desperate evaluation of life. A moving example of this need of balance is related by Petrullo about the nomadic Yaruro, a moribund ethnic remnant on the upper reaches of the Orinoco. The outstanding priestly activity of the shaman seems to consist exclusively in prophesying a paradisaical future. In imaginary journeys to the beyond, he visits the supreme female deity and then relates to his tribal brethren her comforting promises of an Eden-like existence after death (cf. chap. xii, sec. 2).

8. THE PROMETHEUS AND HAINUWELE MYTHOLOGEMS

On the one hand, the transformation from primeval myth to Edenic tale involves a culture-historical process by which the myth loses some of its original significance to an emphasis on fairy-tale characteristics; on the other hand, there undoubtedly are constellations in the psychology of culture where concepts similar to Paradise develop independently of each other for the satisfaction of human longings and as defenses against hopelessness. Beyond this—and disregarding the Christian image of Heaven—descriptions of Paradise never seem to have attained major importance in the history of religion. A much more significant process of transmutation, purely culture-historical in nature, took place with respect to the concept of the Dema-deities. Here the original ritual killing became that which we are wont to call blood-sacrifice. We shall speculate on this event later (chap. viii, sec. 4). At this time we only wish to anticipate the surmise in its broadest application in order to carry forth our ideas concerning the relationship between High God and Dema.

On several occasions we have stressed that the idea of the High God received its clearest formulation in the cultures of the cattle breeders, even if its origin were to lead back into more ancient times. In contrast, it is almost entirely absent in the earliest stratum of the archaic cultivators. Schmidt acknowledged this (I, 469): "The two-class culture contains no evidence of a Highest Being." It again plays a role, however, in ethnologically younger cultures where it coexists with Dema-deities, spirits, and ancestors. Between the world view of the more recent primitive cultures and that of the archaic cultivators, there extends a discontinuity which up to now has often been ascribed to the "invasion of the steppe peoples." Plausible and seductive as this theory may sound—does it not explain why the ethnologically more recent peoples of the Old World know the breeding of large cattle?—serious doubts have recently been cast on it by the archeologists (cf. Jettmar). But even if the cultural break was not caused by cattle breeders, there remains the explanation, the only possible one, that racially alien elements brought about a fundamental change in the culture of the archaic cultivators.

107

The process is especially obvious in the so-called Nilotic cultures of Africa, which extend from the populations of the Upper Nile southward to the Masai in Tanganyika. These tribes by and large constitute a single linguistic, racial, and cultural entity. Almost all grow cereals (several varieties of millet) and practice very intensive cattle breeding. Their close ties to cattle are most strongly expressed in the "cattle complex"—which reflects a specific relationship between man and bovine and is composed of a long list of prescriptive rules of conduct. We rediscover this cattle complex among many tribes of east, southeast, and southwest Africa who do not belong to the Nilotic linguistic grouping. Since all of these peoples also show an alien racial admixture, which might well be traced to Nilotic influences, we may assume that credit for the diffusion of cattle as well as cereal grain should go to the wide-ranging Nilotes. The resemblance between the Herero (southwest Africa) and the Nilotes of northeast Africa is, in any case, quite startling.

The culture of the archaic cultivator lives on among many of the Nilotic peoples as an ancient population substratum—usually relegated to the status of despised outcastes. This subject, not quite germane to our present topic, has been treated in some detail in my contribution to the *Festschrift* for Paul Radin (Jensen, 1960).

In northeast Africa a myth is narrated that concerns the origin of food plants that is totally different from any we have come to know within the framework of the mythology of the archaic cultivators and their Dema-deities. We shall call the former the Hainuwele mythologem after its Indonesian prototype, while the latter, which tells of cereal grains and how they were stolen from heaven against the will of the deity, will be called the Prometheus mythologem. Almost all peoples of northeast Africa except the tubers from the theft. The origin of tubers is either said to be unknown or said to have existed from the beginning. In its most frequent form the story of the cereal theft relates that man received the grain seeds through a mouse that had climbed a cobweb to heaven and there secretly ate of the abundantly growing cereal before returning to earth.

The myth of the cereal theft is also found in other parts of Africa. The Dogon tell of a primeval blacksmith who stole the grains from the sky-god and brought them to earth hidden in his

108

hammer (Griaule, 1938: 98, n. 4). According to the Wa-Tawa (Tabwa) who live at the southwestern tip of Lake Tanganyika, the first man came from the heavens and carried the seed grains to earth in his hair (Janssens, pp. 552 ff.). Though the terse myth says nothing of theft, the fact that he carried the seed in his hair suggests that he was hiding stolen grains. The Gula (Gule) and Kulfa of the Central Sudan leave no doubt that millet was gotten through theft, against the will of the deity. A female spirit presses beeswax to the soles of her feet so that the grain which the sky-god had spread out would adhere (Griaule, 1938: 94 ff., nn.). This motive occurs in Indonesia repeatedly and in quite similar form.

In Indonesia a clear example of this younger stratum, which must be associated with the spreading of cattle and cereal grains, may be found in the Middle-Malayan culture which already possesses the water buffalo but makes no economic use of it. On Celebes and in the Philippines, for instance, the water buffaloes are kept only for the "purpose" of blood-sacrifice at funerals or other festivities. The Middle-Malayan culture stratum is thereby clearly distinguished from the Late-Malayan where—on Java, for instance—the water buffalo serves as a draft animal.

Another basic innovation distinguishes the Middle-Malayan stratum from the older stratum of archaic cultivators: the totally different mythic reason given for *the origin of cereal grains*. In southeast Asia, both mythologems, Prometheus and Hainuwele, are neatly delimited: *rice was stolen from the sky; the tubers sprang from the murdered deity*. Despite some overlaps, the distinction between the two mythologems can be made clear in the plurality of cases. Frobenius noted the distinction. He had assembled the data shortly before his death but could not publish the planned work.

Conversely, there is a myth in Polynesia that tells the heavenly origin of the roots and tubers. Our illustration will be taken from Stuebel's collection of myths (pp. 142 ff.). The taro root was stolen in a manner often heard in Indonesian narratives: a man hid it in his penis. We can imagine this as possible with a grain of rice but hardly with a taro root. This form of the myth, then, can probably be traced to the fact that Polynesian culture, though historically recent, possesses no cereal grains. It may be assumed, however, that the Polynesians had been acquainted with cereals for a considerable time in the areas from which they came but had lost them during the migration to Polynesia (Heine-Geldern, 1932: 607). At the same time they also probably knew the myth of its theft which, in their later home, they adapted to roots and tubers. In all of Polynesian mythology, sky and sky deity play an important role, and that is the prerequisite for any myth which bespeaks the celestial origin of the principal food plant.

Differential mythic causes for grains and tubers, respectively, are occasionally even given in America. The Chami, for instance, a subtribe of the Choco in Western Colombia, tell that maize was stolen from heaven (Chaves, p. 150), and from the Taulipang, Koch-Grünberg (*Roroima:* II, 90) reports the mythologem of the theft of a kernel of maize from heaven by which maize first becomes known to man. We must keep in mind here that for the Taulipang, as for most South American forest tribes, the manioc root is the staple and maize has only minor importance. The origin of yams and taro, less often of manioc (which as the younger addition to the diet is frequently coupled with the maize), but also the origin of other tree and root crops is usually explained by the Hainuwele mythologem: a Dema-deity was killed and its body transmuted into the economically important plant. It strikes us as remarkable, then, that in Africa, southeast Asia, and Indonesia maize as a cereal grain is now and then linked to a very different myth. Of the Chané in the Western Chaco we are told that the Fox God hides the small seeds of the *algarobba* fruit, stolen from its senescent custodian, in a hollow tooth and plants it in an open plain (Nordenskiöld, p. 261)—a fine illustration of the Prometheus mythologem.

A further South American example comes from the Kàgaba. It is not entirely unambiguous, however, since it is concerned neither with grains nor with maize but with all kinds of seeds "which the deer eat" and in particular with the canchi, apparently a tree fruit. According to the myth, this fruit is distributed over the earth by theft exclusively, since one people steals it from its neighbors (Preuss, *Kàgaba:* 174 ff.). The cultural and linguistic affinity between Kàgaba and Chibcha and the culture-historically recent forms which we find among these peoples lend likelihood to the surmise that the myth originally dealt with the purloining of maize from the heavens and that the inclusion of other seed crops is secondary.

These were only a few South American examples of the peculiarly different myths of the origin of crop plants. But a single example would, by itself, prove the culture-historical connection between New and Old World just as convincingly as claims for relationship between plant species made by the botanists. How could men, independently of each other, have hit upon the same type of mythic explanations, though nothing about the nature of the plants makes the explanation appear the "natural" one or makes its independent origination in different continents seem plausible! G. Hatt took the same position in a paper on the Corn Mother (pp. 904 ff.).

Set over against the Hainuwele mythologem, the ideas that make up the Prometheus mythologem are so different that only the culture-historically distinct origins of the grains and root crops can explain it. In addition, the myths make it amply clear that the culture stratum from which the grain crops stemmed was dominated by the concept of a sky-god, the stratum of the root-crop cultivators by a Dema-deity. Not only the concepts of the deity differ; the processes of creation differ materially, too. In the one instance a pre-existent crop plant is withheld in heaven; in the other a biological form is produced through an act of propagation or through bodily transmutation.[3]

In telling of the theft of grain from the heavens, the myths reveal a rather singular relationship between man and deity. Promethean man defies the God, negates his will through cunning, and boasts of his deed. The Dogon call on the blacksmith in case of certain ailments. He strikes his hammer (in which, according to the myth, the seed had been hidden) against a rock. At the same time he names himself in an oration as the oldest of the Dogon, descended from the heavens. "C'est moi qui leur ai donné la nourriture. Il faut pardonner à la famille du malade . . ." (Dieterlen, p. 172). Thus the contemporary blacksmith identifies himself with the Promethean primal blacksmith and

[3] A. E. Jensen, "Das Mythologem vom Halben Menschen," *Paideuma*, V (1950). I simply cannot understand how Schmitz (1960: 231 ff.) can say that the Hainuwele and Prometheus mythologems are not basically different from each other. He sees the relationship as that of a "more archaic, savage form" (Hainuwele mythologem) to a "polished, in the truest sense a refined form" (Prometheus mythologem). The theft in heaven on the one hand and the killing of a deity on the other are said to be "a difference of degrees" only, "merely variations of the same structural type."

calls upon his deed as his authority. Such a relationship between God and man is difficult to imagine in the framework of Dema belief. It obviously belongs to a younger stratum in which, presumably, the diffusion of cereal grains first took place.

These Prometheus-like figures—the blacksmith of the Dogon also brought fire from the heavens—are usually called *heilbringer*, benefactors, or culture heroes in the ethnological literature. The basic difference from those culture heroes whom we have designated as Dema-deities should need no further explication. The Dema of the Hainuwele mythologem lack, above all, the aspect of defiance which distinguishes the heroes of the younger stratum. The relationship between man and God had changed in the new world view: a God enthroned in heaven withholds important cultural benefits: fire, grain, or, in Africa, occasionally the sheep! A hero, in human or animal shape, undertakes to steal the desired benefit from the God through cunning and daring. We shall not discuss in this context what caused the new cultural impulse. Here it is only of importance that the older world view was by no means eradicated. On the contrary, all of its significant features are prominently present in the cultures of the early Neolithic peoples. Considerable shifts of meaning are noticeable, however, in addition to economic changes. We are convinced that the Dema of the archaic cultivators experienced a resurrection in the polytheistic religions of the archaic high cultures (chap. viii, sec. 4). A basic criterion of the "gods" is their *presence*, which we have also pointed out as a characteristic of the High God concept. The assumption suggests itself readily that emphasis of the sky-god in the later stratum is at least one factor contributing to the transformation of Dema into "God."

9. THE HOPE OF HEAVENLY RECOMPENSE

The ideas expressed in the preceding sections invite the accusation of "materialism." After all, cultural formulations are not chemical elements which need only be placed in a retort to combine in prescribed ways. When in the course of the history of culture one fully formed idea is influenced or altogether transformed by another, quite heteromorphous idea, we may expect the existence of certain preconditions. An idea that was vigorously alive to the members of a cultural community would hardly undergo a process of hybridization. Yet, there can be no doubt that such hybrids arose in the course of the history of culture. Among primitive peoples, the religion of the Herero and that of the Southeastern Bantu furnish examples.

In order to define the antecedent process in a way that will lend credibility to such hybridization, we must recall the characteristic cause that leads from "expression" to "application." We must especially restate the factor which can so greatly augment this process, particularly in the religious sphere: the expectation of some sort of consummation (cf. chap. iii, sec. 3). We have seen that in the expressive phase devout activity and fulfilment coalesce; then, as the genuinely religious sentiment abates, the notion easily gains ground that external events of pious activity by themselves can bring about the desired benefits.

It is one of Radin's merits that he pointed out this drive for benefits in the sphere of religion, though he never considered it a degenerative force.

The religion of the archaic cultivators—no less than any other religion—has produced a great number of configurations which are primarily forms in which "knowledge" is expressed. They are especially numerous, and we can hardly imagine how closely the life cycle in those cultures is paralleled by ritual commandments, taboos, and observances through which such peoples try to express the world order as they see it. How could such prospects of heavenly recompense be satisfied by Dema-deities who took to action but once—at the beginning of all things—and established an order in whose trammels all that is to happen, happens— fatalistically and unalterably? This constitutes, in my opinion, the first opportunity for a transmutation from the idea of a God active only in the primal past to one somehow still present.

The change is clearly manifested in the numerous myths telling of journeys into the realm of the dead. There Dema-deities survive to this day and the dead ancestors live among them in intimate community. There, then, is also the place where the expectation of recompense may be immediately satisfied. Most of these myths, therefore, have a common point of departure: either the hero must escape from a present or threatening calamity through succor from the land of the dead, or else he requires a special power which permits him to accomplish the extraordinary. One of the finest examples of the latter motive is told us in the Kalevala, the Finnish national epic. The sixteenth and seventeenth cantos give us two variants of the journey to the nether world: the seventeenth is the older version and closer to the culture concepts of the archaic cultivators.

The idea of a land of the dead is at the same time one of the sources of ancestral cults. Human ancestors may become agents of salvation only by living communally with the primeval deities. The realm of the dead thereby becomes a "place of salvation." The presence of the ancestors at feasts, which is often so drastically enacted, compensates for the general absence of the Dema. Claims according to which masks represent the ancestors often are mere generalizations which should include the divine Dema; many reports which make detailed statements about the significance of masks affirm this. We may compare what Wirz writes about the mask-disguises of the Marind-anim; or the telling episode in a Kàgaba text taken down by Preuss (*Kàgaba:* 142 ff.), in which we learn that the Dema-like primeval priests *took off their faces* at the end of their order-creating activities *so that mortal man might wear them as masks* and thus be able to carry out the ceremonies needed to preserve the order. One of the few tribes whom we know to differentiate clearly between the immortal Dema and the mortal ancestors are the Dogon in west Africa (Dieterlen). According to Griaule (*Masques:* 38), we must distinguish four types of cultic activities among the Dogon; two relate to the immortal Dema, two to the mortal ancestors.

The more fully the hope of heavenly reward penetrated and even supplanted the genuinely religious experiences of reminiscence, the more did the idea of a primally centered deity have to give way to the idea of a "present" deity who actively interfered in the course of events. Sacrificial offerings show to how great an extent ancestor cults have functioned as intermediary elements. An offering of food and drink to humans seems semantically sounder than one to divine beings; usually one had known the persons before their demise, when they were old and needed assistance and were grateful for the gesture of kindness. As we see it, the dead have no need for any offering. However, little as we know about the ideas concerning death held by archaic cultivators, we can say with certainty that their concepts differed from ours. An afterlife of the deceased in quite a concrete sense, at least for a limited time, and the possibility of their non-material presence might well be acknowledged as definite characteristics of that system of concepts.

In the ever more pronounced turn toward the realization of such divine expectation and in the growing importance of the ancestor cult which is probably linked with it, I would expect to find the process which preceded cultural interpenetration with the idea of the ever present Highest Being; then, the primevally active Dema were free to assume the roles of the ever present and beneficent gods of the polytheistic religions (cf. chap. viii, sec. 4).

5

CULTURE HEROES AND ASTRAL
DEITIES AS DEMA

We must now speak of two phenomena which have often been treated by the science of religion and investigate their connection with the concepts of God discussed in the previous chapter. One is typical of the mythic tribal heroes of Australia who seem to count among the Dema-deities, the other of the so-called Astral Deities. In the latter instance, we shall ask the question whether primitive peoples have concepts of God which can reasonably be identified as solar or lunar gods.

1. THE WONDJINA OF THE NORTHWEST AUSTRALIANS

So far we have demonstrated the existence of Dema-deities only in the case of those divine personages which predominate in the culture of the archaic cultivators. There they undoubtedly had received their most vital realization. Though a High God may here and there take his place beside them, he is quite insignificant in the greater religious scheme. The essential relationships between man and reality were given almost complete expression in the Dema concept of God. Aside from ancestor cult and belief in spirits, which in their own right are closely linked to this concept, the religious fomulations are dominated by mythic statements about the effectiveness of the Dema.

This conceptual type is also found outside of the culture stratum of archaic cultivators and is probably associable with other forms of cognitive activity. The divine personages of the Northwest Australians furnish examples. These peoples have a purely exploitative economy and are therefore generally considered of great culture-historical antiquity. I am taking my facts from a book by Petri (*Sterbende Welt:* 97 ff.) which is based on data collected on an expedition in the years 1938–39. It deals with the once numerous population of the Ungarinyin in the Central Kimberley District and also with the neighboring tribes where similar circumstances are to be found.

I shall quote a few paragraphs from Petri, since there can

hardly be a more observant presentation of the world image of the Ungarinyin.

It is the image of a primal time, a legendary past in which the earth was populated by beings who carried out creative actions which determined present existence. According to native belief, they were "more capable" than man of today. They wandered over the earth which was then still flat and without form; they gave the landscape its features, invented all the items of daily use, and called into being the cultic and social institutions of the tribe. To put it briefly, they shaped life and the environment as they confront the Black-Fellow of today. An Ungarinyin from the Sale River in Central Kimberley said that the Wondjina—their term for the heroes of primal time—once were capable of doing what only the banman, the shamans, are capable of doing now.

We have here the structure of a tradition known to us for the majority of Australian tribes. Accordingly, spiritual world and mythic-historical tradition of the Ungarinyin would not be new, but only common Australian manifestations which might be brushed off with a generalization. But it is not quite so simple. The primeval traditions of the Kimberley population have forms of expression which differ essentially from the mythic traditions of other Australian tribes, enough to justify detailed analysis.

One of the names current among the Ungarinyin for the mythic primal era is *Lalan*. . . . For example, our informants used to call rock paintings, rock cairns, corroborees, bull-roarers, and other things associated with the primal traditions "Lalan-nanga," i.e., "belonging to the mythic epoch."

The more frequently used term for the period of the mythic heroes is *Ungud* or, more correctly, *Ungur*. . . . My colleagues and I noted a third, though less frequently used designation. It was *Ya-Yari*, a word perhaps derivable from *yari*, the Ungarinyin term for dream, dream experience, visionary state, but also dream totem. In a narrower sense, the native understands by *ya-yari* his own vital energy, the substance of his psycho-physical existence. *Ya-yari* is that something within him, that makes him feel, think, and experience. However, it also seems to be his sexual potency, for a man's state of sexual excitement was described to us as *ya-yari*. Above all, *ya-yari* is the force which enables man to attain the dream state and trance, the "yari," so important to the spiritual and cultic life. Only in that psychological state can man reach that which is essential and lies beyond everyday experience, the spirit world and the great cultic feasts. Therefore, we might view *ya-yari* as an internal bond between individual men, primal times, its heroes, and its creative events. In this sense we also come to understand how *ya-yari* can become the synonym of *Ungur* and *Lalan* in the Black-Fellow's thinking. On the Sale River, an intelligent native who regarded himself a medicine-man, told me: "*Ya-yari* is the *Ungur* part of me. . . ."

Lalan or *Ungur* time begins with the *creation of the world;* life, nature and human existence in their present forms commence with its end. So, at least, it seems through our eyes. The Black-Fellow himself, though, would hardly be so discriminating, for his time-sense can only with difficulty be brought to harmonize with ours. We are always told that the Ungur epoch was "long, long ago," i.e., Lalan; that the Wondjina heroes then "made everything," and indeed made it "good and perfect." That is, they created something final which is not in need of improvement. On the other hand, however, the Black-Fellow considered as "Ungur" and "Lalan" all phenomena of his environment and the categories of his mental life such as landscape, utensils, laws, but especially cultic implements, mythic traditions and sacred locations. All was created in the great Ungur-period and forms a bridge between past and present. Finally we must not forget that the native conjures up the heroes of the primal past in action and word though the corroborees and chants of his cultic celebrations and that he experiences dreams and visions as "Ungur-time," as a real and creative state. Primal time thus becomes eternal time and a magnitude divorced alike from past, present and future. Elkin coined for it the designation "Eternal Dream-time."

The concept of evolution is alien to the Ungarinyin as it is to all Australian Black-Fellows. Singular and definitive acts of creation determine the primal past. Anything that comes after remains the unchanged result of this epoch, its eternally uniform repetition. So it must be, if life is not to lose its meaning, and cataclysms are not to put an end to the existence of individuals and peoples. Primal law, "Black-Fellow-Law," secures harmony and prosperity; if these laws were disregarded, floods or droughts would come and the equilibrium of life would be gone.

In primal time everything became as it is today and no mortal would ever be able to improve or perfect "Ungur," that which has been created. A banman (medicine-man) or a worthy patriarch might effect minor changes or even impose new "laws"; but such would receive subsequent sanction so that it would not be felt as a break with Ungur-time. We must remember that shamans and old men, insofar as they are strong personalities and exercise influence in the community, are viewed as figures in whom the primal past is alive; in them the great heroes and bringers of culture may be thought to live again and they are believed to form a link between the mythic past and the present. Thus, it may be considered a permissible innovation if, for example, an old "boss" modifies the prescribed course of a corroboree, or if a shaman composes and produces a new one. Both only actualize what they have seen in vision or dream, i.e. in a state of "Ungur"; they fulfill the primal law.

So far the literal quotation from the work of Petri. In passing, it might be mentioned that the ideas of divinity are not limited to the Wondjina figures. The natives differentiate them—not quite clearly—from the Rainbow Serpent Ungud that (according to the creation myth) rose from the depth of the ocean and made the land by throwing a boomerang. But then again, in the many locality-linked myths, Wondjina often become Rainbow Serpents; on questioning it is usually said that Ungud and Wondjina are "the same," sometimes with the proviso that Ungud had been even more powerful than the Wondjina. According to one version of the myth, the Wondjina came from eggs which Ungud had laid in the still soft earth. According to this, the greater creative power of Ungud extended even to bringing forth the Wondjina. Other versions have it that "the Wondjina made themselves" or came out of the earth.

Another independent figure is Walanganda, although it is said he was merely one of the Wondjina. Two aspects, however, elevate his position: he introduced some important innovations as, for instance, hunting techniques and the order of the hunt—which are used to this day—and initiation rites, which he instituted in every detail. The other aspect is Walanganda's more emphatically asserted presence, for despite his celestial remoteness—he may be seen in the Milky Way—he does occasionally intervene in the course of a hunt. Petri is of the opinion that Walanganda cannot be equated with the Highest Being of *Urmonotheismus* but that he—like the creator figure, the Rainbow

119

Serpent—corresponds in some traits more closely to the concept than the Wondjina.

We shall confine ourselves to the Wondjina. Their pronounced Dema-character seems beyond doubt, if we look upon their order-creating labors, their disappearance, i.e., their no longer demonstrable presence in any corporeal form, and think of man's eternal obligation to remain conscious of their divine work, which is the most essential component of this idea of God. We have stressed, as basic to the nature of the Dema, that they continue to be effective in the phenomenological world, especially through the natural order which they imposed upon man, though they have not shown themselves as divine personages since the end of the primal era. This applies in every respect to the Wondjina. Being the totemistic ancestors of the present day Ungarinyin, each clan has its local myth describing the actions of a particular Wondjina. Their main efforts were devoted to the shaping and elaboration of the landscape. In primal days the earth was lutose, flat, and desolate. Only the wanderings of the Wondjina gave the earth its present shape; in their paths arose rivers, water-holes, rocks, and the many geographical landmarks which characterize any given area. Here too—as among the Dema of the cultivators—the manner of "generation" is in the main biological, by urinating, bloodletting, or some such process. The end of the story usually tells that the Wondjina disappeared into the earth, but immediately prior to his disappearance he performed that act which became central to the ceremonial life: he left behind his "shadow" or—as the people are also in a habit of saying—his "imprint" on a rock wall. These pictures, which are found throughout the land of the Ungarinyin, are thus legacies of the Wondjina, and mortal man's most important cultic obligation consists in "touching" them at certain intervals, i.e., in retracing them with fresh pigment, especially before the rainy season. Here then is a very live practice of rock painting, which, however, is not comparable in either style or content with prehistoric rock paintings in Europe and Africa (cf. Schulz).

The representation of the Wondjina in rock painting, as in mythic description in general, is predominantly anthropomorphic but passes into some theriomorphic form with extraordinary frequency, that of the serpent being the most common. As humans they are pictured without mouths, a peculiarity for which there is a mythological explanation. Other traits are familiar to us from the archaic cultivators. In Wemale mythology, for example, the Dema wandered as snakes over the land, calling forth rivers, oddly shaped rock formations, or the like. These are mainly etiological traits and, to that extent, unproductive under an analysis that aims at insights. Myths in which Wondjina are depicted as inventors and makers of weapons and implements are not much more informative. The heavy stress on geographical features and their etiological explanation might support the conjecture that these myths are later rationalizations which cannot disclose much about the original world view of the Ungarinyin. It is in fact difficult to search out anything pertaining to the root-meaning of such mythic-cultic matters.

The little that can be established is definitely linked to sacred places where a Wondjina entered the earth and where he left his imprint. Such a place becomes the local cult center of a group which traces its ancestry back to the particular Wondjina. This gives us some information about the relationship between man and Wondjina. First we must note some points of difference from the conceptions of the cultivators: In none of the Wondjina tales is mention made of the killing of a deity. The Wondjina entered into the earth and, although there is the concept of a subterranean realm of the dead, the Wondjina are not thought to live there. According to Petri, they neither have a part in the very concrete notions of the various realms of the dead, nor do they appear in the descriptions of journeys to these realms. They are not the ancestors of man in the biological sense, as the cultivators would have it, whose Dema became mortals and with whom the living are linked through a chain of many generations. These contrasts with the world view of the root-crop cultivators are basic. If it is true that the cultivators' chief concerns turned about human life, i.e., about the nexus between death and propagation of all creatures, then there seems to be a fundamental distinctness of the northwest Australian situation in spite of many similarities between the ideas of God and other clear resemblances. Neither the idea of a slain deity nor its transmutation into crop plants is to be found. The Hainuwele mythologem of the murdered deity occurs among the Warramunga in north-central Australia. Spencer and Gillen (pp. 279, 434) report the myth of a primal being who, having emerged from the earth, occupies himself only with

121

carrying out ceremonies, while making a sound with his mouth that corresponds to the sound of the bull-roarers. Two giant dogs, likewise primal creatures that leave behind "spirit-children" everywhere, are attracted by the sound, tear the man to pieces, and scatter the bits of flesh through the air so that these too make the sound of the bull-roarer. Where the pieces of flesh touch the ground, trees grow; their wood may be carved into bull-roarers. The motif of the origin of musical instruments from wood associated directly with the Dema-deity and the equation of its sound with his voice is a very typical form of the Hainuwele mythologem; it seems, however, to have influenced the world view of the Australians only secondarily as shown by its sporadic occurrence and some few traces in the ceremonial life.

Similarities with the world view of the cultivators are evident especially in the many cultic activities of the Ungarinyin which are focused—as in all of Australia—on rain and on fertility in nature. But the nexus between death and procreation—the necessity to kill and to die so that new life may be engendered—is not the central idea: it seems rather to turn about spiritual parallels with natural propagation.

As we know from other parts of Australia, the Ungarinyin do not consider biological processes decisive for the origination of new life, either in man, beast, or plant; this, they say, is due to the "finding of spirit-children." The spirit-children stem from the divine personages Ungud and Wondjina, who either left them at holy places, marking the end of their earthly careers, or continue to produce them there. The future father "finds" such a spirit-child in a dream or during a particular experience in which he feels himself one with primal time. He hands the "spirit-child" on to his wife who has a similar dream of conception by which the spirit-child enters her body to develop into a human child, as new life develops from an egg. The spirit-child becomes the most important component of the new human being during his life span, his true life substance, and returns at death to the place of its origin. Despite the seeming spirituality of the concept, there exist very concrete descriptions of the outward appearance of a spirit-child: when it is "found," it is light-skinned as if it were of mixed blood; as life substance, it resides as a small snake in a person's heart. The father's "finding" of a spirit-child need not lead immediately to the pregnancy of his wife. He can carry it with him for a long time. Even unmarried men occasionally find a spirit-child and then either keep it until their marriage, surrender it to their sister-in-law, or give it back to the Wondjina.

This concept is widely met with in Australia and seems to constitute the center of the intellectual universe which circles around the Wondjina idea of the deity. We cannot neglect asking about the cognitive aspects of reality which form its basis. First, we must note that here—as with all genuinely mythic cognition— we are speaking of a subject on which there have been no causal-logical or scientific quantitative statements; none could be substituted for the mythic idea, and no native could arrive at them save through the mythic attitude. The native obviously knows the relationship between sexual act and conception (cf. chap. i, sec. 4). But this knowledge is insufficient to "explain" the miracle of new life. At this point the divine forces of primal time step in to fill the gap. A part of them lives in man; and it is a very important part, for it links man with the creative primal past. We have quoted a Ungarinyin as saying to Petri: "Ya-yari is the primal time in me," thereby expressing the idea that part of his own nature is tied to divine creativity. This widespread notion will occupy us later at some length (chap. xiv, sec. 1). Man shares in divinity. Were it not so, were human nature not to include this portion of the divine, how could man recognize divinity?

Ungarinyin philosophy on the biological and the intellectual concomitants of the process by which new life is engendered is therefore not nearly as absurd as ethnology is wont to picture it. It makes a statement about a mysterious "Just-so" which is a fit subject of discussion for us, too. The philosophical view seems to be at the heart of cultic observances, even though contemporary forms have taken on the designation of "propagation rites." Primitive man naturally says that the ceremonies must be performed so that animals and plants may propagate; thereby the course of any attempt at explanation is largely prescribed: the desire for more plentiful food provides the true motivation, and the actions are said to rest on erroneous ideas about the way in which this goal may be achieved. Our attempt to "understand" moves in the opposite direction, even though we are dependent on conjecture since we lack supporting myths. But let us recall that *the magical explanation of rites rests on conjecture to the same extent.*

Propagation rites again imply the expectation of heavenly recompense. Rain (quite correctly seen as a natural prerequisite of fertility in the plant kingdom) as well as direct multiplication of species is regarded as a consequence of the rites; conversely, draught and barrenness are regarded as consequences of their omission. One of the most widely distributed forms of the rite is the rubbing of megaliths which are considered embodiments or creations of the Wondjina. The abrading produces a fine dust which is dispersed by blowing and is obviously equated with the spirit-children of plants and animals. We lack mythic statements of the reason this kind of rite should be the re-enactment of primeval events as we should like to consider them. Interestingly enough, though, the recoloring of the rock paintings, "imprints" of the Wondjina, is called rubbing, though nothing of the kind is actually involved. Rubbing the stones seems to carry a primary connotation of the act by which the primeval beings gave fertility. Since touching up the rock painting also signifies the re-enactment of a primal event, "rubbing," though not a suitable term, has been carried over. There is an abundance of observances associated with the sacred locations, and there are just as many relationships between human life and the activities of primeval beings, especially in the sociological sphere. The dream that acquaints the father with his spirit-child also reveals its name to him, and the name is identical with that of the Ungud or Wondjina who once upon a time brought forth the spirit-child. It is part of the primal epoch and will be told to the child only at the puberty ceremony. In fact, the works of the deities thread through the Ungarinyins' entire world. It is difficult to ascertain how this strong influence, which probably came from Melanesia, reached Australia! It seems, however, rather likely that it can be ascribed to the Neolithic wave which passed over the continent.

We call Ungarinyin culture distinct because it is based on another kind of cognition. We have here the spiritual process without which the genesis of life would be incomprehensible and which has moved man and led him to a magnificent conception of the close bond between all living things and the divine primal beings—an idea which has long retained its potency, if we may assign its origin to the culture stratum to which the Ungarinyin belong. The full significance of this will be realized only in conjunction with the vast amount of data on "souls" which recur in innumerable reports and have muddled theoretical ethnology ever since Tylor. We shall discuss the concept of soul later (chap. xiii, sec. 1) and shall see that a significant amount of the material is made up of later forms of the primal idea. Especially the tendency to have the spirit-children concretely represented by rock dust, i.e., the human urge to outline spiritual matters with solid and palpable realities, has furthered the development of the extensive lore surrounding the concept of soul (cf. chap. xiv).

The relative antiquity of such a culture stratum is hard to determine on the strength of the Australian material. Compared with the archaic cultivators, as found in Melanesia, New Guinea, and as an ancient foundation stratum in Indonesia, most of the conditions speak for a greater age; racial and economic factors especially bear this out. On the other hand, however, there are major similarities between the outlook of the Australians and of the cultivator populations. They are most clearly evident in the initiation ceremonies of which we have said little so far. It would therefore be reasonable to give some credence to a secondary influence from the direction of the root-crop cultures, the archaic cultivators.

Many objections have justifiably been raised against the culture-historical method of relative chronological placement of specific phenomena. The criteria of form and quantity and the various subsidiary criteria do not seem to carry sufficient methodological weight. *Gestalt* and "meaning" of closed culture complexes call for very different methods of investigation before questions of culture history may be answered. And yet the critics undoubtedly made things a little too easy for themselves when they declared that all of culture-historical investigation devoted itself to posing unanswerable questions and was therefore pointless and absurd.

Mühlmann makes the extremist statement that culture-historical research starts from the most improbable assumption imaginable, from the assumption that early cultures underwent no later changes. No one doubts that constant change is in the very nature of culture, but we cannot overlook the fact, affirmed by plentiful and detailed evidence, that the human mind is remarkably sluggish and that it requires prodigious stimuli to bring on major changes in culture. We mean, of course, changes which amount to more than the replacement of one implement by another or the addition of one more mythological motif to the existing inventory; a people does not readily substitute one world view, one way of dealing with the realities of the environment, with another.

The Ungarinyin material shows almost in every sentence that so balanced a culture has no cause whatever to alter its fundamental attitudes. To the contrary: only the strictest observance of traditional forms, which are thought to be anchored in the divine realities of primal time, can make life bearable. Major stimuli need not have occurred in this desolate region for thousands of years. The only inroad of which we have a historical record, that of Western culture, has induced all kinds of changes in the external image of the culture, but the fundamental attitude toward the world as a whole has not been touched if, for our argument, we do not regard extinction as a drastic form of change.

The Northwestern Australians, who have given us numerous proofs of their quite considerable philosophical gifts, have themselves made attempts to explain the contrast between their own conservative culture and the active culture of the occidentals. They link it—as might be expected—with their divine Wondjina. In their anthropomorphic state, we are told, the Wondjina have no mouths. Many variants of the tale explain this fact. According to one, the Wondjina had mouths during the period of their activity, spoke the language of the Ungarinyin, and named all things. At the close of primal time when the world became as we know it now, Ungud closed the mouths of the Wondjina. But for this fact —adds Petri's informant—the world of the Black-Fellow would be as rich in marvelous things as that of the white man.

2. THE RELATIONSHIP BETWEEN DEMA-DEITIES AND NATURAL FORCES

The important mythological role played by the two largest heavenly bodies was realized a long time ago. We must first distinguish, however, between documented statements of ties between mythical personages and the heavenly bodies and the much more numerous interpretations which rest on aprioristic theories of the significance of the link; after all, the intention was to prove the origin of all religions in the perceptions of such natural phenomena. The purely speculative constructions common until very recently add to the understanding neither of myths nor of the divine figures associated with them. In the literature of nature mythology, many ideas make a nexus between mythic heroes and astral bodies more than likely, but this makes many interpretations which unhesitatingly declare the mythic figure to be a "Sun God" or "Moon God" no less grotesque. Disregarding such flights of the imagination, primitive myths still offer an abundance of attested links between certain mythic personages and sun and moon, be it that they ascend to the heavens at the conclusion of the narrative and become either sun or moon, or that they are designated from the beginning as celestial bodies visiting the earth in human shape. The literature is so enormous that it is impossible to attempt an answer to the question within the limitations of this book. We shall rather only make an assertion and illustrate it with some examples.

According to my knowledge of primitive myths, the question must be answered negatively. In other words: mythic personages —I am speaking of primitive mythology only—are not elevated to some higher plane of divinity by the relationship with sun and moon; they share the same character as other concepts of deity, that is, they are, according to their nature, Highest Being, Demadeity, Master of the animals, or fall under some other concept which we cannot treat here since we are not aiming for an exhaustive study of the primitive notions of God. Neither is there a solar nor a lunar mythology; these names could apply only if the inventory of myths of a given cultural community were either exclusively or at least to a major degree dominated by solar or lunar beings so that all others appear only as secondary accretions. In fact the opposite is the case: at the center of the mythic world of primitive peoples are other basic concerns. References to sun or moon may be more important among some peoples, less so among others, but they are always accessory and do not touch upon the heart of the mythic problem itself.

As an example we cite a report by Nimuendajú about the Apinayé which more than many others would let us assume the reference to a Sun God. The Apinayé are one of the Gé tribes of the eastern Brazilian cultural province. They regard the Sun as creator and father of mankind; he calls men his children and is to be addressed as "my father." One prays to him outside of the village, facing the sun, not with set prayers but by asking that he grant specific wishes. There are no picturizations proper of the sun, but the circular plan of the village, with its radial paths to the houses, and the round meat pies eaten at ceremonies are called symbolizations of the sun. There are ceremonies and songs to the sun. How vivid the idea of "Father Sun" can be is shown in the retelling of visions which had occurred to a village chief and in which the Sun-father appeared to him. One of them follows:

I was hunting near the sources of the Botica creek. All along the journey there I had been agitated and was constantly startled without knowing why.

Suddenly I saw him standing under the drooping branches of a big steppe tree. He was standing there erect. His club was braced against the ground beside him, his hand he held on the hilt. He was tall and light skinned, and his hair nearly descended to the ground behind him. His whole body was painted and on the outer side of his legs were broad red stripes. His eyes were exactly like two stars. He was very handsome.

I recognized at once that it was he. Then I lost all courage. My hair stood on end, and my knees were trembling. I put my gun aside, for I thought to myself that I should have to address him. But I could not utter a sound because he was looking at me unwaveringly. Then I lowered my head in order to get hold of myself and stood thus for a long time. When I had grown somewhat calmer, I raised my head. He was still standing and looking at me. Then I pulled myself together and walked several steps toward him, then I could not go any farther for my knees gave way. I again remained standing for a long time, then I lowered my head, and tried again to regain composure. When I raised my eyes again, he had already turned away and was slowly walking through the steppe.

Then I grew very sad. I kept standing there for a long time after he had vanished, then I walked under the tree where he had stood. I saw his footprints, painted red with urucu at the edges; beside them was the print of his clubhead. I picked up my gun and returned to the village. On the way I managed to kill two deer, which approached me without the least shyness. At home I told my father everything. Then all scolded me for not having had the courage to talk to him.

At night while I was asleep he reappeared to me. I addressed him, and he said he had been waiting for me in the steppe to talk to me, but since I had not approached he had gone away. He led me some distance behind the house and there showed me a spot on the ground where, he said, something was lying in storage for me. Then he vanished.

The next morning I immediately went there and touched the ground with the tip of my foot, perceiving something hard buried there. But others came to call me to go hunting. I was ashamed to stay behind and joined them. When we returned I at once went back to the site he had shown me, but I did not find anything any more.

Today I know I was very stupid then. I should certainly have received from him great self-assurance (segurança) if I had been able to talk to him. But I was still very young then; today I should act quite differently [Nimuendaju, 1939: 136 ff.].

Without a doubt, this circumstantial word picture is impressive. How deeply rooted must an idea of God be that allows such experiences! In any case, the assumption seems obvious that a Sun God is the central figure in Apinayé religion. However, when we consider the myths—unfortunately very few—which Nimuendaju has taken down, the picture changes noticeably. He, by the way, never spoke of a solar religion but emphasized that *both* sun and moon are figures of pre-eminence. The myths depict both as anthropomorphic beings who trod the earth in primal days. Their deeds are reminiscent of the twin myths wherein the sun is the superior of the two and the moon is the simpleton. Later we shall discuss how they created man and why the moiety structure of Apinayé society is ascribed to two groups of people, one of which was engendered by the sun, the other by the moon (cf. chap. vii, sec. 1). The majority of cults, too, refers to mythic events which are ranged about both figures. In myths and cults both appear as Dema-deities, who founded the order which man relives today.

Equation of such primeval Dema with the two great celestial bodies is not rare. Especially in America it is frequent. K. T. Preuss describes two brothers in Witoto mythology, who after some momentous adventures ascend to the sky as sun and moon (cf. Métraux, 1946). Everywhere in this type of myth the superiority of the elder brother is mentioned and, with it, claims to superiority for that group of people which derives itself from him. Among the Apinayé the mythologem of the "Twin Heroes" must have been associated with an entirely different range of concepts which granted an exceptional standing to one of the Dema in contrast to the prevalent myths and cults. There are features which cannot be derived from the Dema-character of this deity: the appellation "My Father," for instance, which is restricted to the sun-figure only, though the moon also had brought forth a portion of the population; then, the prayers to him, and the possibility of visions such as the one we have related. These features make it clear that the image of a High God has coalesced with the sun-figure. But even the High God has no basic connection with the sun. Only the red coloring of the God in the vision may be evocative of this. Essentially, however, we have here the anthropomorphic Father-God whose identification was doubtless suggested by the mythic properties of a totally different religious constellation.

Here we certainly have a connection between Highest Being and sun which came about in a different way. The Highest Being often—but by no means always—resides in the sky. That in such localization the sun is called the eye or house of the god is an obvious embellishment, purely perceptual but hardly a profoundly meaningful association. Apinayé religion, then, does not have a central Sun God; rather, sun and moon are associations for twin Dema. One of the Dema, sun, probably blended with a High God idea secondarily.

Much more difficult to analyze are the numerous reports from archaic hunting cultures in which the sun plays a major role in hunting ceremonials. At times its function is reminiscent of the "Master of the animals," and a connection between the divine protector of the animals and the sun is quite possible. The question is so opaque that we shall not take it up here. We must be aware, however, that there is nothing in the context from which an independent concept of a Sun God might be deduced.

If it can be established that the ideas of High God, Dema-deity, and perhaps that of the Master of the animals have at times fused with the sun, then we must stress the hardly to be overestimated role of the moon in mythology. Though sun and moon appear together in the myths of the archaic hunters and though no preference for the moon can be demonstrated even in Northwest Australian myths, the picture is quite different for the early cultivator stratum. The Dema-deity is here so closely associated with the moon that even myths telling specifically of a sun-figure contain traits and speak of deeds which must be accepted as typical lunar myths even by the most reticent interpretation (Jensen, 1939: 29 and 195 ff.). In itself, this is hardly astonishing. The mythic focus of the culture is on the life-and-death cycle which has been given form in a magnificent world view which places the link between death and procreation at the center of all mythic experience. The moon, in its constant waxing and waning, would symbolize the perception basic to such a world view.

The Dema-deities of the archaic cultivators are related to the polytheistic gods of the archaic high cultures by processes of cultural genesis; in the same manner their mythic world has been preserved through later culture strata. The moon assumed a significance in mythology which could make it appear that all myths were of lunar origin.

However, nothing in this particular mythic setting permits deductions about an independently conceived Moon God. The central problem of the myth is invariably man, beast, or plant; we would have to do violence to the data if we were to make the moon the primary mythogenic factor. Mention of it is always marginal and usually consists of the statement that the mythic personage, after its earthly works, ascended to the skies and became the moon; it is the deeds that make up the decisive mythic statement. In this sense no more is involved than in the no less frequent version in which the Dema becomes a *star*. It is quite likely that, in this early cultivator culture, moon and stars are neither in nor on the firmament but are quite definitely part of the terrestrial environment (chap. I, sec. 6).

Insofar as the moon has had an impact on myth only through the metaphorical relationship of its phases to the death-and-rebirth cycle, we are dealing merely with an allegory; it could be omitted and the myth might not suffer a loss of verity. It remains an open question whether the moon exerts other influences on man and beast. With respect to plant growth and weather such influence has been maintained throughout the ages; much of it is demonstrably false. All may be remnants of an allegorical inclusion of the moon in mythic statements on the meaning of life as formulated by the archaic cultivators. But it need not have been this way: the dependence of the well-being of some individuals on the position of the moon and other, possibly more demonstrable, connections argue against it. However, we shall leave the question in abeyance.

These examples were only intended to clarify what the inadequacy of data does not permit us to prove—that ideas of God deserving of the designation of Sun or Moon God do not occur in the primitive setting. At the mention of sun and moon we are always dealing with attendant phenomena, with predominantly external associations of God and celestial body.

The opposing view has most convincingly been put forth in ethnology by P. Ehrenreich (1906), who undoubtedly was one of the greatest experts on primitive mythology. His evaluation of the original meaning of solar and lunar myths is not lightly to be rejected. It would require refutation of his extensive material by other, better data. For us, however, the task is somewhat different. We are not interested in contesting Ehrenreich's often documented claim that the heroes of primitive mythology have been associated with the two major celestial bodies through countless variants. On this there can be no contest. We criticize his thesis on another plane, however, for we have basically different concepts of the nature of the deity. For Ehrenreich, the *heilbringer*, bringers of good fortune of all sorts who in the majority of cases are the heroes of the astrally interpreted myths, are not gods. They are "mythical beings sprung from a conception of nature" and "can become deities only if they exercise their power permanently and are open to magical (cultic) influences" (p. 599). On the contrary, we called this mythic *heilbringer* a Dema-deity, precisely because he was not permanently effective but exercised his powers only in primal days and later is without any function though present in the phenomenological world and its ordering principles. Ehrenreich's criterion of "constancy of effect" seems to us an arbitrary and unjustified limitation of the concept of God. As for the other characteristic, i.e., cults, it is specifically intertwined with this concept. Cults are not magical practices designed to sway the gods but festive re-enactments of divine primal deeds. Our interpretation of the *heilbringer* is in no way shaken by Ehrenreich's material. His arguments in fact seem to bear out my contentions. Ehrenreich was obviously unable to recognize an idea of God specific to primitive peoples, aside from the known Highest Beings and polytheistic gods of the archaic high cultures: therefore he clung to the designation *heilbringer* for a figure who is only to be called a god in later metamorphoses when he has taken on the *presence* of, for example, the Mexican gods. Ehrenreich seems in implicit agreement with our contention that the polytheistic gods of the archaic high cultures have their cultural genesis in the *heilbringer* Dema.

We again agree with Ehrenreich on the relationship between the Highest Being and the *heilbringer*. He opposes the euhemeristic theory of Breysig who sees in the *heilbringer* the only source and a preliminary phase of the concept of God from which, by way of polytheism, the High God belief is said to have developed later. Using arguments similar to ours (cf. chap. iv, sec. 5), Ehrenreich discovers separate roots for the ideas of *heilbringer* and Highest Being. He rightly stresses that the conveyor of benefits is often considered dependent upon the Highest Being and frequently appears as his legate or helper; because of this, the High God concept cannot be derived from the *heilbringer* concept since the latter presupposes the former. Ehrenreich leans on the theories of Andrew Lang which were then already well established.

We have vigorously stressed that the High God concept can be derived neither from spirits nor from Dema-deities. This is not to say that Dema-like divine figures can never be more than legates of the Highest Being and never are independent deities. The different roots of the two concepts permit them to exist side by side; neither needs to be traced to the other. The statement that the *heilbringer* is the messenger of the Highest Being, though heard occasionally (cf. the Selknam example in chap. iv, sec. 5), is no more than a loose association of ideas in which the High God quite naturally appears as the superior but at the same time less active and vital personage. On the other hand, there are examples of the complete absence of the High God concept where Dema-like deities dominate myth and cult. The Marind-anim of New Guinea have no High God concept whatever (Wirz, I, Part 2, 18) and Landtman (1917: 13) has the same to say of the Kiwai who live farther to the east. On Mentawai Island the concept is also lacking (Mess, p. 79). Both Breysig and Ehrenreich miss the true essence of Dema-deities among primitive peoples, a concept of divinity which is unique and *sui generis*.

This, in the main, covers what must be said about astral deities. For Ehrenreich there is no doubt that personification of celestial bodies or of their characteristics, such as light and fire, was the primary mythogenic process. "Yet, not every solar or lunar hero of mythology was also a *heilbringer*. . . . Only his participation in the work of creation, his specific intervention on behalf of man make him one" (Ehrenreich, 1906: 593). But Ehrenreich would be hard-pressed to name mythic heroes from the more archaic cultures who are nothing but personifications of natural forces and whose fate reflects only the course of the celestial bodies. Those myths to which Ehrenreich's abstraction is most immediately applicable all belong to the "age of symbolization" (*versinnbildlichendes Zeitalter*). This led Breysig to his assumption—convincingly refuted by Ehrenreich—that all astral references in myths must be assigned to a stage no earlier than "antiquity." Nevertheless, they are decidedly of greater, even of the very greatest, antiquity, when myths dealt with the problems that moved man most profoundly. Mythic heroes are deities who created the order or condition obligatory for man. In addition, they are identified with the great celestial bodies and possess attributes which make the association more or less obvious (cf. Ehrenreich, 1906: 555 ff.). This indicates no more than that all major natural phenomena, especially sun and moon, were linked to the experience of the divine at an early date. The designations Sun God, Moon God, God of Thunder or Wind, however, would make sense only if the essence of the god were completely absorbed in the parallelism with the respective natural force. In fact, myths refer to them at best through attributes and allusions while describing much more far-reaching divine activities.

In a recent work (1956), Gösta Kock arrived at an image of the *heilbringer* very similar to the one presented here. Reading the essay drew my attention to an earlier paper of the same author (1943) which expresses his view by its very title, "Is 'Der Heilbringer' a God or Not?"

6

THE MASTER OF THE ANIMALS

Early man's relationship to the animal kingdom differed considerably from that of modern man. We generally assume that there can be little communication between man and beast. Yet, in our attitude to domestic animals, particularly to dogs and horses, we have an intimation of those bonds which once placed man and beast in closer communication. Only by giving a far higher rating to the possibility of intercommunication than we are wont to do can we hope to extend our understanding to those alien configurations of culture by which early man linked even his religious experience to the animal world. As we have stressed before, the understanding of strange cultural elements depends largely on an understanding of experiential background. For the Western observer, this is one of the most difficult tasks. Though mankind is essentially uniform, the answers to questions on the nature of things always differ in historically different cultures; each culture experiences and crystallizes its pre-eminent values in its own way. For the cultures of the archaic hunters, the relationship between man and animal is of the first order of importance; it is not immediately accessible to an understanding by our cultural canon.

In this book we deal with the archaic hunters only rarely, mainly because of our conviction that this most ancient of eras, insofar as it still lives in contemporary primitive peoples, is also the era most difficult to approach with ethnological methods and techniques. Almost all of the archaic hunting populations are ethnic remnants and near extinction. Their restless wandering makes research into their way of life technically difficult. They live in the most marginal areas, from which we may conclude that they are the last representatives of a culture which once flourished under other, richer environmental conditions. They may not be fair representatives of their cultural epoch, and the harshness of their present way of life may have altered and partially extinguished the mode of existence which characterized the culture at its flowering. In our critique of primal monotheism, we have pointed out that the information which must serve us to evaluate their religion is extremely fragmentary. This cannot be due to accident or the qualifications of the investigators but must be predominantly blamed on difficulties inherent in the subject matter itself.

These reasons alone—there are others which we do not need to go into here—justify a certain reticence when we scientifically consider the religions of the most ancient epochs of human history. If, in spite of this, we undertake to deal with the religious forms of the archaic hunters, we do so with many qualifications, renouncing any attempt to "understand" their essence. The specialist fully realizes how urgent field research among these vanishing peoples has become, even in the face of the inherent difficulties. It is one of the many merits of the "Vienna School" that it has taken on this task with great energy and carried it out for several decades. Field work, however, is in vain without simultaneous theoretical effort. Despite these limitations, it is gratifying that theory has shown much more interest in the hunting cultures during the last decades so that here, too, the outlines begin to show faintly.

1. A GOD-CONCEPT OF THE HUNTERS

The hypothesis of *Urmonotheismus* admits only one concept of God, closely resembling the God of the Old Testament. Human history, however, has produced several such concepts—we cannot guess how many—which in sequence and in parallel occurrence constitute the essence of the various religions. The essence of divinity has revealed itself to man in manifold ways during the course of history. So far we have dealt with two formulations of such experiences. The thesis of primal monotheism, the singularity and temporal priority of the High God, is hardly provable at this time. The possibility, however, cannot be discounted. Dema-deities probably flourished in the cultures of the archaic cultivators even though the idea itself may have been older; the Australian situation and American examples of culture heroes supply some evidence.

Not to be answered is the question of how many and what concepts of God existed in archaic hunting cultures. There is a sizable amount of material, however, that traces out an idea of the divine which obviously fits into the religion of such an epoch: it describes a being which is worshiped as master and protector of all game and as helper of the hunter. Numerous examples are collected in the works of Dirr and Baumann (1938). A. Friedrich turns his attention repeatedly to the religious concepts of the archaic hunting peoples. In his paper on the study of early hunting peoples, he collected a number of examples in which ideas of a divine "Master of the animals" and "protector of the game" stand out clearly (pp. 26, 32). To him I also owe references to some of the following examples.

First we should like to cite a mythic narrative of the Labrador Eskimo reported by Hawkes (p. 154): There once was a great shaman who wanted to find the place where the caribou (reindeer) went when they moved in great herds into the interior. His guardian spirit led him there in a journey which took two months. After sunset the shaman saw a big house built of sod and stones. In the door stood a big caribou. He was the king of the caribou. He stood so tall that the other caribou could walk underneath him without touching. The caribou came in great herds to pass underneath him into the house. When the last caribou had gone in, the big caribou lay down before the door and guarded the others.

Speck's report on the neighboring Naskapi (pp. 82 ff.) speaks similarly of a divine Master of the reindeer. He, however, has human shape, white skin, and wears black clothing. In a big cave-house live thousands of reindeer in an inclosure into which the "White Master" allows no one to enter. The conjurer of a group of hunters asks the Master of the caribou for prey. The rules of the hunt which are given to him must be followed exactly. The Master of the reindeer grants the hunter only a specified number of animals as prey. Beyond that number, all hunting is in vain.

Hawkes (p. 124) also tells of two deities, one of which is female and mistress of the land animals, the other male and master of the sea animals. The two are man and wife and on their help, for which the shaman asks, depends the outcome of the hunt.

The cited instances are quite typical. Similar ones are found not only among many hunting peoples but also among more recent cultures all over the world. Often it is a particularly large animal of a species important as game, often an anthropomorphic being of striking appearance, uncommonly tall or dwarfishly small, which has the animals in its keeping. The Quiché of Guate-

137

mala consider the wanton killing of animals an offense against the God of the Mountain who has charge of the animals in the interior of the earth and knows their number (Schultze-Jena, I, 20). The "Master of the animals" is protector of all game. At the same time he leads it to the hunter and generally determines the relationship between hunter and prey, since without him there can be no successful hunt. The significance lies in the limited and measured taking of animals and the observance of many rules; their violation would transgress the religious ethos. Many of these precepts aim at the revitalization of the slain animal through the divine master; for only so is it possible that there will always be fresh game for the hunters (cf. Friedrich, "Nordasien": 194).

However, beyond these in-themselves rather impressive characteristics, nothing is ever said that would emphasize the God concept. Many practices that are generally labeled "hunting magic" are doubtless connected with this concept and are therefore truly religious in nature and not related to magic or sorcery. Unfortunately, magic is often invoked where we cannot readily give rational explanations. This, as we have seen from the examples, is true especially of the hunting customs. Hunting magic should only be spoken of in full awareness of the fact that the term explains nothing, that something incomprehensible is given a name and probably a wrong one at that.

It would be tiresome to cite much more on the "Master of the animals," because—at least in the sources known to me—the same traits occur again and again. Two more examples will bear discussion for the questions which they raise. Koch-Grünberg (III, 176) presents a great deal of material in his work on the Taulipang, a Carib tribe in northern South America. They are root-crop cultivators in whose economy hunting and, especially, fishing play a major role. Their name for "the father of all animals, game, birds, etc." is Keyeme. When an animal dies, its soul goes to Keyeme (p. 174). Keyeme resembles a man, but becomes a large water snake when he puts on his colored skin. He may be seen in the rainbow. All waterbirds are his grandchildren. In addition to Keyeme, there are a great number of very similar "spirits" with very similar functions. Rato, for instance, is the "father of all fish" and other aquatic creatures. He is also called "water-father" and his spouse "water-mother." Fish and aquatic

animals are "his sons and grandchildren." Before fishing, the
Taulipang call on Rato, and this is always done at night. For the
expected catch Rato is paid with tobacco; he admonishes the
fishermen not to let the fish spoil. Besides these "animal spirits,"
there is also a "mother of the fever" and a "father of the fog."
Koch-Grünberg subsumes all these figures under "spirits." This
is understandable, since their divinity, clearly expressed in the
reports on hunting peoples, has faded in the younger culture
strata. It is not rare, but rather the rule, that the deity of an antecedent cultural epoch lives into the next as an "evil spirit." The
Indians call all of these beings evil, though there is no evidence
in the record that they actually behave harmfully or with hostility
toward man. Many of the spirits which occur in the tales of erstwhile hunting peoples could probably rather easily be shown to
have been divine Masters of the animals, living on in new guise.
Their bizarre appearance usually betrays them and so does their
special relationship to the hunter, whose good fortune depends on
them. Even in Homer (*Odyssey* iv. 450) there still occurs such a
"spirit": Proteus, who lives among the seals and counts them,
probably is a "survival" of a "Master of the seals" (cf. chap. xvi,
sec. 5).

In the reports about younger cultures, the great number of
such "Masters" is conspicuous. Each species has its own "Master," and every phenomenon in nature is subject to a "Master"
who disposes of it, be it fever, fog, earthquake, or thunderstorm.
The archaic hunters seem to have known only *one* "Master of all
animals," on whom they felt themselves dependent (cf. Zerries,
1954).

Whether this deity was originally conceived in the singular or
in the plural is not so important as its relationship to other concepts of God. Schmidt was of the opinion that the "Master of the
animals" is not an independent idea but something which he
terms an *absplitterung* (splintering-off) from the personage of
the Highest Being. The few criteria of the High God concept are
insufficient to do justice to the full complexity of the subject as a
whole, although some very essential traits correspond closely to
the attributes of the Highest Being. There are, for instance, the
solicitude in providing sustenance; the "presence" of the deity;
the ability to communicate with man; intervention in the life of
man so that established order is maintained or that transgression

may be punished; and, finally, paternal feelings toward man. In the majority of cases, however, the solicitude about food is so much at the heart of man's relationship to this deity that the "Master of the animals" should be considered no more than the degeneration of the more inclusive idea. The idea so produced is important merely in the satisfaction of economic needs. Such a development lies within the range of possibility and positive refutation is difficult.

To me, the figure of the "Master of the animals" seems of so individual a type as to be non-derivable from the idea of a Highest Being. This applies especially to its animal shape, which does not harmonize with the High God concept but fits excellently into the hunter's view of the world. That the divine may be revealed in animal form presupposes an attitude which seems by and large comprehensible to us but accords more properly with the situation that produced the abundance of vivid links between man and beast which we find in proto-totemism (cf. chap. vii, sec. 2). According to my knowledge, we are told neither that the Master of the animals created the world nor that he is omniscient and omnipotent. He lacks the characteristics of a first cause so dominant in the idea of a Highest Being.

The conceptual affinity between the "Master of the animals" and the High God is undoubtedly closer than between the "Masters" and the Dema-deities which share few important characteristics. The criterion of primeval effectiveness, which we stressed, is absent. There is no palpable relationship to myth which is decisive for the idea of a Dema-deity. The mythic narrative of the Master of the reindeer is a rather isolated case, and the many stories about the peculiar figure of Kagn which the Bushmen tell and which Bleek has taken down are of such special nature that their meaning for intellectual history remains to be "discovered." Tales of hunters in historically younger cultures in which "Masters" appear as "spirit-being," are only conditionally useful for interpretation; the divine personalities have already lost much of their essence in them. It does, however, seem beyond doubt to me that such "animal spirits," whom the hunter frequently coerces into yielding a "charm," stand in a genetic relationship to the genuine God concept of the "Master of the animals." However, degenerative forms in the younger culture strata are not of this type alone; often they have produced highly complex forms of religious expression in which the "Masters" have entered into close association with other conceptualizations.

The Japanese ethnologist Kindaichi gave a new interpretation of the bear festivals of the Ainu. He places particular value on the fact that the (always ceremonious) killing of the bear has nothing in common with sacrifice (p. 349). The bear itself is the deity. All animals are gods and inhabit another world in human shape, a world very much like our own. Now and then, they come to our world to play. Then they appear in the shape and dress of animals. The bear is the supreme God. His name means God. Any animal that is not caught, killed, and eaten by the Ainu suffers a sad fate, for it wanders over the earth without purpose. Killing of animals is a sacred act because through it the animal enters the house as a spirit; its meat and hide are gifts. The divine animal itself is satisfied, for now it returns to its proper homeland.

Reports such as this are of great value; they give us a much truer picture of the otherwise obscure animal ceremonies. To be sure, the inventory of ideas of this particular description is not attributable exclusively to an archaic hunting culture but must be a blending of culturally and historically distinct ancient ideas. Always, however, does the figure of the Master of the animals show through. All in all, discussions of the divine Masters remain unsatisfactory as long as the totality of religious concepts cannot be sharply outlined. It exhibits a concept of God of great antiquity which has no features in common with the Dema-concept and probably did exist independently of the High God concept; the available material, however, fails to disclose its true nature.

2. THE COMPLEX NATURE OF SEDNA

Though the "Master of the animals" and the Dema-deities are essentially distinct, both ideas may nevertheless on occasion unite in a single divine figure. A case of this kind is Sedna in Eskimo mythology, a very vital but exceedingly complex figure. Ehrenreich (1906: 542) declares her to be neither *heilbringer* nor animal spirit. He speaks of her as a true goddess, and this is surprising since he is not very generous with this predicate. His judgment was probably influenced by the vividness of the accounts of Sedna which, in turn, are conditioned by the strikingly vivid spiritual life of the Eskimo. We will show that Sedna is an animal spirit as well as a *heilbringer*, i.e., Mistress of the animals as well as Dema, and that she thereby is also a true goddess, even though a very complex one. (It must be mentioned at the start of any such analytical treatment that we stress not the specific nature of Sedna alone. A particular deity of a particular people has its own proper character in a cultural integration of which unity and wholeness are indissoluble. However, only part of the culture-historical question addresses itself to this specificity. Those questions which are today of greatest scientific interest are concerned with the comparability of specific instances.)

Boas (1888: 583 ff.) gives a number of accounts of Sedna and her correspondences in different Eskimo groups. Further variants of the Sedna myth may be found in Rasmussen's work (1929: 63). The most conspicuous motivic elements in these traditions are the following: the maiden Sedna, who lived with her father, rejected all suitors. (In some versions she is called "The one who wanted no husband.") At last she married a dog with whom she lived on an island. She bore a number of children, some of whom were dogs, some humans. One day her father killed her husband who sank into the sea. Now Sedna sent her children, whom she could no longer support, out into the world. The dogs she sent across the sea. They became ancestors to the Europeans. Her human children she sent across the land. From them descended the Eskimo. Sedna then lived with her father again until she was abducted by a petrel in human form. Her father brought her back in his kayak but was pursued by the petrel who caused a tremendous storm to rise over the sea. In his fright the father finally threw his daughter overboard. Sedna clung to the boat with her hands. Her father then chopped off her fingers which fell into the sea to turn into the seal and the walrus. Sedna herself sank to the bottom of the sea where she resided ever after as "Mother of sea animals." Her father, too, was later swallowed by the sea and lives in Sedna's house. The entrance to the house is guarded by a huge dog which, in some tales, is called Sedna's husband. When man violates the taboos, Sedna withholds the sea animals. Then privation and famine occur, and the shamans must appease Sedna. Some variants tell that filth collects in Sedna's head due to infractions of taboos, of which only a shaman can free her. She holds back the sea animals to insure that a shaman will descend to her (Rasmussen, 1929: 127, 173; Boas, 1888: 586).

Sedna is at the same time mistress of the realm of the dead. The Eskimo fear her, and she is often called "the terrible one below" (Rasmussen, 1929: 62, 94; Boas, 1888: 588 ff.).

Intimations of prototypical Dema myths are not to be overlooked: in mythic primal time, a deity—even among the cultivators it is frequently a female deity—is killed by other primeval beings, and from the dismembered body—in this instance the hands—arise the natural species most useful to man, in one instance the crop plants, here the indispensable sea animals. To this extent Sedna may be regarded as a hunter's variant of the Dema concept. Man's descent from her, her residence in the nether world where she rules over the dead, fit the image.

However, Sedna's labors are not completed in primal time. She is a very "present" goddess whose wrath may be provoked and appeased and who constantly intervenes in the affairs of man. As Mother of the sea animals, she can withhold prey and throw man into bitter want and need, or she may release the animals and thereby provide abundantly. Shamans are intermediaries between her and man. They visit her on perilous journeys to the depth of the sea and plead for release of the prey. Withholding of the animals is considered "punishment": Sedna is incensed by breaches of taboos, especially on the part of women. Such infractions settle in her hair as filth and parasites of which she—fingerless—cannot rid herself. A shaman must soothe her and comb her hair until she is moved to free the animals. Returning to the gathering, the shaman demands of all a public confession of their taboo infractions so that Sedna may be appeased (Rasmussen, 1929: 123 ff.). Thus Sedna is an avenging and punitively intervening goddess who guards the established order.

According to another, though isolated, version the shaman must try to strike off Sedna's fingers whereby the sea animals are released (Lyon, in Boas, 1888: 585). In this instance the mythic event is re-enacted, not as we know it from the root-crop cultures, by the community as a whole, but by the shaman alone as its exponent. The community partakes as a quasi-audience.

Conceptions of other divine beings occur among the Eskimo

and sometimes overshadow Sedna in importance. For the Central Eskimo she is indeed the supreme personage, and the other divine figures seem to act on her orders without, however, being expressly subordinated to her (Rasmussen, 1929: 62).

These statements must suffice to give an impression of a particular concept of God, uniting characteristic features which, according to findings made in other contexts, should be ascribed to different culture strata. It exhibits specific properties of the Dema-deities, though it also shares outstanding characteristics of the "Master of the animals."

There is another surprising feature which is expressive of the relationship between Sedna and man. Her name, "the terrible one below," gives an indication; a ceremony reported by Boas (1888: 604) makes it even clearer: At the time of the autumn storms, when nature is in an uproar, Sedna has to be "driven off" by specially endowed shamans. First she is lured by songs, and those present believe that she climbs up from her realm under the sea, through the rocks, till she arrives below the floor of the hut. There she is harpooned like a seal by the shaman who thereby "drives her off." The same lack of reverence is revealed in one of Rasmussen's accounts (1929: 100): Sedna, irate over infractions of taboos, will at times remove the culprit or one of his relatives to her realm in the depths of the sea. There are cases where a powerful shaman can recall these victims to their earthly existence; in so doing he may have to threaten or even thrash Sedna if she does not willingly give up her victim.

Such a relationship between man and deity is totally different from anything discussed heretofore. It is, however, reminiscent of many variants of the Hainuwele mythologem in which an animal controls the hunter's luck and man attains magical powers. We had viewed these animal spirits as "survivals" of erstwhile "Masters of the animals." Many accounts give the impression that the person of Sedna shows hints of such degeneration. We may be generalizing excessively when we say that cultic actions are exclusively in the hands of the shaman and that this is the mark of a certain degenerative tendency; for the shaman is by nature a *heilbringer*, a go-between through whom advantages are obtained. Aside from this practical utility, there is no need for his psychic abilities which, in the context of purely religious ceremonies, primitive man often feels to be disturbing qualities (cf. chap. xi).

If our opinion is correct and the concepts of divine "Masters of the animals" and Dema-deities stem from different origins and if it is also correct that Sedna is in the main within the definition of the "Masters of the animals" while clearly possessing traits of the Dema-deities, then we must ask how the ambiguity arose. In principle there are three possible answers: (*a*) the Dema-like features—especially in the origin myth of the aquatic animals—may be unique creations of the Eskimo mind, unconnected to any outside phenomena; (*b*) they originated with the Eskimo or in a related culture stratum and were from there taken over by the presumably younger root-crop cultivators; or (*c*) the opposite situation holds: they originated among some archaic populations of cultivators and were taken over by the Eskimo as alien acquisitions.

As in most difficult questions of culture history, we can hardly make a conclusive decision in favor of any one of the three alternatives. The first one must always be considered as a possibility. Of the remaining two, likelihood, in my opinion, seems to be on the side of the third one. The mythologem of the origin of plants from the bodies of slain deities does not only have world-wide distribution among cultivators; also, it involves profound religious commitment in all cults which involve the taking of life. Only rarely, however, is the origin of animals explained in this mythic way, and, where done, no reference to this mythologem is made in cultic activities. Therefore it seems to me that the Eskimo in particular must have had some early contact with populations of cultivators to which the personality of Sedna owes Dema-like traits. This explanation, of course, is no more than a possibility.

We return briefly to an individual element of the Sedna myth because it may shed light upon a peculiar custom which has sporadic distribution in the Americas. As related, Sedna cannot rid herself of the filth in her hair because she has no fingers: among some groups in North and South America there exists a prohibition against scratching one's head with one's own fingers. This injunction applies, for instance, to all Hupa girls (California) at the time of their first menstruation (Goddard, p. 53);

the same is true among the Taulipang where the precept also is extended to the relatives of the deceased (Koch-Grünberg, III, 130, 168). Among the neighboring Macuschi, parents may not scratch either head or body for some time following the birth of their child (Schomburgk, in Koch-Grünberg, III, 130). In all cases a suitable implement is used as substitute for the hand. Koch-Grünberg was told that the people concerned were in a state of impurity, as expressed also in other customs at such occasions.

If we suppose that at one time the Sedna myth was more widely distributed than we can ascertain today, we might explain the odd custom as a repetitive rite. In borderline situations men—or here women—recall their essential relationship to the deity and take on its role.

A connection is constructed all the more easily since the idea of the impurity of women at certain times is a part of the Sedna myth: shortly after giving birth and during menstruation, women are considered unclean and dangerous. Impurity emanates from woman as an invisible kind of smoke or steam and drives off the game. If the woman breaks a taboo at that time, which is almost unavoidable, considering the numberless interdictions to which the Eskimo woman is subject (Rasmussen, 1929: 132–41), then the steam collects as filth in Sedna's hair (Rasmussen, 1929: 173). The periodic impurity of women and the uncleanliness which besets Sedna are of a kind which suggests one more link between the myth and the custom to the extent that it is prescribed at menstruation and after parturition.

This interpretation claims to do no more than offer semantic contexts for a curious custom. Even if it were based on completely different conceptions, it must originally have possessed a similarly meaningful nexus with some mythic reality.

7

SOCIAL ORGANIZATION, TOTEMISM, AND THEIR TIES WITH RELIGION

The literature of the science of religion gives much space to the consideration of totemism. Frazer (1910) dealt with it in greatest detail. The theories of Sigmund Freud became much more widely known, although they met with decisive and justified rejection by ethnologists. Without expert knowledge Freud gave the data an interpretation which—though it exhibited extraordinary internal "fit"—only rarely conformed to known fact. Even ethnologists, better informed on the data, were never reluctant to interpret totemistic phenomena. Several scholars see in them the oldest form of religion. According to Durkheim, totemism was the motivating force in the formation of human society, which, in turn, seemed so important to early man that he elevated society itself to godlike status.

Radcliffe-Brown, too (1945:33 ff.), tried to explain the nature of religion by its social functions which had constituted positive and important factors in the development of mankind, independent of the truth or error of the religious contents.

There is no doubt that the history of religions has been in great part a history of error and illusion. In all ages men have hoped that by the proper performance of religious actions or observances they would obtain some specific benefit: health and long life, children to carry on their line, material well-being, success in hunting, rain, the growth of crops and the multiplication of cattle, victory in war, admission of their souls after death to a paradise, or inversely, release by the extinction of personality from the round of reincarnation. [Emphasis added.]

Rightly he sees that the scientific attitude would have difficulty explaining how formulation and acceptance of these beliefs can have come about in the history of mankind. He thinks to circumvent the difficulty—due, I think, to a misaimed question—by assigning the nature of religion to another plane; he sees it as an important part of the "social mechanism" by which communal life is regulated.

In this part of our presentation, we do not consider it our task to give all the data and the theories developed from them. We limit ourselves to the question of whether or not it is justified to speak of totemism as a distinct form of religion. To do this, we must come to terms with possibly the primary meaning of two fundamental characteristics of totemistic formulations, exogamy and unilateral descent.

The point of departure for all considerations of totemism is given in a sociological phenomenon which, with minor variations, can be observed over the entire earth. Peoples or tribes are subdivided into clan units whose members regard each other as kin, though it is impossible to speak of consanguinity in the sense familiar to us. Each unit has its own name, borrowed from the natural environment, animal designations prevailing. The members feel a bond of kinship with this animal or with whatever the group may be named for. They consider the animal their ancestor, or believe that their anthropomorphic founder changed himself into it; he may have had some adventure involving the animal, causing a close relationship between it and his own descendants. The Bororo (Brazil), as a tribe, have such a bond (tribal totemism) with a certain type of parrot, the Arara; Von den Steinen was told (pp. 352, 512): "We [the living Bororo] *are* red Arara. Likewise, the red Arara *are* Bororo." Usually the flesh of such a bird may not be eaten by the members of the clan.

A further important feature of totemism is the prohibition of marriage within the clan. The various clans of a tribe are exogamous: the marriage partner must be sought in another, sometimes a specified, clan. Clan membership is usually regulated by descent rule, so that all children belong either to the mother's clan (matrilineality) or to that of the father (patrilineality); here and there it happens that boys belong to the father's clan and girls to that of their mother.

With minor variations this is the sociological background against which most theories of totemism have been constructed. Here also begin our first doubts about those theories. No one will claim that this sociological phenomenon is "understood" as it stands. The fact that man feels himself related to animals, that clan members will regard themselves related in the absence of close consanguineal ties, that marriage within the group is forbidden, though one may marry a close blood relative just as long as he or she belongs to another clan—none of this is self-evident. The form in which totemism is most often encountered is a petrified end product which as such is incomprehensible. Even the members of the tribe no longer understand it. They are unable to recall anything about the cognition that led to these curious manifestations in their culture. At best, we hear fairy stories about ancient ancestors who turned into totem animals for reasons that sound rather adventitious to our ears. If we are ever to be able to "understand," we shall have to gain access to pristine forms which can still convey a "meaning" to us.

1. MOIETY AND CLAN ORGANIZATION

Helmut Petri has shed new light on the subject of totemism ("Kult-Totemismus":44). His treatment of the totem cults of Australia furnishes the main data for our brief discussion of totemism. Besides America, Australia shows the totem in its most developed form. If we are to aim at understanding, Petri's material will be decisively helpful, for it offers far more genuine and original forms than the late, sociologically ossified configurations which we have already described.

The data show clearly that the "totemistic ancestors," among whom we must count the Wondjina, are to be regarded as Dema-deities in the full sense defined in the second section of the fourth chapter. They are predominantly anthropomorphic, as are Dema-deities in other regions and culture strata. But by the same token, they are also animals. Their external appearance is not fixed, for in the primal era men were animals and animals were men and could interchangeably assume either shape. This is an important and recurrent characteristic of Dema-deities which we stressed when we discussed the Wondjina Dema (chap. v, sec. 1).

The sociological forms to which early mankind had committed itself reflect only one of the reactions by which man transferred to his own regime an order recognized as divine in origin (cf. chap. i, sec. 5). All religious cult activities are such reactions; they, too, stem from a re-creative attitude toward divine deeds of the primal past. The so-called moiety division shows better than anything else to what extent sociological and cultic reactions are identical: Nimuendajú (1939:158 ff.) relates a myth told by the Apinayé in which sun and moon lived on the earth as manlike beings. The various episodes of the narrative bring to mind some of the twin-hero myths widely distributed over the Americas. The elder brother is clever and adroit; the younger one is a bungling simpleton. Such twins are frequently associated with sun and moon. In the present example Sun is superior and gets the better of Moon through all sorts of trickery. Finally, Sun and Moon each engenders a group of humans, ancestors to the Api-nayé, as it happens, at two different points along the course of a river. The two types of people are then settled in a common circular village which—obeying the original dichotomy—is divided into halves: the solar group in the north, the lunar in the south. To this day the Apinayé are so divided and settle in separate halves of the village, with a common chief who is always taken from the solar faction.

Some of the episodes of the myth in which Sun outwits Moon recur in ceremonies. Sun, for instance, challenges his companion to pick a fruit, knowing there is a wasps' nest in the tree; Moon is stung painfully. A planting ceremony makes an obvious reference to this: members of the Sun-moiety dance covered with red paint. A dancer from the Moon-moiety, his face painted black, rushes out to the steppe to beat down a wasps' nest from a tree; naturally, he gets badly stung.

This example, which can stand for many, is mentioned only to show that ways of behavior are the same in principle; on the one hand there is the moiety system and, in conjunction with it, many particulars such as the layout of the village, and on the other there are the ceremonial re-enactments. In both cases we have the same basic attitude toward mythic descriptions of the primal period. Sun and Moon are in this case the ancestors of the two groups. The Canelo who belong to the same Timbira family of tribes have even today a number of parallel moiety systems (Nimuendaju, 1946:79). The exogamous halves of the tribe settle separately in the east and west portions of the village. For the Timbira, as for peoples who think of their world order in terms of polarity, all of nature is dichotomized; to one side belong east, sun, day, dry season, fire, earth, red, all red plants and animals, maize, and manioc; to the other: west, moon, night, rainy season, firewood, water, black, all black plants and animals, sweet potatoes and pumpkins (p. 84).

150

If the Dema, in addition to having anthropomorphic form, also appear as theriomorphs—as happens in the greater number of cases—the people genealogically associated with the Dema must naturally also stand in a kin relationship to the animal. If, among the numerous forms in which man re-enacts the labors and actions of the divine Dema, there were indeed some of a sociological type there, then this point of reference to mythic models should be the only one of consequence to a study in the science of religion. Whether or not tribal moieties or clans explicitly take on the name of an animal or natural object is totally irrelevant in view of the determining relationship between Dema-deity and man. In the majority of cases the animal character of the Dema will be present and demonstrable even where moiety and clan names do *not* make a point of it.

The Marind-anim of the south coast of New Guinea, who have a particularly vivid tradition of the mythic world view of the culture stratum of root-crop cultivators, are divided into a number of clans, each of which may be traced to Dema-deities known by name. There is a Dema, Geb, that caused the first bananas to grow and thus, obviously, became the banana-Dema. The myth tells that he was ugly and bristly and that his body was covered with pockmarks. He lived in an ant hill but later ascended to the sky and became the moon (Wirz, II, 43 ff.). The contemporary Marind-anim have a "totemistic" clan which derives itself from this Dema. The clan members do not name themselves after an animal but after the Dema (Geb-ze) and feel themselves linked by a common force to anything mentioned in the myth, i.e., to banana, moon, pocks, termite hills, and ants (Wirz, II, 49), an aggregation of totems which we would have to think irrational without knowledge of the myth. This kinship tie to the Dema is expressed not only in social organization and totemic relations but in a like sense in various cultic acts.

Clan organization and moiety system, and at the same time exogamy and unilateral kinship reckoning, are united by bonds of common meanings. We shall discuss their chronological relationships later on. They may be mythically traced to the Dema-like founder of the group—insofar as we are dealing with active conditions and not with sociological petrifactions—and everything that the myth tells of the Dema is of significance for the

clan members. Totemistic relationships are only a part of a rami-
fied system which enters into many departments of culture, of
which the social order is but one.

We know, of course, of many cultic re-enactments of primeval
events that do not touch social organization in the slightest. The
history of culture must therefore be vitally interested to learn in
which epoch man discovered, as it were, elaboration of social organization, especially unilaterality and exogamy, in accordance
with mythic models.

Exogamy, for instance, can hardly be derived from totemism
or a similar notion of man's descent from the divine beings of
primal time. To the contrary: it should have been far more natural to find a mate within the same totem. Exogamy may be far
better understood through the—usually exogamous—moiety systems. They rest on concepts of polarity, on the incontrovertible
contrasts of day and night, man and woman, right and left, above
and below. True polarity strives toward unity, analogous to the
sexual drive in organic nature. Exogamy "fits" into the moiety
schema. Therefore I suppose it to be the oldest form of such
social orders, while the plurality of exogamous clans seems to be
the result of later developments and accretions. In a sense we are
dealing with variations of a basic idea.

As in the genesis and formation of a cult, there would have to
be a creative act as origin of the particular social organization.
Once it had taken place the thereby established ties between human and divine order alone mattered. We have seen that the
respective Dema-deities are in the main theriomorphic. Whether
the theriomorphism is stressed in the bond, as in totemic situations, or whether it is not, as in non-totemic settings, is really quite
irrelevant to the sense of the social organization. *Since, however,
the animalistic criterion plays an insignificant role when compared to the other relationships, it is pointless to distinguish between non-totemistic and totemistic clan or class systems.* In most
cases, accident would decide which receives the greater stress.
*Totemism embraces only one of many groups of relationships be-
tween living man and his divine ancestors, and nothing speaks for
a special and independent value and significance of the totemic
relationship.*

To illustrate our view of the so-called totemic social system with still another example, I will cite a work by J. Haekel, collaborator in Schmidt's "Viennese school," about moiety system and totemism among the Sioux Indians. The author has a holistic view of totemism, that is to say, includes links between man, animal, and the exogamous clan organization form in an inseparable organic unity. This statement, however, is left an assertion; nowhere in the work, which in other respects is quite valuable, is there an attempt at "understanding." However, a complex phenomenon such as totemism can be called an organic whole only if the components stand in some meaningful relationship to each other. The author might as well have assumed that moiety division and totemism form an organic whole. With regard to most of the Sioux tribes, this assertion would, in fact, have been much better justified; the moieties are divided into individual totemic clans and both constitute a single comprehensible social system. According to Haekel—and in keeping with the familiar precepts of the School of Vienna—dual organization is said to be generically distinct from totemic clans. Both are thought to have been taken over from two different culture strata.

Now, the Sioux data in particular demonstrate the primary unity of dual organization and the basic elements of this social order, i.e., exogamy and unilaterality. Polarity is expressed through paired contrasts: male-female, sky-earth, right-left. Thus, the sky is considered male, the earth female. The "union of both forces" is regarded as necessary, just as first life goes back to a union of the male sky and the female earth (1937:797, 801). Can exogamy be justified more reasonably than through a statement that the masculine and the feminine principles are polarities that must join for the continuance of life? If a human community divides itself into two polar groups analogous to the God-ordained world order of which one is identified with male-ness, the other with female-ness, *then exogamy is the very natural consequence.*

But when there are two exogamous groups, unilateral descent is just as natural a consequence; for the newborn child must belong to one or the other, and since father and mother always belong to opposite groups the child can belong *either* to that of the mother *or* to that of the father. *Tertium non datur* (Mühlmann, 1938:177). Both solutions occur with approximately equal fre-

153

quency and, therefore, have nothing to do with either original *"Mutterrecht"* or *"Vaterrecht."*

Exogamy and unilaterality are most reasonably explained through moiety organization as a human adaptation to a polarity of the divine order. If this is conceded, the greater likelihood is on the side of the greater age of the dichotomy; clans then are secondary subdivisions of the moieties.

Some recent works controvert the hypothesis. Schlesier writes (pp. 115 ff.): "If one form can be derived from the other at all . . . then the clan was *certainly* the first and earliest unilateral grouping" (emphasis added). He does not tell us wherefrom his certainty stems. Haekel ("Mutterrechtes":3, 13) also rejects my views as a psychologizing and oversimplifying attempt at explanation because "it usually cannot be proved that clans go back to erstwhile moieties." I ask, then, if it has been "proved" that "the pre-existence of a clan organization" must be seen as a "determinative and prerequisite for the development of moiety systems"? In my opinion, nothing has been proved so far, neither the one nor the other; but evidence can and must be presented in support of both solutions so that they may be weighed against each other. And furthermore, why should "psychologizing" carry the derogatory meaning which Haekel and the Viennese school tend to give the word? Does not psychology—used with caution—have much to offer to ethnology?

We must, however, keep in mind the third possibility that the two complexes, moieties and clans, are discrete, especially if one recalls the view that clans developed independently and anew in each region of the globe as Schlesier holds in conformity with Baumann. This touches on the old quarrel between diffusionists and parallelists. Each side has marshaled ample arguments in its own support without ever convincing the other. I personally am on the side of the diffusionists and confess that I find it difficult to imagine how clans—or the dichotomies—could have arisen twice, and even hundreds of times, in complete independence.

Olson examined the American situation extensively. He too arrives at the conclusion that, in America at least, moieties have temporal priority over clans, though in fact each arrangement occasionally does occur separately; in the majority of cases, however, they appear in conjunction (pp. 405 ff.). In Africa, strangely enough, moieties were found last. Koppers (p. 115) had assumed, as late as 1944, that there were no dichotomies on the entire continent. In the first edition of this book, I myself stated "that the last word about moieties in Africa has not yet been spoken." This conviction has in the meantime been borne out very nicely. First there appeared Jeffreys' work on "Dual-Organization in Africa." He does not maintain enough separation between the true, old dichotomies and the later forms, but he has gone through a lot of the literature and was first to deal with dual organization in an African context. The origin of dual organization he seeks—true to his school of thought—in ancient Egypt.

Haekel then took up the subject in "Die Dualsysteme in Afrika" (1950). Relying mainly on the material provided by Jeffreys, he arrived at the view that "White Africa must be regarded the area of origin of African dual-organization" (p. 23). This would mean that, in Africa, we would have to ascribe dichotomies to a completely different culture stratum than in any other part of the world. On the other hand, Haekel believes that the (usually exogamous) tribal moieties of northeast Africa "possibly represent a more rudimentary state of dual organization so that a link may be established with dual systems of other continents" (p. 24).

For northeast Africa the data on dichotomy can be considerably increased (Jensen, 1953). In particular, I have been able to evaluate and publish material gathered on two Frobenius-Institut expeditions to southern Ethiopia. In almost all tribes visited, we clearly found dual organization. On the basis of this work, the African situation with respect to binary order seems much similar to that of the other continents. Without a doubt, this type of social organization is very old. Its oldest forms must, perhaps, be placed at the beginning or in one of the initial phases of the Neolithic period. Though I have expressed the opinion that northeast Africa should properly be assigned to the Nilotic culture, i.e., an economy linked to cattle and cereal grains (p. 752), much also speaks for its inclusion in the culture of the pre-Nilotic cultivators who possessed tree and root crops. Carl A. Schmitz stated in a recent article on New Guinea (p. 404) that dual social organization is an element of archaic Austronesian culture and might possibly be identical with a pre-Austronesian stratum. Whatever the answer to this question may be, it is certain that dual organization precedes the archaic high cultures and is firmly rooted in primitive cultures.

Excellent material for our argument comes from the Sioux. Of the animal totems, we are assured that members of the totemic group are not related to the contemporary representatives of their totem species but to a primeval ancestor from whom both men and animals descended and who later was turned into the animal. A true Dema-deity, then! (Cf. Haekel, 1937:501.) The dead seem to unite again with the deity, for the clans possess sacred death chants which are sung so that the deceased be recognized as a clan member; for the same end the corpse is painted in a prescribed manner (*ibid.*: 461, 490). Very specific personal names are associated with the clans and these likewise take account of the mythic primeval figure (*ibid*: 463, 493). Burial forms differ for the members of each moiety; the dead of the group associated with the sky are placed on platforms, those of the earth-associated group are interred.

Hardly any data can be more suitable than these on the Sioux to show that clan organizations refer to Dema-like primeval beings who, along with many divine attributes, also have animal character, and to demonstrate that the differentiation of totemic and non-totemic clans in no way touches on essentials. Exogamy and unilateral descent, on the other hand, find their most reasonable corroboration in the dual systems, while they cannot be derived from totemism itself. Clan organizations possessing both characteristics are therefore in all probability secondary derivatives from the dichotomies.

Against this concept of totemism it might be objected that so-called totemic clans do possess a ritual which makes them distinct from all non-totemic clans and which can be understood only if we accept totemism as a discrete phenomenon. We are speaking of the so-called fertility (proliferation) ritual. Allegedly, it assures the increase of a single species, and only the group which feels itself linked to that species practices the ritual. In chapter v, we have dealt with the original meaning of fertility rites and need therefore add only the following: Petri's material shows clearly that cultic totemism not only knows fertility rites but that there exists an abundance of cultic ties between individual and his group on the one hand and between individual and totemic ancestors on the other. Of course, if we were to interpret fertility rites as magical acts, motivated by the food quest, we should have to drop our view of totemism. This does not seem justified to us; we cannot accept that men who created such momentous ceremonials were simple enough to believe in the attainment of such goals by such means, not even if their present-day descendants can give no better reason than "to make them plenty." Even Christians will tell us that the consecration of the seed results in an abundant harvest. Cults are by their origin primarily representations of a mythically perceived world order (cf. chap. ii, sec. 1). As we have seen, mythic ideas concerning Australian Dema-deities focus on questions about the genesis of new life. A primeval deity had left behind "spirit-children," and those humans would be particularly responsible for this cult who "are" kangaroo and descend from him. Aside from this, however, the many specializations of Dema are probably not primary but are variations of the single theme of a great Dema who was responsible for all things (cf. chap. iv, sec. 4). The importance of the totemic ancestor for the inception of life in the present was also realized by the Sioux, who believe that the human body is made of the totem (Haekel, 1937:494).

2. *"PROTO-TOTEMISM" AND THE MYSTICAL RELATIONSHIP BETWEEN MAN AND BEAST*

We cannot put aside the subject of totemism without touching upon one other point: we stressed the fact that Dema-deities in addition to their anthropomorphic form also have the character and appearance of some animal. In this, however, they do not stand alone. Many concepts of God, reaching even into the latest archaic high cultures, show close associations between God and beast. This is not integral with the nature of the Dema; if it were not so, nothing said about them so far would be affected. These almost stereotypical relationships have strengthened the idea that totemism is a phenomenon of outstanding significance in the history of mankind; Freya's cat and the wolf in the myth of Romulus and Remus and many other such god-animal associations have been diagnosed as symptoms of totemism.

So far in our discussion we have designated the deities connected with totemism exclusively as Dema. However, their theriomorphic nature needs separate consideration. H. Baumann's material on the culture of archaic hunters in Africa gives us valuable clues. Baumann draws on a great many little noted but seemingly quite ancient tales, customs, and ideas which all have relationships between man and animal as their subject; he subsumes them under the term "proto-totemism" (Baumann, 1938).

Any connection of these ideas with the known forms of group totemism is by no means obvious and cannot even be documented with any great degree of certainty. Only in instances of "individual" totemism is the genetic nexus with generally recognized forms of totemic social order convincing, at least to the extent that the singularity of the man-animal experience, which lives on in many later cultural configurations, is perceptibly present in the social systems. Baumann regards the proto-totemic complex as older, original, and more genuine; only later did the rigid totemism of social groups crystallize among sedentary cultivators.

The farther group totemism moves away from its original state the more strongly evident will become its social aspects; religious and mythic significance, still present in its purity throughout the proto-totemic phase, will congeal or die. Group totemism must be considered the older and more autochthonous, the more elements of the proto-totemic complex are discernible and the greater the religious replenishment of its formalisms is (through animal-reconciliation rites, sacrifices, conscious group loyalty, regard for the totem animals as being a solicitous ancestor, etc.); negatively we may say: group totemism appears the older, the less elaborate the social sector is (through clan totemism founded on individual totemism, absence of exogamy and defined marriage systems) [1938: 209].

In speaking of the "Master of the animals" (chap. vi, sec. 1), we have noted the intensity with which archaic hunting cultures view the relationship between man and beast. The "Master" seems to have been the focus of all these ideas. With such a concept of the deity as a starting point, a better understanding of the archaic notions may someday be achieved. An immediate connection between proto-totemism and group totemism exists only insofar as the proto-totemic experiences of an individual can be transmitted to a group or inherited by his descendants. After all, explanatory myths purporting to explain the origin of totemism almost uniformly trace it to individually or generally proto-totemic events. Usually, in fact, the founder of the clan has a specific encounter with the animal for which the clan is named. This motive appears in another form, for instance, among the Australians. The father of a child yet unborn, dreaming of the totemic primeval being and thereby "finding" the spirit-child, has an individual totemic experience. At the same time, the child has been assigned to a certain group, in this instance to one which is defined not by descent but through a common tie to a particular cultic spot.

Although individualized links between man and animal have undoubtedly been transposed to groups, the specific character of the totemic social organization, with exogamy and unilateral descent, can hardly be explained by it and must be credited to other impulses. Thurnwald (p. 361) agrees with this and stresses that totemism does coalesce with exogamous institutions, "though in essential beliefs it has nothing to do with exogamy, 'Mutterrecht,' 'Vaterrecht,' or the like."

Just as surely as social organization is anchored in the actions of the Dema-deity, it cannot be derived from the concepts that led to totemism. It presupposes a different recognition of reality to which man tries to conform through social organization. The "totemic" social systems must therefore have their beginnings in processes of culture history which were independent of the totemic complex.

Among the data on hunting cultures, emphasis on the relationships between man and beast seems supremely important, for they make clear that, at that early period, man saw the divine mainly in animal guise: " 'Game-animals are like human beings, only more holy,' say the Navaho. 'They are like Holy People' " (Hill, p. 98). The theriomorphism of Dema-deities could thus be viewed as a continuance of the idea of the divine animal. This, however, cannot be claimed without mentioning another contributing factor: extraordinarily numerous accounts tell us that where Dema-deities play a major role, it will be stated explicitly that man and animal were "closer to each other" in primeval times. This adumbrates an idea which, by itself, might have led to the theriomorphism of the Dema concept, an idea which in the last analysis is rooted in the equivalency of the biological existence of man and animal. The Luiseño of Southern California say that in primal time all animals were still "people" (Du-Bois, p. 133); the frog still was a beautiful woman (*ibid.*: 132);

159

Wiskun, the squirrel, was the strongest man (*ibid.*: 134); and the glowworm an old woman (*ibid.*: 146), etc. The Eskimo give vivid expression to the dual nature of the mythic being who lived "when animals were often men" and when "all living things were very similar to each other" (Rasmussen, 1931: 217).

In summarizing, we may say that totemism proper confronts us most vividly during the phase which Baumann calls "proto-totemic." In a later phase, that of the so-called totemic clans, it appears in conjunction with a social organization that is characterized by exogamy and unilateral descent. Totemism has no intrinsic link with these characteristics and can therefore not have been instrumental in their genesis. The creative act from which this social order stems must have been inspired by a perception of reality differing in kind from that which led to totemism. The social system is mythically rooted in the actions of primeval beings and must be understood as a cultic adaptation to certain "verities" of an accepted divine order. To this extent, it is the result of ethical attitudes and thereby—especially in cultic activities—related to many other cultural configurations. We have conjectured that social organization first took the form of the moiety systems, in response to the cognition of polarity, and that all multiclan systems are later variants.

Totemic and non-totemic units cannot be differentiated along lines of the single criterion that relationships to natural objects are specified in one case but not in the other, for both types make reference to divine Dema-beings whose animal nature almost always parallels their predominantly anthropomorphic form. This theriomorphism has two roots; first, the Dema are linked to the concept of a primal past when man and beast were less clearly differentiated; second, there are the widely distributed forms of intimate ties between man and animal which are typical of the more archaic hunting cultures which Baumann subsumes under the term "proto-totemism." Although social systems cannot be derived from these manifestations of older culture strata, ideas of the divine animal obviously have continued to be effective in all later epochs and are thus part of the Dema nature. This is borne out by the fact that, in totemism, references to kinship with animals frequently make explicit such proto-totemic experiences.

Our initial question, "Are there in the primitive world original and truly religious phenomena which are distinct from all others and therefore are justifiably set apart as 'totemism'?" is therefore to be answered partly negatively and partly positively: that which commonly is called totemism is not a form of religion but is, as a social system, the result of a type of behavior which corresponds to the behavior in cultic activities in all significant particulars. Baumann's proto-totemism actually is totemism proper. Without doubt, it incorporates a body of ideas which had been active in very archaic cultures and still reflects a religiosity closely allied to the God-concept of the "Master of the animals." While Haekel (1937: 213) wishes to separate totemism completely from the belief in guardian spirits, this belief in particular and many related phenomena seem to us typical of totemism proper. *To that extent, true totemism is a distinct form of religion.*

8

RITUAL KILLING AND BLOOD-SACRIFICE*

The killing of human beings and animals, more than any other cultic practice, has lent weight to accusations of barbarity in early cultures. Not only human sacrifice and head-hunting but the ceremonial killing of animals seems repulsive to us. The killing, however, is an unavoidable concomitant of the respective acts, while the true motives of the ceremonies may be sought in other contexts. In many instances there can be no doubt that the killing is essential, that it constitutes an important, even decisive, part of the event.

Wherever we know of animal sacrifices—almost exclusively of domestic animals, for they all occur in agricultural cultures—eating of the flesh or offering certain portions to a deity is part of the total event, and the animal always is brought to the cult place alive to be killed there. That this is no accident, at least for some primitive culture strata, becomes clear in the glorification of the killing and its presentation as a deed necessary for the preservation of the world order.

In the discussion of man hunts attention has generally been focused up to now on the trophy to be won—usually heads or genitalia—and the motivation has been sought in the acquisition of potent magical substances or the like. Important as the ceremonies may be in connection with the collected trophies—they do, in fact, usually get preferred mention in the description of the events—we should not be deluded into the belief that the act of killing is of primary importance to primitive man. There are differences, for instance, between head- or genitalia-hunting and the so-called human or animal sacrifices. For example, in head-hunting the killing cannot be performed at the cultic center. The specific importance of the act of killing is underlined. Successful participation in a head-hunt often is the prerequisite for marriage for a young man and, in this respect, it does not matter whether he is in actual possession of a trophy or not. The fact that he has killed is alone decisive. Among some Ethiopian peoples there is a "counting-up of killings" in conjunction with religious festivals

* This term is used throughout the book. It might be more correct to speak of "bloody sacrifices," as R. H. Lowie does in *Primitive Religion*, for not blood but an animal is sacrificed, at the killing of which blood is shed.

in which each killing is assigned a point value; the value varies with the tribal affiliation of the victims, but even the killing of animals is included in the count. Actual possession of the trophy is not decisive.

The number of examples attesting the importance of the act of killing within a given cultural configuration is very large. The most telling formulation of the idea may be in an Ethiopian song reported by Cerulli (II, 125 ff.). Enumerating the things worthy of special praise, the song says: "My Gada is a Gada of abundance . . . of riches . . . of peace . . . may your milk vessel be full . . . your mead vessel shall run over. May your calf grow so large that it excells the bull. *He who has not yet killed, shall kill.* She who has not yet borne, shall bear" (emphasis added).

1. THE ATTITUDE TOWARD KILLING IN HUNTING CULTURES

These and many other examples do not come from cultures which count among the oldest in the history of mankind. Killing is glorified especially by the older and the younger root-crop cultivators, who are also the chief exponents of such phenomena as man hunts, head-hunting, and cannibalism. Early archaic high cultures did not reject ritual killing, which may certainly be traced to its "cultivator" component.

With regard to our moral scruples, we must keep in mind that the act of killing should not be confused with unrestrained carnage. Murder is no less a punishable offense in primitive cultures than in ours. The permissible act of killing is strictly regulated by religious rite. It is not a deed which sets aside moral scruples or does not know of any (cf. chap. ix). Our perplexity remains, however, insofar as it seems to us an aberration that the idea of the divine should be related to man in ways which find expression in such acts. This problem will be discussed later.

First we shall deal with a phenomenon significant in connection with the act of killing itself. It is the fact that ritual killing not only is completely absent in the oldest known strata of culture, that is among the hunting-and-gathering peoples, but that here we encounter a totally different mental attitude. The hunter kills, as it were, for professional reasons; to be a successful hunter, i.e., to kill much game, is a natural wish dictated by the urge of self-preservation. In stark contrast to the naturalness of killing, however, a major part of the hunter's ceremonial is oriented, not to glorify the act of killing, but to nullify and negate the unavoidable deed. We find corresponding customs in all regions where hunting peoples still live, at the southern reaches of the ecumene as well as in the Arctic.

We hear, for instance, that the successful hunter will try to shift the blame by telling the slain animal his arrow "had lost its way" or that not they, the hunters, but "the toad" or "the sun" had killed it. At the same time, as we have seen, the "Master of the animals" watches that no more game than necessary is killed. The customs and ideas show clearly that killing is not viewed as a desirable or laudable act but as an encroachment into a non-human realm, forced upon man by the struggle for sustenance. These examples may suffice to support the assertion that ritual killing is not only absent in the earliest period of man's history but that we must assume for it a different, often opposite mental attitude (cf. here Friedrich, "Jägertum":21 ff.).

2. A PSEUDO-RATIONALE FOR RITUAL KILLING

If peoples at the oldest cultural and economic stage of history did not practice ritual killing of animals, incisive events indeed must have introduced such cruel practices. What are the causes of animal sacrifice? Tylor, for instance, explains ritual killing as a desire for the liberation of souls (II, 42). He refers in particular to the widespread retainer killings, performed on the occasion of the death of a king or nobleman whose soul proceeds to a world where the souls of his wives, servants, and slaves are to be of perpetual service to him. This interpretation has the advantage of being supported by native statements. There is no doubt that very concrete concepts about the potential separate existence of souls are current in certain primitive cultures. The idea that such souls might be put to some service was also present obviously. Yet we find this idea only in relatively late cultures which are characterized by state organization and complex political power structures, while it is absent in the stratum of archaic cultivators.

The question arises whether ritual killing in both strata is attributable to the same concept at all or if retainer killing may not have originated in a complex of ideas quite distinct from that which produced, for instance, head-hunting. In my opinion it is not difficult to furnish proof that this custom goes back to the same root as the ritual killing of men and beasts in the archaic cultivator stratum. The fact that (in America as well as Africa) the respective cultures are not only geographically adjacent to archaic cultivator cultures but have carefully preserved their ideology in myths and cults suggests this. If, however, the two sets of customs are connected, the later form, naturally, cannot give us any hint of the *original* concepts behind ritual killing. Later cultures took over killing as an established trait from former times and restructured it in line with other sets of concepts to become a sacrificial death of the king's retainers.

In another form of ritual killing, i.e., blood-sacrifice, the meaning has been thought to lie in an idea of sacrifice to a deity. The term "sacrifice" always connoted an offering to the god, and in this sense it was widely distributed, even throughout the latest archaic high cultures. It is described to us as an essential part of religion in India as well as in ancient Greece, though it will forever remain incomprehensible why it should give the gods pleasure to see man engaged in killing and subsequently in feasting. The Greeks themselves noticed the disparity in the allotment of portions of the sacrificial animals and traced it back to a ruse of Prometheus. Very like the sacrificial death of the king's retainers this leaves a residue of unsolved problems which makes it impossible to ascertain the "origin" of the curious feature from adduced motives.

The archaic cultivator cultures did not have the concept of blood-sacrifice. The act of killing is not a gift to the deity. Just like other sacrifice, it is a religiously founded ethical action. This already seems to me to bespeak a common root of sacrifice and ritual killing; it would mean that blood-sacrifice draws its essential meaning from this common root and that the transformation into an "offering" is a relatively incidental, late, and rationalistic reinterpretation. The nexus between killing-ritual and sacrifice will be taken up again later, and at that occasion we shall revert to an earlier idea (cf. chap. iv, sec. 4): the relation between the older Dema-deities and the polytheistic gods of the archaic high cultures.

One further element should be considered from which the act of killing seems inseparable and which is therefore regarded as

165

the motive par excellence for the origin of the ritual: heroic mentality, which to our day constitutes the ethical imperative of masculinity. Soldierly bearing in war or in duels in defense of one's honor constitutes high values in ancient cultures as well as in ours; in the oldest of the archaic root-crop cultures these are not notable characteristics of the killing-rituals. Here and there in songs of praise for successful head-hunters we may hear verses in which courage and bravery are stressed. In fact, the act of killing, whether in battle with other men or savage beasts, is hardly to be accomplished without a display of courage and thus its mention is quite natural. But the heroic orientation toward courage and bravery is almost totally lacking in the ancient cultures, though, among the Nordic peoples of the period of the Sagas, it led to an extensive battle code (injunction of killing by might and of attack on the defenseless). Killing is often done in a manner most unheroic; it would have to be called cowardly if such an evaluation were called for. The defenseless as well as women and children are killed, and raids are conducted as perfidiously as possible to insure success and reduce personal danger to a minimum. The glorification of killing is therefore more likely to stress the fact of having killed than the courage exhibited in the act, though there is an occasional intimation of that idea.

One thing the head-hunter and the Teutonic heroes have in common, however: their deed and success meet with the approval of the community which even demands the deed as part of the divine order. The creative event which engendered their attitude toward killing and which has shown such tenacity in maintaining itself at the center of significance in manifold transmutations must be sought in the most archaic cultivator strata.

3. RITUAL KILLING IN ROOT-CROP CULTURES (HAINUWELE MYTHOLOGEM)

At another place I have attempted to clarify the original meaning of killing-rituals from the world view of the cultivators (cf. "Weltbild"). I shall therefore give a brief résumé only and limit myself to highlights of the data.

The world view of the archaic cultivators in general may be concluded from a number of accounts which describe the ceremonial life of some decidedly archaic cultivator populations and contain at the same time—and this is most important—an extensive collection of their myths. Reference of the cults to the myths has been stressed by several researchers. The accounts deal with peoples of India, eastern Indonesia, New Guinea, and the Americas. The lack of corresponding reports from Africa is undoubtedly an accidental lacuna in field research; there are enough clues to show that the same forces must have been at work in Africa also. But the area outside of Africa from which we have clear statements is large enough to demonstrate that the cultural homogeneity, borne out in religious utterance, must be credited to world-wide diffusion of one of the most magnificent cultural epochs in the history of mankind. All these peoples know the idea of a mythic primal past which antedates the world as it exists today. Not men, but Dema lived then on earth; sometimes they are thought to have human form, sometimes the form of animals or plants. Prominent among them are the Dema-deities (cf. chap. iv, sec. 2). Always central to the myth is the slaying of the Dema-deity, but the reason remains obscure. In Ceram (eastern Indonesia) the slain deity is Hainuwele. I proposed to call the mythic theme of the murdered deity and of the origin of crop plants the Hainuwele mythologem.

For the present we must take it for granted that the deity is killed by the Dema, an event with which the primal era ends and today's world begins. The Dema become men, mortal and propagating—this is a main point; the deity henceforth exists in the realm of the dead or transforms itself into the house of death. From the body of the deity originate crop plants so that the eating of the plants is, in fact, an eating of the deity. Since the supreme deity often also had animal shape—especially that of the pig—the killing of pigs, too, qualifies as a "representation" of the deeply disturbing primeval event. Its repetition means no less to mankind than a constant remembrance of the divine act which stands at the beginning and from which all things stem.

This ever renewing reminiscence constitutes the charter of a whole series of cultic activities which become typical of this culture. Diverse as they seem at first glance, they are related to the same primeval event and try to make this prototype live again. Puberty rites are reminders of the act of procreation which originated in conjunction with the first mythic act of killing and of the fact that mortality is inevitably a part of this. The death ceremonials which refer to the journey to the land of the dead are commemorative celebrations, since every death journey repeats the journey of the Dema-deity. Most important is the constant re-enactment of the killing itself. It does not matter here whether men or certain animals considered "identical" with the deity are slain. Thus the human and animal sacrifices (to which head-hunts belong) are the most frequently recurring motive; canni-balism is the festive remembrance of the realization that the eat-ing of crop plants in reality is an eating of the deity in its trans-mutation.

In our context, these are the fundamental features of a religion in which everything of significance to the bearers of the culture is traceable to institution by a deity, whose unmotivated slaying constitutes the basic idea of the mythology. It turns out that the human and animal sacrifices carry none of the connotations of "sacrifice" for the genuine representatives of the culture which they have assumed in later cultures. For them it is neither more nor less than the festive reformulation of a primeval event; the sacred event is made to occur again, primarily for commemora-tion but also to initiate another generation into the order of all things. To this extent the slain being—man or animal—repre-sents, of course, the deity itself in the sense in which an actor represents King Lear on the stage and is "identical" with him for the duration of the play. The deity is not "sacrificed to itself" as it has been put on occasion. It would be more cautious and more correct if the term "sacrifice" were entirely avoided in respect to these specific acts of killing among the genuine archaic cultivators. It can be shown that among cultivators in particular even killings that take place in definite ceremonies—regarding the fertility of the fields, rain-making, the curse of barrenness in man or beast—are not rain sacrifices, fertility sacrifices, etc., but re-enactments to keep alive the memory of primeval events.

4. THE CHANGE IN SIGNIFICANCE OF RITUAL KILLING IN YOUNGER CULTURES

If we admit the validity of the mythic world view, the killing ritual appears reasonable. Now we shall ask to what extent the mythically expressed propositions are comparable with other, for instance, scientific statements and their "truths." First we shall

look at the mythic justification of ritual killing in the most archaic root-crop culture, where the slain deity offered the prototype. Thereby killing became a cultic, i.e., religious-ethical activity. Ritual killing, however, occurs not only in that stratum but
in similar forms in younger cultures also, where they are usually
designated as blood-sacrifices. We ask then to what extent there
may be a genetic connection between these forms of killing in the
various culture strata and also whether significatory changes did
perhaps occur.

In treating this topic, we are dealing with three major epochs
of culture history. Living forms of the two older ones, the cultures
of the root-crop and cereal cultivators, still confront us on almost
all continents; the younger is known to us through numerous
sources of the archaic high cultures. All three epochs knew ritual
killing. It is especially notable that the occasions at which the
killings take place, besides some variations, show remarkable
similarities. Such occasions might be the death of a chief or a
nobleman; the construction of a house, especially a temple; rain-
making; observances to insure fertility; the suppression of epi-
demics; reconciliation ceremonies after a war; expiation of a
transgression, etc.

Whatever may have caused the great restructurings in the history of mankind which make us speak of epochs—vexing, in any
case, for culture history—we shall leave undiscussed. We can,
however, distinguish epochs by a proper set of criteria.

It is not the killing ritual alone that runs through all three
epochs; it seems to me that many fundamental traits of the religious world view can be ascertained in them, often in different
dress but never so changed that one cannot recognize the material from which the dress was made. Problems of culture history
are not the real topic of this book, which strives to discover the
original meanings of phenomena. But to find the meaning of
cultural configurations we must also consider changes in that
meaning. Therefore it may be permissible to speculate on relationships, on the one hand, between the cultivators' idea of the Dema-
deity and the divine figures of the polytheistic high cultures, and,
on the other hand, between legitimate killing rituals and semantically depleted blood-sacrifices.

The term "sacrifice," in the sense of an offering, has been
carried over in scientific usage from the archaic high cultures to

169

similar though more primitive manifestations. In accounts of head-hunting expeditions, however, the word would be rarely found, if for no other reason than that the external course of events is more evocative of "war" or "chase" than of "offering." The word may be employed, however, when a pig is killed and eaten in a death ritual of a head-hunting tribe. But, as I have shown at another place ("Weltbild": 54), the killing of the pig is fully equivalent to the head-hunt in the mythic frame of reference. Thus "sacrificial offering" in the sense of a sacred act (sacrifice) should either be extended to include head-hunting or be dropped entirely. The designation "ritual killing" emphasizes precisely that which the archaic cultivators stress. We ask, then, whether sacrificial offerings in the younger cultures signify something completely different and perhaps stem from different roots, or whether they are semantically depleted "survivals" of ancient ritual killings.

With respect to peoples with stratified societies it can hardly be doubted that blood-sacrifice is no more than the persistence of ritual killing in a degenerated form. Head-hunting expeditions become formal wars whose aim is to take as many prisoners as possible, to make them slaves, and to kill them at the cult site (or temple), as was formerly done with the sacrificial animals. That the slaves are also exploited economically is a very characteristic culture trait; for the first time, the idea was grasped that man, too, can be "utilized," thus instituting social stratification.[1] Degeneration of the original concept of ritual killing is evidenced especially by the emphasis on the number of victims. We have already seen (chap. iv, sec. 9) the expectation of some future good functioning as a major factor in the process of semantic depletion. If killing is a sacred act which involves rewards, its root meaning will be corrupted by the primitive (though human) deduction that the more killed the more benefits are engendered. This corruption through adoption of a quantitative principle is observable throughout the younger cultures. Here belong the "feasts of merit" which increase the recompense in accordance with the number of animals killed.

Another factor contributing to degeneration is the primitive substantialization of the idea of the death journey. The archaic cultivator did not know the association of ideas which makes the slain victim servant to his conqueror, if for no other reason than the

[1] Trimbon suggested this in a conversation.

absence of the concept "servant." The claim that the magical powers of the victim become the victor's spoils, as it were, has been advanced by the advocates of the hypothesis of pre-animistic magic, and whenever it is made there is the suspicion that it derives from that very source. In the younger archaic high cultures, already at the threshold of literacy, killings at the death of a noble are explicitly justified by services the sacrificial victims are to render their master in the beyond. This is a very natural conclusion among peoples that have such concrete ideas of a continuation of life after death (cf. chap. xiv, sec. 2). Yet this is also a gross oversimplification or else a clumsy embroidering of the sublime concept of a journey into death—typical "application-thinking," compared to the "expressive thinking" of the older culture stratum.

The above applies more or less to all socially stratified cultures. I should like to advance the following idea, though as an assertion only: the world view of this epoch is based almost exclusively on the mythic insights of the archaic root-crop culture without addition of essentially new ideas. Just as exclusively, the cultural configurations are "applications" of those mythic concepts and thereby very "successful" elaborations of social, technological, or economic life. But, weighed ideologically, the "successful developments" constitute pauperization and semantic depletion. By the same token, there is no concept by which the offerings could be differentiated from the ritual killings among archaic cultivators, and there is nothing that would suggest separate origin. Such ideas, supported by like arguments and often in a like form, are found only in the head-hunt or in the genitalia-hunt, as we are tempted to call it by analogy, since genitalia or foreskins are brought home as trophies as in northeast Africa (Jensen, 1936: 437 ff.) and as already told in the Old Testament (II Sam. 23:8 ff.).

As we stated before, the term "sacrifice" was transposed from the archaic high cultures to primitive situations. But how can we ever understand—in spite of any theory—that it can be satisfying to any god or many gods that men or animals be killed and eaten for their glorification? By comparing it with this old and familiar practice, primitive actions do not become one whit more comprehensible. We get further if we go in the opposite direction and accept per se the meaning-filled and therefore understandable

171

ritual killing which the cultivators practiced as the more ancient and original rite; the sacrificial offerings of the high cultures would then assume their place as no-longer-understood, depleted "survivals." This view, applied to the sacrifices of the Greeks, was held by K. Meuli in an article (1945) which adduces material so convincingly that doubt of his basic contentions seems hardly possible. His attention is mainly directed toward details of sacrificial ritual, and he shows us how among the Greeks, to whom the sense and meaning of these sacrifices already appeared doubtful, such rituals corresponded to those of the Asiatic pastoralists down to minutiae. But even among Asiatic pastoralists the strictly observed rites attendant upon the eating of the animals were only survivals from a much older hunting culture which had carried out the very same commandments in the killing of animals. We have to go back to the hunters to find act and meaning in a one-to-one relationship. To the hunter, resurrection— the regeneration by the "Master of the animals"—is an important (almost too practical) but in any case natural concern, and the rules strictly followed serve this regeneration. That, at least, is the impression that emerges from the data. Where the hunting cultures are concerned, we do best to hold back on a definitive judgment, for the ultimate sense of many actions has not yet revealed itself.

According to Meuli, the practices associated with offerings in archaic high cultures reach back into earlier periods of history than we had contemplated. Regarding the ritualistic handling of the several sections of the offering, comparison with the hunters seems to be confirmed; we have much material to corroborate it. However, significant features of the "sacrifice" are lacking among hunters, and in particular those that make of it a sacred act. The fact that the killing of an animal is associated with the deity at all (irrationally as a present, as a gift), the fact that many peoples never kill or eat their domestic stock outside the ritual setting, not even by subsequently elevating the action from a meal to a religious feast, the fact that animals are actually killed and eaten only at truly religious occasions, the fact that the killing of animals can expiate an ethical infraction—all this receives its intrinsic meaning only through making reference to the mythic slaying of a deity. The relationship of man to the fact of killing is, as we have seen, an important element in the hunter's intellectual quest for an understanding of his environment, in a quite idio-syncratic sense, however, from which the later idea of sacrifice can hardly be derived.

In any event, the killing and eating of a "sacrificial victim" makes sense only if it constitutes a sacred act, i.e., a cultic re-enactment of divinely creative events and is both commemoration and internalization. How, otherwise, are we to understand expia-tory sacrifices? How can guilt be atoned by the killing and eating of an animal? It can make sense only if the guilt itself consists in the fact that the internalization and commemoration have not taken place on some occasion which should properly have evoked it, so that guilt must be consciously revived. This, in fact, consti-tutes "ethical guilt" in the religious world view of the archaic cultivators. The entire existing world order and with it actions that have to conform to this order were the result of that event, and any infraction of the order—the disregarding of a taboo—is a guilt of omission, of forgetfulness. Such forgetfulness, however, is expiated by a particularly intensified act of commemoration (cf. chap. ix, sec. 3).

An expiatory sacrifice is meaningful only, then, if linked to a primeval event in which killing is an intrinsic element. It is the same with sacrificial offerings at a house raising, which we en-counter in their most meaning-filled form in the archaic head-hunter cultures but which have persisted throughout all the ar-chaic high cultures and into latest occidental history; it neither preserved its original, nor did it gain any new or comprehensive significance. Here, too, the genuine meaning is given in the Hainuwele mythologem: the slain deity is the first being to em-bark upon the death journey and is transformed into the realm of the dead, represented on earth by the cult edifice, and con-structed to this day according to the indications of the myth (cf. Landtman, 1927: 9 ff.). The temple, as representation of the land of the dead, and the original slaying, as inception of the world order, are mythologically very closely linked, so that it is not astonishing if among occasions for cultic re-enactments of the primeval drama the erection of a sacred edifice is frequently mentioned.

If we are willing to concede the original, true, and understand-able sense of blood-sacrifice only in connection with the Hainu-wele mythologem, it may be objected that a phenomenon which first appeared in a specific context often enough persists, completely changed in significance, in some other cultural setting. This is not to be denied, but sacrificial offering is mentioned as one of the—actually rather plentiful—examples where cultic acts were taken over from the older, truly religious practices and were carried on without a paralleling world view. In these instances, the activities were not meaningfully integrated in the new perception of the world. This would hardly have been possible, considering the wide distribution of sacrificial offering, if ritual killing had not long before degenerated to a fixed but no longer understood routine throughout a lengthy process of semantic depletion.

We must mention, however, that certain religious spheres in the archaic high cultures—as Kerényi ("Kore") has shown for the Eleusinian Mysteries—do represent a thoroughly meaningfilled cultural heritage from older strata. This applies especially to much that is important in Christian ideology. To this retention cult owes its place in occidental history and *Lebensgestaltung*.

The transformation of ritual killing into sacrificial offering seems to have gone hand in hand with the even more telling transformations of the conceptions of god which dominated the respective epochs. Primitive peoples with highly developed state structures already have "the gods" and also have the metamorphosed relationship between man and god, as for instance on the west coast of Africa and in Mexico. But the gods obviously still possess full Dema character. Mexico shows it most clearly, and we shall return to it.

The same fluctuation of significance between individual gods and the Dema nature of long-past primeval deeds can be demonstrated at closer range, in India, as H. Lommel has recently done in an interesting essay. The ancient Aryan gods Mitra and Varuna already possess individuality, divinity, and constant presence characteristic of gods of the archaic high cultures even in the oldest documents, reaching back to the second millennium B.C. It is said of them, as of all gods, that they "guard the right, punish injustice, maintain the order of the world, and bestow manifold blessing upon their devout worshippers" (Lommel, p. 207). In one myth, however, which tells of the institution of sacrifice, we see an entirely different aspect of the gods. They are hardly differentiated from the Dema-deities of primal time who decide upon the decisive deed of slaying a Dema-god and thereby initiate the present order.

The Yaiur-vedic texts give innumerable instances of sacrifices performed by the gods. Sacrifices carried out by men must emulate the prototypical sacrifice and sacred act performed by the gods. . . . To carry out the sacrifice, the gods must slay, murder, their fellow god Soma. They do this jointly; not a single god is named with the exception of Mitra, and he precisely because he refused participation. . . . But the gods nevertheless succeed in persuading Mitra to take part in the sacred crime, the beneficent murder [p. 215].

In all its detail the Indo-Iranian descriptions correspond to myths about the primeval past told by root-crop cultivators. Common action in particular often is a characteristic feature. Schärer (pp. 21 ff.) reports of the Ngadju-Dayak of Borneo that the torturing of the sacrificial slaves at the stake is essential only because *every* participant in the death feast must have stabbed the victim. The stabbing takes place in a rigidly fixed sequence. In animal sacrifices the process is the same. At the burial of the slain slave all the participants in the ceremony join in trampling down the earth over the grave, just as the Hainuwele myth reports that all the Dema trampled down the earth on her grave. Mitra's hesitation, however, is a new motive; primitive examples give no evidence for it. It probably already exhibits an element of a new mental attitude which attaches a new ethical evaluation to the primeval murder.

We learn further from Lommel that the god Soma (Haoma in Iranic) is identical with a being that existed prior to all other life and whose appearance, not clearly stated, as is typical of all Dema-deities, is sometimes related to a bull, sometimes to a plant, or to the moon. His death brings forth all life, vegetal as well as animal, and the pressing of the Soma plant, a cultic re-enactment of the slaying, yields the potion which gives immortality to the gods but confers upon man only immortality of the genus. "In the Soma sacrifices of the ancient East Indians, the highest and most solemn sacrifice, the offering to the gods was clearly not the main point; the chief object was the iconic repetition of the primeval sacrifice."

Mitra's initial scruples against the act of killing appeared to us to stand in contrast to primitive attitudes and to be the mark of a changed mental attitude and new ethical valuation. Zoroastrian evidence makes the changed relationship to the ancient mythologem even more obvious. Zarathustra, in condemning the old gods and their worshipers, turns with particular vigor against the slaughtering of cattle. He calls his adversaries "dissemblers [who say] the bull must be killed." But all his vigor could not prevent Mitra's being reinstated in later Zoroastrianism. However, since cattle sacrifices were now branded sacrilegious, the primeval deed could no longer be attributed to the reinstated god; it was said, rather, that Ahriman, the spirit of evil, had killed the primeval bull in his attack upon the perfect creation of Ormuzd. "Nevertheless the salutary effect brought about by the death of the bull was related piously and credulously, though, of course, without mention of his Haoma-nature" (p. 216).

This is an especially graphic example of the potential transformation from meaningful belief to absurdity, where the nuclear thought has been lost in historical changes but the externals are reverently preserved and brought into harmony with new concepts. It is an astounding fact which obtrudes itself in every aspect of culture history that a culturally shaped idea may persist through unlimited periods of time, even when that which we might call its verity is no longer discernible in the new guise. Thus every cultural configuration has, in addition to its principal verity, other characteristics which guarantee its life and continuity.

Mitra religion had another historical continuation and even experienced a renaissance in the Hellenistic-Roman Mithraic Mysteries which reached their apogee at the time of the Roman Empire and even penetrated our northern latitudes. Central to its iconic representation is again the killing of the bull, unmistakably of beneficent effect, since all food and medicinal plants derive from the slain beast. "Haoma is no longer known in Hellenistic and Roman Mitra religion. The killing of the bull has preserved its chief symbolic contents, the renewal of life, but it is considerably weakened since it is no longer the killing of a god who, by his death, confers benefits" (Lommel, p. 214).

Lommel's informative researches show us the problem of culture change from many sides. We are particularly interested in the Dema-like nature of the Indic gods insofar as they are part of the dramatis personae of the mythologem that deals with the slaying of Soma, their fellow god. Neither in Zoroastrianism nor

in occidental mysteries is the divinity of the killed bull conceptualized as a primeval being that existed before all forms of life.
In the Hellenistic-Roman cult the triumphant figure of the divine
bull-slayer usurps the center of attention as any celebrated mata-
dor in a Spanish bullfight. Parenthetically one may mention that
in primitive cults it is often a high dignitary who performs the
killing of the "victim"; among the Marind-anim he is called the
"father who kills" (Wirz, IV, 32). The Indic rite of obtaining the
Soma potion is still clearly related to the primeval slaying of
Soma who is killed anew in the pressing of the plants. It is the
"highest and most solemn sacrifice" of the ancient East Indians.
However, no matter how great the vitality of the mythic inventory of the archaic cultivators that confronts us here, the displacement of emphasis concerning essential relationships between man
and gods is already very apparent. In spite of the conservation of
the semantic contents of the old, we yet find ourselves in another
world.

Ideas related to Soma show other specifically Indic characteristics which are missing from primitive examples. We refer to the
particular character of the plant which is not the main crop plant
but an intoxicant. This variant of the mythologem which is related
mainly to the origin of extraordinary plants such as medicinals,
poisons, or intoxicants, is especially frequent in South America.
A surprising parallel to the Indic Soma cult is found among the
Huichol in Central America who give similar ceremonial recognition to the peyote cactus, a narcotic plant (Lumholtz, pp. 17 ff.).
According to Huichol myth the plant was brought forth in primeval time by a male deer which thereupon "disappeared." Even
today the Huichol embark on forty-three-day ceremonial expeditions to distant regions where the plants are collected. They shoot
at the plants with bow and arrow as they would at game; the
primeval deer appears to them in visions. In addition, a male
deer is the chief sacrificial victim in all religious celebrations.
The outstanding importance of the peyote feast, when the plant
exerts its intoxicant influence upon the participants, is connected
with cultivation, rain, and the fertility of the fields.

It seems to me that the ambiguous nature of the Indic gods
shows itself again in many divine figures of the archaic high cultures, especially in myths that tell of the killing of a deity as, for
instance, the myths of Osiris or Dionysos. It is particularly ob-

vious in ancient Mexican religion. Here the Dema character of the gods is preponderant, and the numerous human sacrifices were without a doubt primarily re-enactments of the slaying of the god. Yet, gods of continuous presence are described from whom man expects the gift of favorable destiny and to whom he sacrifices in token of this hope. Thus, Xipe-Totec—"our Lord, the Flayed One"—is still a potent force in the mind, but while the special god of the goldsmiths' guild (Seler, II, 1073), at the same time he is a fertility god to whom pleas for rain are addressed (p. 1075) and who is promised the first fruit of the fields in return (II, 1077 ff.). The name Xipe-Totec brings to mind a peculiar but by no means rare ambiguity: the god himself was slain and flayed but also had slain and had put on the skin of his victim. The name indicates the first aspect, but in the cult, the "Feast of the Flaying," the second aspect predominates; in the killing of the captives, priestly officiants take part who perform the cruel act in the garb of gods, especially that of Xipe-Totec. At the ceremony a priest appears in the guise of the god Opochtli (Sahagun, p. 70), and the killing itself is done by the "Night Drinker" (an epithet of Xipe) in the shape of Totec (pp. 68, 71). Those, however, who put on the skin of the dead captive are characterized by their designations as representatives of the god Xipe (p. 67); the god himself is always depicted draped in a human skin. The fact that all of these cult actions are related to a myth about Xipe, which has, however, not come down to us, is evident from the following sentence from Sahagun: "As told in the account about Xipe, so it happened afterwards in the same way . . ." (p. 67).

In a not quite comprehensible way, the slain captive and his owner are equated: when the flesh of the sacrificial victim is eaten the person who brought in the captive is not allowed to partake in the feast. "He speaks: Shall I then eat myself? . . . [p. 72] The one who took the prisoner is called sun, white paint and feathers, because he is like one painted white and covered with feathers [i.e., like one garbed to be sacrificed]." His relatives greet him with tears (p. 65). The lost myth about the god Xipe must therefore have told of something that would explain the ambiguity.

The peculiar position of the polytheistic gods—primevally active Dema who themselves perpetrate the killing, and ontological gods to whom sacrifices are offered—speaks for a direct culture-historical nexus with the older Dema-deities. Now, if we ask how the ones are differentiated from the others and what the cause may be for the change from ritual killing to a semantically empty sacrificial custom, we can undoubtedly point out many character-istics in the individual cultures by which gods may be distin-guished from Dema; each god, of course, is by nature an ex-ponent of his culture. One criterion, however, seems to me to possess greater and more general validity—the element of *presentness*. Despite their primeval deeds, the gods were not absorbed by the phenomena to which they gave rise, as would be expected of Dema, and their existence is not restricted to the land of the dead with which the living have no contact. *Presentness* as an essential characteristic of polytheistic gods, however, is the mark by which the "Highest Being" is differentiated from the Dema-deity (cf. chap. iv, sec. 3).

This much abbreviated chain of reasoning suggests that the ambiguous nature of many polytheistic gods was brought about by the blending of two originally separate concepts of deity. One would be the idea of the deity that reigns in heaven, to whom the creation of the world is attributed, who is ever present, holds hu-man destiny in his hands, and can reward or punish; the other would be the primeval divine being through whom the things of this world came to be as they are and thus bear the mark of their divine origin for all times. The ability to perceive this constitutes the ontological essence of humanity. Culture-historically speak-ing, such a blending would point up the impulse to which we should like to ascribe the genesis of these younger, socially differ-entiated cultures. As we have stated, the High God concept has had its clearest elaboration among Northeast African Hamitic cattle breeders; it also appears alongside the Dema-deities in the younger primitive cultures, i.e., in the cereal-grain cultivating strata which, in the Old World, usually possessed some cattle breeding. In such settings Dema-deities usually exhibit that am-biguous nature which we have noted about Indic and Mexican gods. That means in this case that the Dema have already been transformed into ontological gods. We leave open the reason for the appearance of the Sky-God and the nature of the impulse that initiated the change in the Dema concept. If our conjecture that the idea of a High God played a major role in that change makes even *one* of probably many connections seem credible, then the summary treatment of a very difficult problem will have been justified.

We must again stress the hypothetical nature of our conjecture, presented as it was, practically without illustrations and data. Even the best documented scientific results usually stem largely from an understanding of culture history that accrued from innumerable impressions and through constant immersion in the subject matter; this gives understanding in broad and general outlines although it does not prove our contentions. The terms Highest Being, Dema-deity, and polytheistic gods are in themselves summarily conceived. For each people, the substance of beliefs naturally has a proper and specific aspect which is the principal object of monographic descriptions.

Our attempt to demonstrate the culture-historical connection between polytheistic gods and Dema-deities of the archaic cultivators could not go into the question of the deeper nature of high-culture gods or inquire into their proper position in the larger historical process. Our intention of comparing them to the older Dema figures must per se stress "semantic depletion." Viewed differently, they would undoubtedly have shown still other aspects. It happens to be characteristic of all cultural configurations that their essence, because of the creative process of their genesis, seems partly incased—as if in eggshells—in the remnants of prior states. If we dealt only with this residue, it was as a result of the problem discussed in this section.

It is, however, quite possible to treat concepts of God typologically and to compare common features over long distances. This is, in the last analysis, due to the fact that concepts of God neither arise out of nowhere—possibly from occasional notions or accidental sports of man's imagination—nor are traceable to natural predispositions which are reflected in everyday living. Rather, they are results of unique and powerful creative events that determine the course of history. Once they have become reality, all cultural configurations lead their own existence. In this manner originate the numerous variants of a basic idea which are the subjects of phenomenological consideration. Whoever denies this premise would naturally not be willing to enter into a discussion of our views.

5. *THE SLAYING OF THE DEITY AS PROPOSITION OF A MYTHIC VERITY*

Up to this point it has been our aim to establish ritual killing as a cultic and therefore genuinely religious phenomenon. In a largely speculative digression we tried to show that blood-sacrifice in the younger culture strata does not rest on a novel concept of sacrifice but, basically, is a survival of older killing rituals. Having described killing rituals as anchored in myth and thereby linked to a form of reason, it now remains to demonstrate their sense not only in the framework of alien mythic propositions but to make them comprehensible within the range of our own experiential capacities. A custom will appear more plausible when we take it out of isolation and bring it into a context with other expressions of its own culture with which it harmonizes free from contradictions in logic. If a cultic activity such as ritual killing presents difficulties to the understanding, little is gained by making reference to myths. Our insight into the cycle of associated images may deepen, but, on the whole, myths are made up of the very same type of incomprehensibilities. To gain full understanding we should have to lay ourselves open to mythical thinking and that is, of course, the one seemingly insurmountable difficulty.

Mythic and Scientific Insight

Assuming that man has acted from reason throughout his history and that even in the earliest phases unreason had no greater share in his cultural creations than it has now, we may also assume that the significance of his early action may be expressed in the language of our day. In other words: we should understand, even from the standpoint of our scientifically influenced thinking, why early man gave over to killing so large a proportion of his design for existence. We should have to comprehend the aspect of reality which seized primitive peoples when they made killing the subject of deeply felt cultural representation.

This should be possible to achieve. The only obstacle is the wide gulf between the mythic and the scientific attitude. Rationality, which is not out of place in the scientific attitude, already implies something of the sobriety—in extreme utterances even banality—of science and forms a contrast to poetic creativity or the mythic world view. If we make the effort, then, to use the insights at the root of mythic statements as scientific judgments, we must be fully aware of the consequences of such abstraction. The true, essential, and vital content of the myth will be lost.

Let us take up one more illustration before we discuss the act of killing with the attitude of science. Most striking in almost all puberty ceremonies is the idea that the initiates must die before they can awake to a new life as fully accepted and procreative members of the community. Other assertions refer to the same inseparability of procreation and death. Formulated in the language of science, they say everything that lives is mortal and propagates. Without death, propagation would be a logical absurdity, just as absurd as the converse would be. Such a statement would be prosaic and would not produce any reaction from us if we confronted it without "involvement." Only when we realize that we are here dealing with the most significant characteristics of all living things and that we must gain insight into its sense and meaning will we "feel" with an intensity that approximates mythic perception. In meanings and significances so perceived, the divine in nature is revealed to mythic thinking. When the creative primal principle brought about life *for the first time*, the die was cast about the "Just-so" of all life. Biological science can say no more than that it is so.

Does myth tell us more than science? First of all we may perhaps note that it does not say any less. Mythic perception clearly recognized the characteristics common to all living things and separated them from the inanimate. On Ceram a myth tells (Jensen, 1939: 39 ff.) of a quarrel between the rock and the banana tree about the ultimate nature of man. The banana tree, wishing man to beget children and propagate, is victorious in the dispute. Resigned, the rock says: Very well, but then he shall also die as you have to die. Thus man did not become like the rock, but became part of the animate world and shares in its fate. Could he have become like the stones and shared the characteristics of stone, especially immortality? This is the mythic question and through negation the answer affirms the given state as the realization of a divine principle.

Such a myth actually transcends the phenomenology of science. The additional quality lies in affective experiences which have been deliberately excluded from scientific judgments. Among other things, the manner in which mythic insights are transmitted from generation to generation shows the difference clearly. In the cultures we are considering, cults are the most important means of communication (chap. ii, sec. 2): insights are not conveyed by verbal teaching alone but are "experienced" in ecstatic ceremonies and communal celebrations. Youths, participating in the cults, undergo the revelation of something unknown and profound, in which the essence of things shows itself as a vast mystery for which our occidental culture lacks expression. The scientific equivalents of such insights, in their sobriety, are not capable of being "experienced" to this extent. Myth and cult make the fuller statement, for not only do they convey insights but, in addition, they place man into immediate relationship with perception.

While scientific formulations are comprehensible in a general sense, mythic and cultic representations of religious insights are far more culture-bound. The outsider's difficulties in understanding the "teachings" of cults that have lost touch with the prevailing world view are to be seen in the reports of Christian writers about the cultic activities in Eleusis. Kerényi (1945: 55) writes:

Of the ear of corn which is silently raised at the climax of the ceremony and of the simple supplication "Let it rain, and bear fruit" [the Christian writers] mockingly say "that is the great, the unutterable Eleusinian Mystery." They are beside themselves in the enumeration of unworthy, lowly objects of worship said to constitute the "Mystery." By this they prove that the pagan *arreton*, the sanctifying principle, was lost to them in its characteristic quality.

We must keep in mind that the Eleusinian cult, in origin as well as cognitive values, shows close spiritual affinity to the primitive cults that are our main concern.

Cognitive Values

After the preparatory discourse, we now take up the cognitive values contained in killing rituals. What moves man to kill creatures of his own kind—not from a moral or unthinking semi-bestiality, guided only by ignorance or the lowest instincts, but from a quest for deeper meanings and from a will to transmit these meanings as cultural *Gestalt* to successive generations? When we attempt to express this as a judgment about reality, our

183

statement will appear pale and lifeless compared to the affective fervor of mythic experience. Mythic thinking turns to *primal* events, to creative acts, in an awareness that their evidence must be the more vivid. Whoever wants to fathom the true nature of reality must be able to state how it came about that this or that manifestation turned out to be as it is.

At the core of the mythic world view is the statement that a deity was *killed* in affirmation of the verity that all that is animate is mortal. Myths lack comprehensible motivations for killing. Motives which are sometimes alleged are invalidated by the fact that the deity itself commands the Dema, the ancestors of man, to perform the act, and holds out promise of a magnificent earthly reward. Many other variations of the myth could be imagined, all expressive of approximately the same thing: the deity might die; it might in so many words or by its removal to the realm of the dead institute mortality and provide the promised abundance. But when myths, almost without exception, tell of the killing of a deity, and when in the re-enactments of these events killing assumes such a decisive part, then we must attach some superior significance to the statement.

Our object was to rephrase this cognitive value in the form of a scientifically phrased statement of reality. Dispassionately and stripped of all that is affective, it would read: all animal life maintains itself solely on organic materials, i.e., through the destruction of other forms of life. Thus, killing is a fundamental and common characteristic of animal existence whereby we must keep in mind that primitive peoples have justifiably associated the harvesting of plants with killing, with the destruction of life; we know it in the image of the "reaper," Death.

To us this is so obvious that we feel just as the Christian writers on the Eleusinian Mysteries: such cognition, after all, is not sufficient reason to kill human beings. What kind of cognition is this, and what mystery is hidden in it? In fact, however, this is no argument against mythic experience. It is an expression of noncomprehension in the face of a revelation of sanctity.

When the deity was actualized in animal existence, a decision had been made that things should be so and not different—life should be life-destroying. Is another form of existence conceivable? Doubtlessly so. Could there be no life very much like human life in a differently constituted world? Life which does not kill? Perhaps such life may yet be in some far-off future. But the world we know and to which we belong has qualities precisely as received from the self-actualizing deity that engendered life-destroying life.

Affirmative and Negativistic Views of Life

Human behavior can take many forms. Two opposing attitudes are often found through history. Briefly formulated, they might be called an affirmative and a negativistic dialogue with reality. All we have said concerning the world view of the archaic cultivators shows a basically affirmative attitude. It is true that *sin* occasionally appears as a motive of the primeval death, or regret that the serpent and not man received the power of immortality. This makes room for the idea that human fate is not viewed as "right" but as something avoidable and something that should have been avoided. But these are only intimations. The majority of myths leaves no doubt that the deity wanted this and only this fate. The fact of the repeated killing alone speaks for the basically affirmative attitude of the archaic cultivators toward the facts of existence.

It might be said that, after all, man can do nothing but come to terms with set conditions and submit to his fate. Viewed in the history of culture, however, this is by no means an obvious fact. In our own cultural environment, at least in its most recent phase, we find very stringent taboos relating to the human body. In extreme cases we are constrained almost to overlook the fact that we have bodies at all. Much that is unavoidably corporeal is hushed up entirely or felt as an embarrassment. Anything that has to do with metabolic functions, sweating, or unpleasant body odors, not to mention sexuality and the genital organs themselves, is treated as non-existent in interpersonal dealings and even by individual consciousness. A wealth of circumlocutions and euphemisms serves to avoid having to call a spade a spade.

Since most other cultures do not know of our taboos, the ethnologist is often in the embarrassing dilemma either of having to disregard the cultural record or of breaking the taboos of his own society. Other cultures have devoted particular attention to sexual practices and have given them much space in their cultural formulations. The same can be said about excreta (cf. Preuss, "Ursprung": 325). Both attitudes are based on realities of the

185

environment and of human nature. The sensibilities underlying our particular taboo are not unknown to primitive peoples, as is evidenced by the fact that even primitives whose cults are highly charged with eroticism usually conduct their love play in private. The affirmative or negative attitude toward aspects of reality rests on a definite stand taken by man and is conditioned by his proper culture.

From this point of view we must also regard man's attitude to the act of killing. Despite its incontestable reality, it also produces a certain feeling of revulsion. Hunting peoples seem to have made this aspect of the reality of killing the object of cultural formulation in a sense paralleling the occidental taboo of the corporeal. Objective reality is suppressed, denied, and submerged under euphemisms. The hunter who has killed acts as if he had not killed. It is a negative attitude toward certain areas of reality which states: that which is real were better not real.

A Special Obstacle to the Understanding of Ritual Killing

If archaic cultivators regarded the reality of killing as something natural and viewed it affirmatively, we are still at a loss to "understand," even though our inability may be ascribed to cultural parochialism. We find it hard to accept the view that man should ever have felt so few of the revulsions which seem normal to us and all hunting peoples, and that he could set them aside so easily and draw cruel conclusions from his own experiences which urge the killing of his own kind. The facts are indisputable, but we are inclined to make allowances and to grant extenuating circumstances. Even if we concede that early cultures do not credit human life with the unique value which we give it and that dying possibly comes easier in other cultures, we yet maintain that something more, something extraordinary was needed to persuade man to assign to the act of killing such a realistic and momentous significance. The obstacle to our understanding ritual killing is increased by the fact that primitive peoples in particular possess a highly developed faculty for symbolic representation. Almost all cultic activity is based on it. Cult is the great language of antiquity and the preferred means of communication about the meaning and essence of nature—a language, by the way, which in the course of history has receded more and more into the background. The actual act of homicide, however, pertains to that characteristic of realistic behavior which is not inherent in the language of symbolism. Ideologically speaking, the initiates of a puberty rite must die though, of course, none is actually allowed to die; however, there is an arsenal of graphic and at times quite drastic means to give adequate expression to the thought.

Even in Mexico where, in a hypertrophy of human slaughter and cannibalism, cultic forms had assumed especially horrific and exaggerated proportions, there existed an almost too disingenuous variant in which the slain deities were eaten at the sacrificial offering in the shape of kneaded dough (Sahagun, p. 218). Sahagun, in Seler's translation, tells us in his description of the sixteen-year festival, Atemoztli, that at the feast of the

"Descent of the Waters" sacrifices were offered [to the rain god] on all the mountains. It was said that the rain gods came down [for the first time]. In the houses of the rich the kneaded [dough images of the rain gods] were made; at midnight the little mountain gods were born and songs were sung in their honor. At the time of the sunrise the little mountain gods were sacrificed and at that time sacrifices were offered [to the rain gods]. Some kneaded ten, others only five; they were given the appearance of men, supplied with a crown cut from paper and with a paper garment. Afterwards their heads were cut off with the weaving blade of the women; thus they were killed [sacrificed]. And their paper garments were burned in the court yard of the temple and their bodies which were made of the seed of the notchweed were eaten. The feast took place in the month of December, on the third day.

Another example of the many that Mexico offers is also related by Sahagun (pp. 15 ff.). He speaks of Omacatl, who was a god of banquets, of invitations to guests, and of the serving of food:

When his feast is celebrated he who takes part in the divine meal first makes the roll of the god which was the bone of the god. Only priests and headmen of the gens may make it. It was half an arm in length, very thick and like a roll (cylindrical). And before the division takes place, they eat and drink, drink wine. When dawn has come they stab Omacatl in the abdomen and kill him. Then he is divided up, the roll of baked dough is broken into pieces and the pieces are eaten.

We see that we may give primitive peoples credit for cultic forms which do not cause us horror and aversion. Neither is it obvious that such horror was unknown to them. Why then did early man have to formulate the cognition of the significance of killing in so final and soberly realistic a manner? The actual performance of the cultic act of killing under avoidance of the alternatives of symbolic representation does not fit our over-all picture of the archaic root-crop cultures. It seems a hypertrophism, originated at some time by religious zealots who pursued an ideology to its utmost consequence inexorably and frantically. Zealous representatives of such a religious attitude are rarely found in contemporary primitive cultures. We may think of the peaceable image which has been drawn, especially of the archaic cultivator. The past may have been different, of course. Yet all such ideas are hypothetical, and it remains uncertain whether the urge to find such reasons does not stem from a preoccupation which translates our occidental aversion to killing into a universal human quality.

Overly literal interpretations and, in that sense, realistic elaborations of religious ideas are found in other religions. Mendicant poverty as a religious ideal presupposes that not all the people make this ideal their own. In the same way generalized celibacy would put an end to mankind, though this would not be the ideal aim. All such extreme measures have in common an absurdity that would become manifest under universal application. If killing were to take place without sense or limit because it pleases the deity, mankind would literally exterminate itself, and that is not what the rite aims to achieve. The less archaic cultures were apparently well on the way to prove the absurdity by forgetting all moderation or bounds set by nature. How modest appear the achievements of head-hunts among the archaic cultivators when we compare them with the slaying of thousands of human beings in the late "high culture" of Mexico. Mills, an expert on the notorious Naga head-hunters of Assam, points out that it is not commonly realized how small the number of victims in a raid actually is. He was able to establish that two Naga villages managed to carry off a head only four times in the sixteen years during which they were feuding. A village which lost on an average a head a year would consider itself subjected to a series of stunning blows—and this despite the fact that all the concepts connected with head-hunting are central to the thinking of these people and that their entire life receives its tension from them (Mills, 1926: 209 ff.).

We have dealt only with questions as they presented themselves in a discussion of the true primeval myth of the slain deity. The totality of these questions is far more comprehensive as is the case with every genuinely mythic prototype. They capture a profoundly searching look into reality which cannot be fully translated into another medium. Other questions arise, for example, from the mythic statement that killing is part of the masculine principle, an idea which recurs in conjunction with warfare and hunting.

We have not gone into the meaning of the cruel tortures which are often part of the rite of killing. As one example of many, we mention only the feasts of merit of the Naga during which the "sacrificial animal," the buffalo, must be killed with great cruelty. Its four legs are hamstrung, and it is belabored with rice-pounding poles while lying helplessly on the ground (Mills, 1937: 194). Among the Ao-Naga the festooned animal is tied to a post, beaten, and thrown to the ground. Then the young men dance on it till it is half dead. The next day after further torturing, it is speared and then—whether quite dead now or not—cut up and eviscerated (Mills, 1926: 259 ff., 391). The entire description gives us the impression that the torturing is not the concomitant of a ceremonially elaborate ritual killing but that it is very closely connected to the essential meaning of the event. Just as the ritual killing is related to mythic prototypes, there may be mythic prototypes for the torture. Especially the motif according to which the animal must be pounded with rice pestles might find explanation in the mythologem associated with root-crop cultivation and its significance for the origin of crop plants. Other motifs, however, the beating itself, the dancing on the helpless animal, the evisceration of the living beast, etc., require separate researches. Since ritual torment takes on extraordinary importance among primitive peoples—at puberty rites, for instance, or at the initiation of a shaman—and plays a major role in the archaic higher cultures, such an investigation would lead far beyond ritual killing; we would expect that psychology would have to contribute significantly to the explanation.

Here we were chiefly concerned with the nuclear idea of ritual killing, its cognitive value. If we have undertaken to translate the mythic statement into our own language, we do so with the awareness that the true myths contain more, much more, than an enunciable inventory of basic cognitions concerning a defined state of reality; enunciable only is the fact that the characteristic of all animal life is that it must maintain itself by the destruction of life.

9

THE RELIGIOUS ETHOS

Theories about the origin of religion which attempt to uncover the *essence* of its early forms are in remarkable accord on the claim that primitive religions lack "ethos." Since the ethical principle is usually thought to be a basic part of all religious behavior, it was logical to conclude that primitive forms are not yet religions in the full sense of the word. For that reason, more recent authors speak of formative or incipient stages, of proto-forms of religion, from which indisputable religion developed later, so gradually, however, that the exact moment of the transformation cannot be fixed. Tylor, for example, states that lower animism is not immoral but merely amoral. The belief in a moral government of the universe is said not to be a component of natural religion, and morality is said to have been added to religion only in the course of a long history. Originally, moral precepts and moral laws were totally independent of animistic beliefs and rites. Such a non-religious morality—often admirable and praiseworthy—could be found even among the most barbarous tribes. Only at a much later stage, it is said, have such practices and customs, based on "tradition and community conscience," been attached to religion. Others, of course, have judged the early forms of religion far more harshly. Human sacrifice and head-hunting as part of religious ceremonial, especially, have repulsed occidentals.

We feel justified in invoking Tylor, though his works were written more than eighty years ago; his ideas are still current in ethnology and he offers what still is, in many respects, the best systematic presentation of primitive religion.

The hypothesis of *Urmonotheismus*, of primal monotheism, stands in isolation and is unique among the theories of religious origin. W. Schmidt stresses, in contrast with all others, that the ethical element constitutes an important part of original religion. However, this image of an ethos, so closely akin to occidental ideas, follows only if Schmidt's contention is granted that most religious expressions of primitive peoples are products of degeneration; his proof of the genuinely ethical character of the primal religion postulated by him is limited to a few assertions of the kindness of the Highest Being, manifested in benevolence toward man and in the fulfilment of human desires. God, who imposed some of the ethical tenets, watches over their observance, meting out punishment or reward. *Urmonotheismus* alters the image of the non-ethical nature of primitive religion only insofar as it notes some features which we would call ethical in the life ways and ideas of the most archaic primitive peoples. Only sporadic features fall into the category, however, while the ceremonial life of primitive man that confronts us in the majority of the accounts is characterized as degenerate and thereby virtually non-ethical. According to Schmidt, even the oldest culture possessed a belief in one God, the Highest Being, and therefore also possessed an ethic. Later, in primitive cultures, religion degenerated, turned into its opposite, and became totally immoral.

Theory, then, denies the ethical element to most primitive religions. In contrast, the *secular life* of primitive peoples—as we learned from Tylor—is described as being governed by ethical norms. Many an extensive account comes to the conclusion that savages are better men than we are. Kindliness toward fellow men, readiness to help in emergencies, respect and even reverence for the aged, strict upbringing of the youth, and insistence on politeness and etiquette—indeed all that we consider ethical in interpersonal action can be found in primitive populations, often in a highly developed state. The opposite, of course, is also reported, especially the cruelty of primitive peoples. But since the same may be reported of later cultures which admittedly do possess ethical religions, the absence of morality from primitive religions cannot be explained through instances of cruelty or crudity.

There is then quite a break in the view that the savage is a "better man" but that, on the other hand, his religion (or its preliminary phase) has no element of an ethic. The very assumption of such a break invites doubt and suggests that it hides fuzzy thinking about basic concepts such as religion, ethos, divine commandment, and perhaps others. When Hellpach, for instance, expresses the view (1946: 62 ff.) that the contents of the Homeric epics cannot be linked with religion because, though gods are spoken of, duties toward the gods are not mentioned, then doubts about the proper application of terms become certainty; if we are not permitted to connect the Homeric epics with religion, we simply reject everything that is customary and common usage. If we hope to find a solution to the problem of ethics in early forms of religion, we must treat terminology with greater care.

1. ETHICS AND CUSTOM

The term *ethics* has varied meanings even if we do not consider at all those that are confined to sexual behavior. Nietzsche sees ethics as "a respect for custom," i.e., a way of life guided by usage and mindful of it; he regards its effect as stultifying since it opposes the evolution of new and better usages. But when we keep in mind the compound ideas of ethical behavior or ethical decision, ethics, or that which is ethical, stands out against custom as something more spontaneous, more genuine, and more germinal. In the primitive world, however, we are dealing primarily with custom, since ethical decisions of individual personalities are practically never mentioned in the reports. Our task, then, consists in finding the ethical nucleus in the many layers of customs. This, of course, can be accomplished only if we understand the customs, that is, if in accordance with our own postulate, we can isolate within our own consciousness a measure of empathy that permits us to regard whatever may be the custom as natural, reasonable, and even self-explanatory. How difficult a task this is we see when we reflect that we do not apply such measures even to our own usages. However natural it may seem that we bow or remove our hats as a form of greeting, few of us could claim to "understand" the custom.

Every human usage arose at some moment of history. As we shall emphasize again and again, at the time of its origination it was "expression" of a very specific attitude toward the environment. Just as surely it can be said of most customs that they will continue to be practiced even after their original meaning is forgotten and that no one will give a thought to their primary significance. Like all other cultural phenomena, customs relentlessly move from the "expressive" stage into that of "application." It is therefore necessary to examine any cultural configuration to see the extent to which it has maintained contact with its original and proper meaning. According to an inescapable law, anything that culture has created must grow more distant from the content of the creative idea; finally, it will be only a pale reflection of its original "expression" and may even be transformed into its exact mirror image. Between the extremes of expression and application lies a continuum of intermediate values which makes any cultural manifestation seem closer now to one, now to the other of the two poles. To judge a tradition, we must provide ourselves with an estimate of its position within the continuum and this we can usually do only because we encounter the same complex among many peoples, though with greatly altered semantic contents. Thus, in individual cases, we are able to study the process of gradual semantic depletion along the way from "expression" to "application."

Custom generally is a formula of application which makes a creative idea useful for the human community. The deeply religious recognition that death is part of the divine world order has brought forth a multitude of customs which relate man to death and to the deceased. They can be carried out with reverence even after all traces of their original sense have been lost.

Custom incorporates more than the ethical element, for it constitutes the more or less exhaustive representation of an entire idea and is therefore rite or ceremony. In fact, the ethical element is part of the religious mode of behavior and to this extent is also discernible in the primitive cultures. We know primitive life to be filled with an extraordinary number of taboos. Actions are forbidden or demanded without stipulated reasons. We on our part are inclined to seek meaning exclusively in defined goals. It is plain why stealing is forbidden, but why should a man not speak to his mother-in-law or why should one person not call another by his name? According to our "knowledge" of things, no immediate disadvantage should arise from an infraction of such a taboo, either to the transgressor or to anyone else. And yet, primitive peoples act as if dire consequences were to be expected, not only for the transgressor but for the whole community. Taboo commandments are strictly adhered to, and when someone fails to conform the community acts to atone for the misdeed. Nothing could be more obvious than that according to primitive belief, the commandments incorporate the correct ethical behavior, based on the ethical code related to the idea of the divine.

The particular difficulty then is that these precepts which

represent the ethical content of religion make no sense to us. We will not overcome this lack of understanding until we stop searching for purposes. If we see sense only in practical advantages or palpable disadvantages, we will understand neither customs nor their original ethical content. We are moving in a vicious circle, for common-place purposes engender no ethical decisions, at least not of a religious nature. If we inquire after the ethical concomitants of customs and usages, our eyes fixed on a practical goal, we shall of course find no trace of the ethical element in religious precepts but only commerce with "corruptible and corrupt spirits" (Andrew Lang).

It may be remarked parenthetically that, in our opinion, even actions which serve most mundane purposes stem, basically, from the cognition of the divine order; they, too, owe their existence to a truly creative process. This applies largely also to legal norms; though purposive, they must at intervals be re-examined with a view to the sources from which they sprang. However, this is not the object of our inquiry; it is a relationship that was forgotten in ancient days when man drove himself from Paradise by subjugating himself to the rule of purpose. Purposive acts are judged by the standard inherent in the purpose itself. Tylor's thesis applies to them: they are amoral, though not immoral. The ethical code to which they are subject is earthly law which in the final analysis—with us as with primitive peoples—serves only the attainment of the very same goals. Transgressions of such laws are not sacrilege (though they may, on occasion, be sacrilege) but punishable acts, in aggravated cases even crimes; and punishment has the defined purpose of safeguarding the one order under which normal life can thrive. Commandments based upon taboos leave deeper roots. Bollnow (pp. 65 ff.) quite correctly linked taboos with the emotion of awe. Therefore it is not astonishing that a misdeed which infringes upon no law may affect us more violently than the transgression of a legal prohibition. Our codified law also covers some such misdeeds as blasphemy or the desecration of sanctuaries, such as churches and cemeteries. It so happens, however, that the impunity with which—according to our lights—mother-in-law avoidance may be violated also holds in the case of blasphemy. For insights that draw upon causal logic, both injunctions are equally irrational. Both are established customs, i.e., the community accepts them as formulas.

At first glance, primitive life seems to be more intensely en-
meshed in the bonds of such commandments and interdictions
than our own. This is probably true, but we must keep in mind
that we too are not solely governed by statute and law; there are
many other regulations, no less binding, even though we do not
officially, as it were, take cognizance of them. The sanctuary need
not be a church or cemetery; we all know sacred precincts toward which we feel similar reverence and awe. To mention one
other example: in several regions of Germany it is considered
disgraceful for a man to eat in a closed room while wearing a hat.
Among us, uncovering the head expresses respect and reverence;
eating, as an out-of-the-ordinary event, is associated with a particular psychological attitude. How completely the spiritual basis
of such a custom can vanish, a glimpse into any cafeteria will
prove.

If we search for the ethical component of the taboo, we must
forgo comparison with the ethical base of our Western social
order. Primitive taboos differ in principle; rational, i.e., purposive, meanings cannot usually be stated. Some other Western
precepts which we do not count among taboos show a certain
affinity with primitive customs; they are negatively defined by
the fact that obvious disadvantages cannot be demonstrated. Because of our indoctrination, these Western usages seem eminently
plausible: blasphemy, desecration of churches or cemeteries are
outrages, and no one who has been brought up to these verities
will doubt it. Any attempts at rationalistic suasion to contrary
values will leave at least a residue of awe. The many taboos of
primitive peoples are, however, neither compelling nor even
sensible in our eyes. But primitive man lives in an entirely different cultural context. Customs are products of culture and can
therefore be understood only if we are able to see all the cultural
expressions of a people from the inside out, as it were; then we
can assign specific customs to their proper places in the over-all
scheme.

2. CUSTOMS AS REFLECTIONS ABOUT
A DIVINE WORLD ORDER

Ethnology cannot be expected to provide us with insights into
the meaning of customs. It is too much to hope in view of our in-

ability fully to understand cultural totality. If we nevertheless make a tentative attempt in that direction, we do so in the hope of clarifying areas in which the ethical element in custom may be sought. This in turn may suggest ways of supplementing the usual ethnological procedures with other techniques. As an example I again choose the Wemale of Ceram. The Wemale know of a ruling principle of life which they call *holine*. Wherever inquiry leads him, the ethnologist is told that this or that is *holine*, often, unfortunately, with the implication that one may not speak of it. Now and then there is an uncertainty whether a thing is *holine* or not. If the opinion prevails that some thing or some event is *holine*, then it is certain that one must act in accordance with *holine*-precepts. About this the members of the community have no doubt.

Holine extends to all significant events of the life cycle, to anything that has to do with childbirth, childhood, puberty, marriage, or death, and to many activities pertaining to tilling of the fields, house construction, the preparation of food, etc. We shall briefly relate some of the childbirth ceremonials and especially one of its most important rites, the "bringing-in of a coconut." The palm from which the coconut is taken must stand mountainward, as seen from the house. In the opposite direction lies the ocean. These two directions play a considerable role in the ideology. On the one hand, they are the principal geographical directions, but in addition they carry a great number of religious and mythic connotations. For the newborn child the direction "toward the mountain" is most propitious; at a man's death his corpse is carried "toward the sea." Bringing in the coconut is hedged about by many more conditions: the man that scales the palm tree carries with him a valuable kerchief, the so-called *sarong-patola*. The coconut may not be cut down with the bushknife and permitted to drop to the ground, as would be done under ordinary circumstances. It is decisive for the entire life of the newborn that the coconut must not drop; it must be carefully wrapped in the *sarong-patola* and gently handled during the difficult descent. In the house the child is then washed in the coconut milk.

This custom, naturally, is *holine*, and observance of every detail is of the utmost importance. That the custom might be omitted is inconceivable. It so happens that in this particular instance the significance, in context with other religious concepts, is not difficult to ascertain. One of the most prominent deities of the Wemale is the maiden Hainuwele. Her name—it means palm frond—associates her with the coconut tree. Of the elaborate myth which we have frequently drawn on, we shall here relate only one episode: after the maiden's miraculous genesis, her foster father wraps her in a *sarong-patola* and carefully carries her to the house from the palm tree in which she had grown like a fruit. How could he allow this precious fruit to drop to the ground? From it is to blossom forth the maiden whose divine destiny establishes the order of the world and all life. The parallelism between the gathering-in of Hainuwele, the divine, and the careful plucking of a coconut at the birth of a child clearly shows man reminiscing about the sublime event of the birth of a deity. The miracle of childbirth is related to the divine events and the involvement of man's destiny is depicted in the custom. This is not the sole parallelism between human and divine events. Essential moments of the rites of passage establish similar analogies between Hainuwele and individual human destiny.

If parallelism makes customs more comprehensible, the question of ethical content must be raised again. Living up to usage, as we have seen, is *holine*. Its neglect or inept execution would be sacrilegious. An appeal is thus made to ethical consciousness. A religious commandment demands of man a particular way of behavior. The community raises it to a binding law and sees that it is carried out. Without a doubt we are dealing with a religious ethos. What then is the ethical imperative? In the instance of the Wemale we should say: myth refers the order by which the cultural community guides itself to a unique divine event. (Again it should be said that this is viewed as an eternal verity which, as such, is irrefutable and is not the outgrowth of misapplied causality.) The ethical imperative to which every member of the community subjects himself and to which the community subjects each of its members culminates in the commandment that the individual's whole existence be integrated into the total world order. *To act "ethically" means to live by the universal order.* Not to subordinate the self to the divine code or to act counter to it would be sacrilege and therefore unethical.

Preuss comes to a similar definition of ethos in primitive religions (*Glauben und Mystik:* 52 ff.). Unfortunately, however, his valuable contributions to the understanding of primitive religion are doomed by his unshakable loyalty to the hypothesis that religion originated in magic. In his youth this was considered correct, but his own data should have convinced him of the opposite. For him the divine world order is a manifestation of utility devised by man for his own advantage. The supposedly ethical behavior is therefore limited to what are more or less coincidences in which the allegedly useful demonstrates its immediate advantages. True utility, however, can be determined only by Western scientific thought, not by the thought of primitive man. The example of Preuss shows how even an idea which is incipiently correct may be distorted when purpose becomes the yardstick; a utilitarian act, centered on advantages and therefore undertaken for the attainment of some end, cannot mirror ethical behavior. Purpose is an arbitrarily introduced motive; only preoccupation with the hypothesis of magical origins leads Preuss to accept it.

3. SACRILEGE AND EXPIATION

The example from Ceram has revealed ethical contents in primitive religion. We now must ask if this constitutes a principle of universal validity. Can it be applied to every religious ethos? We deliberately chose an example in which the significance of the custom was much clearer than in most other instances. Yet, the example is not unique. Many others could be similarly presented and would lead to the same conclusion. In addition, however, there is the great number of those which obstinately resist comprehension. Why, for instance, do so many peoples pierce their lips and ears, or disfigure and maim their bodies? The disfigurements are *holine*-precepts and thus are ethical commandment; there can be no doubt of this. Can the originator of such practices really have been so foolish as to expect practical advantage as a causal outcome? Preuss would seem to think so. Rather than satisfy ourselves with such artificial explanations, we should forgo any attempt at gaining theoretical insights. Man's need to assimilate himself to the recognized divine principles of the world order, to integrate himself into them, is so obvious in the early cultures that we must seek here for primary motivations.

The significance of the two basic directions "toward the mountain" and "toward the sea" of which we spoke before will exemplify another point. We have already indicated how greatly the Wemale are concerned with polarities. We have also made the point that reference to polarity is made in the cultural formulations of many peoples and that their entire way of life may be determined by it—social organization, settlement patterns, etc. (chap. ii, sec. 1; vii, 1). The urge to adapt to this bisectioning of the world may be expressed in numerous distinct customs. Some of these peoples have a rule, for instance, that in certain dances one group of dancers may stamp down hard only with the left foot, the other only with the right. Reference to the divine world order, however, is always to be taken as ethical behavior, as a persistent memory that everything essential has a divine aspect; recognizing it and living up to it raises human life to the level of the divine.

Separate acts of this kind never are isolates as long as they still touch upon essential configurations of a culture. The divine aspect of the world is not analyzed into disjoint cognitive units; it is formulated as a single magnificent image. As a result not only the customs attendant upon childbirth but most other customs show themselves to be discrete features of a single image, interrelated as a reasonable and even logically close system of meanings. Ritual killing, head-hunting, cannibalism, and child-birth ceremonials make reference to the primeval divine act (cf. chap. viii). We must add, however, that they also share in the ethical content. In no other way can we resolve the apparent contradiction that primitive man regards as ethical commandments some things which, to us, appear ethically objectionable.

How did early man view sacrilege, *the violation of the ethical commandment?* A custom of the Wemale will again furnish an illustration. *Holine*-rules play an important part in customs associated with menstruation. During their menstrual days women either stay in separate houses or in designated places under the pile-dwellings; conversation with the segregated women or any sort of approach is forbidden to the men. Menstruation is linked to the moon, which the Wemale consider the manifestation of Rabie, one of the three chief Dema-deities. Rabie is said to menstruate at the time of the new moon, and since she remains invisible for a few days and nights, the various menstrual customs, especially isolation and seclusion, may be assumed to emulate the divine model.

When *holine*-rules are violated, a ceremony of expiation is required. The woman brings a rooster, a shoat, or even a hog—according to her wealth and the magnitude of the transgression—to the meeting house where the important men, especially the priestly officiants, are gathered to receive the expiatory offering. The woman acknowledges her guilt and retires; only the men carry out the ceremony. (We are here in the realm of the secret-society culture in which women are also excluded from many other religious observances.) The killing, roasting, and eating of the "sacrificial animal" are parts of the ceremony whereby the smoke of the fire is observed by men "who know smoke."

The real sacrilege is *to have forgotten* the divine act which had become the prototype of all human acts. To violate a *holine*-rite literally is "not to remember" that any particular human situation, e.g., menstruation, is traceable to a primeval divine event and thereby to the divine order of existence. "Not to have remembered" is a crime and sacrilege, fittingly expiated by a specially intensive act of commemoration. Blood-sacrifice, in its original sense, is such an intensive commemoration. Viewed in this light, it is neither a gift to corruptible, nor a pacification of angry, gods who keep a pedantic watch over the observance of their decrees. Of course, there are enough examples where the sacrifice appears to fall under the one or the other of these types or even under both. There is no cultural phenomenon which, during the passage from expression to application, does not show similar semantic displacements. We are interested, however, in understanding cultural creativity as a serious and essential, i.e., properly creative, process which results in reasonable and logically meaningful configurations.

It can be pointed out that there could be an even simpler expiation: the sacrilege might be undone. At the very beginning of the *Iliad* there is such an instance. The seer finds that a priest of Apollo has been outraged by the abduction of his daughter. The Greeks and especially Achilles are of the opinion that restitution must be made so that the deed be annulled. Most acts of sacrilege, however, are irreversible; to have spoken to a man, to have broken a food taboo, cannot be undone. In all of these cases—whether or not the offense can be undone—it is not so much the deed itself as the forgetting of the divine prototype which constitutes the sacrilege. In the episode from the *Iliad*, expiation consists not only of the return of the daughter but also of a festive hecatomb, a blood-sacrifice of many bulls. In this case, however, sacrifice is already a standardized rite with scarcely a sense of reminiscence; the sacrilege, too, is seen as a personal offense against the god—a considerable semantic displacement against primitive conditions.

To summarize: primitive religion does not lack the ethical element. Since all the precepts of the taboo present themselves as divinely ordained commandments, they must mirror the ethical will of early communities. A religious and ethical element revealed a human volition to live according to the divine world order. Not to do so, and especially not to be aware that all that is truly human is reducible to divine prototypes, is sacrilege. Expiation either undoes the deed as far as this is possible or—conscious of the sacrilege—enforces a particularly intensive reminiscence of the prototype.

4. THE RELATIONSHIP OF THE PRIMITIVE TO THE WESTERN ETHOS

It is always instructive to test our knowledge of primitive conditions against correspondences in our own cultural community. If forgetfulness of the divine prototypes is sacrilege, then much of our cultural life must be brimming over with it. There can be no doubt that this is actually so. The realization that neglect of some religious practice will not have any detrimental consequences has, for the last one hundred and fifty years, successfully battled against every kind of ethical standard. This alone would say little about the actual ethos of our culture; as we stated initially, custom is not ethos. We still must establish the lack of this true ethos in wide sectors of our communal existence. It is precisely this, however, that so chastened the occidental mind when it reflected upon the catastrophic consequences of an ever expanding rationalism. An individual, unencumbered by religious commitments or any capacity for artistic experience, viewing purposive action as the sole determinant and complete fulfilment of human existence, may have subdued much that is essentially human and yet may have attained a leading position in public life. According to primitive belief, his life would be a single sacrilege, and entrance to the realm of the dead would doubtlessly be denied him. The rationalist argument that such sacrilege has no detrimental consequences cannot be proven by rationalistic means. It is a mere assertion which relies for confirmation or refutation on immediately visible causal connections. The profound despair that extends to the roots of Western intellectual culture insistently speaks against this claim.

Still, no cultural community should be judged by its intellectually least qualified members. That which it recognizes as valid speaks more eloquently through the works of its most celebrated creative minds. If, however, we look to Kant for confirmation, we will be disappointed. In the fourth part of *Religion innerhalb der Grenzen der blossen Vernunft,* he defines "religion (subjectively regarded) as the recognition of all duties as divine commands." In a detailed explanation he takes a stand against the "erroneous interpretation of religion as an aggregate of *special* duties having reference directly to God; thus it prevents our taking on . . . *courtly obligations* over and above the ethico-civil duties of humanity (of man to man)," or "even to make good the deficiency of the latter by means of the former." Two sentences, apparently, exclude from ethos that which we have designated as the ethical content of primitive religion: "There are no special duties to God in a universal religion, for God can receive nothing from us; we cannot act for Him, nor yet upon Him. To wish to transform a guilty awe of Him into a duty of the sort described is to forget that awe is not a special act of religion but rather the religious temper in all our actions done in conformity with duty." The last of these notably contradictory statements is applicable to primitive religion without restriction. While we characterized taboo-rules as obligations toward the divine, we were saying no more than that they express the religious outlook. That, however, already subsumes the ethical element which is to be sought there and nowhere else. It need not be pointed out that the God concept of primitive ceremonials differs from the Kantian idea of God. The remote and inaccessible deity, the only one with which Kant is concerned, may possibly be found as a "Highest Being" even among most archaic primitives (cf. chap. iv, sec. 1). Because of his abstract nature and unrelatedness to earthly happenings, he had been excluded from our present consideration; we have restricted ourselves to the more active manifestation of divinity in primitive religions. Even for those divine powers which we designated as Dema-deities, the second portion of Kant's first sentence applies: they cannot gain anything from us and we cannot influence them or benefit them. The ethical element as we have ascertained it does not consist of an effect upon the deity—as the hypothesis of original magic would assume—but in a deeply rooted human predisposition always to be aware of the existence of the divine.

In the last sentence Kant adumbrates the idea which led us to see ethical values in primitive religions; that which he calls the religious mentality already contains the ethical element which is not to be sought in special religious acts. Yet, religion among primitive peoples is not recognition of man's duties as divine commandments but recognition of the divine character of reality; then reverence is not a duty but a natural attitude toward the perceived. Man may fail to use his gift of perception as he may neglect the resulting natural (i.e., reverential) attitude. Both omissions then constitute immorality, i.e., sacrilege against which the community of the coreligionists takes its stand, as opposed to the ethical, the naturally human.

The religious-ethical base of our culture is particularly difficult to ascertain. In our culture, the ethos is sought in exclusively individualistic attitudes, and we are therefore prone to reject any rigid definition. This is, in fact, of great significance. Any normative limitation imposed upon the ethos leads to the institution of a custom and thereby draws away from its pristine expression. The fact that our culture ultimately leaves ethical decisions to the individual is a most convincing expression of its creativity and cultural vitality. Contemporary primitive populations, on the other hand, live in a state of cultural petrifaction, that is, they no longer command a significant number of members who have either creative or re-creative contact with the spiritual sources of their own culture. This compels us to infer the true ethical content of their religion from traditional usage. In contrast, the individual ethos of our community is, without doubt, far more closely culture-linked than we imagine. A later period will certainly note how narrow the trammels of our ethical decisions were.

We should like to illustrate the applicability of the primitive religious ethos to ethical decisions in our time by one example which we take from Goethe's *Egmont*. In a crucial conversation with the Prince of Orange, Egmont must decide his future course of action. Two personalities that hold different views of the world, of man, and of their own worth, confront each other. Their decisions are not made lightly. The consequences of possible alternatives are carefully weighed and the arguments of the politically wise prince do not completely fail to make an impression on Egmont. Yet he wishes "to see with his own eyes" and will not "think unworthy of a king." After the prince has left, Egmont ends his hesitation with an ethical decision prescribed by no norm: "That other peoples' thoughts should have such power over us! . . . That is an alien drop in my veins. Benevolent Nature, drive it out again!" He does not wish to be seduced by the "cleverness" of the prince but makes his decision depend solely upon his own relationship to the world as it is traced out for him in his idea of "Benevolent Nature." The essential thing here is the integration of the self into an observed world order. The position taken by the Prince of Orange was by no means unethical. In any event, his was the wiser choice, as later developments showed. Still, it was not ethical, since it was determined by goals to be achieved. Because of this, his concern is neither the nature of this world nor its eternity but that which is a pragmatic and immediately present event.

This example may stand for many that could show how ethics is revealed in a defined relationship between the self and the world. Never do intellectual arguments or purposive considerations of advantages get to the heart of the matter. For this reason, even altruistic actions, those undertaken to the advantage of a person other than the actor, do not automatically fall under the religious ethos; they may very well take place on the level of prosaic goal directedness. And yet, such actions are much more frequently encountered among the truly ethical personalities to whom the image, of a higher, a divine world order is a living and present thing, not because of an inexorable sense of duty, as Kant would have it, but, quite to the contrary, because of the blessed gift of a humanity born to higher things. Egmont's ethical decision is inevitable; his nature and his destiny place before him a basic choice. The decision lies outside all considerations of purpose. He appeals only to Benevolent Nature which, in the language of primitive peoples, would say that the divine ideal precludes all other choices. Goethe guides our senses so that we do not condemn the Prince of Orange for having done the wiser thing and having decided on a pragmatic basis. Obviously, he does not want to picture him as a transgressor who can exist only on this one niveau. In this situation, rather, the prince does not see himself confronted with the decisive ethical question.

Sacrilege always constitutes a forgetting of the fact that man, and everything that has life, must in certain situations be measured against norms other than those of everyday existence. Often this is true of borderline situations, even in instances where sacrilege seems the mark of a criminal act. Thus it may be sacrilege to trouble the waters or to heedlessly eat of a certain food. Therefore, we consider the ethical basis of our cultural community different from that of primitive peoples, but different in content only, not in its essential nature. To act ethically means to live, in certain situations, according to a higher (among primitive peoples invariably a divine) world order; it clearly contrasts with the everyday order by the immediacy of the experience, free from all intervention of the intellect, and by its aloofness from all purposive considerations.

PART III | Magic

10

THE THEORY OF PRE-ANIMISTIC MAGIC

Of the three bodies of theory which dominate the ethnological literature on religion, it is probable that none has caused more harm than the one dealing with magic. It is drawn on for rationalistic explanations of many perplexing customs, not only in ethnology, but in all of the cultural sciences (*Geisteswissenschaften*). It is also called a theory of pre-animism, since it asserts a phase of culture history which preceded animism. Its adherents considered it a noteworthy advance over the animistic theory of Tylor. In the literature of the twenties, Tylor is repeatedly accused of overestimating the intellectual capacities of early man (cf., for example, Naumann, pp. 18 ff.). Yet Tylor always maintained a certain measure of respect for the true nature of man, while for some of the other proponents of the theory nothing was too foolish to be attributed to early man.

We have objected to this view several times in our discussion so far, but because of the attention which it commanded until very recent times we must treat it somewhat more extensively. Its proponents, Marrett (1900), Preuss (1904–5), Vierkandt (1907), and others—all, according to W. Schmidt (I, 493), preceded by J. H. King (1892)—are in basic agreement, and therefore a discussion of the work of Preuss, its leading advocate in Germany, will suffice.

Preuss, in his first article in *Globus* (1904), regards all expressions of a religious nature among primitive peoples as emanations of an aboriginal belief in magic. In any case, he wished to derive from magic the *origins* of all religion. For this he went beyond what most authors had considered to be acts of magic and included all expressions of religion. The important characteristic is primitive man's orientation toward purpose; we have already demonstrated how deeply "pseudopurposes" penetrate this thinking (chap. i, sec. 3). In the earliest phase of his history, man, intellectually not yet mature, strove to attain his purpose through direct action—actions which are said to have been the first, though unsuccessful, steps in the natural sciences and technology. Thus belief in impersonal "powers" preceded belief in personified gods. In communication between man and deity the magical element was dominant. Man believed that he was capable of coercing the gods and forcing the fulfilment of his desires. *Everything* religious, especially the ceremonial life of primitive peoples, seems subordinated to the concept of magic.

These ideas are gleaned not only from the older writings of Preuss but even from his works written in the twenties and thirties, in which he expresses other and undoubtedly more sophisticated views of the nature of religion. But he remains faithful to his view that the spiritual life of primitive man, as distinct from the genuinely religious life of man in later cultures, was dominated by belief in the efficacy of magic.

In his work on evolution and retrogression in religion ("Entwicklung und Rückschnitt in der Religion," 1932), he formulates the difference:

Undeniably, there exists a fundamental opposition between "magic" and "religion"; where magic is concerned, tradition, myth, custom— all that is related to a primeval time—and all that God had instituted at the outset, is predominant. . . . In prayer, on the other hand, one turns not toward primeval myth and cult, but to a present God, to whose kindness man addresses his requests.

Similar distinctions recur frequently in the writings of Preuss. To him, religion is "the devotion to the deity, expressed in prayer, gratitude, and humble obedience" (*ibid.*: 241)—an attitude found only faintly in primitive cultures and stifled there by ceremonials, which, "as compulsive causes" (*ibid.*: 247) instituted by deities and culture heroes, are purest magic. He gives no thought to the fact that ceremonies, too, may express gratitude and humble obedience. The supplicative religions are said to have risen in later phases of history, since prayer seemed to offer an easier path than the sometimes superhuman exertions demanded in the ceremonials. On the other hand, Frazer (1928: I, 237) saw man led to reverence for God by recognizing the failure of magic (cf. the counter argument to Andrew Lang in chap. iv, sec. 2).

We are not concerned here with the background of this particular view of the nature of early religion. Preuss, though he furthered ethnological research by his clear insight into the significance of myths for cultic activities, held fast to his views to the last. When applying myth to the explanation of cults, he again speaks of "alleviation of the magical element" in primitive religious expression (1933: 9). That primitive peoples carried out their cultic activities for the attainment of some purpose remains central to Preuss's view.

Indisputably, primitive man is almost always ready to give a reason to justify a cult: it might be to forestall barrenness of the women, to guarantee the fertility of a field, to assure sufficient rain, etc. We may call this magic, if we are concentrating on the expression of will alone. In this sense, magic does, indeed, color the cults of primitive peoples, at least in the forms which confront us today. But there is no proof that the purposive element deserved temporal priority or should be viewed as the very essence of cults.

Cults do not owe their origins to "pseudopurposes" (chap. iii, sec. 1). But neither can we agree with Preuss's concept of prayer and oppose it to ceremonialism as an expression of genuinely religious feeling. First, all primitive peoples that worship a deity they imagine to be present have prayers with which to address it; then, of course, prayers may shift in the direction of "application" and thus partake of the quasi-magical nature of cults that have deteriorated into purposive actions. We need think only of the prayer wheels of Asia, the Catholic practice of saying a specified number of paternosters for the repose of the soul of the deceased, or of prayer for any other "purpose." The same attribute of magic may be found everywhere, including our own culture. It is not involved in the *origin* of ritual but, quite the contrary, does not appear until—after constant faithful repetition of the ceremony—the expectation of a future benefit becomes dominant.

At another place (chap. i, sec. 1) we rejected the image of man which had to be constructed to support this claim of the priority of magic and ceremonial activities; we need not repeat the refutation here.

The theory in support of magic had a telling influence. Usually, ethnology makes room for the parallel existence of these three main bodies of theory: *Urmonotheismus*, pre-animism, and animism. It more or less sanctions their attempts at explanation, does not replace them with other or better ones, but applies them widely to all areas of religious expression among primitive peoples.

When the more or less clear concept of a High God is found in a particular ethnographic setting, *Urmonotheismus* is cited; any belief in souls, spirits, and life after death is classified as *animism;* and all else—especially anything that defies rationality—is called magic or sorcery. One then speaks of sorcerers, love magic, fertility magic, and all other kinds of magic, assuming that the theory is sufficient to explain the concept. The designation of "pre-animistic belief" in magic usually entails a claim that the original condition of the human mind has been uncovered, although there may be some qualms about the term "religion" in such a context. Often the popular hybrid "magico-religious" is expected to raise the argument above all obscurity. Even dissenters to this view, however, consider pre-animism an antecedent of religion, assume a relationship between the two, and hold that religion grew from a belief in magic.

A quite similar concept is to be found in Lord Raglan's *The Origins of Religion* (1949: 122): "If we do not allow ourselves to be obsessed by the belief that savages are 'primitive,' but study the facts, we can find plenty of evidence that magic is degenerate religion. It consists in performing rites without having learnt, or through having forgotten, their theological background."

A somewhat different concept has also gained some standing in the science of religion. Magic and religion are juxtaposed as related, though clearly differentiated, expressions, not derivable one from the other. Even among the earliest cultures, some attitudes may be said to be religious, while the magical attitude exists, as it were, as a counterpart to religiosity. This is expressed, for instance, in *Religion und Magie bei den Naturvölkern* by Karl Beth. The essence of religion is seen as humility before God, to whose kindness man appeals, while magic is expressed by practices oriented toward specific goals.

The influence which the theories of magic exert up to the present may be seen from the publication (within the year 1947) in Germany of three books containing the word *magic* in their titles. The authors aprioristically accept the correctness of the view implied by the term. (The books are those of Spranger, *Die Magie der Seele;* Ratschow, *Magie und Religion;* and Hellpach, *Das Magethos.*) It seems problematical whether the basis of the hypotheses can be examined from a non-ethnological point of view; yet the philosophers took over "magic" in the specific sense, without further examination.

Theories and hypotheses in support of magic claim to have

discovered and clarified the origin of religion, or the protoforms from which it sprang. Even those who will not recognize the generality of this claim do not usually doubt its validity for a variety of expressions and configurations of the intellect.

If, in the following sections, we deal with magic itself, we must treat completely different aspects, each in its own context; in each area the given conditions must be tested separately to find out whether or not the assumptions of the hypotheses are justified.

Since we do not doubt that genuine magic exists, though on the basis of quite different assumptions than those that support the prevalent theories, we will deal with the facts and data of this "genuine magic" and discuss the activities of the shaman and the phenomenon of "black magic" in detail.

11

SHAMANISM AS EXPRESSION OF
GENUINE MAGIC

Ethnologists have become accustomed to calling a certain type of officiant "shaman." His most striking characteristic is a special psychic ability that gives him power to act as intermediary between man and his deities or spirits, as the case may be. Opinions differ on which of the many attributes that characterize the shaman are to be considered typical. We need not give an exact definition because here—as everywhere else—there are imperceptible gradations between neighboring phenomena. One of the most important functions of the shaman is the healing of sickness, and from this it follows that the medicine men, even if we do not consider them shamans, are not only related to them in this respect but often appear against the same intellectual background; this is essential to our "understanding." For us, the decisive criterion is the psychic ability which differentiates shamans from the cult priests whose office is usually hereditary. The derivation of the word *shaman* is uncertain (cf. Nioradze, p. 1; Eliade, 1957: 457 ff.); it has come to us from the Tungus by way of the Russian (Eliade, *ibid.*: 14). We think it advisable to retain the accepted terminology; our meaning of the term will become clear in the course of discussion.

The areas of greatest concentration of shamanism are in northern as well as inner Asia, the Americas, India, and Indonesia (in the latter, quite strikingly among the culturally more recent peoples, as also in South America where shamanism appears mainly among the Aruak, Carib, and Tupi). True shamanism is only weakly developed in Africa. It is rarely encountered in the culture stratum of the archaic root-crop cultivators and even then only in a weakened form and not as the focal concern of the religious life.

Shamanism has often been designated and treated as a distinct form of religion. It is reported that even official Russian statistics list it alongside Islam and Christianity (Nioradze, p. 3). A religion has a defined world view that encompasses *all* the phenomena which the culture regards as important. Man sees his religion as the work of divine powers; through it he perceives the world and reads from this cognition his obligations. If shamanism were to be a distinct form of religion, we should expect to find the same religious image of the world wherever we encounter officiants that qualify as shamans. As we shall see presently, however, the cultic phenomenon of shamanism is not dependent upon the form of religion; shamanistic practices are carried on within the framework of quite heterogeneous religious world views. Shamanistic formulas and techniques, though, are often uniform and parallel to each other, even to minute detail; it seems permissible, therefore, to assume historical ties between the various areas of distribution.

As in every instance of cultural diffusion, many factors have determined the spreading of shamanism. The particular psychic predisposition which shamanistic practices require makes it very likely that shamanism must be counted among the specific cultural forms which Ruth Benedict has described as "patterns of culture." As the style of a culture is determined in some respects by temperament or personality traits which may possibly even go back to racial traits, so the diffusion of shamanistic practices will have been dependent upon just such factors. One factor, however, quite independent of any so-called ethnic character, also favors the transmittal or increasing significance of shamanism: a mood of depression, anxiety, or some form of psychological disequilibrium might engulf a people which lived in an immitigable historical situation or in an environment that weighs on the spirit, such as the desert or the Arctic. In such circumstances, shamanistic practices show themselves particularly suited to give a feeling of deliverance from unpleasantness. It is hard to say to what extent such environmental factors have contributed to the origin of shamanism. It is certainly an oversimplification to trace it exclusively to Arctic hysteria, as many recent authors have done (cf. Ohlmarks, pp. 19 ff.).

Rasmussen (1929: 127 ff.) gives an account of a shamanistic séance which is usually held at the occasion of impending famine or at other moments of distress. In its closing phase the shaman, having returned from the nether world, demands public confession of any breach of taboo and, if necessary, brings pressure to bear by insistent and ruthless questioning. The mood of imminent doom gives way to a pervasive feeling of deliverance and renewed confidence.

Many accounts stress this social function of the shaman; it cannot be doubted that the psychic experience which frees the community of its anxiety constitutes an essential part of shamanism. It is no accident, therefore, that the office of the shaman is, as a rule, not hereditary. It draws on manifest abilities of specially endowed personalities which must be developed in an apprenticeship. The shaman heals sickness, prevents disease, prophesies; he acts in situations, then, in which man is in particular need of deliverance in the most concrete and direct sense.

1. CURING BY COMBAT

We have many excellent and detailed accounts and shall let them speak for themselves. Here we only want to make note of a few characteristics, and since we do not aim at completeness in their distribution, we limit ourselves to a few instances.

The entire spiritual culture and within it especially the activities of the shaman are graphically described for the Taulipang, a Carib tribe which inhabits the region of the Roroima in northern South America (Koch-Grünberg). The Taulipang are forest cultivators, though hunting and fishing are economically important. The importance is not only economic. Koch-Grünberg's description leaves the impression that their mental life is very much governed by concerns which belong to the sphere of hunting and fishing. This is true, above all, of the significance which is credited to spirit-beings which belong to the "Master of the animals" category (cf. chap. vi, sec. 1). There are a great number of these, some of them quite outstanding. Supreme is Keyeme, the "Father of all animals," especially of the aquatic birds that are his grandchildren. "He is like a man but, when he puts on his many-colored skin, he is a great water snake. . . ." Next to him there are Rato, the "Father of all fish," who is also called "Water Father," and his spouse, whose name is also Rato and who is called "Water Mother" (Koch-Grünberg, *Roroima:* III, 176 ff.).

If we retain the name "spirits" for these beings, we do so for the sake of simplicity. We must, however, keep in mind the vagueness of the term. The same may be said of "soul." We hear, for example, of the "soul" of the shaman which sets out on a journey into the beyond while his body remains behind, though

the nature of this soul is not precisely defined. Among the Taulipang in particular, ideas of this so-called soul and the souls of the
deceased are evidently linked closely with those of the spirits.
The name "Mauari" is given to the more important spirits, to the
"Masters of the animals," as well as to all other spirits, especially the souls of departed medicine men, to all sorts of "helper
spirits," and to the souls of the departed in the land of the dead.
The soul which may dissociate itself from the living body has a
human appearance to the degree that it may be confused with a
person or may, at least, be regarded a complete person. In the
same way, the idea of the souls in the realm of the dead is more
concrete than ours: not only do the dead eat and drink, they also
procreate, the women bear children, and all may die again (*ibid.*:
III, 170 ff.). It is the typically monistic concept of life which
we find among the archaic cultivators, although the Taulipang—
as a Carib tribe—largely belong to the culture of the more recent
cultivators. In the last part of this book the "soul" and "spirit"
concepts will be subjected to more specific analysis; for the present we only want to caution against equating them with our ideas.

The healing ceremony carried out by a Taulipang shaman takes
a course typical of many shamanistic practices. In the completely
darkened hut the patient lies in his hammock; the shaman sits beside him on a low stool carved in the shape of an animal. In his
right hand he holds a bundle of branches with fresh leaves which
here takes the place of the rattle customarily used by Indians.
Chanting monotonously, he rhythmically slaps the ground with
the branches. He forcefully draws on a long cigar and then, puff-
ing noisily, blows the smoke over the ailing part of the patient's
body. Choking and rasping, he drinks the tobacco juices, an
important narcotic, until his "soul" has left his body and has
ascended to the realm of the spirits, thought to be in the mountains, and summons a helper spirit, often a deceased shaman.
Then, through ventriloquism and incredible variations of voice,
he relates his experiences to his audience. Hoarsely and savagely
the summoned helper spirit speaks through him; he has brought
his dog, a jaguar, and we hear him growl. By and by, more
spirits form and make their presence known in the darkness
through many voices; among them are the "Master of the animals" and the "Water Mother." The spirits speak with one
another and those present speak to the spirits, put questions to

them, and receive cryptic answers. A special kind of spirits is the *ayug*, whose nature unfortunately never becomes quite clear; in any event, they are connected with certain trees from which remedies are obtained. They are considered most powerful helpers. "Water Mother" herself flees before one of these *ayug* as he triumphantly boasts and the audience laughs loudly (*ibid.*: III, 190 ff.).

Thus, a very abbreviated description of the externals. Koch-Grünberg is convinced that the shaman's activities exert a strongly suggestive influence on the patient. He mentions (*ibid.*: 200) that an eyewitness to such a treatment, Im Thurn, himself fell into a stupor after a short while so that he no longer was in control of his will and lost all recollection.

It is natural that a person gifted with such extraordinary capabilities, acknowledged by himself and his fellow tribesmen, should attain a prominent place in the community. He can travel to the beyond, into the land of the supernaturals, can give them commands, can transform himself into a jaguar, a tapir, or a king-vulture, by putting on the proper "garment"; after his death he does not go to the realm of the common mortals but remains forever in the mountain region of the "spirits." He is omniscient (Roth [p. 343] was told by a shaman: "I know all things"); he can correctly interpret his own dreams and those of others; and he knows the tribal myths better than anyone else. All this enables him to be the spiritual, and not rarely also the political, leader of his people.

His extraordinary abilities correspond to the rigor of his training which sometimes takes up to twenty-five years. He must pass unbelievably strenuous ordeals: long periods of solitude and what seem like incredibly protracted periods of fasting and physical torment. There is no doubt that these are more than mere psychological techniques for inducing mental concentration and that every single ordeal has a mystic prototype, as reported to us in many instances.

In Koch-Grünberg's account we are especially interested in a statement by which a shaman described the deeper meaning of a curing ceremony (*Roroima*: III, 211 ff.). A hostile "spirit," possessing appropriate "weapons," is to blame for the sickness. Treatment is a robust struggle in the realm of the spiritual between the shaman and his adversary. To be victorious in any combat, one must be the stronger and possess better weapons and auxiliaries than the opponent. All this is enacted graphically and realistically. By means of a ladder, the shaman must ascend to the house of the "spirits." He makes the ladder by cutting a few sections from a liana which he eats, finely ground and mixed with water, until he vomits. (The liana as a ladder to the sky is a frequent motif among the mythic ideas of the Taulipang. According to one myth, the moon is said to have climbed a liana to assume his place in the sky.) The first struggle is over this ladder. The hostile spirit, who also comes to the land of the spirits (usually the "soul" of a living, evil shaman of an alien or hostile tribe), tries to cut it down so that the benevolent shaman cannot return. The shaman's helper spirits—especially the *ayug,* the "spirits" of the "curative" trees—prevent this. However, these helper spirits come into operation only when the shaman is actually stronger than his adversary. If they see that the balance of power is reversed, they may even turn against the shaman and kill his "spirit." In general, however, the opponent is considered to be weaker from the start.

The duel begins with a boasting contest in which each shows the other his "weapons." They consist of various kinds of tobacco, certain crystals that are called the "arrows" of the helper spirits, and *all the leaves which the witch doctors use in their cures, from the very thinnest to the thickest.* Thus it becomes evident that the benevolent shaman has far more and far better "weapons" than his opponent. Then begins the dramatic combat, involving all kinds of transformations on the part of both adversaries; it ends in a victory of the benevolent shaman who kills his foe. In consequence of this, the living person who is associated with the "evil spirit" will also die unless he manages to save himself with appropriate "weapons."

The events in the "land of the spirits," as the shaman "acts them out," are vividly experienced by the audience. *The whole ceremony is a drama* which stereotypically presents events relative to the nature and cure of the sickness. *To this extent, shamanistic séances are not different from most other religious ceremonies,* which also are *dramatic representations,* usually of primeval events.

In still another respect shamanism and other religious cults arise from the same background: *Phenomena of this world that are ascertainable facts are regarded as parallels of spiritual proc-esses met on a distinct level of experience.* Puberty is regarded not only as a biological manifestation but as a spiritual process by which mortality and propagation are understood as a unity. Among the Australians this is clearly expressed. Pregnancy is not viewed as a biological consequence; of greatest significance is the spiritual process, the "finding of the spirit-child" by the father and its entry into the mother's body (cf. chap. i, sec. 4). In the same manner, the Taulipang do not see disease as a process that takes place in the organic sphere. Essential is the spiritual parallelism seen here in a duel between *spiritual forces* in which medicinal plants make up the curative armament of the shaman. But even they are not merely vegetal substance; they have spirit-ual doubles of the order of the *ayug*. "If a man allows a fish to rot, they will shoot arrows at him so that he falls ill and has a fever. He does not notice the shot. Only when he returns home he feels pain in his belly, in his head, in his ears, in arms and legs. Only the fish that shot the little arrow knows of it" (Koch-Grünberg, *Roroima:* III, 179). We would say that the eating of spoiled fish may lead to a dangerous case of ptomaine poisoning, and this concrete fact is also expressed in the statement of the Indians. What does "the fish shot the arrow" mean? Are we justified in taking this literally, in its crudest sense, and then to deduce from it the "magical mentality" of primitive man? Is it so strange that a people which customarily hunts with bow and arrow uses the image to describe a process which can be under-stood only by way of an intellectual detour? In order not to an-ticipate, we will point out only that the helper spirits, too—es-pecially the *ayug* of the medicinal trees—have such "arrows." But let us emphasize that all the leaves employed in the cures likewise are counted among the "weapons" of the shaman, for we shall return to this fact and to the primitive view of the nature of sickness (cf. chap. xvi, sec. 3).

Koch-Grünberg's account has clarified the special physiognomy of shamanistic practice. Most of its traits recur in numerous re-ports about other peoples: the higher social position of the sha-man; his strenuous apprenticeship; the use of narcotics to free the shaman's "soul" from his body; his roaming in the beyond; his close contact with the "helper spirits," among which certain animals (especially large predators) take a prominent place; and many more. At the center of the described ceremony stand, however, the *idea of combat* and the test of strength between hostile powers. The shaman leads and directs those friendly to the patient and his immediate community, while the opponents intrude from without, as evidenced by the sickness. Even though the duel is fought on a spiritual level, it is still closely tied to the life of man. The hostile "spirit" is commonly said to belong to an "alien" shaman. It all gives the impression of combat between two groups of men in which each side is joined by its own friends. Throughout the description we feel that the thought of the people is completely dominated by a dichotomy in which men, animals, plants, and all things confront each other either as friends or foes. Anything alien is prima facie hostile; all that is familiar and of one's own environment is friend.

Koch-Grünberg (*Roroima:* III, 216 ff.) clarifies *kanaime,* a concept which subsumes everything alien and evil and is known to almost all Guayana tribes. All nearby hostile tribes are *kanaime.* "It is the name one tribe calls any other tribe. . . . Even close linguistic relationship does not protect against this aspersion." The shamanistic ceremonial clearly shows this to be rooted in the world order rather than in prosaic human enmity. One is reminded of Zarathustra's teachings of the struggle of good against evil in which all things of this world are put in one category or the other. Without a doubt, we are dealing here with an older form of the dualistic interpretation of reality, where the place of good and evil is taken by the much more pragmatic distinction between friend and foe, the favorable and the unfavorable, but which is already accepted as the spiritual primal cause of the "Just-So" of the world.

We shall see that shamanistic ceremonial is not always enacted against a dualistic background. The ceremony, as described, had all the aspects of very real combat *in which divine figures seem to play no part,* unless we concede divine qualities to some of the numerous "spirits." This, however, cannot be found in Koch-Grünberg's description. The great personages of Taulipang mythology do not appear in shamanistic practices, with the single exception of "Water Mother" who shows up among the spirits summoned by the shamans. "Water Mother," however, seems to belong to the divine "Masters" which no longer dominate belief in this culture stratum and persist only as "spirit" survivals. We see from this instance, as from the Sedna myth of the Eskimo, that this class of divine beings does not—or not any longer—stand in high regard; as a matter of fact, the Taulipang characterize most deities of this kind as evil, without giving any evidence for the accusation (cf. chap. xvi, sec. 5).

2. TRANSMISSION OF DIVINE RECOMPENSE

Although the course of external events may be similar, shamanistic ceremonies differ in spiritual background for each people. Among the Taulipang no connection could be established between shamans and divine powers, though in other forms of shamanism such a connection could be of central importance. As a brief example, I cite Petrullo's (1939) account of the Yaruro, a declining ethnic remnant that lives on one of the small tributaries of the Orinoco in southern Venezuela. The group visited by Petrullo comprises only 150 people who eke out an existence as other nomads do, living on fish, crocodiles, and turtles, but also by hunting on land and by collecting plants and wild honey.

Their meager creation myths revolve about Kuma, a female supreme deity. Besides, there are the divine serpent and jaguar, and an anthropomorphous goddess, Hatchawa, who called man forth from a cave. The shaman is the political head of a group that forms an economic unit. In the face of rapidly approaching extinction, the Yaruro are comforted by the idea that Kuma will take them into her realm where, as chosen people, they will have a far better life than their mortal enemies, the so-called *Racionales,* peoples of mixed origin that inhabit the llanos of the Orinoco. Kuma's realm is not accurately defined. On the one hand, it is thought to be in the sky; then, again, it is thought to lie in the west, probably below the horizon, from where a mysterious light occasionally emanates which the Yaruro value as a comforting message from Kuma.

While Koch-Grünberg described only curing ceremonies but emphasized that shamans are also prophets, seers, and dream interpreters, Petrullo reports only ceremonies in which the shaman appears as a herald of divine messages. The Yaruro shaman does not go to some realm of the spirits but directly to Kuma's land, speeded by the consumption of enormous quantities of cigars and cigarettes; ritual smoking plays an important role, as in the

Americas generally. Having arrived in the land of the goddess, he meets the deities of the primal past one by one, and, usually last of all, Kuma herself. Through the shaman, they speak to the assemblage; his act consists in versification and the composing of songs which he will present in astonishingly large numbers (up to 6,000) since the séance lasts through the night.

The style of poetry and composition, as well as the thought content, is always of the same type, though slightly varied. Its principal content is the prophecy that the deities love their people, the Yaruro, and that each member of the tribe will be well taken care of when, after death, he comes to Kuma's land. Even the outsider Petrullo—who apparently managed the difficult task of establishing a bond of friendship with so shy a people of so archaic a culture style—was included in the prophecy. Kuma greeted him through the intermediary, the shaman:

Greetings, man, greetings! Your wife is waiting. She is not dead, nor is she sick, but she is thinking that her husband has been away so long perhaps he is dead. . . . But it is good that he is with me [Kuma speaking] and with my people. He is a good man. He gives me a cigar. I shall give him a horse when he is born again in my [Kuma] land. I shall give him much silver [then] when he is born again in Kuma land. . . . I love him, the good man, and I shall love him in my land. . . . In the other land, my land, he gave me drink like you my people. Like you my people, everyone will come to my land, the Yaruro land [Petrullo, p. 252].

This prophecy is only for consolation. The shaman has, here at least, not developed any "second sight"; Petrullo was not even married but had said that he was for the sake of simplifying matters, a white lie which the shaman failed to discover.

The souls of the deceased who already are in Kuma's land avail themselves of the shaman to speak to their relatives. These, in turn, embrace the shaman in the conviction of embracing their departed relative; the shaman is given a cigar or the like which is thereby given to the deceased. On the following day, the shaman knows nothing of his experiences. In his own eyes he has been a medium only, and everyone tries to describe to him in detail what had happened during the night.

Here, then, we have a shamanistic ceremony in which no mention is made of combat; emphasis is on the divine figures. It is also said of Kuma that in her land there is a single, specially large specimen of every animal and plant species (Petrullo, p. 237); we have already encountered a similar form of this motif as a characteristic mark of the "Master of the animals."

Conceivably, the absence of combat might be due to the fact that Yaruro séances deal with prophecy and not with curing. Yet, we have a sufficient number of accounts of other peoples where the séance does not pertain to curing but where the contents of the ceremony agree fully with the one described. Röder (pp. 49 ff.) reports a ceremony (from Ceram) in which a shaman undertakes a journey to the heavens in order to receive a bowl of water from the deity that rules in the ninth, highest, heaven; in the meanwhile the assemblage apprehensively waits to learn whether or not the shaman receives the beneficent water.

Journeys to the heavens to seek out the deity, to request rewards in a most general sense, or to ask for curatives, have a wide distribution. Eliade (*Schamanismus:* 465) regards this as the true and genuine practice and sees other forms, such as journeys to the underworld, as secondary developments. We can add a few arguments that favor this view, though other facts speak against the priority of the celestial journey. Indonesian shamanism—at least, in some regions—seems to support Eliade's view; this cultural phenomenon is usually found where the concept of a sky deity is prominent; it is absent where there is little or no belief in a celestial deity.

Then there are examples in which the mythic rationale gives clear indications of the celestial journey. Nimuendaju (1914: 327) reports of the Apapocuva of southern Brazil that the son of the creator-god had invented shamanistic practices so that he could communicate with his father who had removed himself to the "farthest reaches of eternal darkness"; as a typical otiose creator- and sky-god he no longer maintains any connection with man. In this instance, the mythic explanation of the origin of shamanism is so closely linked with the dominant religious concepts that an original unity seems highly probable.

We have stressed the amythical nature of the sky-god. If we were to assume that this idea of God was dominant at a very early time, we would also have to assume the absence of cults, for cults are based on the mythic world view. Assuming this, however, the nature of shamanism would lend a great deal of probability to the priority of the celestial journey, for the lack of communal cults could allow free reign to many divinely inspired personages.

There is another argument in favor of Eliade's contention. The shaman's journey to the subterranean regions of the dead often serves the same end as the celestial journey: the transmittal of a boon. However, the realm of the dead is a place of good fortune only because it is the home of the deity (cf. chap. xiv, sec. 2). We have already shown this deity to be a special kind, a Dema-deity. We have characterized the Dema-deity as effective in primeval times but now aloof. This aspect of the God-concept might be adduced as a negation of shamanistic activity.

On the other hand, the realm of the dead is frequently believed to be a place of a better life, quite aside from shamanistic considerations; descriptions of a shaman's journey into the beyond— as, for instance, the sixteenth canto of the Kalevala—seem by no means contrived. In any case, the fact remains that shamanistic activities are associated with many varied conceptions but that no single one deserves to be called the one and only true one. Thus we leave unanswered the question of priority and also the question of historical origins. Some peoples may possess only the external forms of shamanistic techniques, elaborated along the lines of the dominant world view. A people not given to ideas of a celestial God will not know of a shaman's celestial journey. Yet there are cases in which the shaman may employ a variety of forms, if different world views have contributed to the structure of his culture. The remarkably complex Eskimo culture is a good example of such coexistence of heterogeneous shamanistic forms. The shaman may travel to the heavens, as he may also travel to the underworld, especially to Sedna. We also encounter the combat between good and evil, without the participation of divine beings, which was so significant in Taulipang shamanism.

Rasmussen (1929: 43) describes such a scene which he saw among the Iglulik Eskimo: One evening, a small, weeping boy came running into the hut without anyone knowing why the child cried. A shaman who happened to be present jumped from his seat and ran excitedly out of the hut. After about half an hour he returned, breathless, with torn clothing, and covered with blood. He declared that the boy had been attacked by an evil spirit whom he had just conquered in terrifying battle. Though it could be easily guessed that the shaman had torn his own clothes and smeared himself with the seal blood stored in front of the hut, the assembled Eskimos doubted neither the reality of the battle nor that the shaman had saved the boy's life. Rasmussen, who came to know this shaman well, is even convinced that he—despite his gross deceptions—had actually in cold and darkness gone through an imaginary combat with spirits.

In one version of a shaman's journey to Sedna the combat motif stands out. (It will be remembered that we have viewed Sedna [chap. vi, sec. 2] as a blend of "Master of the animals" and Dema-deity.) The shaman must go so far as to threaten the goddess with a stick or even, if the need arises, to thrash her until she releases a soul which she had stolen (Rasmussen, 1929: 101). On the one hand, this shows Sedna already to have lost the aura of divinity, since otherwise such disrespect exercised in the procurement of favors—quite unusual among primitive peoples—would hardly be thinkable. On the other hand, it gives spontaneous expression to the idea of combat between the antagonistic forces of this world, the "spirits."

3. SHAMANISM AS A PHASE OF APPLICATION

If we are to assume a single origin of shamanism, we seem to imply that it appeared in only one of its variant forms at the place of its origin. This primary form must have conformed to the formulations of a certain religious world view. This primary situation, however, we can hardly reconstruct at the hand of present-day conditions. It so happens that the activity of the shaman is "application" and must have been that from the start, since its very essence is application. There is no shaman that does not wish to confer benefits or ward off evil. The basis is his special ability, which he can exercise only within the framework of notions of the where and the how of attaining the good or warding off the evil. These, however, must always be part of a people's world view, quite independent of the existence or absence of shamanism.

To evaluate shamanistic activities, we must turn our attention to two basic questions. First, there is special ability. What enables some men to be more effective transmitters of divine bounty than others? Are the shaman's outstanding abilities only deceitful or are they real? This is the principal question concerning the nature of true magic. We shall deal with it in the next section. Second, there are the concepts of which the shaman makes use. Here our examples indicated two distinct complexes: first, the struggle between friendly and hostile powers, usually without divine participation; then, the shaman's journey to the land of the deity to receive the bounty directly and transmit it to his people. The principle is not affected by the direction of the journey, whether it leads to the heavens or the nether world. In either case the goal is the same: to supplicate or to coerce the deity into conferring benefits. The grander aspects of religiosity are revealed in those forms of religious expression which see in the deity more than mankind's benefactor. The divine is seen in its undiminished grandeur, and only secondary, all-too-human ideas, oriented toward practicality, look to it with expectation of philanthropy. The expectation of good fortune and salvation is doubtless a natural quality of man; its penetration into the religious, originally only cognitive, world view is a first step toward an inversion of genuinely religious behavior: the universal wish to receive divine bounty misleads to the assumption that it is the result of ritual performance.

In this context we shall take up a subsidiary question: can a shaman properly be called a priest? The answer sheds some more light on shamanistic activities. If we take the priest as leader of a community that unites for devotional activities, then the shaman could not be a priest for the simple reasons that neither his actions nor the sentiments of his community are "devout." Piety is a reminiscing about divine actions and deeds; pious works are faithful conformance to the divine world order; salvation and bounty are encompassed as a part of true humanity. If, however, the benefits are expected as a consequence of pious acts, then the ceremonial leader becomes a go-between. In this respect only do shaman and priest resemble each other and for no other reason, in my opinion, have shamans been regarded as priests. We shall come to know primitive peoples that make a sharp distinction.

The appellation of priest does not apply to the shaman in his purely combative role. What is the verity that underlies the curing ceremonial of the Taulipang? We have already seen that the activities of the shaman are not linked to the workings of divine powers; figures of the order of the "Masters" no longer have divine character but already have degenerated into spirits. Shamanistic activity is rooted in the recognition that the world reveals itself in two aspects, one benevolent, the other hostile. Once seen from this point of view, everything resolves into a struggle, into a friend-and-foe relationship. This form of shamanism, totally given over to the idea of struggle, is one of the most vivid pieces of evidence. Nothing among the Taulipang—or among many other peoples—suggests that the friend-foe relationship among all things would have been incorporated into the religious world view. Obviously, it is a "Just-So" which is not referred to divine activity. The hostility indicated by the *kanaime* concept can take on very realistic forms as, for instance, wars between populations. But it is more than that, and, especially, it is of a different order. *Kanaime* describes the hostility between all things; mainly, however, it means the invisible spiritual forces which stand in inimical opposition to each other. Sickness, especially, comes under this. It is an understandable view since it is suggested by the human element. The thought fit the opposing natures of all things and probably even led to some cultural advances; we will show this in our later discussion of disease and medicinal plants. However, there is no conception of the actual nature of the phenomena; a statement about the *nature* of mosquitoes, for instance, will not begin with the question of whether they are friendly or hostile toward man. Therefore, the shaman, in interfering with the conflict between things and processes, should not be viewed as a priest, since the divine order is not involved.

There is another indispensable cognitive insight that forms one of the roots of shamanism: psychophysical dualism. We have seen it in the ceremonial of the Taulipang and before that, even outside the framework of shamanism, among the Northwest Australians, i.e., in the notion of "spirit-children" (chap. v, sec. 1). There can be no doubt that the dichotomy was arrived at independently of shamanistic techniques, for we find it expressed in the most heterogeneous cultural contexts. But, wherever shamanistic practice occurs, it is tied to this dualism; the ability of the shaman's "soul" to separate from his body would bear this out.

Dualistic division into knowable and discrete, though parallel, spiritual processes is widely distributed but by no means universal among primitive peoples. In the stratum of the archaic cultivators, for instance, we have a thoroughly monistic idea of life (cf. chap. xiv, sec. 3). But since shamanism is connected by technique and nature with the dualistic view, it is only natural that it should be rare among archaic cultivators. W. Schmidt (IX, p. 217) agrees with us on a major point: shamanism avails itself not only of the religious conception of the world but also, secondarily, of genuine religious cult activities; he disagrees, however, with respect to the relationship of shamanism to root-crop cultures. He and others of the "Viennese School" often expressed the conviction that any trait that does not belong to the High God religion may not be ascribed to the so-called *Urkulturen* (primal cultures) but arose only in later epochs, as for instance in the culture of the root-crop cultivators. In many cases this undoubtedly is so, as for example in head-hunting, cannibalism, or human sacrifice. In my opinion, the data now under discussion seem to make it impossible to "blame" shamanism on the archaic cultivators. We may also object that the will and power aspect that is part of all shamanisms and true coercive magic will not properly fit the religious mentality of the cultivators.

There are other conceptions which are of significance. We must, for instance, inquire into the nature of the "spirits" against which the battles are fought. This will be dealt with separately later. We shall then also delve into the nature of the medicinal plant and primitive man's attitude toward disease (cf. chap. xvi, secs. 2 and 3), although all three questions can hardly be detached from shamanistic activities. Here we will anticipate only that the answers given by primitive man are quite sensible and contain a realization of reality which could not be gained by any other form of cognition.

4. THE NATURE OF GENUINE MAGIC

We shall now discuss the shaman's special abilities and that particular something which enables one man to transmit divine beneficence to a degree greater than another. We may confidently eliminate the accusation that the claims to special abilities are no more than lies, at least where the origin of the phenomenon is concerned and even if many shamans may be shown to be liars. Liars are often gifted with imagination but are not so creative that they can produce truly new phenomena and deep beliefs; they usually make use of what exists.

As we have seen, all shamanistic practices are based on psychophysical dualism, although the concept of spirit-beings arose independently of shamanism. Shamanism adds a concept which gives it its specific stamp: man, as a spiritual being and as *a link in the chain of spiritual events* which parallel the sensory, perceptual processes, is capable of *affecting these spiritual events through psychic concentration*. All shamanistic activity that has not degenerated to sleight-of-hand trickery contains this characteristic. In the eyes of the believers, the shaman can cause sickness or death, not by physical action, but by controlling the parallel spiritual processes. By the same means he can heal sickness, divine future happenings already outlined in the spiritual sphere, or see realities beyond common experience.

There can be no doubt that man actually possesses such abilities. The possibility that suggestion can influence the course of events would alone make it certain that psychic concentration can operate in the absence of direct physical action. Its efficacy, in general as well as in particular, cannot be denied in certain healing practices. This, however, answers the most important question as to the possibility. Whether all the effects claimed by the shamans are based on suggestion can be neither affirmed nor denied; nor does this matter very much. That many of the shamans' assertions are based on real experiences, that there is much in the psychic sphere about which science can tell us little, of this I feel a personal certainty, for which I do not feel obliged to plead guilty to occultism. To the contrary, I have a deep aversion to the primitive magic which holds wide circles of our Western community enthralled. When we go by our own experience, it matters little how often accident confirms prophecies and visions; decisive is a *sense of the self-evident* which inheres in certain psychic experiences.

For our purposes it matters only that there is the possibility of exerting influence through purely psychic processes; where the line is drawn is immaterial. If the shamans, in their claims, should have exceeded the set limits, it would be no fundamental objection to our interpretation. Just as countless members of our own cultural community exceed it considerably, so may shamans in primitive cultures.

The only authority to judge the true ability of any personality is the "congregation," which either believes or does not believe. A "living" cultural community is distinguished from a "petrified" one by the presence of a sufficiently large number of members who will discuss the spiritual foundation of their culture creatively and critically and who possess the ability of differentiating between true greatness of ideas and imitation. The more "primitive" a community (in the only admissible sense of the word), the easier it is for the ignorant to have their pretended abilities believed. Primitive cultures predominantly count among the "petrified"—in contrast to our own, at present still "living" culture—but we have sufficiently credible reports to show that "primitives" well know how to tell the genuine from the spurious.

Shamanism, as we have pointed out, is connected with religious forms of expression not only through utilization of concepts of established reality. Shamanism actually resembles them through enactment of concepts taken from the religious world view. In dramatic representations we saw the criterion of cultic activities. Yet a wide gap separates shamanistic practices from religious cult by the very fact that *an individual takes the place of the community*—the community which would recall its essential humanity in joint activity. If we have not decided the position of shamanism in the history of culture before, let us now touch upon the much discussed relationship between genuine magic and religion.

It seems impossible to us that a religious world view—a part of every genuine form of religion—can be derived from the mental attitude that lies at the root of all forms of genuine magic. Conversely, true forms of religion can exist without any magical concomitants. That magic is secondary follows from the fact that it always makes use of the religious world view. We are not implying, however, that in the beginning there was an Age of Religion followed by an Age of Magic, as maintained in the hypothesis of primal monotheism; we are dealing with totally different attitudes of mind. Why should man not have possessed the aptitude for both from the very beginning? Volitional influencing of the environment presupposes a cognition of this environment. In early human history the cognition was predominantly religious. Magic is related to the religious world view, as applied physics is related to theoretical physics; nothing prevents a great technician from being a great theoretician also. This analogy naturally applies only in a very general sense; *it should not be supposed to prove, for instance, that the shaman is the spiritual precursor of the technician,* oriented toward the rationalistic evaluation of religious insights.

The secondary nature of magic—as seen from the vantage point of true religion—has put the "sorcerer-priest" in an ambiguous light even among primitive peoples. Much as his services are in demand when misery and sickness turn all thoughts toward help that can be expected to come only from the deity, still we have much evidence that a sense of tact and style draws a sharp line between ceremonies related to the religious world view and the "practical" activities of the shaman. Among the subject peoples in the Barotse kingdom, for example, the sorcerer-priest (called Nganga) is healer, prophet, and oracle. He has no function whatever in the purely religious ceremonies, such as puberty or funerary rites. There he gives way to others, usually to hereditary priestly officiants. The sharp separation between the "sorcerers" and the usually hereditary priesthood, where communal cults are involved, is found among many African peoples (cf. Friedrich, 1939: 174 ff.) and on other continents also. Mills (1926: 244) stresses that medicine men must not be confused with priests, since their tasks and proficiencies are completely distinct. Medicine men ascertain the proper time and place, but ceremony and sacrifice are carried out by the priests. The only ceremony which the medicine man—and only he—can perform is the journey to the beyond. The priests are part of the normal religious life of the community, the medicine men part of the extraordinary. The Gilyak of the Amur region also differentiate clearly between cults proper and shamanistic ceremonies. Schrennck (p. 722) reports that whenever the Gilyak celebrate the bear festival—their characteristic cultic feast—shamans may not be active within the homestead. "This may be due to the fact that the art of the shaman, uncanny in the eyes of the Gilyak, might repress the festive mood and might, because of its power over the spirit world and human soul, spread confusion and distress among the participants."

Here we have the basic difference between shamanistic practice and solemn cult. Shamanism—as we encounter it today—is inseparable from acts of volition, which in extreme forms do not even hesitate to make the deity subservient to human will. This is "genuine magic"; through it, shamanism attains its exceptional position. The religious world view finds its outlets at all times solely in cognition, imitation, and re-enactment. Genuine magic was aware of man's ability to interfere at will with mental processes. If it was natural that man made use of this ability, especially to his own benefit, then it was equally natural that the true and original religious sense would view the use with reservation and awe.

Contemplative mysticism no less than ecstatic trance has produced a great number of psychotechnical expedients to facilitate the concentration of will power. Darkness, monotonous chanting, rhythmical drumming, hours of inertia, solitude, fasting, narcotics of all kinds, physical fatigue, and dancing—all these are expedients of undoubted efficacy. None of them, however, can substitute for the strong-willed and spiritually susceptible personality which forms the prerequisite of all genuine magic. The employment of the techniques alone presupposes such personalities and, as it were, constitutes a selection of those who are "called." It is therefore not astonishing that, according to most accounts, shamans are indeed strong personalities. If only the shaman has been treated here as a true and real magician, we must recall that the word *shaman* has been used in a most general sense. Our shaman is very much like that personage who is called "sorcerer" or "medicine man" in most accounts. In our view, his effectiveness is based on specific psychic capabilities which can, of course, take many forms according to his greater or lesser personal commitment. Practices, however, which make reference to existing rites or superficially imitate rites but actually are only incomprehensible vestiges in the form of superstitious activities—such practices cannot be called magic.

5. BLACK MAGIC

Shamanism, then, is not a form of religion; it does not encompass a uniform image of the world composed of all those phenomena which, at one specific historical epoch, were understood to be a manifestation of divine powers. Rather, shamanistic activities are phenomena arising within culture history; their dissemination was furthered or hindered by ethno-psychological factors and by the historical situation; they are applicable to the respective religious forms of expression. The shaman can journey to a High God residing in the heavens or to subterranean Dema-deities, and he can stage a battle between benevolent and hostile forces.

The latter form appears often in contexts that have been treated separately from other shamanistic practices. Ethnological literature usually differentiates between white and black magic depending on its aim, whether it is carried out to help or to harm man. On the other hand, we emphasized the separation of genuine magic from all those phenomena which, in our opinion, are wrongly called magic. We have illustrated genuine magic through the prominent figure of the shaman and have restricted its meaning to those phenomena for which man possesses certain aptitudes and of which he may make conscious use to influence the course of real events. Such genuine magic must be assumed to exist when the possibility of suggestion wherever man or animals are introduced into a chain of events is admitted. The extent to which the influencing of reality may transcend psychic suggestion may be left to individual preference; it produces no fundamental changes.

Magic of this kind can, of course, begin as intent to inflict harm as easily as an effort to heal the sick; to this extent we need not discuss black magic. Its manifestations offer no insights which cannot be found in the sphere of white magic. If we consider it here nonetheless, it is done chiefly out of interest in the behavior of the human community.

In general, harmful magic is considered unethical, both as a matter of attitude and as interference with interpersonal relationships. This evaluation agrees with the views of primitive peoples, who consider such uses of magic a serious crime against the community. Science would have it that they overestimate the capabilities of the black magician exactly as the instigators of the witch trials in the West overrated the power of witches only a few centuries ago. In this respect, again, we shall never find agreement between the two extremes: How much or how little credit should be conceded to the efficacy of magic? Furthermore, the boundaries between black and white magic are probably not static. They oscillate not only in the individual but also in ac-

cordance with the relative historical situation of a people. Preoccupation with the idea of eternal bliss in the realm of the deity
as we found it among the Yaruro (cf. chap. xi, sec. 2) would, in
this form, hardly be possible in a "vigorous" people. In the over-
all view—though exceptions certainly exist—primitive peoples
must be granted greater psychical lability and therefore greater
susceptibility to genuine magic processes.

It will still be shown (chap. xii, sec. 3) that those spells to
which we denied the predicate magical because of their originally
mythic properties were "applied" in both ways. Since the myth
reported the origination of a disease as well as its cure in primal
times, words could "bewitch," bring about sickness, and effect a
cure. The "application" of mythic values of spells to "magical"
purposes is apparently not subject to religious-ethical considerations. To the extent that the world is divided into friendly and
hostile spheres, there exists a natural need to bring harm to the
enemy and help to the friend. Hostile acts, with the approval of
the community, are to be directed against the world at large as it
lies outside the communal boundaries. We have already spoken
of the *kanaime* of the Indians of Guayana (chap. xi, sec. 1), and
the Bakuena rainmaker of whom Dr. Livingstone told (chap. i,
sec. 2). He said: "We never love each other. Other tribes cast
spells around our land to hinder the rain so that we will be scattered by hunger and will have to go to them to increase their
power" (Livingstone, I, 31).

We could quote an infinite number of examples of such hostile
feeling toward all outsiders. In fairness, however, we should also
have to mention the many forms of politeness shown to strangers,
especially the hospitality which characterizes even the most
archaic peoples. Such behaviors probably would not have arisen
were it not for that primal consciousness of antagonism and hostility. A criminal in the full sense is anyone who directs his knowledge and gift of black magic against members of his own group.
The opinion seems unanimous that there can be no greater crime
than such abuse of magical powers. One who, from passion or
sheer pugnacity, has killed a member of his own tribe, is almost
invariably judged far more leniently than one who is suspected
of a misuse of magical abilities.

In contrast to the theory of magic, we have started from the
idea that magic did not arise from intellectual error. We hold

that there are genuinely magical phenomena and that cultural configurations attributed to magic are thereby based on a true perception of reality—like everything that is factual in human history. Here we would have to answer the question whether witches and black magicians really do exist. According to customary usage, we would deny it. If someone were to point out some person, some old woman, for instance, as a witch, we would reject this as a superstition. But, for the converse, we have a designation not connected with superstition. When someone is called a "spellbinder," when it is said "that he holds us entranced," we know instantly what is meant. Actually, though, the statement relates to something genuinely magical. There are personalities that weave such spells, and we mean what we say in a quite literal and positive sense. Why, then, should not the analogous negative statement be equally correct? Do we struggle against this only because witch trials are still too disagreeably close to our historical consciousness? If we accept the statement that someone is a witch or a sorcerer in the same sense in which we accept the parallel statement that another weaves a spell over his audience, we have no need for refutation, for we all have had ample occasion for such experience. Of course, even if we are ready to concede black magic in this sense, we cannot grant it the same measure of potency which primitive peoples find in it. Many, for instance, would trace the death of any man in the prime of life to the machinations of black magic.

Nimuendajú (1939: 13 ff.) reports such a case of the Apinayé, a tribe of eastern Brazil. An alien to the tribe was suspected of having had a hand in a noticeable increase in the number of deaths. The weary black magician learned of the intention to kill him (this is generally considered the proper punishment or defense measure) and fled to his own tribe which he was able to persuade to make war on the Apinayé. Some years later, though, he was killed by his own people, again because he was linked to several deaths in his capacity as a black magician. Thus, we at least cannot discount that there was something about the man that justified a suspicion of evil acts or evil intent even if we consider the accusation of magical killing unjustified.

Granting much of this, we must keep in mind that the primitive view of magical acts usually differs from ours by fundamentally different mythic concepts. We have seen that the ideas

which dominate the inspired magician are so completely integrated into the mythic world view that it is usually impossible to
tell what part of his activity is attributable to his special psychic
gifts and what part stems from the mythic ideology. The participants' faith lets both spheres blend into a unity, and thus the
wildest tales are reported of benevolent shamans as well as of the
practitioners of black magic. Yet, the experiential element cannot
in any way be isolated from the account.

To explicate the close bond between accounts of magical acts
and mythic conditions by an example, I return to H. Petri's data
on northwestern Australia in which we find detailed descriptions
of events and their mythic backgrounds. Powerful spirit-beings,
usually called *djanba,* are linked to black magic. They live among
neighboring tribes where they inhabit a labyrinth of underground
passages from which they emerge to kill some victim with their
bird-headed boomerang. By magical singing they separate the
flesh from the bones to consume it, for human flesh is their favor-
ite food. When they come out of the earth, they wander restless-
ly, leaving no footprints. Within them they carry a mysterious
force (*groare*) which may emerge from them as a spirally wound
thread (*Sterbende Welt:* 258 ff.).

The Australians relate several ceremonies to these not readily
understood spirit-beings. These must be considered black magic
even though the nexus between ceremonial acts and the nature of
the *djanba* becomes in no way clear. We are dealing here with
characteristically Australian ceremonies; one of them, the "killing chant," is practiced in the following way: The men who wish
to "sing an enemy to death" isolate themselves from the community at a secluded spot in the bush. There a small pit is dug in
which a fire is lit. Around the hearth are placed pieces of cork-
wood bark on which crude outlines of human figures have been
drawn. They are to represent the "enemy" (though the plurality
of images seems to break through the analogy). A lizard whose
limbs have been broken is placed on crude paintings; the participants form a circle, take blood from their forearms, let it spatter
on the lizard, and several times call out the name of the "enemy."
Then follows the chanting of very specific songs, while one man
jabs the lizard with a wooden cult implement until it is dead and
shredded. It is then thrown into the fire and everything is covered

with sand. As a result, the object of the ceremony is expected to die.

It can hardly be doubted that the most significant elements of this ceremony are of mythic and cultic origin; this may be seen especially from the fact that the natives themselves relate this to the *djanba* spirits. Petri conjectures that the *djanba* may have been culture heroes, i.e., Dema, in their land of origin. In accordance with our earlier findings, we should not call these ceremonies magical, since they are re-enactments and, thus, cults in a phase of "application." The magical elements would here only be secondary and could not be related to the origin of the custom. One feature, however, seems to me to indicate genuinely magical origin just as in shamanism: the idea of hostility and the imaginary combat with the enemy. We have seen how strongly the shaman is affected by the notion that man is threatened by adversaries that must be vanquished. Again the decisive element is not a physical hostility which can be fought out with physical weapons; rather, we are concerned with the spiritual parallel which, when acted upon by spiritual devices, will bring about concrete results. In an evil and in a benevolent sense, this is the actual root of true magic and its link to reality. Since they are psychic processes, man can insinuate himself by volitional acts. Every magician, however, who does this is a member of his cultural community besides and is swayed by all the ideas of its world view. For this reason his actions blend so well with the cultic customs.

If we are still inclined to speak of black magic, we do so because these ceremonies are unimaginable without great feats of psychical concentration. How potent the evil intent is in all this we shall leave undiscussed. According to the account, the ceremony is placed completely at the service of the spiritual effects. If they originally were true cults—which I consider probable—then they are magically "applied" in a sense quite distinct from that which we came to know in our discussion of Preuss's views. If primitive man wishes to kill with non-physical means, he can do so only by utilizing the mythic, religious concepts of the nature and cause of death. The cultic aspect of magical ceremonies is rooted in this. But the magical aspect of the ceremony is determined by the special psychic power of the true magician.

Pechuël-Loesche gives a vivid description (from the Loango

coast) of the verities which underlie the belief in black magic and which in that environment take hold even of Europeans:

About witchcraft, about the human demons and black magicians who fill all hearts with horror and awe, about their abilities and tricks, much is known though without any consensus. Doubtlessly, it is the most sinister and fearful thing to be known. . . . We may hardly doubt that there are indeed persons who regard themselves witches in the most evil sense of the word and who even acknowledge themselves as such. Their hostile intent suffices perhaps to do harm, even to kill. Evil will begets evil deeds. It works as directly as the warming rays of the sun, as the cooling breezes . . . [p. 335].

At another place Pechuël-Loesche gives us a fine description of a concrete case: A recently married man received a confidential post in a plantation and therefore moved to another village where his wife was a "stranger." In keeping with her husband's position, she lived better than the other villagers; she owned pretty dresses, lived quite comfortably, and had servants of her own. Envy and ill feeling were added to the fact that she was a "foreigner" and tension developed between her and the other women of the village. Among the "enemies" one stood out who would rather have seen her own daughter in the young woman's place. Then the young woman grew sickly. The author thinks it possible that general animosity caused her ill health. The same suspicion grew among the villagers as her condition worsened, despite the ministrations of many medicine men. Not only was the hostile attitude blamed, however; all were convinced that some individual magical act must have been performed to bring about the ruin of the young woman. The main adversary, mother of the rival, was now accused of black magic and the sorcerer-priests carried out the painful ordeal of poison to ascertain the woman's guilt or innocence (pp. 423 ff.).

These few accounts must do, for the problems of black magic do not differ from those of genuine magic. The questions which are raised are essentially the same. If magic "works," it works in either case. The use of magic does not depend on ethical considerations. Black magic is quite "legal" if directed at enemies only. Aimed at a friend, it constitutes the most grievous and antisocial of crimes. Every member of the community is involved and its very real dangers are warded off according to the laws of inter-

239

personal conduct by which other perils to communal life, such as theft or murder, are controlled. These defensive and deterrent measures are fundamentally different from the attitude which the community assumes toward offenses against religious-ethical obligations (cf. chap. ix). Neglect of religious obligations is a sacrilege, which the community will not counter with defensive measures alone. Then, human existence itself is jeopardized and expiation encompasses an enhanced awareness of the roots of man's experiential capacities. This difference in conduct, better than any other symptom, reflects the distinctness of spiritual attitudes, rooted on the one hand in religion, on the other hand in magical experiences.

12

CULT AND MAGIC

The general "expectation of a divine recompense," though not necessarily detrimental to religious experiences, has been shown (chap. iv, sec. 9) to further the degenerative process. Specific expectation tied to equally specific acts will tenaciously persist and jealously preserve every ceremonial detail long after the original meaning has been lost.

1. RAIN-MAKING CEREMONIAL

We now ask whether the hypotheses of pre-animistic magic are justified in transferring the ceremonial life of contemporary primitive peoples to the prehistoric past. Are they justified in their well-known conclusions concerning the origin of religion?

David Livingstone (I, 29 ff.) left us an account of the difficulties he encountered when a long drought was blamed on him. The Bakuena, a Bechuana tribe in South Africa, claimed that his missionary successes had paralyzed the effectiveness of the rainmaker. The Bakuena have "many medicines" to induce rain. Livingstone describes one instance in which the rain-maker chooses a particular tuberous root, pulverizes it, and gives part of it as a cold infusion to a sheep which after five minutes dies in convulsions. The rest of the root is then burned to produce a great cloud of smoke. Rising to heaven, the smoke is believed to bring rain within one or two days.

Livingstone then relates his conversation with the rain-maker, a fine refutation of the assumption that primitive man has an "undeveloped mind." The rain-maker is never at a loss for an intelligent reply; and beyond that, even in a conversation conducted by all the rules of logic, he makes his point so well that his European questioner has to surrender. He remains superior because he has a better understanding of the nature of cognition than the European, who labors under the error that his own culture has attained ultimate and irrefutable insight. The rain-maker realizes that perception is linked to a world view; what is valid for him is not unconditionally valid for the white man. He expresses this by saying that God has given to the Bechuana one single, insignificant thing of which the white man knows nothing, i.e., the knowledge of certain medicines by which he can make it rain. The Bechuana, he says, do not underrate the white man's possessions, though they do not understand them; they cannot understand the white man's books yet do not scorn them. Therefore, he feels, the white man should not scorn what little knowledge the Bechuana possess, though he knows nothing of it (pp. 31 ff.).

The ceremony described by Livingstone would usually be classified as magic, as Livingstone himself classified it. The smoke of the burning root resembles a cloud; this is a common observation. The resemblance is said to have misled the ignorant ancestors of the Bakuena that they need only make smoke to attract rain clouds. It is a clear case of imitative magic, a common argument often encountered in the literature.

But it is just as common that the greater portion of the report is disregarded. Why have there to be specific "medicines," in this instance a very particular poisonous root; and why must a sheep be killed, and in a way that is doubtless unusual and cruel? (Livingstone, unfortunately, does not tell us what becomes of the sheep.) Neither is it taken into account that the rain-maker specifically ascribes any possible success to divine powers: God is said to send the rain. All these decisive factors are disregarded by the cliché "imitative magic."

Livingstone's account is not productive and offers no conclusive data on the original meaning of the ceremony. However, if we are to proceed by a purely phenomenological method, the entire account, meager as it may be, should be considered. No doubt it would be better if we said: God sends the rain, and the rain-maker believes that he is doing something to induce God to end the drought. In no sense can we speak of coercion, for the rain-maker is quite aware of the possibility of failure. If we are to gain deeper understanding, we must ask: what makes the rain-maker believe that the poisoning of a sheep and the burning of a poisonous root are God-pleasing acts? For this question we have no answer. The rain-maker himself would probably not have been able to supply one. Neither, however, does the hypothesis of pre-animistic magic have an answer; it does not even ask the right question. Asking the right question is often more fruitful and always better than an erroneous interpretation which is not based on the totality of available data. Livingstone's scanty account was deliberately chosen because the bulk of field data at our disposal is equally deficient. Often the data will not allow us to answer even a correctly phrased question. Then we must turn to analogous cases from other reports and about other peoples. A reasonable answer based on all of the factual material can often be applied—at least as a surmise—to the people who were the first subjects of the investigation.

We possess enough accounts of rain-making ceremonies to know beyond doubt that their practitioners have clear ideas in mind when they consider certain acts of devotion necessary after a prolonged drought recalls to them that rain was first created as a consequence of a divine deed in primeval time. Stevenson's comprehensive description of a rain-making ceremonial among the Zuñi (pp. 180–204) shows with all desirable clarity that every detail in the elaborate episodes of the great dramatic performance goes back to divine primeval events related in accompanying myths. They are, therefore, not purposive means, devised to coerce the powers, but representations which are to assist recollection and reflection. Only the expected boon, in this instance the rain, lends the ceremony its pseudopurposive aspect. As with other rituals, we are justified in seeking an explanation for rain-making ceremonies primarily in mythic contexts.

If we apply the principle to Livingstone's much more meager account, understanding would have to be sought elsewhere. In describing the world view of the archaic root-crop cultivators, we stressed the great significance of ritual killing: the present condition was brought about by the original act of killing. In all killing ceremonies in which either men or animals are victims, the myth-cult context readily suggests itself.

In an analogical myth of the Khond (India), the tears of the "victim" are equated with rain (Macpherson, p. 130). Applied to Livingstone's account, this would seem to say that the killing of the sheep, disregarded by the hypothesis of pre-animistic magic—and performed in a quite extraordinary way—is in itself the central event. Furthermore, the smoke of the burned tuber can have been associated with the cloud only in an analogical, secondary way. We know of many ceremonies in which smoke, generated in particular ways, plays a major role but is unrelated to clouds or rain. Thus, the hypothesis of pre-animistic magic offers a poor explanation, even for this single characteristic and is at that so badly supported that alternative explanations can make equally strong claims.

2. FERTILITY CEREMONIES

The importance of killing in those rudimentary ceremonies which tend to be interpreted as magic is illustrated by an example reported to me during an expedition to the Molucca Island of Ceram. If a woman is barren, three pigs must be slaughtered and a piece of each pig must be placed on a plate of Chinese porcelain which, under the name of a Pusaka-piece, is used in many ceremonies. These items of trade were imported by the island peoples in very early times but are not regarded as importations; rather, they are woven into the mythology and are said to stem, as presents to mankind, from the divine beings of the primal past.

The bowls and the pieces of meat are buried while the pigs are consumed at a ceremonial feast. Later the bowls are dug up again, filled with water, and left standing during the night. On the next day the participants in the ceremony wash themselves in the water.

The significant moments of the ceremony are the killing of the pigs, the ceremonial consumption of the meat, the burying of the pieces of meat, and the ceremonial ablutions. The porcelain bowls are specifically called presents of the primeval deity in the description of the ceremony; the deity specifically prescribes the ceremonial treatment of the gift and equates it with the human genitals. According to a myth, the bowls originated from parts of the body of the slain Dema-deity in the same manner as the crop plants. They recur in many ceremonies and are closely tied to head-hunting.

In ethnology, such a ceremony is classified as fertility magic, even if nothing in it corresponds to the cloud and smoke analogy of Livingstone's account. The equation of porcelain plates and human genitals would in itself be seen as an intellectual aberration and, as to the rest, it would be felt as pointless to trace out the abstruse thoughts of primitives. But we cannot pass by the question of how man ever hit upon the idea of overcoming barrenness by such means. The only possible answer is that no one had any such idea at all at the institution of the ceremonial.

In this instance, fortunately, we are in the position to come to a fuller understanding. The essential actions are as directly related to primeval myths as we can ever hope to find. Hainuwele, the Dema-deity, was killed; her corpse was cut into pieces and buried. This act ended the primal epoch; the human condition and life as it is lived were instituted, and with it came the precious gift of procreativity and the fertility of the women. But not the desire for offspring alone "causes" the ceremony. Similar cults take place on the occasion of a death, the founding of a village, the initiation of youths, and on many other "occasions" with which we became acquainted through the example of the expiatory ritual in discussing the ethical contents of religion (cf. chap. ix, sec. 3). In all of these cases, vivid recollections of the divine origin of life take the place of prayer. It is no more and no less than devotional action. When piety takes the aspects of *Heilserwartung*, an expectation of divine recompense, and when the vital sense of a cultural nexus is lost to the community, then cultic acts may indeed become pragmatic. At first impression, pragmatism may then appear the ruling characteristic and builders of theories may be misled into circumstantial "magical explanations" which explain nothing.

It may be objected that we present here interpretations, justified in some cases, doubtful in others. In the same way pre-animistic magic, it might be said, can be demonstrated in individual instances and, once demonstrated, can be extrapolated to others, even if the precise link cannot be immediately proven. Assuming this to be correct would imply a severe narrowing of the hypothesis, and allowances would have to be made for other possible explanations. To counter the defense of the hypothesis of pre-animistic magic, however, every single case adduced by its advocates would have to be refuted separately—a task which we shall not even undertake here. The attempt would be doomed to failure, since rational explanations cannot, in most cases, be given —at least for the present.

The hypothesis of pre-animistic magic rests solely on interpretations and, by no means, represents assured results. This can be shown in the case of mutilation, a very ancient custom with obscure origins. Ethnological literature consistently treats mutilation as magical. About the origin of dental mutilations, Preuss says ("Ursprung": 363): "The causes behind this custom are, of course, forgotten everywhere and replaced by secondary statements. Only one girl on Formosa gave the relatively proper answer: 'So that they can breathe more easily and more wind can get into them.'" Preuss ties this assertion to some others about the necessity of the man's breath entering the woman's mouth during the sexual act because a live, i.e., breathing, child could result only in this way. He concludes correctly that the incisors then should be struck from the mouths of the women only (though it would seem simpler if they opened their mouths to achieve the same magical result). In central Celebes there are indeed three tribes which practice dental mutilation on girls only and at the time of puberty. Beyond this, however, and despite the wide dissemination of the custom, no preference for the female sex can be established. We shall not pursue this subject any further (cf. chap. xii, sec. 6); we only wish to show that the magical explanations are by no means self-evident from the statements of primitive man but are usually quite farfetched.

Preuss, as an Americanist, bases his ideas chiefly on Mesoamerican material. Mexico, however, had a pronounced polytheistic religion. He reasons in the following manner: The divine acts related in the myths are exclusively magical. His leitmotiv in the study of primal religion is the dictum that the "gods carry on magic by the same methods as earlier ordinary beings [i.e., at the stage postulated by Preuss, when man supposedly had no concept of a god]. *If this can be proven the genesis of gods from [magical practices] is assured. Animism then is only the bridge between the two*" ("Ursprung": 362; emphasis added). This theory rests on similar interpretations. At that, it requires an image of early human mentality deserving of Preuss's (p. 419) term *Urdummheit*, primal stupidity. In fairness, we must admit that cultic activities often confront us today in a state of deterioration which seems to justify such assumptions. Elaborate observances, performed with solemnity and care, would be more evocative of religious and cultic origins than "abbreviated" actions. When we read, for instance, of the numerous and heterogeneous activities that make up the preparation for war among some peoples, we gain the impression that they are not connected by any unifying idea. It appears as if anything once considered pious or worthwhile had been "poured into one pot," to be brought out indiscriminately on important occasions. But even such catch-all activities should not be discussed simply as magic. Some original

meaning should at least be assumed, and this might in some cases
—if not in all—be ferreted out by patient and detailed analysis.

3. "SPELLS"

Critical investigation does not even stop before the so obviously magical "spells." We must ask the general question: *what
transforms some utterances into spells?* Something must have
given the words a special significance. Available accounts usually show that the magical nature of spells is by no means primary
but that spells are essentially mythic and religious. Only the loss
of original meanings makes them appear as something properly
called a spell.

Koch-Grünberg has taken down a sizable number of spells
among the Taulipang (*Roroima:* III, 219 ff.) and makes the
point that usually—just as the Merseburg spells (*Roroima:* III,
220)—they originated in short mythic narratives which introduce
the formula. If animals are mentioned, they are usually mythical
beasts that play a part in the conjurations of the witch doctors.
Some of the spells relate to sickness. Koch-Grünberg says (p.
221):

The "Ancestral Maiden," the "Ancestral Youth," the "Maiden of
the Savanna," the "Youth of the Earth" are prototypes, *primal men*
who *for the first time* experience human suffering and to whom "contemporary man, the children," i.e., their present-day descendants, are
to be juxtaposed; these then are to *apply* the spells. [Emphasis added.]

Koch-Grünberg's introductory remarks show the personages mentioned in the spells to be Dema who, in the primal past, were first
to suffer human ills, as the myths relate. At the same time the
divine powers of assistance are spoken of and are said to be able
to put an end to the suffering.

One spell (pp. 233 ff.) tells of a beautiful "ancestral maiden"
who is very reluctant and, lashing out and biting, rejects Makunaima, one of the most prominent Dema, and his two brothers.
Makunaima and his kin "make her ugly by conjuring fish-eggs
into her face," i.e., cause her to suffer from suppurating pustules
"so that she never again will be beautiful." Simultaneously, Makunaima casts his spell: "The people of today, the children, must
say these words. They must call us by our names when they want

to make others ill. I am Makunaima." The mythic significance of this episode probably means no more than that Makunaima, as a primeval Dema, first caused the pustules, a common symptom of pubescence, to afflict mankind. The recollection of the mythic act (in this case not by re-enactment but through recounting of the myth) is expected to bring forth analogous suffering. Even disease has its prototype in primeval occurrences.

The myth goes on to tell how the "maiden of our ancestors" encounters various other Dema, especially personifications of various kinds of rain and some kinds of pepper. She replies, upon their questioning, that Makunaima and his kin had made her sick with thorns in her face. The rains and the peppers then say in turn: "I am such and such a rain! I cleanse the face of the 'maiden of our ancestors' so she will never suffer from thorns. The people of today, the children, must speak these words. They must call us by our names. With water I cleanse her face." Or the peppers will say: "I will frighten these thorns. I will make the pain disappear. . . ."

This second part of the myth constitutes the spell that heals the pustules. It always states explicitly that the descendants, "the people of today," must repeat the words of the myth. This is done whenever someone is afflicted with pustules: the "spell of the rains" is repeated six or seven times and the patient is washed as often with lukewarm water. Then the "spell of the peppers" is repeated the same number of times and ground pepper is rubbed on the patient's body.

These then are the spells of the Taulipang in which the myths appear, sometimes in great detail, sometimes much abbreviated, but always containing the instruction to repeat the pertinent phrases. Quite commonly, the myths contain a command to the descendants to re-enact this or that event at some time. Narrating the myth is in itself—just as the cultic act—part of devout behavior. If retelling of the myth has here become a spell, it is the same process that has transformed the genuinely cultic act into that which ethnology likes to call "magic." It is the same process of degeneration which leads, by way of pragmatic expectations (here the expectation of healing), from expression to application. So, at least, it would appear from the Taulipangs' own statements.

From the available data, it is also difficult to determine

whether or not we are actually dealing with genuine myths. Do these myths contain statements about the essential nature of disease? Koch-Grünberg himself is not of this opinion: "These are magical devices which are still rooted, far from any belief in soul or spirit, in the analogies of everyday existence *and belong therefore among the most ancient concepts*" (*Roroima:* 222; emphasis added). He explicitly refers to the theory of pre-animistic magic, but his claims are not supported by his own data. Analogies do occur but never predominate and usually occur quite sporadically. Were it true that the concepts are indeed "rooted in the analogies of everyday existence," we would have discussed them in section eight of this chapter rather than here. Unprejudiced reading of the myth fosters the conviction that many truly mythic motifs are touched upon, although it is not easy to advance from critical analysis to intuitive understanding.

4. SCOURGING

Koch-Grünberg speaks of scourging (*Roroima:* III, 232, 375), another magical practice by which the Taulipang endeavor to prevent the evil consequences of eating wild game, such consequences being sickness and boils. When a tapir, deer, or wild boar has been killed, all who partake in the meal are scourged in front of the oldest of the men. They step in front of the head of the tapir; children receive only one, though quite painful blow; young men and grown girls several, from one leg to the shoulder and then from the other leg to the other shoulder. Scourging is a widespread custom in South America. Koch-Grünberg (*ibid.:* 375) offers further examples. We find scourging as magical prophylaxis, not only in association with the eating of large game, but also attendant upon moving into a new house. The *candidate for the chiefdom* is violently flogged by the "leaders." During the main planting activities, the young people are scourged by the old. Among the Manao of the lower Rio Negro and also among some tribes of the upper Orinoco, men and women were scourged on the occasion of a harvest festival. While the warriors were on a raiding expedition, Caribs flogged two boys to bring about victory. At the end of the death ceremonies of the Aruak, all the men of the village whipped each other's calves until shreds hung down. The list can be extended: in a Timbira tribe the participants in a ceremonial contest, the so-called log race, are scourged by an old man after they have arrived at the place of celebration (Nimuendaju, 1946: 138). This motif is also evident on the pottery of the Chimu culture (cf. K. Hissink, who gives further examples of ritual flogging in South America).

The designation "preventive magic"—especially in view of a long list of very different "occasions" for the employment of the ritual—says little about this peculiar phenomenon. Again we must ask what it was that could have led to the idea that whipping could stop sickness or insure victory. R. Karsten (1926), who gives further instances of scourgings from South America, attempts an explanation in which he closely approaches Frazer: the girls who are flogged at initiation are thought to become immune against the influence of evil spirits (*ibid.*: 169 ff.). The whip is said "probably" to possess some supernatural power; on the whole it is assumed that we are dealing with a purification ceremony in which evil is scourged away (*ibid.*: 174). We need hardly say that this is "pure interpretation," unsupported by data. If we are to proceed phenomenologically, we must admit that we know only one kind of fact—aside from the descriptions of the flogging—which can help our understanding: the various occasions for flogging. It is immediately clear that understanding can be gained only with difficulty, if at all, and then only hypothetically. In this case, however, the occasions tell us at least enough to justify making assumptions.

What are these occasions? After the killing of a large animal, especially the tapir, and before its consumption; before occupation of a new house; during the main work of cultivation; at the harvest; at puberty ceremonies for boys and girls; at burials; before the installation of a chief; at the end of a contest; before first marital coitus; before the remarriage of a widow (*ibid.*: 169 ff.). The South American tribes that practice scourging predominantly represent the archaic cultivator stratum. The implication is clear. The situations are almost identical with the one great occasion, the one great cult which is related to the one significant mythic theme: the killing of the animal parallels the killing of the Dema-deity; the new house—especially the cult house and then, by transference, any house—uses the house of the dead as prototype; field and harvest labors began when the Dema-deity was transformed into a crop plant; puberty ceremonies are festive reminiscences of the origin of propagative faculties through the slaying of the deity; the same may be said of wedding rites; the chief is to be seen as the living representative and direct descendant of the Dema; contest was instituted as a ceremony at the occasion of the primeval murder; etc.

All instances point to the Hainuwele mythologem, the mythologem of the root-crop cultivators. It is all the more astonishing that we possess no version of the myth which mentions scourging as a comprehensible part of the specific primeval event. I owe it to the astuteness of Dr. O. Zerries that I can cite two pertinent, though rather fairy-tale-like, instances from South America. Métraux (1948: 22 ff.) quotes a myth of the Tupinamba of Bahia from an old French source which tells of a poor woman who sends her children to look for edible plants during a great famine. The children meet a strange child in whom, unknown to them, a divine being is hidden. They fall on the child and beat it. Immediately, sweet potatoes and all kinds of edible fruits rain down on them. When the children stop in astonishment, the strange child tells them to continue the thrashing so that they may have still more food. They are, however, not to tell anyone what they have seen. But the mother discovers the secret. She plants what the children have left, and from then on the region knows no lack of food.

Another myth is reported by Tessmann (pp. 199 ff.) of the Shipibo and Conibo (Chama), a Pano tribe that lives on the banks of the Ucayali in the Peruvian mountains. It tells of a time when men did not yet possess any crop plants. A man went to the forest with his wife, and only their daughter remained at home. Then a boy came (who actually was a bird). When the girl could not satisfy his demands for food, he made her strike his knees with a stick. Ripe bananas fell from them. On later visits the process is repeated: the girl strikes the boy's legs and, in time, receives all the crop plants known today.

These examples have more the character of miracle tales than of genuine myths, but the motif of the origin of crop plants still is strikingly similar to the main motif of the Hainuwele mythologem, the mythic theme of the archaic cultivators. Conceivably, it could be an episode of that myth, perhaps of a variant elaborated in South America. We know of numerous motifs which became independent stories and fairy tales. Scourging would then

again be a rite of re-enactment. In origin it would have nothing
in common with magic.

In my opinion, reference to the scourging ceremony is also
made in an account by Karsten (1926: 169 ff.): the Uaupé of
the South American forests dip a whip into prepared food; after
the scourging a girl will take the food by licking it from the whip.
The custom may be directly related to that myth according to
which, through whip and flogging, crop plants originated. This
explanation would seem more natural than the involved and artificial ones of Karsten and Frazer.

5. HOMEOPATHIC MAGIC

The main purpose of our discussion so far has been to suggest
an alternate way of thinking about so-called "magic." Of course,
our method cannot immediately discover the mythic-cultic origin
of all the phenomena that might be categorized as magic. In
many instances no statement can be made, and we must wait to
see if new semantic links can be forged from newer and more
specific data. Setting aside some few exceptions which shall occupy our attention later (chap. xii, secs. 6–8), I should like to say
that *none of the ceremonies customarily called magic in ethnological literature involves anything on the order of a "magical
mentality" but that they, as all other phenomena in intellectual
history, are to be traced back to a perception of a (usually myth-
ic-religious) reality.* Many factors favored their degeneration
to "applied action," particularly the hope and expectation of
practical reward for devotional acts. This can be said even of acts
of genuine magic (cf. chap. xi). The more curtailed and mechan-
ical a ritual has become, the more difficult is it to understand and
the more readily is it called magic.

Prehistorians and ethonologists like to use the term homeopathic or imitative magic. Wherever pictorial representation enters ritual, imitative magic is offered as an explanation. Frobenius (1933: 127 ff.), for instance, observed that African pygmies, prior to the hunt, would draw an antelope in the sand, at
sunrise; when the first rays of the sun fell on it, they would shoot
an arrow into the picture. This they believe to have assured the
success of the hunt. It is an ethnological commonplace to interpret this as "homeopathic magic." Among all conceivable expla-

nations this seems the least probable to me. It requires us to believe that the pygmies actually thought that the shot at the image would magically bring about a shot at an animal. Aside from the fact that a very significant element, i.e., the sun, is disregarded by the interpretation, the information given in the tale is too meager to lend it conviction. With equal right we may say that we are dealing with a repetitive rite for which a corresponding myth is lacking.

There is no justification for representing prehistoric rock paintings as "magical art," as we see it done with great regularity (cf. Obermaier, pp. 145, 155). Actually, we know nothing of the motivations behind the rock paintings. The arrows are cited as parallels to the homeopathic magic of the pygmies or to similar ceremonials of other hunting peoples. These then are extrapolated to show the magical character of all rock paintings. If ethnological findings are to explain prehistoric phenomena, only proven facts and not dubious conjectures should be admitted. Such data can be found among some archaic peoples who even today draw rock pictures. Here everything affirms that the practices are cultic acts performed in genuinely religious spirit. Clearest are accounts of Australian rock paintings (cf. chap. v, sec. 1). The deity left behind an image of itself and, as in all cults, its restoration is regarded a pious act. This motivation corresponds better to our ideas of the nature and grandeur of art. How could the creative beginnings of art, which we regard as the most exalted sphere of human endeavor, be rooted in an incomprehensible mentality and error? This seems all the more strange, when we consider that their documentary remains—the paleolithic rock paintings of southwestern Europe, for instance—speak to us directly as works of art. This would seem to affirm the enduring sameness of human mentality.

Another example: the Kwakiutl (northwest coast of North America) used to make a rock engraving at the spot where a slave had been killed and eaten on a cultic occasion (Boas, 1897: p. 439). The engraving, then, is a memorial to the religious ceremony, as were, in other settings, the megaliths often erected on similar occasions. During puberty ceremonies, the Kissi of West Africa paint on mud walls (Germann, pp. 112 ff.); Indians of Southern California painted on rock walls at similar occasions (Du Bois, p. 96). Griaule (1938: 405 ff.) gives a detailed description of the restoration of rock paintings within the framework of an elaborate ceremonial of the Dogon in the Western Sudan. All of this speaks against the magical origin of prehistoric painting.

6. IMITATIVE ZEAL

Having asserted that the true religious ethos is to be found in the attitude which prompts man actively to contemplate and recall divine actions, we must now speak of some restricting facts which we can study in our own environment and which must therefore also have been part of early human history, although it may be difficult and even impossible to cite concrete cases of them.

We have spoken of ritual scourgings (cf. chap. xii, sec. 4), have denied their magical character, and have favored the idea of their origin from presumably mythic sources.

It so happens that the great myth which reflects the world view of the archaic root-crop cultivators in all its essentials and which should incorporate the scourging ceremonial has no variant in which the motif of flogging occurs. On the basis of some fairy-tale-like instances, we conjectured that it must have appeared in a relatively insignificant episode of the mythic narrative. And yet, ceremonial scourging is conscientiously carried out by many South American peoples despite its painful consequences. Our train of thought, though burdened by many assumptions, was followed only to indicate how the otherwise reasonable relationship between myth and cult might—*even in its beginnings*—have had an element of irrationality. The inconsequential and the external might have obtruded, while truer and deeper meanings might hardly be ascertainable. We see this disparity in our own culture: between creative ambition and its realization by zealous disciples or dry and unimaginative latecomers.

It is not easy to demonstrate such disharmony for primitive conditions. The example of the scourging ritual shows that, even if we discount the conjectural nature of the idea and accept it as fact for the sake of the argument, it would still be almost impossible to affirm the secondary quality of the motif with any confidence. Seen against the totality of the all-encompassing mythologem, it would certainly be inconsequential, for the myth focuses on the organizing primeval act and the slaying of the Dema-deity. Who could say to what extent flogging or other tortures correspond in some ways to essential mythic events in the mind of primeval man? Psychology may have the answer and might see ritual torture as an expressive response to fundamental psychic predispositions. This would at least make it improbable that flogging became a rigidly observed rite by accident and without significant motivation.

Psychology, however, can hardly be expected to offer an explanation for the importance given other odd and incomprehensible customs. Mutilations—the removal of teeth, circumcision, subincision, monorchy, excision of the mammillae of men—can be linked neither to cognition of reality nor to universal psychological predispositions. These acts remain obstinately obscure. If we assume, however, that the meaning of creative acts is at all times subject to distortion, we may also assume that some incomprehensible acts are due to similar distortions of the myths.

Some explicit motivations for such abstruse customs turn our ideas in a new direction. It is, for example, reported of Mohammed that he lost two teeth in the battle of Ohod. Thirty-seven years after the Flight of the Prophet, the archangel Gabriel appeared to one Oweis of Karn in Yemen and commanded him to renounce the world. In homage to the Prophet, and in commemoration of the battle, Oweis has all of his teeth pulled and then required this sacrifice of all of his followers. We can leave aside the questions of whether he knew of the widespread and undoubtedly ancient custom, whether it was godfather to his action, or whether it was a spontaneous innovation. Of significance here is the fact that the desire to approximate the revered ideal, even in minor respects, inspired a zealot to institute such a practice and that the practice came to seem plausible to his adherents. The Herero (southwest Africa) have a similar rationale when they file down two of the upper incisors and knock out all four of the lower in the puberty ceremonies; the initiated boys are to become more like the sacred ancestral bull (Irle, p. 105).

Another case of conscious assimilation comes from the Semang, a remnant population of hunters on the Malayan peninsula. They believe in a celestial deity, Kari, that sits in the heavens, leaning against the slanting trunk of a tree. In the branches of the tree sit the souls that Kari sends out to be incarnated in men and beasts. For this reason, women must lean against a slanting bamboo pole at parturition. It is said that woman thereby assumes the position of Kari and that the slanting trunk is the tree against which Kari leans (Skeat and Blagden, II, 3).

We cannot deny ourselves a short digression. It is easily conceivable that the position prescribed for the birth act will persist as a custom longer than the myth of Kari, and it would then be said that woman had to assume such a position "so that the child may get a soul"; nothing would prevent the custom's being declared a "magical act."

The examples should demonstrate that even incomprehensible and rudimentary customs may originate in mythic concepts. Though the possibility remains that their meaning was more profound at an earlier time, it is clear that the venerability of the prototype suffices to explain the derivation of such customs, even from the less significant traits of the prototype. Customs may have been engendered by the desire to emulate. To smile at such zeal is easy. One may call it stupidity or inability to tell the significant from the trivial. On the other hand, all of these traits are undoubtedly of the essence of the religious attitude. The great pedagogical value that the idea of God has for mankind consists specifically in the fact that man accepts the deity as his august prototype and, deeply impressed, attempts to adapt himself to the image. True discipline lies not in the order-preserving interpersonal acts but solely in the affective prototype. When a romantic schoolgirl wears a red blouse because an adored teacher wears one, or when an overenthusiastic student will write only with black ink because Schiller and Goethe preferred it, we may smile. But we must admit that the red blouse and the black ink carry along some of the emulated prototype, just as the dental mutilations of the Herero actualize some of the sacred essence of the ancestral bull. If this urge to emulate exhausts itself in trivia, we are reminded of the soldiers of Wallenstein who tried to live up to the image of their admired general by imitating *"wie er räuspert und wie er spuckt."*

Many incomprehensible customs may stem from a zeal concerned less with the deeper meaning of myth than with one of its unimportant and superficial aspects; only with some limitations could we call them true religious phenomena. *Urdummheit* would be too harsh a word, for, despite its simplemindedness, zeal often possesses a spark of genuine reverence.

Psychology might perhaps call even the ideas that support imitation sensible expressions of human nature. No one will object to this, if for no other reason than the unlikelihood of man's ever coming to make a statement through sheer accident. But the actual meaning could then be demonstrated only at the hand of the mythic prototype. Imitative zeal would even remain a characteristic of human behavior but not of the primary creative behavior to which the great and true achievements of culture history owe their existence. Among the other categories of cultural phenomena, such as scourging, psychological interpretation might be of importance for the cultural formulation itself, not only for the understanding of the mythic prototype. It might be possible to establish not only that mythic statements are sensible and significant but that ritual repetition, too, is based on psychological predispositions and that these predispositions have evolved these repetitions as a fitting expression of the central mythic event.

Whatever alternative may be preferred, in no case is there a link with magic; taking this point of view, we cannot imagine what magic should be performed in the execution of the actions.

7. THE CONSERVATIVE ATTITUDE

A second category of phenomena shall be dealt with only very briefly. Its presence and the pertinent mental attitude can best be illustrated from our own cultural setting. We are again speaking of the "survival" phenomena, for it seems that a residue of ideas from the entire long history of culture has been preserved in some Western redoubts (which, for that matter, might be in the middle of our most populous cities). We have shown through many examples that these ideas have nothing in common with magic but that their fuller meaning must be traced back to prior cultural epochs from which—semantically depleted—they were taken over as empty formulas. The mental attitude which lies at the root of this conservatism prompts us to speak of "survivals." The verity of cognition is tied to the cosmological basis of each cultural epoch. Belief in a system of statements which dispenses with this basis is not only non-creative but no longer even reproductive; it is divorced from genuine religious experience, in any case. Spiritualism and faith in astrological prognoses offer illustrations from our own cultural environment. Both are demonstrably anchored in a mythic background and have, therefore, the characteristics of an original semantic complement which we have contrasted to the hypothesis of pre-animistic magic. And yet, the present-day practices of spiritualism and astrology are superstitious and devoid of sense only because the respective cosmological assumptions which vouchsafed their verity were not taken over.

This latter idea is of extraordinary importance, since it points up the fact that the taking over of one cultural expression by another cultural environment does not inevitably bring about semantic depletion. The Eleusinian Mysteries, as I conclude from Kerényi's exposition ("Kore": 361 ff.), are based on the world view of the archaic root-crop cultivators. The Olympic pantheon reveals to us a perception which is separated from that of the archaic cultivators by several major historical epochs. And Eleusis was, at that very time, experiential reality and in no sense a "survival" phenomenon. It continued on its proper and original spiritual foundations. Our latter-day believers in astrology are far from its true mythic sources and possess none of its experiential values. They rather refer themselves to the last vestiges of cosmological mythology, which has already passed completely into the stage of "application." But they still believe in the verity of astrological statements, and in this lies the discrepancy which makes superstition of their faith.

Astrology is a superstition which has its true prototypes in a none too remote cultural epoch, in the archaic high cultures. Concepts from much older, even from the most ancient phases of culture history have, here and there, maintained themselves in popular belief. The following story, for instance, is told as a "true event" in the village of Weisingen on the Upper Danube: Without any visible cause, many of a farmer's young geese died. A man from a neighboring village, who had a reputation as an oracle, advised him to roast a live young goose in his oven; the guilty party would then announce itself. The desired success came. Soon after, a woman appeared; the left side of her face was burned, and she pleaded that he take the goose from the oven, since otherwise she would have to burn alive. What actually happened can certainly not be ascertained from the statements of those who were involved. But it is significant that many concepts still lead a ghostly existence here, though they undoubtedly are part of man's most archaic ideologies, which we have encountered as genuine beliefs among the proto-totemistic phenomena (chap. vii, sec. 2). Such intimate links between man and animal must be founded on a world view in which their common destiny is a central experience.

Astrologers and spiritualists are, of course, no supporters of the principles of the hypothesis of pre-animistic magic; they will have nothing to do with magic. But in their mental attitudes they justify many of the claims of the hypothesis; only because of this are they mentioned here. What was said of *our* cultural community applies of course in a wider sense also to the early stage of history. Ethnology is full of such actual "survivals" which are without any cosmological referent. Through the formalized and faithful respect which they receive, they exemplify the spiritual attitude which the hypothesis of pre-animistic magic mistakenly ascribes to the creative process.

8. STERILE AND IMITATIVE MENTALITY

The two categories of phenomena could not confirm the magical postulates because magic did not enter into them. But they betrayed a spiritual attitude which approached the hypothesis and this leads to the question of what its chief criterion may be. There can only be one answer: *It is the ever non-creative, which neither today nor at any time has produced anything of any consequence.* We may try to excuse imitative zeal by calling it re-creative, insofar as it aims to actualize mythic statement in cultic activity; but its most prominent characteristic is precisely overly literal aping and arid and petrified stultification. The second category cannot even lay claim to such limited re-creativity; it contains only the reproductions of semantically depleted reproductions—and no longer has access to the creative source.

Absence of creativity marks everything that habitually is designated as magic—except of course those phenomena which we have found to be "genuine magic." The proponents of the hypothesis of pre-animistic magic have shown little sensitivity to the creativity which clings even to the latest repetitions. Until now we have concentrated on making note of this creativity in all cultural configurations, in order to protect them from fatal aspersions like the hypothesis of pre-animistic magic. Concluding the subject, we ask: Is there any cultural configuration which *owes its existence* to the non-creative attitude?

If we hesitatingly give an affirmative answer, we do so only with several reservations. Can we even speak of "cultural configurations"? We might do so by extending the term to encompass all of man's traditional acts. On the other hand, we may not be justified in calling the underlying mentality absolutely non-creative. It, too, is ultimately re-creative—at second, third, or fourth hand, so to speak—for non-creativity cannot create from the void. This mentality has brought forth, and still brings forth, totally absurd and sometimes perverse mutations of phenomena which belong to the assumed cultural inventory; they are absurd and perverse because the proper sense of the prototype is not— or is no longer—understood. Since there are food taboos, the mentality postulated by the theory of pre-animistic magic can invent new ones which differ from the genuine ones in that they have no meaning of their own but only that conferred on them "from the outside." A third reservation corresponds with the limitation demanded in the previous section: We can never know with certainty if phenomena—even if they come close to the theoretical idea of magic—were not originally part of a rational context and only now confront us in secondary reinterpretations.

We do not want to continue the enumeration of examples; ethnological literature is full of them. The majority of cases are listed under the heading of imitative magic. Food taboos are often explained as in the following manner: The men of the Chamacoco (Gran Chaco) eat deer meat only because it gives them the ability to run fast; only old men and women eat ostrich eggs; if a young man eats them, his wife will die and leave many small children in his care, for it is the male ostrich that cares for the brood. Eating of capybara meat will make one an expert swimmer on the very next day. Turtles are eaten by women but not by men lest they become sluggish and be exposed to blows in quarrels (Baldus, p. 96).

The rationale of these injunctions is interpreted as imitative magic. The observed qualities of an animal are supposed to be transferred to man through ingestion, either to his advantage or detriment. Unless these reasons are ex post facto explanations of customs that have lost their original meaning, they indeed are examples of *Urdummheit*, of primal stupidity. But further facts feed the suspicion that they are secondary explanations, especially where the Chamacoco are concerned: normally, mature men never eat armadillo, lest symptoms of old age befall them. There is, however, a secret men's ceremonial which constitutes the main cultic event. At that occasion, at the height of the celebration, armadillos are eaten, though the women are never told of this. On the other hand, old men will eat the animal in public. This is reminiscent of a widespread notion that only old men (beyond the age of procreation?) may, without peril, eat human flesh or other foods reserved for ceremonial occasions. This is said of the meat of the tapir, and in South America the tapir is the outstanding mythological animal. It is always stated in explanation that the younger men would immediately turn old and senile if they ate of the tapir. These explanations recur for tapir and armadillo in conjunction with the explicit statements that old men may eat both animals openly and without any danger. This suggests that the taboos must have been related at some time to specific meanings. To my knowledge, the possibility has not yet been thoroughly studied; such an investigation might lead to the idea that the custom is rooted in mythic concepts of male procreativity belonging to a specific culture stratum. Among the archaic cultivators, as we have seen, ritual killing of men and animals and the cultic eating of their flesh are dramatically re-enacted reminiscences. Old men, who are considered to stand outside the cycle of destiny, may eat of these essentially cultic foods without danger. The magical hypothesis would probably hold the pebbled armor of the armadillo and the wrinkled skin of the tapir responsible for the analogy to old age. According to our view, the rationale is quite different: Old men may (for mythically established reasons) eat the flesh of certain animals without detriment; if a young man were to do so, he would then also be an old man, for he does as the old men do. If, however, the Chamacoco have food taboos, aside from the one discussed, which are based only on imitative reasoning, then there must have been prior, mythically fixed taboos. These may have degenerated to the state of "application" and may then, in turn, have encouraged a superstitious frame of mind which would "invent" similar "applied" taboos. But the imitatory acts would not then stem from a creative process but would be a direct aping of an already decadent cultural inventory, a re-creativity of the third or fourth order.

In this section of the work we have taken issue with the so-called pre-animistic theory of magic, though it goes back more than fifty years and is rooted in the thinking that characterized the turn of the century. In other spheres it has long been passed over. In the literature of the cultural sciences and even in philosophy, however, its premises still dominate the interpretation of phenomena.

On the one hand, we have argued against the underlying conception of early man and have emphasized that explanations of spiritual phenomena among primitive peoples along the lines of the hypothesis of pre-animistic magic are no more than interpolations. We feel justified, therefore, in offering interpretations which are founded on a different evaluation of the mental abilities of early man. Beyond this, we feel that we have found more solid support for our assertions in the available data, at least in some instances. Of more weight in our argument is the conviction that primitive forms of expression can be understood only when their creators are viewed as human beings who are urged on by motivations similar to our own, whose world view is not composed of a chain of errors, whose actions must not be explained as symptoms of unimaginable stupidity, especially when these same abject fools possessed a reasonable and wise regimen of life and were technologically and mechanically gifted.

PART IV | Souls, Ancestor Cults, and Spirits

13

TYLOR'S THEORY OF ANIMISM

In the sphere of the cultural sciences, rarely has a book had the effect of Edward B. Tylor's *Primitive Culture* (1871). Ever since its publication the view has taken hold and hardly been doubted that the various concepts of souls, the dead, and spirits constitute the fundamental elements of primitive religions. Even theories which saw the origin of religion in other phenomena admitted that so-called animism was the form of religion most prevalent among primitive peoples. Statistical tables listed "animists" along with Christians and Moslems. Tylor's ideas were not only accepted in ethnology; all other disciplines of the cultural sciences made them the basis of religious-scientific discourse.

Such widely felt effects are not accidents. There is no doubt that the greater portion of the available data describes exactly the concepts with which Tylor deals. Add to this that Tylor was a scholar of admirable scope whose compelling presentation one can resist only with difficulty, if one agrees with his premises. Even Tylor, however, does not base his conclusions on data alone but establishes his intellectual edifice—as it lies in the nature of the thought process—on unproven assumptions, treated as self-evident, which can be regarded as his world view and his view of man. Images of mankind and environment are essentially time-bound. Only in rare cases are they personal intellectual property; more often they are concepts produced by the co-operation of all cultural forces and inculcated into each human being from the cradle onward. Our critique of Tylor's theories is directed, not against his data, though these are affected by the passage of time, but against his self-evident and unproven assumptions.

1. THE SOUL CONCEPT

Animism has been described so often that we can limit ourselves to the tersest summary. First, we must emphasize Tylor's positive contribution in areas which had been dominated by obviously erroneous ideas. He was one of the few true ethnologists of his time, and he recognized the importance of his science for all problems in the history of mankind. His is the observation that

no more can he who understands but one religion understand even that religion, than the man who knows but one language can understand that language. No religion of mankind lies in utter isolation from the rest, and the thoughts and principles of modern Christianity are attached to intellectual clues which run back through far pre-Christian ages to the very origin of human civilization, perhaps even of human existence [II, 5].

His passionate espousal of the historical view is founded on Bastian to whom he acknowledges his debt. Tylor rejects the migration or diffusion theory with Bastian's arguments, but here and there even he is impressed by the striking correspondences between concepts in widely separated peoples. He at least toys with the question of whether such similarities should not be explained by transmission of the same thought from tribe to tribe (II, 130).

Of inestimable merit also is his argumentation against the degeneration theory, which sought to see in the intellectual life of primitive man nothing more than the degraded achievements of higher cultures. Wherever there are similarities between the illiterate and the higher cultures, the former show the fuller, more vital, and meaningful forms. Primitive mentality can, therefore, not be understood from the viewpoint of the high cultures. On the contrary, many manifestations in the more recent strata can be understood only as persistent ideas of older provenance. The designation of "survival" for many such manifestations dates back to Tylor. The implication that a cultural configuration possesses a "life of its own" surely counts among the most fruitful ideas in the science of culture.

Tylor builds his ideas about the origin of religion on a minimum definition: *"Religion [is] the belief in Spiritual Beings"* (II, 8). With this definition he believes himself to have eliminated all prejudice while encompassing all phenomena among all peoples which belong in the religious sphere. Spiritual beings are found chiefly in two forms: as souls, first of man, later of animals, plants, and even inanimate objects; and then as independent, disembodied souls which, as spirits, have an existence of their own. Spirits are said to have developed later from individual souls. A scientifically unbiased answer to a question about the genesis of the concept of soul could only make reference to natural conditions. Causally oriented man investigated the distinction between living and dead bodies, between sleep and waking, and also the contents of dreams and had of necessity arrived at the answer that something like a soul must exist which leaves the sleeping body and which ultimately departs from it at the time of death. Departed souls formed the basis for a belief in non-individual, independent souls, i.e., spirits; they were regarded as the causative forces behind those happenings for which other causes could not be established, as, for instance, meteorological phenomena.

The rationalistically developed concepts of animism always contain the belief that spiritual beings are held to effect and control the events of the material world and man's life here and hereafter, that they hold intercourse with men and receive pleasure or displeasure from human actions. Thus, the belief had to lead "naturally, and it might almost be said inevitably, sooner or later, to active reverence and propitiation" (II, 11).

This at any rate, corresponds with the actual conception of the personal soul or spirit among the lower races, which may be defined as follows: It is a thin unsubstantial human image, in its nature a sort of vapour, film, or shadow; the cause of life and thought in the individual it animates; independently possessing the personal consciousness and volition of its corporeal owner, past or present; capable of leaving the body far behind, to flash swiftly from place to place; mostly impalpable and invisible, yet also manifesting physical power, and especially appearing to men waking or asleep as a phantasm separate from the body of which it bears the likeness; continuing to exist and appear to men after the death of that body; able to enter into, possess, and act in the bodies of other men, of animals, and even of things [II, 13].

These views of archaic beliefs Tylor supports with a wealth of data: even the term for the soul is, among many peoples, identical with the term for shadow or breath; usually, the soul can be thought to be localized in some part of the body; many peoples believe that in severe illnesses the soul leaves the body even before death occurs, and efforts are made to catch the soul and return it to the patient; if successful, the patient recovers. His copious material is well known, some of it even still active in our own cultural environment, and needs no elaboration here.

The further development of religion, from spirits originating in departed souls *to the gods* of the high cultures, Tylor described in these words:

The higher deities of Polytheism have their places in the general animistic system of mankind. Among nation after nation it is still clear how, man being the type of deity, human society and government became the model on which divine society and government were shaped. As chiefs and kings are among men, so are the great gods among the lesser spirits. They differ from the souls and minor spiritual beings which we have as yet chiefly considered, but the difference is rather of rank than of nature. They are personal spirits, reigning over personal spirits. Above the disembodied souls and manes, the local genii of rocks and fountains and trees, the host of good and evil demons, and the rest of the spiritual commonality, stand these mightier deities, whose influence is less confined to local or individual interests, and who, as it pleases them, can act directly within their vast domain, or control and operate through the lower beings of their kind, their servants, agents, or mediators. The great gods of Polytheism, numerous and elaborately defined in the theology of the cultured world, do not however make their earliest appearance there. In the religions of the lower races their principal types were already cast, and thenceforward, for many an age of progressing or relapsing culture, it became the work of poet and priest, legend-monger and historian, theologian and philosopher, to develop and renew, to degrade and abolish, the mighty lords of the Pantheon [II, 334].

2. TYLOR'S IMAGE OF MAN

Many ideas in this book make reference to data which seem to confirm one of Tylor's principal theses. It was undoubtedly an early discovery of mankind that there are spirits that are of decisive importance for events in the natural environment. On the other hand, Tylor's developmental sequence from souls to spirits to gods is pure speculation. Neither do we know anything about the events which led to the discovery of such spiritual beings. It is certainly useful to refer to such natural phenomena as sleep, dreams, and death, for man's reflections are usually derived from his natural surroundings. Nevertheless, the process is not quite as simple as Tylor wishes to have us believe. Try to empathize with the described process. Tylor's "scientific lack of prejudice" postulates an original state when man existed as a biological creature devoid of any "belief in spiritual beings." In that state man must have known sleep, dreams, and even death, without ever reflecting on them. He accepted them as he accepted all other phenomena, as realities; he lived with them with the same assurance as children and animals do. The phase may have endured for uncounted millennia. It is by no means self-evident, however, that early man had—by contemplation—to work out the idea of a soul. Other kinds of explanations may be imagined through which which man might have conceptually mastered the nature of these phenomena. The most questionable aspect of Tylor's deductions is the purely causal-logical character of his postulates. The discovery of spiritual beings and of psychophysical duality must undoubtedly go back to a significant creative event in history. But creative events never are limited to causal-logical connections but lead from direct observation to living, obligatory configurations. That it was the nature of death and sleep through which spirituality first revealed itself is likewise gratuitous speculation; a culture phase which knows the concept of soul but lacks the idea of divinity exists nowhere on earth, a fact Tylor himself emphasized.

I am certain that it needed no meditation on sleep or death to convince man of spirituality and its importance to existence. That which we call moods, the feeling of solemnity, that "awe" which Goethe called *"der Menschheit bester Teil,"* the awareness of sublimity or triviality—all point to a spirituality which translates the quantitatively defined "Just-So" of concrete appearances into kaleidoscopic images which let reality appear now so, now otherwise. Though speculation about the "how" of the discovery of spiritual beings may seem a waste of effort since we have nothing to go by, I find it only natural to imagine the process to be the same as that which has produced great new insights in historically documented cultures. In our culture, creative minds direct our attentions to that which has in fact always existed but to which they give expression and form, the more "compelling" the more perfectly they trace out the sphere of perceived reality.

The question of how the concept of soul was formed is of importance after all, since the answer clearly shows the intrusion of history into Tylor's image of man. Tylor makes a stand against theological solutions which seek the origin of religion in revelation. In the need of being "scientifically unbiased," he himself introduces a new prejudice; i.e., the assumption that man is causally oriented only. The philosophy of Auguste Comte and the ideal of scientifically abstract man were godparents to the thought. We have already dealt with this much too narrow image of man's nature and want to repeat only that the limitation holds true neither for the present nor for the beginnings of human development. Even early man's experiential range was far wider, and many of his inherent possibilities could have and would have led him to recognize the importance of spiritual processes. Only by the narrowness of his "unbiased" questioning could Tylor arrive at a concept of soul which, so he supposes, could have been the basis of all religions. An as yet godless Man is said to have had this conception.

This, however, does not correspond to the data even of the careful Tylor, not even with the data he cites specifically; in particular he has repeatedly rejected the claimed godlessness of the most archaic peoples and has demonstrated that, among them, conceptions are to be found that are quite reminiscent of our familiar idea of the High God. On the other hand, all concepts of God have—according to his theory—"developed" from the abstraction of soul. Methodologically, at least, this constitutes a gap in Tylor's system.

More problematical even than Tylor's image of man is his notion of the several ideas of God. From a peach a peach tree can grow; this is inherent in the fruit; but how Tylor's abstract idea of the soul can have developed into an idea of God will probably always remain obscure to the truly unprejudiced. The missionary A. C. Kruijt, author of a book on animism in the Indian archipelago, who came to know primitive peoples and their life and work, says in his Introduction: "It has always remained a riddle to me how Christianity can have been considered a development from this nature worship." He thus turns sharply away from Tylor. I would add: had he not viewed this "nature worship" too much through Tylor's eyes, but as expression of a genuinely religious look at reality, it might have been less of a riddle to him that at least some of these religious ideas have been preserved in Christianity and are even basic parts of the Christian view.

Tylor's image of God betrays his scientific prejudice even more than does his image of man. That a concept of God should be motivated by the causally oriented nature of man is a prejudice which is rooted neither in the nature of religious experience nor in the true nature of man. Tylor's claim that independent spirits can have been derived in a causal-logical way only from the souls of the deceased does not agree with the facts, which show a far more complex nature for the spirits, close as their connection to the dead may be. Söderblom has already spoken out against this all too schematic derivation of all spirits from "souls"; we shall later discuss the heterogeneous character of spirits (chap. xvi). That spirits have been linked to unexplained manifestations of nature by pure pursuit of causalities, that this gave them their power and brought them close to godhood is pure surmise on Tylor's part and in itself unlikely. Quite to the contrary, when souls and spirits appear in connection with concepts of God, it is more likely that power was primarily linked with the idea of God and only secondarily transferred to souls and spirits. This cannot be proven, any more than Tylor's sequence can be proven. Preference for one or the other hypothesis comes exclusively from the image of early man's mentality that one chooses to employ. We hold that neither prehistory nor ethnology supports the common claim that early man—to the extent that we discuss him in a cultural context—was not yet "Man" as we regard him. Since awareness of the divine nature of the universe is independent of technological progress and expresses qualitative insights only, there is no good reason why man should not at all times have possessed an idea of the divine.

14

THE DIVINE SOUL

1. THE DIVINE PROVENANCE OF THE SOUL

Data on concepts of soul among primitive peoples are more copious than on any other subject. From the numberless questions which they suggest for the scientific study of culture, we shall pick only a few of special importance. One of these questions we have already touched on (chap. v, sec. 1) in the discussion of the Dema-deities in northwestern Australia. The basic religious concern of the people was the condition prerequisite to the inception of life. Like many other peoples, the Australians are convinced that the sex act offers only an insufficient explanation of propagation. Their attention is focused on manifestations of spirit-beings which make the natural miracle comprehensible by establishing a connection between man and deity. We learned that pregnancy depends on a father's "finding" a spirit-child in a dream, a spirit-child which might well be considered a "soul" in Tylor's definition.

Decisive, however, is that which we are told of the origin of the spirit-children. Dema-like primeval deities left them behind or generate them anew at the sacred places of their earthly accomplishments. The divine endowment makes up the total personality of the human being. We must keep in mind that these ideas are to be found among extremely archaic peoples with a purely acquisitive economy but that they should not be assumed to reflect the pristine condition of human society. In any event, it will not do to derive such a concept of soul from Tylor's causally oriented ideas. It is more natural to interpret these ideas as we encounter them among Australians and many other peoples, i.e., as a testimonial to early man's capacity for experiencing the divine aspects of reality and his ability to assume their place as partakers of the divine. Such examples urge that man cannot have discovered "soul" at a period when the idea of God was not yet known to him. The conception of the divine was primary and fostered the discovery. His own spiritual nature and the spiritual nature of all things were revealed to man through the

272

experience of divine beings who introduced him to the idea of spirituality.

The explicit statement that manifestations which we translate as "soul" stem from the deity and return to it after death is heard among many peoples. We take a somewhat detailed illustration from a report on the Apapocuva by the German author Unkel who was adopted into the tribe and given his Indian name, Nimuendaju. The Apapocuva are a horde of Tupi-Guarani speakers in southern Brazil. The central figure in their religious life is the medicine man. One of their most important cultic activities is a sort of baptismal ceremony which follows the birth of a child. The details of the ceremony would not be comprehensible without some knowledge of Apapocuva mythology ("Apapocuva": 316 ff.).

"Our Great Father" is a High God who "discovers" himself in the middle of darkness. He "finds" his helper, called "Our Father, the one who knows all things." Later, both "find" a woman, "Our Mother," with whom both have intercourse; she becomes pregnant and bears twins. The older of the twins, the son of "Great Father," is the more powerful of the two; the other shares the insignificance that characterized *his* parent, "the one who knows all things," in the epoch of creation which had passed before. The two fathers withdraw after their creative labors: the "Great Father" into the farthest distances where eternal darkness reigns; only on doomsday will he again intervene in human destiny.

The pregnant woman remains on earth and is devoured by jaguars when she attempts to follow "Great Father." The twins in her womb are saved miraculously. After "Great Father" has taken back his wife, he begets another son, a younger brother (or half brother) of the twins, who is given the name Tupan. He has no real career on earth but sits on a boat in heaven, in the "farthest west." His mother resides in the east, and when she longs to see her youngest son he sails his boat across the sky, thereby setting off a thunderstorm.

Of the twins, the son of "Great Father" is called "Our Elder Brother," and the son of the helper, "His Younger Little Brother." They are typical Dema-deities that carry out their order-producing activities in primal time. Thereafter, the elder assumes his place in the zenith of the heavens, while the younger goes to his mother in the east. From there the younger twin is supposed to have gone to his father, "the one who knows all things," whose abode is unknown. The more powerful Dema is "Our Elder Brother," whose main achievement is the institution of the medicine dance which receives a genuinely mythic rationale—as already indicated in the discussion of shamanism—by the fact that the older twin wishes to communicate with his father to receive alleviation of his terrestrial solitude. He is able to make contact even with the farthest reaches of eternal darkness to receive the requested assistance. The technique for journeying into the beyond which he originated was inherited by present-day medicine men, involving two concepts of soul which we shall discuss immediately.

The far removed "Great Father" and his helper, as well as the latter's son among the twins, are relatively insignificant in the religious context; not so, however, "Our Mother" in the east, "Our Elder Brother" in the zenith, and Tupan, the younger brother of the twins who resides in the west. They influence even present-day life of man and are especially linked to the concept of soul of which the naming ceremony can give us an impression (*ibid.*: 302 ff.).

Shortly after the birth of a child, the horde gathers and the medicine man conducts a nocturnal ceremony to establish "which soul has come to us." The newborn is thought to have had *existence long before*, either in the realm of "Our Mother" in the east, with "Our Elder Brother" at the zenith, or with Tupan in the west. From one of these places of residence the child comes to earth; the medicine man is to determine from which one. In accordance with his findings the child is named. From this name —in contrast to those given at the Christian baptism which have no such function—the individual's provenance in one of the three realms may later be known. Some of the names refer to immediate attributes of one of the deities. One, for instance, is derived from the boat-shaped benches on which Tupan sits in the West. The bearer of this name, then, received his "soul" from the realm of Tupan. The Apapocuva are puzzled by the Christian priests' habit of asking the parents the name of the infant to be christened. Is it not the priest's task to ascertain the correct name? An Apapocuva is not "named" but "is" who he is. His "real" name is usually kept secret for it is linked with the essence of a person in too direct a fashion to be revealed casually.

The naming ceremony lasts the whole night; from time to time the medicine man receives supernatural "magical powers" from the forces to which he sings. These gifts are thought to be quite material, though invisible to common mortals. The medicine man catches them from the air above his head, rolls them up, and then spreads them over the child. Medicine men also seem to possess the ability to produce such invisible gifts from their own persons: "He pulls it like a shirt over his back or takes it from his chest, by describing a circle over it with his hand; then he carefully spreads it on the child."

At sunrise the singing reaches a climax, a particularly ecstatic chanting with which all ceremonies end. All bow low in the direction of the rising sun, their arms raised, their knees slightly flexed. Now the medicine man has "found" the proper name. It usually relates to personages, objects, or episodes from mythology or ritual.

Without a doubt, the "soul" here is of divine provenance. At the same time, the ritual shows how seriously this fact is regarded. It remains unexplained, however, what is to be understood by supernatural "magical powers." Presumably, these are typical actions which stem from a desire to delineate events more graphically; as the body of the newborn needs protective covering, so the "soul" needs to be sheltered. The protection seems to take the shape of kerchiefs or blankets—all of course as invisible as the soul itself—which are sent from the divine realm or which the medicine man can in part provide.

The Apapocuva concept of soul forms only one, though the most important, part of the spiritual nature of man. To the "plant soul," as Nimuendaju calls it, an "animal soul" is added some time after birth, though the author provides no information as to its source (*ibid.*: 305 ff.). Man's good and gentle impulses, as well as his appetite for bland vegetal food, stem from the soul which came from divine regions. Evil and violent impulses and the carnivorous appetites belong to the animalic soul; it, too, is later recognized by the medicine man in some way. A man's temperament is essentially determined by the animal whose soul he possesses. A woman who bore her paralysis with good grace was said to have the soul of a butterfly; another who was lively and a little malicious, that of a capuchin monkey. The latter had already been diagnosed by a female shaman during the woman's earliest youth, for from the nape of her neck, the place of the animal soul, she had heard the call of a capuchin monkey. Souls of predators are dangerous because they completely dominate the plant souls. They are "not 'like' tigers (jaguars), or comparable to tigers, or symbolized by the tiger; no, they are themselves and by their nature tigers, though in human shape (*ibid.*: 306).

After death the soul immediately dissolves into its two components again. Nimuendaju tells us nothing of the fate of the animal soul apart from a special case which we shall discuss immediately. The plant soul embarks on its journey to the land of the dead, i.e., it returns to the location of its divine origin. If a person had been very fond of life, it might happen that his plant soul would return once more in a child. The medicine man would be able to see this and would give the child the name of the deceased. When a child dies, it is always assumed that it had been a soul returning from the dead to visit its kinsmen once more.

When a person meets a violent death, he usually remains as a ghost in the company of the living. It is the medicine man's task to remove the feared specter. He must know precisely whether he is dealing with the plant or with the animal soul. The plant soul is regarded as the less harmful of the two; the relevant ceremony is designed to catch it with the greatest care and deliver it to the realm of the dead. There everything is set right. Nimuendaju witnessed a case in which a ghost could not be removed because the medicine man erroneously assumed that he was dealing with a plant soul. The much more difficult procedure against animal souls was therefore invoked. It is not a gentle treatment; as a matter of fact, the animal soul is to be annihilated, not captured. Nimuendaju himself succeeded in shooting the ghost. Naturally, he could not see it but followed the directions of the agitated medicine man and aimed in the indicated direction. The entire episode which Nimuendaju describes very graphically (*ibid.*: 309 ff.) shows that spirits are seen in very concrete terms, for the simple reason that non-imaginative spirituality is unimaginable.

According to Nimuendaju, the two concepts of soul go back

to the dichotomies which are so widespread in the Americas, to the recognition of the polarity of nature; they reflect the opposite temperaments of man, the phlegmatic-melancholy and the sanguine-choleric. The twin heroes of the myth also stand for the two opposing temperaments and the members of the moieties traced back to them are usually said to share their temperament (*ibid.*: 314). The Apapocuva settle the dichotomy within the individual. For his practices the medicine man depends especially on the plant soul, because it constitutes the link to the beyond; he must therefore often abstain from eating meat, for a vegetable diet is said to "make him light."

So far Nimuendaju's account. We gave it in detail because of its perceptiveness. Numerous other accounts reproduce the concept of soul, here linked to the plant soul more or less clearly. The idea that the soul stems from a divine sphere and returns to the same place seems to be basic. We find it also significant that here—true to the prevailing ideas of psychophysical duality —the bond between man and the divine relates to his spiritual nature, to his "soul," alone. We shall see that, when based on other conceptions, the derivation from the divine can take other forms. The belief in animal and plant souls is peculiar to the Apapocuva but may be derived from the widespread idea of the polarity of nature. Also widespread is the belief in two or more souls inhabiting a single person; it must be explained through the particular cultural condition, a task which is not demanded of us within the framework of our topic, since the principal question about the nature of "soul" is hardly affected by it.

The ghost in whose annihilation the author participated belongs among the spirits that we shall yet discuss. We cited this portion of Nimuendaju's account to show the connection of certain spirit manifestations with the concept of soul. In anticipation, we shall only point out that we are here dealing with the soul of a murder victim, a fact which is significant in the identification of certain spirits (cf. chap. xvi, sec. 4). As to the soul concept of the Apapocuva, the account clearly shows a need to concretize purely spiritual phenomena. The dramatic gestures of the medicine man who equips the child with invisible substances show the human desire to translate the unfathomable into realities and thereby make it intelligible.

If we summarize this discussion of the concept of soul, we find that we have no proof of the idea that man must have discovered "soul" before he possessed any idea of God. The greater part of the evidence speaks against this and for the view that the concept of soul is unthinkable independent of the concept of God: "soul" is the spiritual nature of man which stems directly from the deity. The inception of a new human life is not even possible without the divine "breath." Only this *Gotteskindschaft*, this participation in the divine, makes man capable of experiencing the divine. Soul concepts, therefore, need not be based on ideas derived from causal logic but can be explained far more reasonably by regarding them as concretizations of experiences through which man became aware of the spiritual and divine aspects of the world and to which he was predisposed by his natural endowments.

Again, the implications of the concept of soul point to the fact that man, if he were incapable of experiencing the divine, would not be man at all. This capacity requires a spiritual partaking in divinity. For this reason, then, do all statements concerning the provenance of the human soul point so uniformly toward the deity as benefactor.

2. THE REALM OF THE DEAD

The descriptions of journeys to the land of the dead belong among the most impressive episodes in the oral traditions of primitive peoples. Their most splendid achievements in sculpture and painting, too, make some reference to death. This is specifically true at least of the time span that extends from the archaic cultivators to the threshold of historical cultures. All this makes a convincing case for death and an existence after death being considered significant in the ideology of most primitive peoples.

In the following pages, we shall occupy ourselves with the part which "soul" has played in the thoughts about existence after death. We shall attempt to show two separate ideological spheres, each reflecting a unique view of the nature of man. First, we shall show the uniformity which governs the ideas about the realm of the dead. The description hardly ever leaves us in doubt that it is the entire human being that embarks on the journey, the entire man in an invisible shape. In the description of shamanistic excursions to the beyond, too, the soul is pictured as being like man in form and essence. In the same manner does the existence in the beyond duplicate the ways of the living in all particulars. The departed live in houses, till their fields, celebrate the traditional feasts, marry; in some instances we even find the notion that their stay there is transitory as their life on earth had been: they propagate, age, die, and move on to a further beyond.

Among the myths which Dr. Niggemeyer and I collected in Western Ceram, many tell of the land of the dead and give vivid accounts of the life there. One of the most impressive tales (1939: 88 ff.) speaks of two chiefs who were such close friends that they made a ceremonial pact by which one would follow the other into death in order to assist each other on the difficult journey. The journey is almost always described as perilous or strenuous. When one dies, the other fails to live up to the obligation but follows the deceased secretly in order to kill him so that he cannot demand the fulfilment of the pact. He does not succeed but does manage to save his own life. While following his friend, who appears exactly as in life, he experiences the various stages of the death journey which leads across a nearby river and over certain mountains. He hears the lonely wanderer groan under the burden of his possessions and curse the faithlessness of his friend. Finally, arriving at the mountain of death after days of traveling—it is a prominent mountain in an uninhabited part of the island—he hears the voices of the departed who come to meet the new arrival and he hears the welcome by the herald of the goddess of the dead. She had once, in primal time, been the sovereign of the Dema and now plays this august role in the realm of the dead.

This example, paralleled by numerous others from many parts of the world, makes it immediately clear that one should here not speak of "soul" concepts. It is the whole person that continues to exist after death, though without its earthly body; the body is worth nothing: "it rots like a decayed tree when its time has run out."

The Ceram myth does show a difference between the forms of existence here and in the beyond. Most of the petty annoyances and the enmities of the world drop away in the hereafter. Annoyance over a lost object, hunger, lack of compassion, and the fear of evil drove the heroes of the narratives to the beyond, where such provocations do not exist. "Land without evil" is the Apapocuva's name for the realm of the dead. Often the idea is elaborated to paradisaical lengths, as among the Yaruro (chap. xi, sec. 2); to them the realm of the dead is the eternal link to the Highest Deity and the fulfilment of all conceivable wants. Description of life in the hereafter may go into such detail that the narrative loses its characteristic grandeur. Though it is then no more than a continuation of the most ordinary existence, we cannot blame the deficiency on the original thought, if we remember the ethical significance which the concept of an afterlife possesses. Admission to the realm of the dead characterizes *the fulfilled life*. In discussing the ethical content of religion (chap. ix, sec. 2), we have already pointed out that the beliefs of many primitive peoples contain the conception that man gains true humanity only to the extent that he becomes aware of the divine nature of the world. In no other way can life find fulfilment; there is no other way of entering the realm of the dead.

It is therefore quite natural that the dead are subjected to appropriate tests. We have many accounts of such examinations. Among many peoples, proof that the deceased participated in certain ceremonies during his lifetime is of significance. Among the Kayan, on Borneo, tattooing indicates the deceased had been a successful head-hunter (Hose and McDougall, II, 41). These cultic activities include the attainment of the fulfilled life through which man first achieves true humanity. Layard (p. 255) describes the extensive ceremonial life of the inhabitants of the New Hebrides, which makes explicit reference to the great difficulties involved in gaining entrance to the realm of the dead, over which a female deity presides. Only since the corruption of these activities has the bond degenerated into a causal relationship in which admission to the land of the dead is pictured as a consequence of the meticulous observance of ceremonials or even as a reward. It is not surprising that the performance of ceremonies is now a matter for anxiety and that great sacrifices are made.

We will always be confronted with the question of how man came to hold his concrete notions of an afterlife: the afterlife can hardly have been "experienced." Though such a question seems obvious, we cannot accept the notion as the aberration of a prelogical mind. Though the embellishments and the details may stem from the ordinary working of a popular imagination, the basic idea must be of the human essence which lives in us as it lived in earliest mankind—quite independently of the powers of discernment which accept only what is ascertained or ascertainable fact. Goethe repeatedly expressed his thoughts about the afterlife in his conversations with Eckermann, and his ideas might have been those of some creative mind of the remote past:

Wenn einer 75 Jahre alt ist, kann es nicht fehlen, dass er mitunter an den Tod denke. Mich lässt dieser Gedanke in völliger Ruhe, denn ich habe die feste Überzeugung, *dass unser Geist ein Wesen ist ganz unzerstörbarer Natur;* es ist ein fortwirkendes von Ewigkeit zu Ewigkeit. Es ist der Sonne ähnlich, die bloss unsern irdischen Augen unterzugehen scheiht, die aber eigentlich nie untergeht, sondern unaufhörlich fortleuchtet [*Gespräche mit Eckermann,* May 2, 1824].

3. SOUL AND THE SPIRITS OF THE DEAD

Though we dealt in the foregoing with a concept that should perhaps not really be called "soul," since it actually refers to the whole person, much evidence points toward a soul which departs from the body at death. Kruijt was probably the first to direct attention, in contradiction to Tylor's theory, to the fact that among many Indonesian peoples the *Seelenstoff* (his term) or soul-substance is by no means identical with the "soul" which leaves the body after death. According to Kruijt, this soul or *Totengeist* does not even exist during its owner's lifetime. It manifests itself only after his death, while the soul-substance, which constitutes man's actual vitality, has a fate other than that of the *Totenseele.* The distinction has since often been applied in the ethnological literature and has found confirmation through data from non-Indonesian areas. As differentiating terms, *Lebensseelen* and *Totenseelen,* as well as others, have been used (cf. W. F. Otto, *Manen*).

We shall briefly sketch the distinct destinies of the two souls. We have learned that the goal of the journey into death is a reunion with departed tribal or clan members and, especially, union with the deity that receives the deceased in the land of the dead. About the soul-substance, or *Lebensseele,* Kruijt tells us (pp. 166 ff.)—as do many others—that it returns to its origin after the death of its owner; in the overwhelming number of cases this means a return to the celestial deity from which it started out at birth. On Nias, an island west of Sumatra, for instance, the notion prevails that Lowalangi, the son the highest celestial deity, controls this soul-substance, which he apportions to each human being. After death the divine gift returns to the storehouse from which it may again be distributed.

According to another, also very widespread, notion, the *Lebensseele* hovers near the grave of its owner, frequently as a bird or some other winged creature, then to transmigrate into a newborn child or some animal, after whose death it would again begin a human life. If we disregard, at this point, the concept of soul which centers about the common destiny of man and beast (cf. chap. vii, sec. 2), there remain two basic ideas which deal with the destiny of the soul-substance. It either returns to its place of origin or enters into another creature. Neither necessarily excludes the other, and both have in common *the immortality of the soul.* In its very first beginnings it comes from God and can fulfil its purposes for all eternity either in proximity to the deity or by continuous reincarnations. This idea of a psychophysical dualism does not require the conception of a realm of the dead in which the individual being continues his existence. The conception of a celestial realm in which the souls of the departed reside is part of it. This land of souls is, according to our view, not a realm of the dead in the indicated sense at all but a divine precinct from which the soul comes forth and to which it returns after death. Only under the influence of the alternate idea of the true land of the dead are the usual descriptions applied to this abode of the souls.

The idea of a true land of the dead is found especially among the archaic cultivators. They have a thoroughly monistic view of life which sees man as a union of mind and body, directly derived, i.e., biologically descended from the deity. According to its distribution, this ideology seems to include primarily the conception of a realm of the dead in which man continues his individual existence. In this realm, the deceased are not "living dead"; rather they are men *without* their bodies that continue their eternal existence in proximity to the deity.

This is not the place to insert an essay on concepts of soul, but we may express a conjecture on the nature of these two views of life and their position in the history of culture. It would be all the more difficult to demonstrate because ideas about destiny after death have occupied mankind at all times, resulting in a profusion of philosophical speculations. Among most peoples, the most heterogeneous views have currency.

One belief stands out among the many accounts: that, with or without a specific concept of soul, man is of divine origin and reunites with deity after death. In analyzing the data, assumption has turned into probability for me that the various statements about the form of the afterlife represent a historical sequence or perhaps an ancient synchronism of two conceptions of the nature of life. The continuing life in a land of the dead, which is at the same time the abode of the deity, would be one of the primary conceptions; the separate destiny of two souls, as described by Kruijt, constitutes the amalgam of two ideological spheres. The most convincing descriptions of Dema-deities in the cultures of the archaic root-crop cultivators permit the conclusion that the dominant deity was the first to embark on the journey into death and to choose the land of the dead as his permanent abode. Thus Sido, the most important figure among the Kiwai of New Guinea, transforms himself into the house which represents the realm of the dead and which is duplicated in the cultic houses here on earth. In Western Ceram, Satene, the ruler of primeval beings, exercises power in the land of the dead. Entrance into the land of the dead, then, means not only reunion with the ancestors but, especially, reunion with the deity.

Among these peoples *Gotteskindschaft*, the filial relationship to God, is thought of quite biologically. No spirit-children are "found" and there is no need for a soul-substance; but every newborn human being is directly related to the divine Dema of the primeval past by a long line of ancestors. Chiefs and priestly officiants are therefore immediately, i.e., by biological descent, representatives of definite divine personages. When such chiefly ancestors are worshiped as deities—and this may occur even with historically determinable personages—then they usually were not elevated to godhood at their death but had always possessed divine character, even during their lifetime. Among the Herero one of the names of God is *Mukuru*. He, his wife, and the first cattle sprang from a tree. Now every chief calls himself Mukuru. The missionary Irle (pp. 72 ff.) relates many conversations with such a chief, who always asserted: "Am I not Mukuru, that is God? After all, I am Mukuru of my people!"

In such a view of life the actual soul concept has no place. The birth ceremonial in Western Ceram speaks of no adscititious soul. The events, however, do dramatize the fact that the child is related to the primeval Hainuwele by a long line of beings (cf. chap. ix, sec. 2). After death, then, it is not two soul-substances that embark on separate destinies but the deceased, i.e., the entire person with the exception of his body, who journeys to the beyond and fulfils his existence if he is admitted into the company of the deity and if he is permitted to continue an individual life in the realm of the dead.

Returning to Kruijt's observations on Indonesia, the duality of the soul concept, particularly in this island world, seems to constitute a more recent element, which is linked with the infiltration of the concept of a celestial High God. In Indonesia especially—and I am inclined to believe in Africa, also—the religious significance of a celestial deity belongs to a younger stratum, which I should call Middle Malayan (with a view to Indonesia), since it must obviously have preceded the high-cultural, Late Malayan influences. The sky-god has, however, not been able to displace the Dema-deities, just as he was unable to exert decisive influence on the cultic life; the peoples of Celebes or Borneo have remained passionate head-hunters, though by their social life (tendencies toward slavery), economy (cereal agriculture and cattle), and many other cultural factors (megaliths) they are clearly differentiated from the stratum of archaic cultivators (cf. chap. iv, sec. 8).

The introduction of new ideas of God undoubtedly also resulted in changes in the ideas of life. Here, it seems to me, belongs the belief that a particular soul-substance stems from the deity, later to return to its source while, according to the old belief, the *Totengeist,* the spirit of the dead, undertakes its journey to the land of the dead—an idea retained in the later culture stratum along with the idea of a *Lebensseele.* This historical derivation of two distinct souls, first traceable in Indonesia, is not meant to exclude the possibility that the idea of a celestial deity should be very old. Great age is even more probable in the case of the belief in the soul's return to the celestial deity, the belief in pre-existent souls, or the belief in the separate existence of spiritual beings which operate parallel to perceptible reality. Thus, the world view of the Northwestern Australian presumably antedates that of the archaic cultivators. It joins the belief in Dema-deities to the idea of the discrete soul, the spirit-child, without which new life cannot be generated. It is hardly an accident, however, that the archaic cultivators devote less (or no) attention to man's spirituality and see individual existence as predominantly biological. A newborn child is understood as a complete entity, directly descended from the divine primeval ancestors. Such a view of life had to see the act of procreation as a great and mysterious miracle and had to assign it great significance in the religious cults. At the root of all this is a conception which senses the harmony of human life with the *sterb und werde,* the life and death cycle of nature, especially in the plant kingdom, and to which the spiritual is somewhat alien.

Any attempt to devise historical sequences for the variety in life views is certainly premature. I think it possible that two quite distinct conceptions have coexisted "from the beginning." One cultural community focused squarely on spirituality, which it placed in dualistic opposition to all that is concrete; the other discovered life to be a unity and found the divine miracle in the biological process itself. Common to both is the thought that man is inconceivable without the divine. According to the dualistic view, he receives his soul from the deity; according to monism he is directly descended from it. In the more recent Indonesian culture strata, we believed we found a parallel existence of the two ideologies, a result of historically caused blending, expressed also in the parallelism of the two conceptions of God—Celestial High God and Dema-deity. Psychophysical dualism engendered the idea of a distinct soul-substance. For this, the idea of a land of the dead is not prerequisite; in our opinion it may belong to the monistic view. Both ideological spheres have joined and produced the notion that a distinct soul-substance or *Lebensseele* returns to the deity after death, but that another soul—essentially the deceased individual himself, as in the monistic view—embarks on a journey to the beyond.

These thoughts are only conjectures. They are abstracted from the concepts themselves, although they are not proven by data. Reference to correspondences in the data is made particularly difficult by the fact that most peoples hold a variety of beliefs about soul, life, and death, side by side. Thus, the archaic cultivator populations, as typical representatives of the monistic view, also possess in some form an idea of spiritual entities that form a part of things. Despite such instances, research need not despair of segregating the genuine and obligatory components from the totality of conceptions which make up the culture of a people; casually accepted ideas can often be recognized by their small significance in religious practice. A central idea of God can often be distinguished from less important manifestations, to the same extent that it should be possible to delimit the original views of life and afterlife from other less compelling ideas. However, in my opinion, the available field data fail us as far as answers to these questions are concerned.

15

ANCESTOR CULTS AND MANISTIC OFFERINGS

We cannot hope to go into a comprehensive investigation of the very complex phenomenon of ancestor cults here. We shall deliberately limit ourselves to those aspects that are concerned with their genuinely religious contents.

1. BIOLOGICAL DESCENT AND NAME-INHERITANCE

After all that has been said so far, it can hardly be doubted that the religious significance of ancestor cults must be understood in terms of their own profoundly spiritual concern with life. Ethnology agrees that the manistic cults have found their most powerful expression among the cultivator populations. A major part of their ceremonial life is oriented toward communion with departed ancestors. No tilling of the fields, no wedding, no puberty ceremony can take place without some communication with the dead. The dead continue to belong to the community of the living; one even gets the impression that they are the more important segment. The life of primitive man is in the trammels of tradition to an extent hardly imaginable. Attention is fixed on the past and on earliest, divine, beginnings. The more recent past is, of course, more given over to life and more closely tied to the present. Thus cultic activities that deal with the dead usually make reference to the last link in the chain of ancestors, but the idea itself extends to all, to the very end of primal time. This is greatly aided by an ahistorical attitude toward time spans; in the thought of most peoples, primal time begins precisely where active memory ends—thus, about the time of one's great-grandfather. The distinction between ancestors that have long been dead and are unknown and those that are still remembered has often been stressed in discussions of religious content among primitive peoples. It is, however, not of a fundamental nature but results only from the personal relationship of the living to the dead. Ideologically, all ancestors are meant.

Of greater importance is another distinction which we encounter in many accounts of ancestor cults. As priestly dignitaries were distinguished from common members of the cultural community even in very archaic cultures, so are those personages among the dead that stand out from the mass of unknown ancestors. For the valuation of ancestor cults as truly religious phenomena, we must find an answer to the question: what criteria place some of the dead and their descendants in contrast to others, even in cultural settings which otherwise know no social stratification? The answer will show that ancestor cult is not a form of religion in its own right but only a specific attitude within religious behavior in general, which is primarily determined by the relationship between man and deity.

Even in the cult of the dead, which cannot properly be counted among the ancestor cults since it deals only with the recently deceased who have not yet entered the realm of the dead, there are rudiments of differentiation, which are, as we have seen, of greatest importance to each member of the community. The survivors are anxious that the departed shall succeed in entering the realm of the dead. Only then will he remain a member of the community of the living and participate in celebrations to which all the dead are solemnly invited. Although the cultic forms are more or less the same for all the dead, departed priests rate disproportionately higher. The priestly officiant, however, does not possess his eminence on the strength of his office, but, quite to the contrary, he holds the office because he can, to a higher degree, be representative of the Dema-deity—this especially by descent through a long chain of ancestors who were all first sons. The beginnings of social stratification, which, interestingly enough, are revealed in the spiritual rather than the economic life, rest on the differential significance of the Dema. As stated (chap. iv, sec. 3), all men are descended from the (usually large) number of primeval Dema that were all, to a certain extent, gifted with divine creativity. Among them, those personages stand out that we have designated as Dema-deities in the narrower sense. Priestly officiants usually trace themselves back to them, which explains their greater prestige in the community. It permits these officiants to portray the Dema-deity at cultic events. The close tie between deity and certain living priestly functionaries and their ancestors or predecessors may be read in many accounts. According to Preuss (*Nayarit:* liii), the Cora Indians regard their dead as intermediaries to the higher deities. Appeals, however, are made only through the departed of the last two generations, evidence of the more active relationship felt with the personally remembered dead. Those who passed on earlier are "mere adjuncts to the overabundance of lesser nature deities," that are subsumed under the term "rain-gods" and are equated with those dead that appear as "our ancient ones" at the cultic celebrations. They are called by the same appellations as the contemporary ceremonial leaders, the priests, who actually are their successors. We see, then, that "ancestor" does not always refer to all the deceased but, at times, only to certain prominent figures among them, as, in our example, to the predecessors of the priests. Succession to certain priestly offices is, among some peoples, determined by biological descent, among other peoples, by transfer of names or titles in the absence of the element of consanguinity.

The Konso of southern Ethiopia have a remarkably complicated social organization. Among the numerous officeholders in a village, a sort of village headman holds the most prominent position. His office is hereditary and is passed on from father to oldest son. The homestead of the headman lies just outside the palisade-inclosed village near a sacred precinct which is visited only on festive occasions and which women never enter. The headman bears the name of the mythic founder of the village. *It is both his name and his title.* He is thought of as the direct descendant of this mythical personage, whom we can regard as a local Dema-deity—whether he had been a historical person or not. The founder of the village is buried in the sacred precinct and this fact lends the location most of its sanctity. The throne on which he "rested" is today the seat of his descendant during the celebrations. The deceased village headmen—his ancestors—are buried nearby. His monument, however, stands separate from the grave and consists of wood sculptures which depict the full range of his religious and social merits. Such monuments are usually erected at crossroads or other conspicuous spots. Sculptures for the village headman, however, are placed at the periphery of the sacred precinct. None of the figures is ever touched once they have been erected; they gradually decay and fall victim to termites. When the monument has fallen into ruin after one or two generations, the vivid memory of the departed has died with it and he has joined the host of ancestors that is apostrophized at every great cultic occasion (Jensen, *Gada:* 563). The same situation is found among the Cora Indians: at the beginning stands the mythic figure of a deity from whom certain officiants trace their descent. The last living descendant represents not only the deity but all of his ancestors. The most recently deceased, whose memory is still alive, evoke a relatively greater sense of presence. The decay of the monument symbolizes, among the Konso, the gradual decline of a living memory.

Often it is not biological descent but the likeness of names that furnishes the decisive characteristic. The meaning is without a doubt basically the same as the Konso headman's taking on the personal name and title of the village founder at the assumption of his office while, at the same time, being his direct descendant. The excellent material which Nimuendaju presents on the Timbira of Brazil clearly shows the significance of the transfer of names. As already mentioned, the social organization of the Timbira is extraordinarily complicated and, incidentally, has a surprising resemblance with that of the Konso in some of its features. Among the Timbira several moiety structures exist side by side. Membership in some is matrilineally inherited, in others through name transfer. Among the Eastern Timbira masculine personal names belong to a defined subgrouping of moieties. The name which an individual has inherited from some relative assigns him a seat at the place of assembly (Nimuendaju, 1946: 85).

That name-inheritance is a parallel to the calculation of descent becomes clear among the western grouping of the Timbira, the Apinayé. Names always stay within one of the moieties and descend from a maternal uncle or a maternal aunt upon niece or nephew. The most important datum, however, refers to the close link between name and ceremonial function. Some of the names are arranged in pairs so that a specific name in one moiety is matched by one from the opposite moiety. The Apinayé even have a name for this cross-relationship which affirms the importance assigned to this practice in the thinking of the people. The ceremonial functions of the bearers of those names are quite distinct. In certain ceremonial races, in which the runners carry massive logs, the two moieties constitute the contesting parties. The initial raising of the logs at the beginning of the race is done by bearers of co-ordinate names from both groups. Other pairs are leaders of particular initiation groups. There also are names which are of significance in only one moiety, while there is no matching relationship in the other. The bearers of such names have definite ceremonial roles in cultivation, hunting, when brush fires occur, and at many other occasions (Nimuendaju, 1939: 21 ff.).

Although Nimuendaju does not tell us, there seems to me no possible doubt that the ceremonial significance of the name goes back to mythic events in which certain Dema with certain names accomplished certain deeds, such as, for instance, the carrying out of the first log race. Name-inheritance placed the living in a special relationship to the Dema, i.e., they are his living representatives and in the ceremonies do what the original bearer of the names did. The behavior pattern is always the same: *The higher meaning of life as revealed in the ceremonial observances lies in its association with the primeval activity of the deity.*

We are not told whether the living bearer of a name feels a particularly close bond with those ancestors who bore it before. Yet it would be only logical that he do so. Such thinking is found among the Eskimos who have a hunting economy but whose spiritual culture represents a stage higher than that of the gatherers (cf. chap. vi, sec. 2). Rasmussen (1929: 172) reports that a newborn child receives the name and the sum of his personal qualities from someone who has died. It is felt that one inherits the mental and physical characteristics of all those who have borne the same name. Shamans say that they can sometimes, on their soul-journeys, see mighty processions of spirits following each individual, to assist him and guide him as long as he observes the rules. They turn against the bearer of their name when he transgresses the code (*ibid.*: 58). The bond among all who have the same name is neatly expressed in the fact that custom obliges them to exchange gifts when they encounter one another. This is to "strengthen" their souls and to delight their departed namesakes (*ibid.*: 183).

In summing up our ideas on the ancestor cults, we are forcibly impressed by the fact that the ancestors themselves are not the objects of cultic reverence but enjoy their distinction in consequence of an over-all religious conception which centers about the relationship between deity and man. Some of the deceased have a special relationship to the deity which may be shared by certain living persons but which receives its final attestation only upon admission to the realm of the dead. The basis of this religious relationship to the dead lies in the (correct) conception that man partakes of the divine—either in being created in the image of God, or in receiving from the deity a spiritual quality which constitutes his true "life substance," or even in being thought to have descended from the deity through the chain of ancestors. Thus, the miracles of procreation and birth share in the divine. These notions of a bond between deity and man logically lead to certain beliefs concerning the relationship between the living and the dead. Those who are admitted to the land of the dead have had a "fulfilled" life; they could not have entered the afterlife if they had not attained fulfilment during their lifetimes. In their case, partaking of the divine has already actualized what is still an uncertainty to the living. The dead, having attained a higher level of humanity and residing in the presence of the primeval deities, are thereby the elect intermediaries between deity and man.

Independent of this source of the divine character of all who reside in the land of the dead, there is the great deed through which a mortal of the distant past became a primeval Dema when he—as village founder or leader in tribal migrations, and just like the mythic figures—had established part of the existing order of things. *The institution of a new and obligatory order which we regard as the primary creative element in man,* and whereby man is distinguished from all other creatures, is generally an individual act. Primitive beliefs tend to identify creative personalities with their descendants, the bearers of their names and titles. The Dema-like leader and founder was in his lifetime already a "descendant" and possessed a greater than normal share of the divine, since he was able to trace his ancestry to a deity. This image of existence, which is most clearly outlined in the cultures of the cultivators, has had great effects upon the later history of culture. Most remote to our understanding is the usually quite concrete idea of existence in the realm of the dead. We are justified in asking what experiences can have led man to such beliefs. We quoted Goethe to show that such ideas are not alien to occidental thought. In any event, early mankind formed beliefs that harmonized with its sensibilities and, therefore, these cannot be eradicated by rationalistic arguments. For us the bridges to the world of the dead no longer exist; we have no statement to make. Primitive peoples, on the other hand, can be quite specific and concrete. Of what kind the experiences—if there be any—that produced such statements might have been, we have no way of knowing.

2. MANISTIC SACRIFICE AS GIFT

We devoted an earlier chapter (viii) to a discussion of blood-sacrifices. We regarded their original meaning as a reiterative ritual killing, related in turn to the mythic slaying of a primeval deity. Totally different is the meaning of the so-called manistic sacrifices, which can in no way refer to the mythologem of deicide, the Hainuwele mythologem. We must distinguish several types, each of which suggests a particular meaning. At the occasion of a death and especially the death of an outstanding personality, a chief, or some other notable, when a head-hunting expedition is undertaken or a slave or animal is killed, then the practice undoubtedly belongs ideologically to those killing rituals that are a *sacrificium*, a sacred act, but not a sacrifice as we understand it in common usage. When the archaic Sudanic peoples on some occasions—there are many that are associated with tilling the fields or the human life cycle—kill a chicken or some animal at a site consecrated to the ancestors, take special measures with the blood, or engage in some other cultic activity, then we do not know what ideas were originally connected with it. Undoubtedly, they, too, point more toward the killing ritual than to the common meaning of *sacrifice*.

But when food and drink are placed on the grave—and this is manistic sacrifice proper—and when native belief states that these are not eaten or drunk by the deceased but that he does consume a "spiritual something" of them, then we are quite within the sphere of "soul" and "death" concepts. Tylor showed at the hand of excellent data that the concept of soul encompasses not only man but animals, plants, and even inanimate objects. This is actually not at all surprising. Once soul stands for that spiritual something which constitutes a spiritual essence, the quality of any object in which this essence is revealed is best expressed as its "soul." We ourselves often use the word in this sense. We may speak of the soul of a tree, a mountain, scenery, or even of an edifice or some cultural artifact, and we know quite well what is meant. I see no reason to assume that primitive peoples use the terms in any other sense, i.e., as the name of the special and unique nature of some phenomenon.

The dualistic view, maintained and demonstrated by Tylor, that there exists the possibility of a separation of soul from substances or of spirituality from the thing itself is obviously one of the spiritual sources of the custom of making funerary offerings of food, drink, or other objects. It might be particularly emphasized that cultivator populations who are particularly given to manistic practices and who are characterized by a monistic world view make explicit mention of the spiritual nature of the gifts. We have already pointed out that the idea of spiritual entities is extraordinarily widespread and is found among peoples of decidedly monistic attitudes.

In the case of gift giving the relationship of one party to the other is always significant. In the foreground are concrete ideas about the difficult journey into the beyond during which the thoughts of the living are constant companions to the departed. We declared ourselves incapable of making any statement about the realities or experiences which may have induced these conceptions. We can do no more than recognize that primitive peoples believe they have knowledge of the fate of man immediately upon his death. It is part of his destiny to be dependent on the succor of the living. Aside from spiritual support during the numerous ceremonies, this dependence consists of substantive assistance such as in providing sustenance, clothing, implements, currency, etc. According to most accounts, gift giving ends with the great festival that celebrates the end of the journey, the arrival at the goal, and admission to the realm of the dead. On the part of the donors the "death offering" carries out the urge to surround the departed with kindness and care: "*Liebe zeigt die schenkende Gebärde.*" Yet sentiment alone never can explain the custom without the complementary explanation that the deceased has need of the gifts. Besides solicitousness for the individual dead during the journey to the beyond, there are many other offerings to the deceased at large, deposited at sanctuaries that are consecrated to the ancestors. They may correspond in meaning to the sustenance provided for the great journey, especially if the deceased is imagined to be present, as at many ceremonial feasts. Seen as a whole, manistic sacrifice is far less a *sacrificium* than the ritual killing; in the final analysis it is a gift to a being that is in need of it and an almost inevitable consequence of the view that the deceased continue to be members of the community. They can be actually present as spiritual guests, and the spirituality of their existence allows them to make use of the spirituality of the offerings. A fantastic and horrifying extension of this thinking is revealed—though exclusively among peoples of younger culture strata that have state organization—in the grisly practice of killing men and animals so that their souls may serve the deceased or in order to send them into the beyond carrying a message to a departed king. These are late and derivative motivations that have strayed far from the sources of the original conceptions and from their true experiential background.

We have not introduced the subject of primitial offerings, which undoubtedly play a major role among many primitive peoples and which are also accorded great weight by the hypothesis of primal monotheism, which assigns them to the most archaic stratum of the High God concept; an interpretation seems beyond present possibilities. As an offering to a deity that is explicitly not in need of it, I find it no more understandable than other, similarly interpreted, offerings.

16

Söderblom pointed out that a great number of spirit-concepts cannot be traced back to the idea of an afterlife. Unfortunately, however, we possess no very searching investigations into the nature of spirits beyond such general assertions. Even a casual acquaintance with the immensely extensive data leaves no doubt that the "spirits" of ethnological literature and of the literature of the science of religion stem from a variety of backgrounds and can hardly be subsumed under any one common denominator.

The heterogeneity of the spirit-concepts, the sheer bulk of the data, and the lack of detailed research are only some of the obstacles. Another difficulty we have already discussed: our inability to comprehend what is so unequivocally plain to primitive peoples. No occidental is in a position to make credible and concrete statements about the nature of an afterlife. Primitive peoples, however, do this not only about the afterlife but also about spirits. In many communities there is hardly a person who has not had in the course of his life some encounter with a spirit which he can accurately describe. Spirits appear not only in dreams, although dream encounters are the most frequent source of experience; they are occasionally seen in broad daylight; and one may have the most varied kinds of contact with them.

1. FEAR AND HOSTILITY

In all probability it is impossible with the means now at our command to understand spirits as they are conceptualized by primitive peoples. Yet we may ask ourselves this initial question: how can such clearly described encounters with spirits take place at all? The most direct answer might be: such experiences come about because there *are* spirits and because primitive people—in contrast to the average occidental—have the gift of communicating with them. The possible correctness of this answer cannot be rejected on purely theoretical grounds. But it brings us no closer to understanding; we would have to discover in ourselves states of consciousness that would make us capable of similar experiences. The answer is apparently not workable.

Another answer might be: primitive man has become a victim of hallucinations. We do know of hallucinations; there is no doubt that they occur, and to this extent the answer makes sense. However, hallucinations do not arise out of nothing; they must be linked to known conceptions. No one previously unacquainted with the idea can have the hallucination of a spirit. In fact, primitive peoples have manifold concepts of spirits; they inherit them from their forefathers. But at one time, in the past, the idea of specific spirits must have confronted man so persuasively that hallucinations henceforth became possible. In other words, the reality of spirits—perceived or not—must once have been recognized, and we must then ask in what spheres of the human psyche perception has its locus. What specifically constitutes the experiential basis will be difficult to say and possibly there will be no solution at all.

We shall leave this for later discussion (sec. 7) and now turn to the forms in which spirits may appear. Misleading as a comparison of primitive peoples with children has proven to be, there may be occasional justification for it, especially when dealing with attitudes that are to be seen detached from the influences of our culture. It can aid us toward an understanding of the behavior of primitive man, for we, too, were once children and carry memories of our experiences. We know through our childhood that it is easy to fill the world with spirits and ghosts, once the child's mind is directed toward them. The guardian angel, Santa Claus, or witches can become so real to a child that an encounter with them seems completely possible. We see again and again that intense experiences of this kind are associated with feelings of fear, just as threatening with such specters is an effective, though dubious, means of giving the adult control over children when other forms of wielding authority fail. Although this pedagogical motivation is entirely lacking among primitive peoples, fear is a primary element of their dealings with spirits. We have already mentioned the oft-repeated assertions that primitive peoples of a certain culture stratum do not believe in divine beings but only fear spirits while worshiping ancestors. It cannot in fact be disputed that fear of spirits plays a prominent part in their everyday lives. Even in our culture, where spirits are not generally credited with any reality, they have preserved their connotations of fear from ancient days.

Childhood experiences, then, demonstrate no more than the ease with which the world view of a people may be populated with spiritual beings. Once the concept has been formed, it can easily assume reality, just as a child may accept the appearance of a spirit (more often perhaps that of a burglar or "enemy") or to read it into some object in a darkened room. The child is much more directly influenced by the "biological proximity" of a familiar environment—here, too, the analogy with primitive peoples is justified—and by the "hostility" of the unknown. Growing into a familiar environment produces a valuation that extends into the biological sphere; everything is treated affirmatively that belongs to this world and, conversely, everything is denied that enters as an alien element. That this is a biological process is shown, not only by the behavior of children, but even more clearly in dogs that love a master who mistreats them. The dog will bark furiously at any stranger, even if he treats the dog with greater kindness than does the master. This biologically rooted feeling that everything strange is hostile is decidedly present in the primitive world.

We have already encountered this in *kanaime* (chap. xi, sec. 1), which plays such a central role in the sentiments of the Guayana peoples. In *kanaime,* "alien" and "hostile" are synonyms; beyond this it includes an element of the mysterious. Hostile tribes may be *kanaime* but so are the spirits that live by day in human form and turn into animals at night. In this sense *kanaime* appears in spirits like the Weddu and Subach, to which we shall refer in section six. The fear of the unfamiliar as hostile and menacing is characteristically associated with belief in spirits. Hostility aims at doing harm; in its very nature it is reciprocal. One expects no good from an enemy and takes protective measures against him, most simply by giving him no chance to carry out his designs. Most of the harm expected from a foe centers about the loss of life, health, or property. For the belief in spirits, harm to health is most significant, although spirit interference in the other areas has also produced a variety of cultural countermeasures. *The nature of sickness* has been the subject of man's questioning since earliest time as it is still today.

2. THE NATURE OF SICKNESS

What is the nature of sickness? The answers given by primitive peoples may be reduced to two formulas which are frequently found side by side. They usually focus attention on the essence and—among peoples of dualistic ideas—on the "spiritual parallels" of the phenomena. They are not satisfied with biologically expressed manifestations, though these are frequently taken into consideration. Primitive peoples see the causes of sickness in man's arbitrary interference with the universal order. The deity itself is then usually thought to be the cause of the disease. (As we saw in discussing the religious ethos, the original idea possesses even greater immediacy: disturbance of the order—and non-ethical acts are just that—already carries the seed of doom, so that there is no call for a punitive deity.) The spirits that have shot their arrows, as exponents of the hostile world, or have caused sickness in other quite tangible ways would seem to be more widely distributed.

These ideas are commonly given short shrift: they are superstitious and foolish. In *Kosmos*, for instance, we can read (1950: 63) the following about epilepsy, the sacred sickness:

Men of earlier cultures, overwhelmed by anxiety and a feeling of helplessness, gave the incomprehensible a mythic garb and fancied an invisible spirit world. As with other illnesses, there were terrifying demons that slipped into the huts and attacked the people. By means of amulets, tattoos, and offerings, primitive man attempted to drive off the spirits.

The same article later quotes Dostoevski, who was himself an epileptic and wrote on the epileptic seizures of Mohammed: "[The Prophet] does not lie; he undoubtedly was in Paradise even though it was in an epileptic attack; I do not know if this ecstasy lasts seconds or hours, but you must believe me, I would not exchange it for all the joys of life." The experiences of the Prophet resemble in all material details those of the shamans, who, not rarely, are epileptics and who are able, according to their own statements, to travel into subterranean regions which often are described as Paradise. We have here from our own cultural environment a statement which is closer to the primitive view than that of the medical author in *Kosmos*, who considers today's ideas on epilepsy basically different, leaving no room for a "mythic view." He is undoubtedly right; he is wrong only in believing that scientific findings about cerebral events create a system of statements which can take the place of those made by primitive peoples. Rather, they belong to a separate sphere of experience which has almost nothing in common with the qualitative psychology of primitive beliefs.

This applies not only to epilepsy but to all sicknesses, more or less. When illiterate peoples, almost everywhere, ascribe illness to the work of spirits, it means only that they believe in spiritual forces which are operative throughout nature. Even if the intrusion of a foreign object into the body of the patient is given as cause, we are often dealing only with the reification of belief in hostile spiritual forces, as Ackerknecht maintains (p. 622). Occasionally, this comes from the fact that substances which the shaman removes from the body are invisible. Scientifically, however, we feel safe in stating that spirits or spiritual entities cannot be quantitatively ascertained as causes of disease. But when a person falls ill with cancer in the prime of life and languishes away, it should not seem absurd to think of a "hostile force" which has destroyed his life. Tracing the illness to an evil spirit seems hardly more than an explanatory image; we should think of it as giving a name to a disease.

In some respects, primitive peoples are no more helpless in the face of sickness than we are. Resignation to disease seems to be no more frequent with them than with us. They have their doctors and their medicines, and their faith in them may well be stronger than ours. Important, then, in view of the measure of truth inherent in their conception of the nature of illness, would be the question of its verity being demonstrated or even being shown to be probable.

Here we approach one of the central problems of the belief in spirits. Occidental medicine has made use of so-called household remedies until recent times—at first to the complete and then to the almost complete exclusion of all others. This pharmacology undoubtedly has its origin in prehistory and rests on an idea of the nature of disease which does not differ from those of contemporary primitive peoples. Primitive medical lore makes use of many such medicines or therapeutic measures as rubbing, sweating, and bloodletting. Little research has been done, but, on analogy with the history of Western medicine, we are justified in assuming that many of their remedies are effective in the same sense in which we believe ours to be. How is it possible that primitive peoples, given their ideas of disease, have arrived at results which—if we think of our own folk remedies—were initially not surpassed by our own medical science? This fact alone gives occasion for reflection.

We do not doubt that medical science is capable of insights which are unattainable to the spiritual attitudes of primitive peoples. But should we not have to reckon with the possibility that earlier ideas, in which the spirituality of the spirits plays a role, were capable in their own right of gaining insights attainable only through this and not any other spiritual attitude?

3. MEDICINES AND POISONS

The Itonama in northeastern Bolivia believe that every animal species is linked to a plant species. In their current reasoning they derive the pairings exclusively from external resemblances. The fact alone that they have a term, *huaboa,* for the relationship speaks for a former deeper significance. The *huaboa*-plant of the alligator is said to have leaves which bear a certain likeness to an alligator head. One who touches such a plant runs the risk of being pursued by alligators. The same is true of the *huaboa*-plants of jaguars and venomous snakes (Nordenskiöld, p. 195). If we knew the belief only in this form, we should try to count it among the incomprehensibilities of which we spoke earlier (chap. xii, sec. 8). We should find a way, however, to make it at least probable that these late and semantically depleted statements conceal an originally valid insight into realities. The same dangerous climbing plants are stuck into the ground around the fields and no Itonama will steal the fruit. They are probably warnings and markers of property as we know them also from eastern Indonesia (cf. Jensen, *Drei Ströme:* 260 ff.). In Indonesia, markers are usually put up that are named after an animal, now and then also after a plant or object. Those who disregard the markers and steal in spite of them are attacked by certain illnesses, such as stomach ache, mental disturbances, or pains in the knee. The interpretation suggests itself that the disregarding of sacred markers results in retribution and that the touching of the plant as such received its implication of danger only secondarily. It should be added that men also have their associated *huaboa*-plants and that these, interestingly enough, are medicinal herbs.

Very similar data are offered by Roth (pp. 281 ff.) on the Guayana tribes. But there the associated plants are not a threat to man but assist him in the chase of the respective animal. The hunter either carries a young shoot of the plant on his person, rubs his weapons with it, or has it rubbed into incisions in his body (Penard, pp. 177 ff.).

About such plants, W. Pelikan (p. 7) says that

it is curious that plants used for such purposes are usually caladium species, i.e., tropical aroids. It is a plant family which does indeed have a unique relation to the animal kingdom. In some respects, they transcend the normal plant processes. For instance, their flowers often develop a specific heat which rises above the ambient temperature. The flowers extend far downward to the root systems and sometimes assume a mushroom-like appearance. The chalice becomes a regular animal trap: it emits odors of spoiled meat and thereby attracts a particular kind of fly, which is prevented, by seine hairs, from escaping the "kettle trap."

If this is correct, the relationship is one between plant and animal, and not a matter of external likeness or similarities of form.

A third type of relationship—the one that seems to me the proper and genuine one—is given in the beliefs of the Apinayé (Nimuendaju, 1939: 146). It is believed that for each species of edible animals there is a corresponding wild plant species which can be used as a remedy when an illness befalls one who eats the meat, i.e., through the harmful effect of ingesting the "soul" of the animal. Mooney (p. 252) reports a myth of the Cherokee in which illness and remedial effect are traced to the operation of spiritual essences of animals and plants. Illnesses were imposed by the game out of revenge. The spirits of the remedial plants decided to place themselves at man's disposal as medicines against disease. The belief that man ingests the effective spiritual essence of a plant is often documented. The spirits of narcotic plants tell things otherwise unknowable—the future, the cause of an illness, the proper remedy, etc.

The pharmacological lore of primitive peoples is built on

assumptions that relate phenomena in ways which are not justified by our sense of reality. A decisive question would be the
effectiveness of the medicines. The absence of research on this
point, however, precludes an answer. Two factors make it likely
that the medication is in many cases actually effective: for one,
the comparison with our folk remedies; and, second, the fact that
the detrimentally operative plants, i.e., the poisons, had been
correctly recognized by primitives with the very same mentality.
In tropical South America there are more than one hundred fish
poisons of vegetal derivation and their efficacy cannot be
doubted.

This also applies to arrow poisons, including the dreaded curare.
The Canelo and Jivaro in Ecuador say forest demons reside in
plants from which arrow poison is made. For its production the
"sorcerer" withdraws to the forest in order to subdue these spirit-
beings and make them subservient to his will (Karsten, 1920:
15 ff.).[1] The effectiveness of curative plants is ascribed to their
benevolent spirit tenants, the effectiveness of the poisons to hostile spiritual entities. Among the archaic Semang on the Malayan
peninsula, this belief is joined to some peculiar concepts of soul:
Kari, the supreme deity, apportions "souls" to all living creatures. He broadcasts the souls of animals like seeds over the
ground; where they fall, mushrooms will grow. Before giving
birth to her young, the animal eats a mushroom which possesses
a soul befitting her species, and this soul enters the unborn young.
All creatures harmful to man receive the souls of poisonous mushrooms. When a person eats a poisonous mushroom, the contained
animal soul attacks him as violently as if it were a fully grown
animal (Skeat, I, 4).

Independent of the belief in spirits, certain forest tribes in
South America possess analogous myths about the origin of medicines, narcotics, and poisons, as well as vestiges of the Hainuwele
mythologem. Medicines, narcotics, and poisons are also often
derived from the body of a dead "spirit." Considering the importance which such plants have in the life of the Indians, this
is not astonishing. How great the significance of the narcotics is
to the religious life we have seen in the discussion of Soma-
Haoma and peyote (chap. viii, sec. 4).

[1] The sources on America are taken from the works of O. Zerries (cf. Bibliography).

Poisonous and medicinal plants are discussed in the same terms, and though we cannot check the effectiveness of the medicinal plants, we do not doubt the effectiveness of the poisons. It can be objected that poisoning is far more obvious and unequivocal and that its discovery could hardly have been avoided. But it seems most significant that the ideas about medicinal plants are analogous to those about poisons and that both convey a particular impression of the nature of plants. Classification of plants into a system is predominantly the result of an attitude that sees the plant not as a source of effective chemical substance but assumes it to possess a spirituality that was taken to be analogous to the spirituality of other living things. The statements founded on this assumption are quite sensible. Moreover, this attitude, oriented toward the spiritual, may have been the creative causation of man's ability to make the discovery. In this he would have surpassed by far the corresponding abilities of animals. Contemporary man would not be in a position to make such a discovery. Our inability is borne out by our changed relationship to plants, and we can therefore no longer say how man came to discover medicinal plants and poisons; we no longer "understand" the underlying attitude.

It may be objected that all the statements of primitive peoples are no more than a late accretion of superstitions which has no connection with discovery. The knowledge might have been gained in the normal way of trial and error and it might be that only the mythic propensities of man linked simple experiences to a belief in demonic spirits. Theoretically this is possible. But how should we imagine this process: not only are there several thousand plants to be tested; all of them are divided into parts: roots, stems, leaves, flowers, fruits, etc. The effective component usually comes from one portion of the plant. In the application there are again many alternatives: remedies are used internally and externally; they are laid on or massaged in; an extract is made, etc. If, then, the number of possible outcomes is enormously large on the side of the medications, it grows to unimaginable magnitudes when we consider the number of possible afflictions which may be larger than the number of remedies. One must try to imagine the process of experimentation which always presupposes that the accumulating positive or negative experiences are taken into consideration in the continuation. This notion receives no support from references to the millennia of human history that could have been devoted to the task; we can imagine that a positive result, i.e., an effective remedy, might be handed down through time, but not so the negative experiences.

If trial and error are eliminated as causes of discovery, only accident remains. Here the history of millennia makes a useful argument: any accident that did not happen within a hundred years may well happen within a thousand. But the word "accident," wherever used, denotes embarrassment and stalling; it contributes no explanation. If the Australians had by accident found a piece of meteoric iron and had, by accident, noted that it can be shaped by heating and hammering, they would nevertheless hardly have had an iron industry thereby. It might have been just such an accident, however, that led man, at some point in cultural history, to switch over to the utilization of iron. This presupposes that the accident occurred in a situation in which his mind was able to integrate it into the particular reality and world view. In the discovery of iron manufacture, accident can have had no greater part than in the discovery of the New World. No one doubts the historical contingency of that event. The discovery of a medicinal plant cannot have been otherwise. The experience can have benefited man only if it "came at the right time." This means only, however, that mankind was mentally prepared for the discovery of medicines and that they would most likely have been discovered even if accident had not helped.

It is always important to have a clear conception of the process in which the cultural inventory originates. In this particular instance we must begin at a cultural level on which medicinal plants are unknown. How might man have formed the notion that a particular plant should be used against a particular ill? A one-time, purely accidental effect would certainly never have been noticed if the "historical situation" had not directed attention to the possibility of interactions. This obviously suggests the exemplifying beliefs which relate plant, animal, and man in reciprocal interplay. Everything is placed in hostile or friendly relationships. It is clear evidence that there had been a "historical situation" in the early history of mankind in which a substantial part of awareness was occupied with this aspect of reality. The *kanaime* concept of the Guayana peoples lets us see only a minute segment of this world view. The information about *huaboa-*

305

plants goes far beyond it and contains far deeper insights into a very specific nature of things. They do not originate in a biological awareness, as the *kanaime* concept, but locate animals and plants in an objective system according to their relationship to each other and to man. Undoubtedly, there is a relationship of affinity and antagonism, and the nature of things is at least in part expressive of it. Not only poisons and remedies are based on it but so are many other aspects of reality; so, for instance, the assertion that certain colors "go together" while others "clash." To have recognized the particular nature of things— especially in the plant and animal kingdoms—is the great merit of a cultural epoch that was enabled to do so only by a very particular relation to reality. Other cultural epochs did not possess this specific ability; they lacked the culturally determined prerequisites.

The conceptions of nature and function of the natural species which we have cited seem to us a precipitate of this world view, as one of its cultural formulations. As such they are subject to the law of metamorphosis from expression to application; many customs and practices among primitive peoples are undoubtedly no more than their semantically impoverished "survivals." The *huaboa* relationship, which is rooted entirely in external similarities, has demonstrated the point. Many other phenomena which ethnology is in the habit of labeling imitative magic fall, in my opinion, into this category. If, in summing up, we once more ask what the characteristic of the historical situation is which might have led to the discovery of medicinal plants, we shall select the attitude which stresses the spirituality of all things of the universe and their possibilities of interaction. It would, then, have been the belief in "spirits" that enabled man to discover the potential of plants to work to his harm or good.

When we speak of a spirit, we tend to think of it as a person. Up to now we have dealt only with spiritual beings that appear in the literature as spirits. Usually, according to primitive beliefs, plant spirits have no shape or are pictured as infinitesimally small creatures. Despite this, they are usually thought of as persons, as, for instance, were the *ayug*-spirits of trees and plants (cf. chap. xi, sec. 1). Their personality is much less defined than the ghosts of the dead, which will be discussed in the next section. To that extent, the spirits discussed so far are identical with the spirits of sickness to which we must return (sec. 6). In both types we are dealing with some agent force of the phenomena, i.e., something spiritual, which undoubtedly is only secondarily personified and, in the final analysis, without significance.

4. SPIRITS AND THE EVIL DEATH

It is quite usual for savage tribes to live in terror of the souls of the dead as harmful spirits—so writes Tylor (II, 197), who does not notice that immediately thereafter his own data resolve into a curious contradiction; on the one hand, horrifying and tormenting spirits are mentioned, outspoken foes of man, and, on the other hand, "deified ancestors" who are regarded on the whole as kindly patron saints, at least to their own kinfolk and worshipers (II, 199).

Fear of the dead is in any case said to be the most natural emotion and at the base of much of the spiritual posture of early man. H. Naumann (p. 52) takes the malicious character of the dead for granted; the dead, he argues, share the feeling of gregariousness with the living and therefore they fetch those they love best. The dead thus become heralds of death and in consequence are feared. Funerary rites supposedly have the only purpose of hindering the deceased in his misanthropic endeavors. Cremation, for instance, stemmed from the desire to destroy the dead totally.

But since cremation was powerless against dreams and fantasies, since the dead and annihilated returned just the same, there was but one conclusion left: life is not lodged in the body but . . . in the soul. . . . The entire animism is probably nothing but a concomitant of cremation, a logical deduction from a fruitless defensive rite [*ibid.*: 59].

Some manifestations of the ancestor cults contradict the view that the fear of death is natural. The attitude is quite different. The dead are invited to the feasts, are portrayed by masks, or participate in their subterranean abode. The contradiction cannot be resolved, as Tylor obviously attempted to do, by declaring that the same dead can very well be evil and benign alternately, like a strict father or ruler who punishes and rewards as the mood strikes him and according to the performance of those under his authority.

The loved and the dreaded dead actually form two completely different categories. The relationship of the living to them differs accordingly, since they do have distinct destinies. Even the examples given by Tylor himself (II, 197 ff.), those of the fear-inspiring dead, show in the majority of cases that they are quite specific instances: unburied corpses, sorcerers that became evil demons after death, shamans that became a particular class of spirits, lepers and beggars, persons who died by pestilence or violence, women who died in childbirth, etc. This list, taken from Tylor, is not complete; but it suffices to establish that the feared among the dead do make up a special category. Most died an unnatural death. It is difficult to imagine that the "evil death," that the violence of the death, should by itself be the cause for which the deceased is subjected to a fate that is not meted out to those who die of natural causes.

The belief that a startling and especially a violent manner of death makes man a spirit, demon, or ghost is so common and widespread among primitive peoples that the generalizing surmise seems permitted: victims of the evil death are the ones to be feared. We shall yet see that the underlying idea obviously is even more general: the feared dead have never been admitted to the realm of the dead. I recall to mind (cf. chap. xiv, sec. 1) the example of the Apapocuva which Nimuendaju reports; in one case a murdered man turns into a ghost so feared by the living that they decide to leave their homesteads and resettle at a great distance. Nimuendaju managed to stop them only by joining forces with the shaman to annihilate the ghost. As mentioned, had it not been an animal soul but a plant soul, a shamanistic ceremony might have succeeded in procuring belated entry to the nether world for the ghost.

How may these hostile attitudes, this destructive rage against the unfortunate victim have developed? The literature on primitive peoples seems to show not a single case where such a ghost had not been considered hostile and where his effect on the community of the living had not been given a most gloomy prognosis. This judgment is by no means made on the strength of deeds that might have characterized the ghost as an evildoer or enemy in his lifetime. Only an unusual manner of death designates him as an enemy of mankind. Does the manner of death turn a benign human being into a fiend or is it a sign that he had always been an adversary whose harmless exterior was only a camouflage? The data speak clearly for the second alternative. To round out the argument, I cite a myth from Ceram which deals with the origin of spirits: Satene, ruler over the yet immortal primeval Dema, conducted a ceremony when the ancient order was overturned by the slaying of Hainuwele. She erected a great gate in the shape of a ninefold spiral (labyrinth?) and bade all Dema to assemble beyond it while she remained within. The Dema now had to come to her, passing through the gate. All Dema that reached Satene, the goddess, became normal mortals. The others became spirits or animals. The mythic conception undoubtedly is the prototype of the death journey; for Satene now resides in the land of the dead, and mortal man must reach her if he is to be permitted to continue the "fulfilled life." Passage through the gate corresponds to the frequent ordeal prior to entry into the realm. That the Dema that failed turned into spirits and animals parallels the assertion that those mortals that fail the test and do not attain the beyond turn into spirits. The tests, however, undoubtedly did not have the effect of turning inoffensive men into malicious demons but constitute criteria to determine who had attained fulfilment.

Now it is remarkable that an evil death should have the same consequences as failure in a trial before entry into the beyond. This may, however, be illustrated by some reports from Southeast Asia which, in their totality, give a good picture of the ideas connected with the evil death.

Mills (1926: 283 ff.) describes the measures which must be taken when an Ao meets with an evil death. Like all Naga, the Ao regard certain forms of death as "accursed": drowning, falling from a cliff or tree, burning, in childbirth, or by wild animals. The victim must be buried immediately and without the usual, otherwise so important funeral ceremonies; if death occurred outside the village, he must be interred on the spot. His name may not be mentioned along with those of the important dead at the major ceremonial occasions, not even if his rank in life would have demanded it. Furthermore, his name may never be given to a descendant (*ibid.*: 286). The village community must undergo extensive purification rites (*ibid.*: 254). To the victim's immediate family the event spells shame and ruin. All domestic stock must be killed; ornaments and utensils are broken up; all clothes are slashed, and the entire household is demolished (*ibid.*: 285). It is to be noted that the Naga inflict very similar devastation as punishment for heavy crimes (Mills, 1937: 147). The granaries are cut open by the priests and the grain allowed to trickle on the ground, and the crops are left to rot in the fields. The family of the deceased must, under certain rituals, leave the village without any of its possessions and settle in the jungle in a small hut of leaves. There they must discard their clothes and put on old ones which fellow clan members have given them. These fellows also place a daily food supply outside the hut without, however, talking to the ones within. Only after a lengthy stay outside the village is the family permitted to return. They are now free from "defilement" but are reduced to utter poverty and have to live on the charity of friends.

This and the terminology for the manners of death show that the deceased is considered "accursed." Everything reminiscent of him must be erased. Refusal of the death ceremony indicates that he cannot or should not enter the beyond. He is expelled from the community of the dead, as his surviving kin must be expelled from the community of the living until they are "cleansed." It all appears like a reaction to an act of sacrilege.

In fact, many peoples regard the evil death as a sign that the departed was guilty of a horrible crime. So, for instance, the Mikir, neighbors of the Naga, believe that anyone killed by a tiger must have committed a serious crime and cannot enter the afterlife unless special ceremonies are undertaken (Lyall, pp. 37, 71). So also is it said on Ceram (Indonesia) that one who died in an accident was carrying great guilt (Röder, p. 70). The same link between crime and violent death is intimated by Gurdon (pp. 77, 94, 122, 135) about the Khasi (Assam): they have an exogamous social organization and consider incest the worst and unremissible crime. Such transgression is punished by expulsion, denial of death rites, and denial of burial in the clan's burial plot. At the same time, it is believed that the guilty will meet with one of those violent deaths which the Khasi regard as sinister so that an especially protracted ceremonial is required if burial in the clan plot shall become possible. It follows from this and many other cases that might be cited that the evil death does not make the deceased an outcast but only brings to light that he was a marked person from whom the community turns in horror and who may not enter the realm of the dead. It even seems to us that the latter is the decisive point and that the revulsion and fear are only consequences of it. In line with our earlier discussion of the religious ethos, this would prove that man does not attain full humanity in his lifetime, since he either had no capacity for experiencing the world order as divine or made no use of it.

The belief that the dead that find no home in the beyond are to be feared as malevolent spirits fits the scheme. We point to Tylor's illustrations in which the dreaded spirits were victims of an evil death and to Nimuendaju's account of the ghost of a murdered person (cf. chap. xiv, sec. 1).

The community is a most direct expression of the duality of the world. The "biological proximity" which unites all members generates in itself a feeling of antagonism against all outsiders. The dead that passed on into the realm of death continue to belong to the community. Not to belong means to be at large, with all the dread consequences to the living and the dead. A ghost is homeless, the enemy to men, who are his enemies.

If a meaningful connection can be established in this way between exclusion from the realm of the dead and a ghostly existence after death, we have made no more than a phenomenological observation; the strangeness itself has not been totally resolved. We too consider a life that ends in a natural death richer and more complete when we view the biological existence without reference to outside values. But we find it difficult to regard the manner of death as the yardstick of fulfilment. In younger culture strata we find, incidentally, quite different valuations attached to the very same deaths; fallen warriors frequently go to a special land of the dead which, however, denotes homage.

This complicated question will not occupy us here any further, however. For the present we shall accept the fact that the deceased are considered evil spirits. Their existence is a continuation of life that differs from the normal. Only specific dead fall prey to this fate, and the criterion usually is the manner of their demise. Fear of the dead and of their return is by no means a universal characteristic of primitive attitudes. Their emotional relationship to the dead is, quite to the contrary, ruled by the belief in their proximity to the deity and therefore emphatically reverential and affectionate. A particular ethical valuation of life has engendered the belief that the fulfilled life brings with it

311

eternal and individual afterlife in the divine precinct. Those, however, who fail the "ordeal" are excluded and must enter into a ghostly existence on earth as evil spirits, hostile to the living.

This kind of belief in spirits makes it clear that the entities with which we are dealing here are totally different from the animal and plant spirits which were discussed in conjunction with medicines and poisons. There we spoke of spiritual essences which constitute the life proper of animal and plant, especially that which is effective in them. Our word *soul* does not describe them perfectly but it serves them better, in any event, than the ghosts of the deceased that are made up of the entire human being save for his body.

5. DEGRADED GODS AS SPIRITS

The typological enumeration of spirits and their origins is not yet complete. Although even widely scattered populations, located in America and Africa, for instance, possess typologically similar spirit beliefs which speak strongly for common origin, the present state of our knowledge does not allow us to attempt an even approximately complete description of all the types. And this quite aside from the fact that we have no way of understanding many of the underlying conceptions. We shall mention only briefly one more group of spirits whose community shall be negatively defined by the fact that it can be equated neither with the spiritual doubles of the living nor with the spirits of the dead; it obviously has its own roots. Many of these spirits which appear directly in mythic or fairy-tale-like narratives are often marked by some physical peculiarity. In my opinion they must be interpreted as originally divine figures that, after a long process of degeneration, took their place as spirit heroes of some tale which at times still exhibits pale reflections of mythic description of divine deeds.

To give only one illustration, I cite a narrative which I took down in Western Ceram (1939: 371). It tells of a man whose genitals grew so that he finally had to carry two baskets, one on his back, the other on his chest, to hide his penis. The motif of hypertrophy of the male genitals is frequent in primitive narratives and usually designates some spirit being. Another example is reported by Zingg (p. 538) of the Huichol in Central America who tell of one spirit-being whose penis grew to a length of one hundred meters. He had to wind it around his body and carry it in a basket on his back.

In the fairy tale from Ceram the male figure with the hypertrophic genitals is undoubtedly a late descendant of an important Dema-deity. The myths which G. Landtman has recorded of the Kiwai in New Guinea show this clearly. There they tell of a Dema-deity, Soido, whose genitals have swollen to unusually large size because he swallowed the fruits of the field without chewing. The myth relates that the first plants arose when the Dema scattered his semen, containing the fruits of all plants, over the earth. The unusually distended genitals of this fertility deity are therefore not only to be understood symbolically but are explained by the factual assertions of the myth that all fruits are hidden in them (Landtman, 1917: 119 ff.). Soido is only a mythic variant of another Dema-deity, Sido by name. It is he that suffers the first death, embarks on the first death journey, and transforms himself into the house that symbolizes the realm of the dead. As usual, this Dema figure is associated with the moon. Quite similar to Sido-Soido is another Dema, Ganumi, who later, as the moon, ascends to the sky. Even the two baskets, which in the tale from Ceram served only to carry the genitals, reappear, while it is said of Ganumi that he carries one in front and one in back and that (as the moon) he hides alternately behind one or the other. The divine nature of the great Dema-deities of the Kiwai comes out clearly in the genuine myths which Landtman collected. In view of the convincing parallelism with the no longer unadulterated myth of the Ceramese—the congruences are even more numerous than indicated (cf. Jensen, "Weltbild": 58 ff.)— and in view of the geographical proximity of the two peoples, it seems permissible to link the Ceramese "spirit" and the deity of the Kiwai. Quite similar forms of the myth are also to be found, however, at a greater remove. Of the Tacana, Hissink (p. 82) reports many variants in which a man sees his penis grow through intercourse with Moon Woman until finally he must carry it in a basket on his back.

This illustration is given to show how often, in inconsequential tales, spirits or similar figures appear that can be understood only through the mythic descriptions of deities and their deeds. Usually they are malformed in some way; the mythic mark has been retained only out of morbidity. A world-wide mythic motif of this kind is the half-sided spirit-men. On another occasion,[2] I have pointed out that this motif goes back to a divine characteristic, the notion that the right half of the deity's body is of greater worth than the left.

Individual connections between such spirits and deities whose outstanding corporeal peculiarities have some mythic meaning can, of course, be established only through extensive comparisons. Especially rewarding should be the investigation of the numerous spirits that have animal parallels and permit the conjecture that in them the divine concept of the "Master of animals" reappears in a corrupted form. The fact that many spirits recur in the most widely dispersed areas of the globe but have astonishingly similar characteristics speaks for a common source. Spirits with a Cyclopean eye, with an iron tail, with pointed legs, those that consist of a head only, and many others are found practically everywhere. In the original conception the physical peculiarity must have been semantically complemented in some way; the spirit tales retain them only for their grotesqueness. We may be granted the conjecture that all were once true mythic personages —and deities at that. The process of degeneration would have made the mythically justified physical peculiarity of the deity the basis of a spirit-concept. Here, then, the direction of development is an absolute contradiction to Tylor's theory: the gods do not derive from spirits; rather, some types of spirits are degraded deities.

6. *VARIOUS SPIRITS IN THE BELIEFS OF THE CERAMESE*

Since it is impossible to make a complete index of the very different kinds of spirit-concepts, we shall conclude our discussion of spirits by indicating briefly the various types that occur in one particular culture. I am selecting the Wemale of Ceram, since I am well acquainted with them (Jensen, *Drei Ströme:* 192 ff.). The religion of the Wemale is dominated by a belief in Dema-deities. Soul-concepts are vague and not of particular importance in their spiritual life. The relationship to death and the dead, however, carries great weight. All deities are reckoned among the

[2] "Die mythische Vorstellung vom halben Menschen," *Paideuma,* V (1950).

dead, with the understanding that death occurred a very long time ago. Normal death gains admission to the realm of the dead, where earthly life continues almost unaltered. Violent death may transform man into a dreaded ghost that manifests itself through howling noises.

Spirits are clearly distinguished from the deities and the deceased, especially by man's attitude to each group. The designation of one type of spirit, *halita*, often becomes the collective term for all. Isolated statements as well as narratives about *halita*, however, make their exceptional position obvious, first of all by the fact that they are not described as conveyors of disease. Nevertheless, most are considered dangerous and hostile, since they are intent upon the abduction of human beings and are especially pleased to capture and eat children. This trait alone reveals their relation to the ogre that appears in the puberty ceremonies of many peoples and plays a major role in the initiation ceremonies of a secret society of the Wemale. All other characteristics of the *halita* confirm the assumption that they are fairy-tale degenerations of the Dema-deity to whom the secret society ritual is dedicated. Many statements show that the *halita* are figures of the lunar mythology in the same sense as is the Dema-deity. They possess great treasures in which the highly valued gongs, which are a major Ceram import, are very plentiful. According to statements of the Ceramese, these are specific lunar symbols. Animals with which the *halita* are customarily associated are marten and mouse, both of which are frequently given lunar connotation in many stories.

The *halita*, therefore, seem not to have been spirits according to origin but are "survivals" of an ogre that initially did not have the aspects of a spirit; dangerous as the effect of this deity was, man's attitude in response was opposite to the one with which he usually confronted spirits. Death is a legitimate part of the world order and it cannot matter if it pleases man. Grandeur and sublimity forbid man to react out of egocentric and self-seeking sentiments. The twin aspects of the deity, its somber and its bright face, shone through even in the fairy-tale-like stories about the *halita*. Though dreaded for their cannibalism, *halita* often appear as benevolent helpers.

Clearly different are the spirits of disease that inhabit sky, earth, and the regions below. Their common name means "the ones that live in the entrails." Emphasis of their small size and their swift motion tells us that we are dealing with the spiritual entities we had come to know in discussing medications and poisons (cf. sec. 3, this chapter). They are personifications of hostile natural substances. One fights against them as one fights with any enemy; the medicine men are in command of the proper weapons and methods. Man's attitude to the hostile face of nature has never changed; even today medical sciences battle against disease with all possible means without being able to say much more about causes than that some substances are incompatible with others. It is to be noted of primitive peoples that they never resigned themselves to disease as to some inevitable destiny as they did in other aspects of life but confronted it in terms of hostility and combat.

Another group of spirits must be distinguished. The Wemale call them *waitete*. Their position is not clear though they resemble the *halita* in anthropomorphous appearance. In contrast to them, the *waitete* do rate as conveyors of disease. Their main functions are in the sexual sphere. They may appear to a person in the disguise of his spouse so that the man or woman believes himself to be dealing with wife or husband, respectively. If sexual intercourse takes place, a serious illness of the sexual organs results.

An old Wemale who had suffered much from a *waitete* begged me to help in its destruction by means of our instruments. He led me to a spot in the jungle, near the village, where the *waitete* supposedly resided, where his provisions were stored, or where he tilled his fields. He knew the spirit's personal name, which the spirit himself had told him in a dream. The *waitete* had a wife and children and they were sometimes visible when they cultivated their field. The *waitete*'s main act of aggression was lying in wait for young women in the guise of a very handsome man. Some who had succumbed to his ardor had become gravely ill and died. Even to walk past his abode was dangerous. The son of the old man who had approached me had recently had a dizzy spell at that particular spot on the path. In a dream the father asked the *waitete* why his son had become dizzy and had been given to understand that his son had urinated on the *waitete*'s supply of palm wine. This supply is invisible; yet it can be damaged by man. The old man felt obliged to place several bamboo containers of palm wine at locations in the jungle to avert further perils for his son. The so-called spirit offering has in this case the outspoken character of a compensation made in order to maintain peace. The Wemale wanted to see the *waitete* and his family annihilated and left no doubt either about the ungodlike or hostile character of the spirit. This statement says nothing of the original idea behind the existence of *waitete*. With the *halita* he shares human form and the human way of life. He also has a physical characteristic, a cartilaginous excrescence on the upper forehead and on his back. The fact that he causes illness, however, relates him to those spirits that "live in the entrails."

The description which the old man gave shows that many primitive peoples are given to self-important exaggeration or elaboration along lines of popular fantasies. When the old man pointed out the place where the *waitete* resided and kept his stores, he probably "derived" this knowledge from some of the events that had taken place at that spot. The greater part of his intuitive knowledge was gained in dreams, which were most certainly influenced by ideas familiar to all members of his tribe. In the majority of cases, knowledge of spirits is a result of dream experience anyway. It has been documented repeatedly that primitive peoples differentiate between dreams that have revealed great truths and normal, inconsequential ones. In the special case it is of course difficult to decide whether the teller is capable of distinguishing the true from the false, the significant from the trivial.

Another, very much feared, type of spirit is the *weddu*. They parallel the *kanaime* of Guayana to some extent. Like them they are not invisible, but normal men, at least in outward appearance. In reality, however, they are spirits given to nocturnal mischief. Entire villages were once populated by *weddu*. The fight against them is an actual armed combat. The corpses of slain *weddu* change into sticks and rocks over night. Naturally, as in Guayana, only remote villages or specific individuals in remote villages are reputed to be *weddu*. To this extent the basis of their existence is undoubtedly the feeling of hostility toward strangers.

In addition, the *weddu* have another peculiarity, also shared with some peoples. This hostility mainly takes two forms. They are considered necrophagous; a corpse has hardly been buried when they come flying through the night to disinter and eat it.

With the same intention they approach the living by severing their own heads from their bodies in such a way that all the entrails remain attached to it and only the empty shell of the body is left behind. Such a head with dangling intestines flies as an owl or as a large bat to other settlements to cut open the body of sleeping folk and devour their viscera. On awakening, the person attacked notices the symptoms of a lingering disease. These fearsome spirits, which will suck the life of sleeping men and women through tubes from outside the house, fly as owls to distant villages and always deprive their sleeping victim of something that constitutes the very essence of his life, though death need not result immediately. Such spirits are found in all parts of the world under remarkable resemblances of the conceptions. From the Western Sudan, where they are called *subach,* they have been described by Frobenius. They remind us of nightmares and belong among the spiritually potent personalities with whom we dealt in our discussion of black magic. They have, however, developed special faculties to satisfy their hostile impulses. The extensive agreement in the description of these abilities leads us to surmise a common origin in a very ancient culture stratum; it is not possible, however, to make clear the underlying concepts.

Finally, there is a last group of—also manlike—spirit-beings about which we could learn but little. The border line between man and spirit is here particularly indistinct, and the living are emotionally too involved. In a large village which had to give in to the Christianizing tendencies of the colonial administration, we learned that the former village headman was living as a *habubunita,* without any human company, in the jungle. He had retired there out of grief and sadness over the vanishing of his people's traditional world. The second component of his name (*nita*) indicated that the man was to be considered a spirit-being. The meager information about his existence bears this out. He probably had discovered within himself the powers of a spirit; according to prevalent belief this is quite within the range of possibilities.

7. THE REALITY OF SPIRITS

If we wish to summarize what we have presented on the subject of spirits, we must first return to the question concerning the special experiential background of the belief in spirits. Our aim remains the discovery of whatever sense of reality underlies the mental constructs of primitive peoples. The reality of spirits, no longer comprehensible to us, is basically the same as the problem of the reality underlying the idea of God. In neither case have auxiliary concepts, designed to explain particular phenomena, been syncretized into concrete generalizations. The desire for clearer delineation may have contributed to the process of personification, but it is not to be doubted that only truly stirring events can have led to the conception of spirits and other such manifestations.

The ideological history of beliefs was a particular interest of Tylor. The discovery of that which he calls "soul" can undoubtedly be traced very far back through the history of mankind. Not needed for the process, however, were rationalistic considerations of sleep, dreams, and death. "Soul" impresses itself upon experience in ways far more direct. The spirituality of all things, in which we must seek the basis of a belief in spirits, reveals itself to man through its effects. The medicinal plant as well as the poisonous one has an effect on or in man; the spirituality of the plant is ascribed to this effect. We have attempted to present the discovery of specific effects which specific parts of plants will cause as the result of a world view which focused on spirituality. From this it follows that spirit-beliefs or any other serious creations of man cannot be interpreted as foolish aberrations. Rather, we hold that his view of the world makes man capable of definite experiences which only this view and no other can disclose.

The category of spirits is chiefly associated with disease. We note with interest that many, though apparently not all, primitive cultures do not accept illness as a part of the divine order in the sense in which death, birth, growth, maturity, and procreation are accepted. Man's attitude toward these elements of the order of existence differs in principle from the attitude toward illness. This becomes most clearly noticeable in the differences between the effective potentials of genuine magic, which finds one of its primary tasks in the curing of illness. We have seen the various ways in which the shaman enters the spiritual contest against the foes of his community. It is not immaterial that the shaman, in cases where he directly communicates with the deity, is no longer paladin against the foes but supplicant for divine recompense or transmitter of consoling prophecies. His ability to mount a defensive struggle against spiritual enemies with his own spirituality is in the final analysis the basis of his exceptional position, which often involves his exclusion from religious ceremonies (cf. chap. xi, sec. 4).

In discussing the mythic world view it was our wish to show that mythic statements about reality are rooted in a specific kind of cognitive ability and that these are not the inadequate forerunners of scientific cognition. We gave several concrete instances to show that the genuine and magnificent creations of culturally and historically early times are almost without exception based on cognition of this kind and that no scientific attitude can supplant it. The same applies to statements about the nature of disease and the various methods of treatment. Our medical science cannot make any statement that would, as solely correct, demonstrate the absurdity of corresponding primitive views. Neuropathology makes use, of course, of a different terminology, but its insights into the nature of illness are not too different in content from those which primitive peoples assert under reference to their spirit beliefs.

That which we call the effect of medication is still steeped in obscurity when it comes to an understanding of the processes involved. The paraphrases with which we attempt to illuminate the process of healing itself are—from the scientific standpoint—just as obscure as the accounts primitive peoples give of the effectiveness of spirits. It is, then, not superstition or foolishness when primitive man speaks of the spirituality of a curative plant which sends its "arrows" against "hostile spirits" but a (for him) sufficiently descriptive mode of expression which represents obscure circumstances for which there are no better or more precise statements at hand. Even the most sober scientific description of a disease cannot remove its demonic aspect, simply because that aspect is quite real. The claim that a hostile spirit caused a disease state is a thoroughly meaningful proposition, even though it is not taken over into scientific usage.

Totally different, however, is the experiential background of the spirits of the dead which, according to Tylor, constitute the primary form of spirit belief; all other spirits are said to have developed from it. On my part, however, I can see no connection between these spirits and the arrow-shooting, disease- and other evil-causing spirits of animals and plants. Only the characteristics of invisibility and fearsomeness are common to both. Spirits of the dead are not spiritual entities to the same extent; they represent the total person with the sole exception of his body. Essentially, they present the same appearance as the deceased that reside in the land of death; they also have retained their individual personalities.

We can hardly hope to tell how the reality of these ghosts may have come about. But the spiritual background from which they stand out in relief is clear. They are human beings whom the deity has rejected, and the fear which the living feel is probably less a fear of practical dangers than a fear of strangeness, a fear inspired by the condition of those marked by the evil death, of those who are outside the community of deity or man and who lead a barely outlined existence.

Again of a different psychic reality are those spirits that we have tried to define as corrupted descriptions of divine personages. The normal historical process of semantic depletion changed them into the quaint figures which we encounter in fairy tales and which tend to be labeled with the designation "spirit." They conform to neither of the two categories previously summarized, although some external elements may have been taken over in description. This does not exhaust the list of sources from which belief in spirits is drawn. We neither aimed at completeness nor could it be attained in view of the present state of research.

The high degree of reality which spirits have attained is attested by the fluctuating boundary between spirit and man, not to mention the close link between spirit and animal. That living men may at the same time be evil spirits may go back to the experience of universal antagonism. The phenomenon of the last-mentioned *hababunita,* who is by no means an evil spirit but simply the redefinition of the human way of life to that of a spirit, reveals the extent to which—in certain cultural communities—the existence of spirits is part of universal reality.

CONCLUSION

In bringing this book to a conclusion, I shall try briefly to summarize some of the ideas which seem of particular importance to me. As I have done in the Introduction, I shall cite an example from a book that represents the results of rich ethnological field work: Mills (1926: 225) reports the belief held by the Ao-Naga of Assam that the soul, which always accompanies a man, lives in his head. To this Hutton remarks (as quoted in the same book): "This theory is clearly the basis of head-hunting, at any rate in this area." The souls of dead men are wanted to fertilize animal and vegetable life and to add to the general stock of vital essence in the village. The soul is located in the head above all other parts and therefore the head is carried back (with the soul in it) to the village—also, of course, because it is easier to carry the head rather than the whole corpse. Hutton (*ibid.*: 254) refers to an account by Marshall according to which the neighboring Karen are reported to state quite explicitly that the souls of human beings become a sort of pupa which resembles an egg filled with a vaporous substance. When these burst, their contents spread over and fertilize the fields, since this vapor is the fructifying substance which again passes into bodies via the eaten grain and so to the seminal fluid, enabling men and animals to propagate life.

There are probably few theories about a custom so difficult to understand as head-hunting that can appeal to propositions stated by primitive peoples themselves, like the one reported by Hutton. When we relate the soul-concept of the Karen to the statements of the Ao-Naga concerning head-hunting, we seem to possess complete information on the meaning head-hunting holds for all the Naga. Accordingly, head-hunting would be *raubmord*, homicide aggravated by robbery; for it is not enough that the enemy be killed, he is also robbed of his most precious possessions for the egotistical use of the murderer: "Head-hunting is really life-hunting, and implies the capture of the soul and its utilization to increase the stock of life-essence already possessed by the village . . . (*ibid.*: 225).

According to a later book by Mills (1937: 160), this theory

does not seem as clearly documented for the Naga as Hutton presented it. Mills refers to Hutton's view and finds confirmed for the Rengma-Naga (in a far more convincing way) that enemies' heads cause the crops to flourish and men and animals to increase. This, however, we know not only of the Naga but of many other peoples. They say nothing of a captured substance that is brought to the village.

But even if Hutton's combined statements could be documented for the Naga themselves—this seems quite possible— even then we could not persuade ourselves to accept his pseudo-cause for the origin of the custom. An unbridgeable chasm seems to lie between such statements of the natives and the possibility of the genesis of new cultural values. Many experts have made an impressive case for the claim that head-hunting must be reckoned among the most fundamental religious utterances in certain culture strata. But if aggravated robbery forms the basis of a religion, then the religion predicates a type of man with whom we share no common spiritual ground. Pseudopurposes which primitive peoples assert, and the occidental theories which rest on them exclusively, make primitive man a creature who glorifies a criminal tendency while the morality he actualizes is the same as that which lies at the base of our own view of life.

It was one of the principal tasks of this book to attempt to close the gap through a new approach. We set out with the assumption that the religious utterances of primitive peoples are to be taken seriously. We should be able to understand them, if we only take the trouble to work out an image of early man that makes him seem deserving of the name. Even in a cruel custom such as head-hunting, we have searched for the more genuine motives that lead to their institution.

In Part One we have discussed human behavior as such to demonstrate that man, in the long course of his history, has always assumed the same, that is, the human, attitude. In the dialogue with enveloping reality, culture has assumed ever new configurations.

For us, the reference of cultic activities to mythic cognition has been the criterion of religious utterances. Man is given to express himself in representations, and the nexus between cult and myth finds its clearest confirmation in the vast amount of data from primitive peoples. Not only cultic behavior in the narrow sense but also everyday regulations, the social structure, and even standardized behavior in technology and economy go back to this fundamental attitude. It may be said of myth and cult that they stem from two elemental human capabilities: man's *cognitive nature* which enables him to grasp reality through observation, and his *representative nature* which eternally urges him on actively to integrate himself into the existing order. The recognition of profundity and magnificence inspires man to emulation, and this explains cult as well as all other human regulations and the ethical aspect of his activities.

A new scientific theory of religion depends on the successful comprehension of mythic propositions about reality; they are, after all, a premise to the cultic acts which by themselves are so difficult to understand. We do not doubt that, from the onset, man was an intellectualizing and an economic being. In these spheres, early man is comprehensible to us. Myths, however, are pure cognition. Two errors in analysis have led into a blind alley. For one, the acceptance of pseudopurposes by which primitive man is said to explain all phenomena; second, the assumption that mythic propositions, making reference to reality, must in some way have counterparts in propositions of the natural sciences. I have attempted to show that *genuine mythic cognition* —the word is chosen with deliberation—makes statements about the nature of reality for which there cannot be any comparable scientific statements; the methods of science are oriented toward a different nature of reality, toward the quantitative and measurable which is never understood through direct impression but only by the detour of "de-anthropomorphization."

Finally, basing ourselves on Frobenius, we stressed a third criterion of mythic propositions. All cultural configurations— once the creative act made them apparent—have a history of their own. The creative attitude of "expression" is opposed by the deteriorated forms of "application," which owe their existence to historical processes characterized by gradual semantic depletion. Forms of "application," no longer understood by primitive peoples, include numerous imitations of mythic embellishments which may no longer be essential. In the area of religious expression it is especially an expectation of divine recompense that hastens the process of degeneration. It is therefore not astonishing that, particularly in primitive settings with petrified cultural forms, religious configurations are given purposive explanations so absurd that their secondary invention is easily guessed. That a captured head does not make a large field fertile must be clear to a peasant people by simple experience. And yet, this pseudopurpose is connected, even in our eyes, with the origin of the custom; for primitive man, however, the link is not one of causal relationships but a mythic cognition which refers mortality and propagation—the essence of fertility—to the primal slaying of a divine being.

Constant reiteration of deeds accomplished by the primeval deity is the important foundation of all cult activities. It is the human attitude par excellence. Reminiscences of divine activities and imitation of divinely inspired deeds form the basis of all true education. They constitute the religious ethos and *imply the expected reward, since man can attain full humanity only through this reminiscence.* Degenerative petrifaction lays stress on externals and expects recompense or the protection from evil, either by the act itself or by the observance of minutiae of performance. Related to this is the universal human inclination to reify purely spiritual processes. Degeneration proceeds through forms similar to those connected with the expectation of rewards, that is, through obversion of original relationships between phenomena and by focusing on external events and visible objects. The divine bounty which originally was part of the action is represented to be its consequence; the symbol is described as "efficient magic."

In Part Two we have concentrated on the idea of God in the primitive world. The data hardly permit completeness. We were committed to present a concept of God that must be distinguished from the concept of a "Highest Being" suggested by proponents of the theory of primal monotheism. We have called it "Demadeity," a concept that up to now has variously been designated by *Heilbringer,* culture hero, or tribal ancestor. As an idea it is alien to our culture but its nature is comprehensible. It was of decisive importance in recent history but may go back to history's most ancient phases. As we see it, the Dema concept has made a permanent impression on the concept of God of the polytheistic religions. The great significance which it had in the history of religion sheds new light on the practice of blood-sacrifice. We have presented it as a semantically depleted, degenerative form of the ritual killings, which in their essence are genuinely religious memorial celebrations. This raises the question whether cultural phenomena can continue to exist when they have lost their original meanings, that is, when they are not successfully integrated into the world view of a later culture phase. We have come to the conclusion that a great number of factors are responsible for empty "survivals." One of these is the character of formal play that adheres to all cults. In them, cognition of reality is given in quite specific ways, insofar as it does not describe a mere "Just-so" situation, but lends expression to man's own nature. Since this is applicable to all human actions, psychology might have to make significant contributions to the investigation of the meaning of cults. To say that cults are only expressions of man's psychological make-up would be going too far.

Man is, by definition, the symbol-using creature. Cultural history asks what was represented in each epoch. The particular way in which experience is represented gives man deep satisfaction by providing an outlet for one aspect of his nature. Thus, ball games may still be played with ecstatic fervor when the ideology that gave rise to them has been lost.

In Part Three we dealt with the relationship between magic and religion. The prevalent theory, chiefly devoted to manifestations of magic, is the so-called theory of pre-animistic magic. It traces *all* religious phenomena to originally magical activities that are thought to harmonize perfectly with the mentality of early man. The consequences to which this theory must inevitably lead were revealed unmistakably in the work of one of its most outstanding proponents, K. T. Preuss. For him, the origins of religion and art—the most sublime creations of man—lie in *Urdummheit*, in a primal stupidity.

We have attempted to reduce magic to its proper significance. Magic, like all other true cultural formulations, has a link with reality. It rests upon certain psychic abilities of all or some members of a community and has found its most striking expression in the figure of the shaman. It cannot matter to the principle whether *all* the abilities claimed by the shaman and believed in by primitive peoples have demonstrable correspondences in reality. Primitive men seem to be no more of one mind about the limitations of magical potentials than modern occidentals. The incontestable possibility of suggestion is sufficient for the justification of the magical conception. It enables man to influence the course of events by purely psychic means. This is the basis of genuine magic.

Beyond this, shamanism is not a form of religion in its own right. Rather, it is a widely distributed, quite uniform practice, which utilizes the religious conceptions that make up a particular world view. Thus, the techniques of imaginary journeys to the beyond are rather stereotyped, both in the shamanistic "performance" and in the means employed. The "place of divine bounty," however, is sometimes in the heavens, the abode of a High God, then again in the underworld, the residence of the ancestors and the primeval Dema. The goal of the journey depends on the religious ideology.

In Part Four we have dealt with souls and spirits which have held attention ever since Tylor made them the center of his scientific theories. Many of his ideas are still valid, but we cannot follow him in the basic contention that the various concepts of God developed from the idea of souls and spirits during later phases of the history of mankind. We maintain that soul-concepts are very ancient and owe their existence to the discovery of spiritual parallels to visible manifestations.

Spirits are by no means solely derived from the idea of souls of the dead. They have many roots. Spirits often conceal divine personages of a past cultural epoch. Where there actually is a belief in the return of the dead, they usually are human beings that suffered the "evil death." The greater number of the departed "live on" in the land of the dead and continue to be part of the human community. Quite different are the spiritual entities of animals and plants that subsume the essence of interactions: effects which medicinal plants or poisons can have upon man are said to be due to spiritual elements in plants and in man confronting each other amiably or inimically.

All cognition in the science of religion deals with the *nature* of phenomena. Mythic propositions are not inadequate forerunners of scientific knowledge. They can neither be replaced nor set aside by them. The most important methodological aid we have employed in the interpretation of obscure phenomena is the twin concepts "expression" and "application." They reveal that we cannot speak of cultural manifestations in a static sense. We must ask ourselves if the known form of a given phenomenon can provide information concerning its original meaning. We have negated this wherever hypothesizers consider it necessary to construct an image of man that differs fundamentally from that in the historical record. On the other hand, we have attempted to show that it is quite possible to come to "understand," even if we accept man of early epochs as a true man with all of our own experiential capacities. All in all, I should like to see this book judged as a step toward a new, a culture-morphological science of religion.

BIBLIOGRAPHY

ACKERKNECHT, ERWIN H. "Medical Practices." In: *Handbook of South American Indians*, Vol. V. Smithsonian Institution. Bureau of American Ethnology, Bulletin 143. Washington, 1949.

BALDUS, HERBERT. *Indianerstudien im nordöstlichen Chaco*. Leipzig, 1931.

BAUMANN, HERMANN. *Lunda. Bei Bauern und Jägern in Inner-Angola*. Berlin, 1935.

————. *Schöpfung und Urzeit des Menschen im Mythus der africanischen Völker*. Berlin, 1936.

————. "Africanische Wild- und Buschgeister." In: *Zeitschrift f. Ethnologie*, Vol. LXX. Berlin, 1938.

BAUMANN, HERMANN, RICHARD THURNWALD, and DIEDRICH WESTERMANN. *Völkerkunde von Afrika*. Essen, 1940.

BENEDICT, RUTH. *Patterns of Culture*. Boston, 1934.

BERNATZIK, HUGO ADOLF. *Akha und Meau*. Innsbruck, 1947.

BETH, KARL. *Religion und Magie bei den Naturvölkern*. Berlin, 1914.

BLANC, ALBERTO CARLO. "Ethnolyse." In: *Paideuma*, Vol. III. Bamberg, 1948–49.

BLEEK, W. H. J., and L. C. LLOYD. *Bushman Folklore*. London, 1911.

BOAS, FRANZ. *The Central Eskimo*. Smithsonian Institution. Sixth Annual Report of the Bureau of Ethnology, 1884–85. Washington, 1888.

————. *The Social Organization and the Secret Societies of the Kwakiutl Indians*. U.S. National Mus. Rep. 1895. Washington, 1897.

BOLLNOW, OTTO FRIEDRICH. *Die Ehrfurcht*. Frankfurt, 1947.

BREYSIG, K. *Die Entstehung des Gottesgedankens und der Heilbringer*. Berlin, 1905.

BROWN, A. R. Cf. RADCLIFFE-BROWN, A. R.

CATLIN, GEORGE. *Letters and Notes on the Manners and Conditions of the North American Indians*. London, 1841.

CERULLI, ENRICO. *Etiopia occidentale*. Vols. I and II. Rome, 1927–28.

CHAVES, MILCIALES. "Mitos, tradiciones y cuentos de los Indios Chami." In: *Boletin de Arqueologia*, Vol. I (No. 2). Bogotá, 1945.

DIETERLEN, GERMAINE. *Les âmes des Dogons*. Paris, 1941.

DILTHEY, WILHELM. *Gesammelte Schriften*. Vol. VIII: *Weltanschauungslehre. Abhandlungen zur Philosophie der Philosophie. Traum*. Pp. 218 ff.

DIRR, A. "Der Kaukaziische Wild- und Jagdgott." In: *Anthropos*, Vol. XX. Mödling, 1925.

BIBLIOGRAPHY

DOSTAL, WALTER. "Ein Beitrag zur Frage des religiösen Weltbild der frühesten Bodenbauer Vorderasiens." In: *Archiv für Volkerkunde*, Vol. XII. Vienna, 1957.

DUBOIS, CONSTANCE GODDARD. "The Religion of the Luiseño Indians of Southern California." In: *University of California Publications in American Archaeology and Ethnology*, Vol. VIII (No. 3). Berkeley, 1908.

DURKHEIM, É. *Les formes élémentaires de la religion.* Paris, 1912.

EHRENREICH, PAUL. "Die Mythen und Legenden der südamerikanischen Urvölker." In: *Zeitschrift f. Ethnologie*, Vol. XXXVII. Suppl. Berlin, 1905.

———. "Götter und Heilbringer." In: *Zeitschrift f. Ethnologie*, Vol. XXXVIII. Berlin, 1906.

ELIADE, MIRCEA. "Le problème du chamanisme." In: *Revue de l'Histoire des Religions*, Vol. CXXXI. 1946.

———. *Traité d'histoire des religions.* Paris, 1949.

———. *Schamanismus und archaische Ekstasetechnik* (German translation by INGE KÖCK). Zurich and Stuttgart, 1957.

FISCHER, H. T. "Indonesische Paradiesmythen." In: *Zeitschrift f. Ethnologie*, Vol. LXIV. Berlin, 1932.

FRAZER, JAMES GEORGE. *Totemism and Exogamy.* Vols. I–IV. London, 1910.

———. *Der goldene Zweig.* Leipzig, 1928.

FREUD, SIGMUND. *Totem und Tabu.* Leipzig, Vienna, Zurich, 1913.

FRIEDRICH, ADOLF. "Afrikanische Priestertümer." In: *Studien zur Kulturkunde*, Vol. VI Stuttgart, 1939.

———. "Die Forschung über das frühzeitliche Jägertum." In: *Paideuma*, Vol. II. Leipzig, 1941–43.

———. "Knochen und Skelett in der Vorstellungswelt Nordasiens." In: *Wiener Beiträge zur Kulturgeschichte u. Linguistik*, Vol. V. Vienna, 1943.

FROBENIUS, LEO. "Rede in der Diskussion zu den Vorträgen von Graebner und Ankermann." In: *Zeitschrift f. Ethnologie*, Vol. XXXVII. Berlin, 1905.

———. *Atlantis I–XII.* Jena, 1921–28.

———. *Des unbekannte Afrika.* Munich, 1923.

———. *Kulturgeschichte Afrikas.* Zurich, 1933.

———. "Denkformen vergangener Menschheit." In: *Scientia*, Vol. LXIV (Ser. 3). Milan, 1938.

GAHS, A. "Koph-, Schädel- und Langknochenopfer bei Rentiervölkern." In: *Festschrift P. W. Schmidt.* Vienna, 1928.

GERMANN, PAUL. *Völkerstämme im Norden von Liberia.* Leipzig, 1933.

GODDARD, PLINY EARLE. "Life and Culture of the Hupa." In: *University of California Publications in American Achaeology and Ethnology*, Vol. I. Berkeley, 1903.

GRAEBNER, F. "Die melanesiche Bogenkultur und ihre Verwandten." In: *Anthropos*, Vol. IV. Vienna-Mödling, 1909.

GRIAULE, MARCEL. "Masques Dogons." Université de Paris. *Travaux et mémoires de l'Institut d'Ethnologie*, Vol. XXXIII. Paris, 1938.

———. "Notes sur l'agriculture des Goula et des Koulfa." In: *Bull. de l'Institut Français d'Afrique Noire*, Vol. VII. Dakar, 1946.

———. *Dieu d'Eau. Entretiens avec Ogotemmêli*. Paris, 1948.

GURDON, P. R. T. *The Khasis*. London, 1914.

GUSINDE, MARTIN. *Die Feuerland-Indianer*. Vol. I: *Die Selknam*. Mödling-near-Vienna, 1931.

HAEKEL, JOSEF. "Totemismus und Zweiklassensystem bei den Sioux-Indianer." In: *Anthropos*, Vol. XXXII. Vienna, 1937.

———. "Die Dualsystem in Afrika." In: *Anthropos*, Vol. XLV. Freiburg, Switzerland, 1950.

———. "Zum Problem des Mutterrechtes." In: *Paideuma*, Vol. V. Wiesbaden, 1950–54.

HATT, GUDMUND. "The Corn-Mother in America and Indonesia." In: *Anthropos*, Vol. XLVI. Freiburg, Switzerland, 1951.

HAWKES, ERNEST WILLIAM. "The Labrador Eskimo." In: *Geological Survey of Canada Memoir*, No. 91. Ottawa, 1916.

HEINE-GELDERN, ROBERT. "Mutterrecht und Kophjagd im westlichen Hinterindien." In: *Mitt. d. Anthropolog. Ges. Wien*, Vols. L–LI. Vienna, 1921.

———. "Urheimat und frü heste Wanderungen der Austronesier." In: *Anthropos*, Vol. XXVII. Viena-Mödling, 1932.

HELLPACH, WILLY. "Numen und Ethos." In: *Zeitschrift für philosophische Forschungen*, Vol. I (No. 1). Reutlingen, 1946.

———. "Das Magethos." In: *Schriftenreihe zur Völkerpsychologie*. Nos. 3, 4. Stuttgart, 1947.

HILL, W. W. "The Agricultural and Hunting Methods of the Navaho Indians." In: *Yale University Publications in Anthropology*, No. 18. New Haven, 1938.

HISSINK, KARIN. "Motive der Mochica-Keramik." In: *Paideuma*, Vol. V. Bamberg, 1950–54.

HISSINK, K., and HAHN, A. *Die Tacana. Erzählungsgut*. Stuttgart, 1961.

HÖLTKER, GEORG. "Zum Problem der Fadenspiele, speziell in Neuguinea." In: *Bulletin der Schweizerischen Gesellschaft für Anthropologie und Ethnologie*, 1942–43. Bern, 1943.

HOSE, C., and MCDOUGALL, W. *The Pagan Tribes of Borneo*. London, 1912.

BIBLIOGRAPHY

HOWITT, A. W. *The Native Tribes of South East Australia*. London, 1904.

HUIZINGA, J. *Homo Ludens*. Boston, 1955.

HUTTON, J. H. *The Sema Nagas*. London, 1921.

IRLE, I. *Die Herero*. Gütersloh, 1906.

JANSSENS, P. A. "Het ontstaan der dingen in de Folklore der Bantu's." In: *Anthropos*, Vol. XXI. St. Gabriel-Mödling near Vienna, 1926.

JEFFREYS, M. D. W. "Dual Organization in Africa." In: *African Studies*, No. 5. Johannesburg, 1946.

JENSEN, A. E. "Beschneidung und Reifezeremonien bei Naturvölkern." In: *Studien zur Kulturkunde*, Vol. I. Stuttgart, 1932.

————. "Die staatliche Organisation und die historischen Überlieferungen der Barotse am oberen Sambesi." In: *Festschrift und 50. Jahresbericht 1931 bis 1932 des Württ. Vereins für Handelsgeographie E. V., Museum für Länder- und Völkerkunde, Linden-Museum*. Stuttgart, 1933.

————. *Im Lande des Gada. Wanderungen zwischen Volkstrümmern Südabessiniens*. Stuttgart, 1936.

————. *Hainuwele. Volkserzählungen von der Molukkeninsel Ceram*. Frankfurt, 1939.

————"Wettkampf-Parteien, Zweiklassen-Systeme und geographische Orientierung." In: *Studium Generale*, Vol. I. Heidelberg, 1947.

————. *Die drei Ströme. Züge aus dem geistigen Leben der Wemale*. Leipzig, 1948.

————. "Das religiöse Weltbild einer frü hen Kultur." In: *Studien zur Kulturkunde*, Vol. IX. Stuttgart, 1948.

————. "Dual-Systeme in Nortost-Afrika." In: *Anthropos*, Vol. XLVIII. Freiburg, Switzerland, 1953.

————. "Beziehungen zwischen dem Alten Testament und der nilotischen Kultur in Africa." In: *Culture in History: Essays in Honor of Paul Radin*. New York, 1960.

————. "Mythos und Erkenntnis: Eine Entgegnung auf W. E. Mühlmann." In: *Paideuma*, IX, 63–75.

JETTMAR, KARL. "Zur Herkunft der türkischen Völkerschaften." In: *Archiv für Völkerkunde*, Vol. III. Vienna, 1948.

JUNG, C. G., and KERÉNYI, KARL. *Einführung in das Wesen der Mythologie*. Amsterdam, Leipzig, 1941.

KARSTEN, RAFAEL. "Beiträge zur Sittengeschichte der Südamerikanischen Indianer." In: *Acta Academiae Aboensis Humaniora*, Vol. I (No. 4). Abo, 1921.

————. *The Civilization of the South American Indians*. London, 1926.

————. "The Head-Hunters of Western Amazonas." In: *Societas*

Scientiarum Fennica Commentationes Humanarum Litterarum,
Vol. VII (No. 1). Helsingfors, 1935.

KERÉNYI, KARL. "Vom Wesen des Festes." In: *Paideuma,* Vol. I. Leipzig, 1938–40.

———. "Kore—zum Mythologem vom göttlichen Mädchen." In: *Paideuma,* Vol. I. Leipzig, 1938–40.

———. "Was ist Mythologie?" In: *Europäische Revue,* Vol. XV. Stuttgart-Berlin, 1939.

———. "Mysterien der Kabiren." In: *Die Geburt der Helena. Albae vigiliae,* N. F. III. Zürich, 1945.

KINDAICHI, KYJSUKE. "The Concepts behind the Ainu Bear Festival." In: *Southwestern Journal of Anthropology,* Vol. V (No. 4). New Mexico, 1949.

KING, J. H. *The Supernatural: Its Origin, Nature and Evolution.* Vols. I–II. London, 1892.

KOCH-GRÜNBERG, THEODOR. *Vom Roroima zum Orinoco.* Vols. I–IV. Stuttgart, 1916–28.

———. *Zwei Jahre bei den Indianern Nordwest-Brasiliens.* Stuttgart, 1921.

KOCK, GÖSTA. "Is 'Der Heilbringer' a God or Not?" In: *Ethnos,* Vol. VIII. Lund, 1943.

———. "Der Heilbringer." In: *Ethnos,* Vol. XXI. Lund, 1956.

KOPPERS, W. "India and Dual Organization." In: *Acta Tropica,* Vol. I. Basel, 1944.

KRUIJT, A. C. *Het Animisme in den Indischen Archipel.* 'S-Gravenhage, 1906.

LANDTMAN, GUNNAR. *The Folk-Tales of the Kiwai Papuans.* Helsingfors, 1907.

———. *The Kiwai Papuans of British New Guinea.* London, 1927.

LANG, ANDREW. *The Making of Religion.* London, 1898.

LANG, KARL. "Mund-, Hand- und Beinverlängerungsgeräte." In: *Völkerkunde,* Vol. III, Vienna, 1927.

LAYARD, JOHN. "Totenfahrt auf Malekula." In: *Eranos Jahrbuch,* Vol. V. Zurich, 1937.

LEEUW, G. VAN DER *Phänomenologie der Religion.* Tübingen, 1933.

LEHMANN-NITSCHE, ROBERT. *Studien zur südamerikanischen Mythologie. Die ätiologischen Motive.* Hamburg, 1939.

LÉVY-BRUHL, L. *Die geistige Welt der Primitiven.* Munich, 1927.

———. *Les carnets de Lucien Lévy-Bruhl.* Paris, 1949.

LINDBLOM, K. G. "The Use of Stilts." In: *Rikmuseets Etnografiska Avdelning.* Stockholm, 1927.

LIVINGSTONE, DAVID. *Missionsreisen und Forschungen in Südafrika* (German translation by HERMANN LOTZE). Leipzig, 1858.

LOMMEL, H. "Mithra und das Stieropfer." In: *Paideuma*, Vol. III. Bamberg, 1949.

LOWIE, R. H. *Primitive Religion*. New York, 1922.

LUMHOLTZ, CARL. "Symbolism of the Huichol." In: *Memoirs of the American Museum of Natural History*, Vol. III. New York, 1900.

LUSCHAN, FELIX V. *Die Altertümer von Benin*. Berlin and Leipzig, 1919.

LYALL, CHARLES. Cf. STACK, EDWARD.

MACPHERSON, S. C. *Memorials of Service in India*. Ed. by WILLIAM MACPHERSON. London, 1865.

MARETT, R. R. "Preanimistic Religion." In: *Folk-Lore*, Vol. XI. London, 1900.

———. *Glaube, Hoffnung und Liebe in der primitiven Religion*. Stuttgart, 1936.

MARTINO, ERNESTO DE. "Religionsethnologie und Historizismus." In: *Paideuma*, Vol. II. Leipzig, 1941–43.

MELLAND, FRANK H. *In Witch-bound Africa. An Account of the Primitive Kaonde Tribe*. London, 1923.

MESS, H. A. "De Mentawei-Eilanden." In: *Tijdschrift voor Indische Taal-, Land- en Volkenkunde*, Vol. XXVI. The Hague, 1881.

MÉTRAUX, ALFRED. "Myths and Tales of the Matako Indians." In: *Ethnologiska Studier*, Vol. IX. Göteborg, 1939.

———. "A Myth of the Chamacoco-Indians and Its Significance." In: *Journal of American Folklore*, Vol. LVI. New York, 1943.

———. "Twin Heroes in South American Mythology." In: *Journal of American Folklore*. Philadelphia, 1946.

———. "Ensayos de mitologia comparala sudamericana." In: *América Indígena*, Vol. VIII. Mexico, 1948.

MEULI, KARL. "Der Ursprung der Olympischen Spiele." In: *Die Antike*, Vol. XVII. Berlin, 1941.

———. "Griechische Opferbräuche." In: *Phyllobolia für Peter von der Mühll*. Basel, 1945.

MILLS, J. P. *The Ao Nagas*. London, 1926.

———. *The Rengma Nagas*. London, 1937.

MOONEY, S. "Myths of the Cherokee." In: *19th Annual Report of the Bureau of American Ethnology* (1897–98). Washington, 1900.

MÜHLMANN, WILHELM. *Methodik der Völkerkunde*. Stuttgart, 1938.

———. "Mythos und Kult bei Naturvölkern." In: *Zeitschrift für Rel. u. Geistesgeschichte*, Vol. IV, 251 ff. Cologne, 1952.

MÜLLER, WERNER. "Weltbild und Kult der Kwakiutl-Indianer." In: *Studien zur Kulturkunde*, Vol. XV. Wiesbaden, 1955.

NAUMANN, HANS. *Primitive Gemeinschaftskultur*. Jena, 1921.

NIEUWENHUIS, A. W. *Quer durch Borneo*. Vols. I–II. Leiden, 1904–7.

NIMUENDAJU, CURT. "Religion der Apapocuva-Guarani." In: *Zeitschrift f. Ethnologie*, Vol. XLVI. Berlin, 1914.

————. "The Apinayé." *The Catholic University of America. Anthropological Series No. 8.* Washington, 1939.

————. "The Eastern Timbira." *University of California Publications in Archaeology and Ethnology*, Vol. XLI. Berkeley, 1946.

NIORADZE, GEORG. *Der Schamanismus bei d. sibirischen Völkern.* Stuttgart, 1925.

NORDENSKIÖLD, E. *Indianerleben.* Leipzig, 1912.

————. *Forschungen und Abenteuer in Süd-Amerika.* Stuttgart, 1923.

OBERMAIER, HUGO. "Paläolithische Wandkunst." In: *Ebert-Real-Lexikon der Vorgeschichte*, Vol. VII. Berlin, 1926.

OHLMARKS, AKE. *Studien zum Problem des Schamanismus.* Lund, 1939.

OLSON, RONALD L. *Clan and Moiety in Native America.* Berkeley, 1933.

OTTO, RUDOLF. *Das Heilige. Über das Irrationale in der Idee des Göttlichen und sein Verhältnis zum Rationalen.* Breslau, 1917.

OTTO, WALTER F. *Die Manen oder von den Urformen des Totenglaubens.* Berlin, 1923.

————. *Dionysos. Mythos und Kultus.* Frankfurt, 1933.

PAIDEUMA. *Mitteilungen zur Kultkurkunde*, Vols. I–VI. Herausgegeben vom Frobenius-Institut. Frankfurt, 1938–58.

PAULITSCHKE, P. *Ethnographie Nordost-Afrikas.* Vol. II. Berlin, 1896.

PECHUËL-LOESCHE, E. *Volkskunde von Loango.* Stuttgart, 1907.

PELIKAN, W. "Geheimnisvolle Beziehungen zwischen Tier und Pflanze." In: *Weleda-Nachrichten*, No. 23. Arlesheim (Switzerland)-Schwab. Gmünd, 1950.

PENARD, F. P. and A. P. *De Menschetende Aanbidders der Zonneslang.* Paramaribo, 1907.

PETRI, HELMUT. "Mythische Heroen und Urzeitlegende im nördlichen Dampierland, Nordwest-Australien." In: *Paideuma*, Vol. I. Leipzig 1939.

————. "Seelenvorstellungen und Totemismus im nördlichen Dampierland, Nordwest-Australien." In: *Studium Generale*, Vol. I, Heidelberg, 1948.

————. "Kurangara." *Zeitschrift für Ethnologie*, Vol. LXXV. Braunschweig, 1950.

————. "Das Weltende im Glauben australischer Eingeborener." In: *Paideuma*, Vol. IV. Bamberg, 1950.

————. "Kult-Totemismus in Australien." In: *Paideuma*, Vol. V. Bamberg, 1950–54.

PETRI, HELMUT. *Sterbende Welt in Nordwest-Australien.* Braunschweig, 1954.

PETRULLO, VINCENCO. "The Yaruros of the Capanaparo River, Venezuela." *Smithsonian Institution, Bureau of American Ethnology, Bulletin 123. Anthropological Papers, No. 11.* Washington, 1939.

PETTAZZONI, RAFFAELE. *La confessione dei peccati.* Vols. I–III. Bologna, 1929–36.

PLANCK, MAX. "Physikalische Rundblicke." In *Gesammelte Reden und Aufsätze.* Leipzig, 1922.

PREUSS, K. T. "Der Ursprung der Religion und Kunst." In: *Globus,* Vol. LXXXVI. Braunschweig, 1904–5.

———. *Die Nayarit-Expedition.* Vol. I: *Die Religion der Cora-Indianer.* Leipzig, 1912.

———. *Religion und Mythologie der Uitoto.* Vols. I–II. Göttingen, 1921–23.

———. *Forschungsreise zu den Kagaba.* St. Gabriel-Mödling near Vienna, 1926.

———. *Glauben und Mystik im Schatten des Höchsten Wesens.* Leipzig, 1926.

———. "Entwicklung und Rückschritt in der Religion." In: *Zeitschrift f. Missionskunde und Religionswissenschaft,* Vol. XLVII. Berlin, 1932.

———. *Der religiöse Gehalt der Mythen.* Tübingen, 1933.

RADCLIFFE-BROWN, A. R. *The Andaman Islanders.* Cambridge, 1922.

———. "Religion and Society." In: *Journal of the Royal Anthr. Institute,* Vol. LXXV. London, 1945.

RADIN, PAUL. *Primitive Man as Philosopher.* New York and London, 1927.

———. *Primitive Religion. Its Nature and Origin.* London, 1938.

RASMUSSEN, KNUD. "Iglulik Eskimos." In: *Report of the Fifth Thule-Expedition 1921–24,* Vol. VII (No. 1). Copenhagen, 1929.

———. "The Netsilik Eskimos. Social Life and Spiritual Culture." In: *Report of the Fifth Thule-Expedition 1921–24,* Vol. VIII (Nos. 1–2). Copenhagen, 1931.

RATSCHOW, CARL HEINZ. *Magie und Religion.* Gütersloh, 1947.

RÖDER, JOSEF. *Alahatala. Die Religion der Inlandstämme Mittel-Cerams.* Bamberg, 1948.

ROTH, WALTER E. "An Inquiry into the Animism and Folk-Lore of the Guiana Indians." In: *Annual Report of the Bureau of American Ethnology,* Vol. XXX. Washington, 1915.

SAHAGUN, FRAY BERNADINO DE. Translated from the Aztec by EDUARD SELER. Stuttgart, 1927.

SCHADEN, EGON. "Ensaio etno-sociologico sôbre a mitologia heróica de algumas tribos indígenas do Brasil." In: *Boletin Antropologia*, Vol. LXI, São Paolo, Brazil, 1946.

SCHÄRER, H. "Die Bedeutung des Menschenopfers im Dajakischen Totenkult." In: *Mitteilungen der Deutschen Gesellschaft für Völkerkunde*, No. 10. Hamburg, 1940.

SCHLESIER, ERHARD. *Die Grundlagen der Klanbildung*. Göttingen, 1956.

SCHMIDT, W. P. *Der Ursprung der Gottesidee*. Vols. I–XII. Münster, 1926–55.

SCHMITZ, CARL A. "Zum Problem des Kannibalismus im nördlichen Neuguinea." In: *Paideuma*, Vol. VI. Wiesbaden, 1954–58.

———. "Die Problematik der Mythologeme Hainuwele und Prometheus." In: *Anthropos*, Vol. LV. Posieux, 1960.

SCHRENNCK, L. v. *Reisen und Forschungen im Amur-Lande*. Vol. III: *Die Völker des Amur-Landes*. St. Petersburg, 1881.

SCHULTZ, AGNES S. "Northwest-Australian Rockpaintings." In: *Memoirs of the National Museum of Victoria*. No. 20. Melbourne, 1956.

SCHULTZE-JENA, LEONHARD. *Indiana*. Vol. I: *Leben, Glaube und Sprache der Quiche von Guatemala*. Jena, 1933.

SELER, EDUARD. *Gesammelte Abhandlungen*. Vol. II. Berlin, 1904.

SHIROKOGOROFF, S. M. *Psychomental Complex of the Tungus*. London, 1935.

SKEAT, WALTER WILLIAM, and BLAGDEN, CHARLES OTTO. *Pagan Races of the Malay Peninsula*. Vols. I–II. London, 1906.

SÖDERBLOM, NATHAN. *Das Werden des Gottesglaubens*. Leipzig, 1916.

SPECK, F. G. *Naskapi. The Savage Hunters of the Labrador Peninsula*. Oklahoma, 1935.

SPENCER, BALDWIN, and GILLEN, F. J. *The Northern Tribes of Central Australia*. London, 1904.

SPENCER, HERBERT. *Die Prinzipien der Sociologie*. Vols. I–III. (German edition by B. VETTER.) Stuttgart, 1877.

SPRANGER, EDUARD. *Die Magie der Seele*. Tübingen, 1947.

STACK, EDWARD. "The Mikirs." In: *Papers of the Late Edward Stack*. Edited by CHARLES LYALL. London, 1908.

STEINEN, KARL VON DEN. *Unter den Naturvölkern Zentral-Brasiliens. Reiseschilderung und Ergebnisse der zweiten Schingu-Expedition 1887–1888*. Berlin, 1894.

STELLER. In: *Handwörterbuch des Deutschen Aberglaubens*, Vol. VI. Berlin and Leipzig, 1934–35. Entry: *Pferdefleisch*. Pp. 1652 f.

STEVENSON, MATILDA COXE. "The Zuni Indians." In: *Annual Report of the Bureau of American Ethnology*, No. 23. 1901–2. Washington, 1904.

STREHLOW, CARL. *Die Aranda-Loritja-Stämme in Zentralaustralien*. Frankfurt, 1908.

STUEBEL, O. *Samoanische Texte.* Berlin, 1896.

TALBOT, P. AMAURY. *In the Shadow of the Bush.* London, 1912.

TESSMANN, GÜNTER. *Die Pangwe.* Vol. II. Berlin, 1913.

———. *Menschen ohne Gott.* Stuttgart, 1928.

THURNWALD, RICHARD. "Totemismus (Soziologie)." In: *Ebert Real-Lexikon der Vorgeschichte.* Vol. XIII. Berlin, 1929. Pp. 348–63.

TORDAY, E. and JOYCE. *Notes ethnographiques sur les peuples communement appelés Bakuba, ainsi que sur les peuplades apparentées. Les Bushongo.* Brussels, 1910.

TYLOR, EDWARD B. *Die Anfänge der Kultur.* Vols. I–II. Leipzig, 1873.

UEXKÜLL, JACOB VON. *Der Sinn des Lebens.* Godesberg, 1947.

VIERKANDT, A. "Die Anfänge der Religion und Zsuberei." In: *Globus,* Vol. XCII. Braunschweig, 1907.

WIRZ, PAUL. *Die Marind-anim von Holländisch-Süd-Neu-Guinea.* Vols. II, III. (Hamburg University, *Abhandlungen a.d. Gebiet der Auslandskunde,* Vols. 10 and 16.) Hamburg, 1922, 1925.

WISSMANN, H. *Im Innern Afrikas.* Leipzig, 1888.

ZERRIES, O. "Geheimnisvolle Beziehungen zwischen Tier und Pflanze." In: *Die Umschau,* Vol. L. Frankfurt, 1950. Pp. 80 ff.

———. "Wild- und Buschgeister in Südamerika." In: *Studien zur Kulturkunde,* Vol. XI. Wiesbaden, 1954.

ZINGG, ROBERT MOWRY. *The Huichols: Primitive Artists.*